Managing Across Cultures:
Issues and Perspectives

e: 020 7 487 7
      @rec

Managing Across Cultures: Issues and Perspectives

Second Edition
Edited by

Malcolm Warner
Judge Institute of Management Studies
University of Cambridge

and

Pat Joynt
Henley Management College and
Norwegian School of Management

THOMSON
™
LEARNING

Australia • Canada • Mexico • Singapore • Spain • United Kingdom • United States

ISBN 1-86152-973-2

First edition 1996 published by International Thomson Business Press

This edition 2002

Typeset by J&L Composition Ltd, Filey, North Yorkshire
Printed in Great Britain by TJ International, Padstow, Cornwall

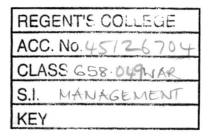

Contents

Part III: Cross-cultural issues

Contributors

Nancy J. Adler is Professor of International Management at the Faculty of Management, McGill University, Montreal, Canada.

Carlos Alberto Arruda is a member of faculty at Fondaceo Dom Cabral, Belo Horizonte, Brazil.

Werner Braun is a Research Student at Darwin College, Cambridge and the Judge Institute of Management Studies, University of Cambridge, Cambridge, United Kingdom.

John Child is Professor and Chair of Commerce, Birmingham Business School, University of Birmingham; and Distinguished Visiting Professor and Associate Director of the Chinese Management Centre, University of Hong Kong.

Philippe Debroux is Professor of International Business, Faculty of Business Administration, Soka University, Tokyo, Japan.

Daniel Z. Ding is Associate Professor of Management, Faculty of Business, City University, Kowloon Tong, Hong Kong.

Vincent Edwards is Professor of East European Management and Culture and Head of the Centre for Research into East European Business and Other Transforming Economies (CREEB) at the Buckinghamshire Business School, Buckinghamshire Chilterns University College. He is also Visiting Professor at the UIniversity of Ljubljana.

Keith Goodall is a Senior Associate at the Judge Institute of Management Studies, University of Cambridge, and Lecturer in Organizational Behaviour at the China-Europe International Business School, Shanghai, People's Republic of China.

Charles M. Hampden-Turner is a Senior Research Associate at the Institute of Management Studies, University of Cambridge, Cambridge, United Kingdom.

Frank Heller is Director of the Centre for the Study of Decision Making Studies at The Tavistock Institute, London, United Kingdom.

David J. Hickson is Emeritus Professor of International Management and Organization, University of Bradford Management Centre, Bradford, United Kingdom.

Richard M. Hodgetts is the Sun Trust Professor of Business at Florida International University, Florida, USA.

Geert Hofstede is Professor Emeritus of Organizational Anthropology and International Management of the University of Maastricht, the Netherlands. He is presently a Fellow of the Centre for Economic Research and of the Institute for Research on Intercultural Cooperation (IRIC), both at Tilburg University.

Frank Martin Horwitz is Professor of Human Resource Management and Industrial Relations at the Graduate School of Business University of Cape Town and Visiting Professor at Nanyang Business School, Nanyang Technological University, Singapore.

Pat Joynt is Powergen Professor of Management Development, Henley Management College, Henley-on-Thames, United Kingdom and on the faculty of the Norwegian School of Management, Oslo, Norway.

Russell D. Lansbury is Professor of Work and Organizational Studies and Associate Dean (Research), Faculty of Economics and Business, University of Sydney, Australia.

Fred Luthans is George Holmes Distinguished Professor of Management, University of Nebraska-Lincoln, Nebraska, USA.

Derek S. Pugh is Emeritus Professor of International Management at the Open University Business School, Milton Keynes, United Kingdom.

Chris Rowley is Senior Lecturer in Human Resource Management and Employee Relations, City University Business School, London, United Kingdom.

Leslie Sklair is Reader in Sociology at the London School of Economics, University of London, London, United Kingdom.

Fons Trompenaars is a visiting professor for the international MBA Programme at the Erasmus University – Rotterdam School of Management and Director of Trompenaars Hampden-Turner Intercultural Management Consulting (previously known as the Centre for International Business Studies [CIBS]).

Rosalie L. Tung is the Ming and Stella Wong Professor of International Business at Simon Fraser University, Canada. She is a Fellow of the Royal Society of Canada and is also Vice President of the Academy of Management for 2001–2. She will become President of the Academy in 2003–4.

Malcolm Warner is Professor and Fellow, Wolfson College, Cambridge and a member of the faculty at the Judge Institute of Management Studies, University of Cambridge, Cambridge, United Kingdom.

Lena Zander is Assistant Professor at the Institute of International Business, Stockholm School of Economics, Sweden.

Preface

This edited volume represents the work of an international network of management scholars working in a wide range of countries (Australia, Brazil, Canada, Germany, Hong Kong, Japan, the Netherlands, Norway, South Africa, Sweden, the UK and the USA) and even more universities and business schools. It also builds on a previous collaboration between the two editors, whose earlier volume *Managing in Different Cultures* (Oslo: Universitetsforlaget, 1986) appeared over a decade ago.

Most of the chapters in this second edition are original contributions to the field and were specially commissioned for the book. Some are revised versions of papers given as contributions to symposia. Others are updated and revised versions of papers published elsewhere. We are grateful to the journals and publishers concerned for their permission to reproduce parts of such papers here or to cite from them.

We would also like to show our appreciation to editorial staff at Thomson Learning for all their help, particularly Marie Osman and Jennifer Pegg as well as So-Shan Au and all other colleagues concerned.

Malcolm Warner.
Pat Joynt.
March 2001

Acknowledgements

We should like to thank the following journals and/or publishers for permission to reproduce parts of, or cite from, articles previously published by the authors.

For Chapters 4 and 5, Elsevier Science for permission to adapt 'Theorizing about organizing cross-nationally', *Advances in Comparative International Management* 13, 2000: 27–75.

For Chapter 4 an abridged version of a paper with the same title that appeared in *Advances in International Comparative Management*, volume 13, 2000: 27–75.

For Chapter 13, Frank Cass, London for permission to adopt an article from *Asia Pacific Business Review* 5 (3 and 4), Spring/Summer, 1999.

For Chapter 19, reprinted from *Management International Review*, special issue 1, 37, 1997, 171–96.

For Chapter 21, *The Cambridge Review of International Affairs*.

Chapter 2, 6, 11, 16 and 17 are adapted from articles written for *The International Encyclopedia of Business Management* (ed. M. Warner), 2nd edition, Thomson Learning, London.

Figures

Tables

Part 1
Theoretical background

Chapter 1

Introduction: cross-cultural perspectives

Malcolm Warner and Pat Joynt

Introduction

As more and more organizations cross national borders, people will need to broaden their views on competition and, more importantly, vis-à-vis other national behaviours. If the world is to survive and flourish, we all need to know more about the differences rather than concentrating on the similarities. Culture and subculture are probably the most important aspects in this change to global behaviours (see Tung 2000).

There are hundreds of cultures and subcultures of consequence that are relevant to the subject of cross-cultural management. The task of integrating all of these into an integrated whole is almost impossible. Not only may the domain vary from the small group, to a department, to an organization, but one must also consider the nation state, the region and possibly the globe (see Ohmae 1990; Warner 2000). The cultural focus may also vary from those factors that are above the water in an 'iceberg' metaphor, such as behaviours and abilities, to those factors that are hidden, such as values, attitidues, beliefs and identity (see Hofstede 1980).

The key concept we focus on is culture, which we believe to deserve some attention as far as a definition is concerned. Culture has been adapted from the Latin *cultura* which is related to *cultus*, cult or worship. *Cult* in Latin means to inhabit, till or worship and *are* is defined as 'the result of'; thus in the broadest sense, one might define culture as 'the result of human action' (Berthon 1993). Earlier, the term was closely associated with socially elitist concepts like refinement of the mind, tastes and manners based on superior education and upbringing. It has also been identified with the intellectual side of civilization, particularly in its German spelling (Heller 1985). In Europe, before the Second World War, the term *Kultur* was used extensively to support arguments on the social and racial superiority of some groups over others. The definition that, perhaps, best fits the concep is that culture is a 'collective programming of the mind', 'collective soul' or some type of 'social glue' that holds people together. Hall (1959) suggests that culture is the pattern of taken-for-granted assumptions about how a given collection of people should think, act, and feel as they go about their daily affairs. Other definitions include:

- common values
- common beliefs
- common attitudes

- common behaviour
- common norms
- heroes
- morals
- symbols
- customs
- rituals
- ceremonies
- assumptions
- perceptions
- etiquette
- patterns of . . .

We often thought of culture in macro-terms such as an American culture, an English culture, a French culture, a German culture, a Scandinavian culture and so on. Today, however, we have expanded the concept to include the organizational or corporate level; thus one can talk of an IBM culture, a GM culture, a PowerGen culture, a Shell culture and so on (Deal and Kennedy 1982; Schein 1985). For our purposes here, we will think of culture in terms of the more macro-examples mentioned above.

There are currently two main approaches towards the application of culture and its consequences in a managerial and organizational setting. One approach, often labelled *divergence*, suggests that we should study culture because management is different in Scandinavia than it is in Germany, the UK, the US, and so on. Another label for this approach that is found in the organizational behaviour literature is *contingency* theory. Divergency theory assumes that elements such as differing values and behaviours, differing stages of economic development and unevenly distributed global resources will guarantee global diversity (see Joynt and Warner 1985).

By contrast, *convergence* theory suggests that because of technology, structure and a global orientation by many firms, it is not necessary to practice cross-cultural management. Convergence theory involves pragmatic issues that can push one in the direction of adopting a 'one best way' approach to the management of organizations worldwide. The two approaches, divergence and convergence (*emic/etic*) represent two sides of the same coin as the debate concerning which approach is most relevant will continue to exist for many years to come. The pivotal question for managers and those studying management to ask is as follows: what is more important, the transfer of behaviours and techniques from country to country in a more uniform world, or the need for more knowledge on a richer variety of management practices and techniques? We hope to make a contribution to this debate in this edited collection.

Plan of the Book

We now turn to the plan of the book of this updated second edition; it is divided into three parts. In Part I, we deal with a number of theoretical issues of interest to those studying cross-cultural management and organizational studies or trying to keep up with new developments in these domains. In Part II, we present a set of area studies looking at managerial behaviour in specific locations across the world, covering the six continents. Last, in Part III, we look at a number of broader issues which we hope will be of close interest and relevance to those interested in trends in international business (for a comprehensive overview, see Tung 2000).

Turning to Part I, which has four chapters, apart from this introductory one. These relate to general theoretical themes which arise from managing across cultures. In Chapter 1, Malcolm Warner and Pat Joynt set out the goals and scope of the book and attempt to provide a short guide to its contents. In Chapter 2, Derek S. Pugh and

David Hickson, two of the most noteworthy writers on organizations, discuss the problem of 'convergence' and the debates surrounding it. In the following chapter, Werner Braun and Malcolm Warner set out the arguments for and against the 'culture-free' approaches to the study of organizations in recent publications in the field, with illustrations from recent developments in multinational firms. Next, in Chapters 4 and 5, John Child looks at the different ways in which we think about organizations cross-nationally, with reference to a wide range of cases, particularly those in Asia. He believes that cross-national organizational studies can embrace both the comparison of organizational forms between nations and the study of cross-national organization.

In Part II, we turn to a number of detailed, empirical area studies which truly span the globe. While we do not cover all the countries which represent the major trends in international business and management behaviour, we have attempted to show off a good number of illustrative cases which exemplify the mainstream currents and trends set out in Part I of this book. Some of these chapters are based on empirical fieldwork; others provide an overview of on-going trends in the locations covered. These chapters may deal with a single country or even a wider geographical area. In Chapter 6, for example, we first turn to management in North America as perceived by Fred Luthans and Richard Hodgetts, who look at how US managers are trying to recreate a competitive business culture. Next, we move on southwards to an Anglo-Brazilian comparison by Carlos Arruda and David Hickson. In Chapter 8, Geert Hofstede, one of the leading scholars in the field of culture's consequences, looks at images of Europe by comparing national values mainly within the European Union (EU) as revealed by his empirical investigations. After this, Lena Zander discusses empowerment in the workplace as revealed in her fieldwork in Europe. In Chapter 10, Vincent Edwards sketches out the evolution of management in Central and Eastern Europe, including the former Soviet Union. After this, we turn to managing in Asia, where Rosalie L. Tung studies the cross-cultural dimensions involved in doing business in that part of the world. In Chapter 12, Charles Hampden-Turner and Fons Trompenaars, a well-known Anglo-Dutch collaboration of cross-cultural management gurus, look at what they call a world 'turned upside down' in Asia. In Chapter 13, we turn to a study of human resource management in Chinese enterprises by Malcolm Warner, Keith Goodall and Daniel Z. Ding. After this, Chris Rowley examines recent management developments in South Korea. In Chapter 15, we move on to a reappraisal of the Japanese employment model by Philippe Debroux, who has lived in Japan for many years. Next, Russell Lansbury looks at how management in Australia has been changing over the last few decades. After this, Frank M. Horwitz discusses the way the new South Africa deals with its business, economic and interracial management problems.

In Part III, we examine wider cross-cultural issues within our remit. These relate to a number of themes which are intriguing and relevant, such as social science, gender and leadership, management education and globalization. In Chapter 18, Frank Heller looks at the role of social science in studies of managing across cross-cultures. Next, Nancy J. Adler presents a study of the role of women in global leadership. In Chapter 20, we move on to a discussion by Keith Goodall of management education across cultures. In the final chapter, Leslie Sklair critically looks at how globalization and management are linked and interrelated. He focuses on the 'transnational capitalist class' as he calls it and how they constitute a further step in the so-called managerial revolution.

What all these chapter try to do is take into account the problems of managing across frontiers and cultures. Today, few enterprises can act locally; they have to look to wider horizons. Those intending to enter the world of business must be prepared to take a wider view and take into account national and cultural variations in how people behave in the organizational world.

Concluding remarks

Culture can have a powerful impact on management and organization behaviour. The challenge for management scholars is to determine what practices will work where and how much cultural adaptation is necessary, if any. Frank Heller (1985) suggests, for instance, that culture should be approached in the same way one would approach an aggressive patient – without prejudice but with a resolute intention not to be bowled over or hoodwinked into prescribing either a placebo or the patient's own medicine. In the final analysis, awareness of culture helps us to understand each other better and understanding is often the essence of successful management. We hope this edited volume not only contributes to analysis and scholarship in the field, but also to more effective organizational analysis in cross-cultural settings (see Warner 1996, 2000).

References

Berthon, P.R. (1993) 'Psychological type and corporate cultures: relationships and dynamics', *Omega* 21(3): 329–44.

Deal, T.E. and Kennedy, A.A. (1982) *Corporate Cultures: The Rites and Rituals of Corporate Life*, Reading, MA: Addison-Wesley.

Hall, E.T. (1959) *The Silent Language*, New York: Doubleday.

Heller, F. (1985) 'Some theoretical and practical problems in multinational and cross-cultural research on organisations', in *Managing in Different Cultures* P. Joynt and M. Warner (eds) Oslo: Universitetsforlaget.

Hofstede, G. (1980) *Cultures Consequences: International Differences in Work-Related Values*, Beverly Hills, CA, and London: Sage.

Joynt, P.D. and Warner, M. (1985) *Managing in Different Cultures*, Oslo: Universitetsforlaget.

Ohmae, K. (1990) *The Borderless World*, New York: McKinsey & Co Inc.

Schein, E.H. (1985) *Organizational Culture and Leadership*, San Francisco: Jossey-Bass.

Tung, R.L. (ed.) (2000) *IEBM Handbook of International Business*, London: Thomson Learning.

Warner, M. (1996) *Comparative Management: A Reader*, 4 volumes, London: Routledge.

Warner, M. (2000) *IEBM Regional Encyclopedia of Business and Management*, 4 volumes, London: Thomson Learning.

Chapter 2

On organizational convergence

Derek S. Pugh and David J. Hickson

Overview

The subject of organizational convergence is concerned with how far organizations in different countries have travelled and may travel in the future along a path to global convergence in operations and management, and how far the influence in this of specific cultural factors must be understood and planned for if the manager is to be effective in cross-cultural situations.

In international enterprises, managers need to know how far the workings of organizations in one country are different from those in another. How can knowledge of their home country style of organizing and its functioning help them deal with organizations in other places in the world? Are the structures and functioning of organizations in different cultures coming sufficiently close together to permit the development of universally applicable approaches with the expectation of obtaining consistent outcomes? Clearly there are international differences, but the key issues are: how important are they and are they diminishing?

For example, are the differences in organizational functioning between the UK and France and Germany, or between the developing and the developed world, fundamental and likely to remain so? Or are organizations all over the world converging so that these differences in management are becoming minor? If that is so then managers can rely on a substantial basis of globally established knowledge and skills which they can transfer from one culture to another. Or must they do things differently in each society (c.f. Hickson and Pugh 2001)?

Three elements of convergence

The convergence argument has three elements. At its strongest it has been suggested that whole societies are steadily moving together so that in social characteristics the similarities between all cultures will become much greater than their differences. This argument was originally presented by Kerr *et al.* (1960). The most obvious way in which we see this now is in the enormous global communications explosion. People are beginning to see immediately via satellite and cable television what is happening all over the world, and this is forming their aspirations. For example, how many teenagers in the world, given the choice, would now prefer to wear some form of distinctive national dress rather than T-shirt, jeans and trainers? Pressures for convergence are set up as people everywhere, particularly the young, want similar clothes, pop stars, automobiles, sports, opportunities for participating in elections and everything else that can be shown on television or networked electronically. The power of modern communications in upsetting controlled political systems is profound. For example, China needs fax and electronic mail communication for business purposes. The possibility of control of these media is limited so they may well contribute to the political opening up of that country, as they did for Eastern Europe.

A second element of the convergence argument refers to economic systems. The most developed countries in the world, those with the highest standards of living, are market economies. The market approach has been so successful relative to any other system (for example, Marxist state control) that it is being adopted worldwide for the economic benefits that it brings. The collapse of the Eastern European communist regimes was primarily economic. They simply could not deliver the Western and Japanese standards of living that were now known about and expected. They were therefore replaced by freer market economies. Of course, capitalist market economies are not completely free. As Galbraith (1978) has demonstrated they have to develop and operate within government-established socio-legal and economic frameworks. There are continuing arguments in market economies about what the precise degree of government regulation should be and what can be left to the market. However, these are merely the kind of adjustments which will be hammered out as organizations such as the European Union or the ASEAN (Association of Southeast Asian Nations) countries develop their common economic systems and more and more countries join. Overall, it can be argued that economic systems continue to converge.

The third element of convergence is that of management. Organizations all over the world need to be managed. If their managers subscribe to aims such as efficiency, growth and increased technological development to produce a higher standard of living then, it is argued, they will be driven to carry out their functions in ways which have been found to be the most effective in comparable situations elsewhere across the world. Add to this the transfer of technology and the proselytizing activities of the multinational corporations and there will be a steady global convergence of management.

The spread of technology

A major influence on all three convergence elements – social, economic and managerial – is industrialization. This is based on technology which speaks a universal language attractive to all, independent of the form of government or the culture of a people. Computers are basically the same everywhere, as are factory automatic machines. Air freight and its handling operates worldwide. Technology spreads out so that the world is divided into countries which are industrialized and those which are in the process of becoming so. Few countries, the argument goes, will forgo the material benefits that industrialization brings. There is a growing realization that there are also costs – excessive urbanization and environmental pollution, for example. Even so, these concerns have made little headway in stopping the process.

This spread of technology from the more advanced nations occurs in four main ways:

1 Through normal channels of trade when developing countries buy products and manufacturing facilities.
2 Through imitation, for example when they set up technical schools and distance learning universities, buy international encyclopedias of business and management and learn from expatriate managers and consultants.
3 Through the effects of economic aid, which usually involves the delivery of more advanced technology and manpower training.
4 Through military channels, since the global scope of defence industry competition has led to the training of workforces to build bases, maintain vehicles and

aircraft, etc., thus yielding skills necessary for wider industrialization (Kerr *et al.* 1960).

The worldwide diffusion of this advanced technology creates a 'logic of industrialism'. A similar range of tasks and problems come into being and the pressures towards efficient production ensure that the most effective ways of tackling these common tasks are adopted worldwide. Thus, inevitably, organizations tackling the same tasks, in whichever culture, become more and more alike. For example, a decision to produce automobiles as cheaply as possible anywhere in the world will require factories of considerable size (individual craftsmen will not do), specialized machinery (hand tools or even general purpose presses will not be sufficient by themselves) and supplies of raw materials (provided through specialist technical processes). Trained people, expert in their particular tasks, would be needed to contribute a wide range of specialist knowledge, skills and effort. Also, professional managers who can raise and use capital (individual, corporate, governmental) to bring all these factors together and to organize putting them to work are crucial.

The spread of industrial technology is accompanied by a structure of industries. For vehicle manufacturing suppliers of steel, of tyres, of paint and of upholstery are necessary, each of which in turn has its own technology and experts. The industrial structure becomes transformed from small craft units showing little technical specialization to a complex structure of large specialized units operating in an interdependent multiorganizational system. This system in turn leads to a particular division of labour: there will be less use for someone who can make sheet steel *and* rubber tyres *and* reinforced glass, increased skill in only one of those tasks being preferred. Production controllers, systems analysts, cost accountants and other staff specialists will be needed. Training in both technical and managerial tasks will develop and the candidate who by ability or training can fill the vacancy best – regardless of colour, caste, tribe, religion, family or gender – will be appointed.

This growth of impersonal organizations (that is, a more bureaucratic structure) has been taking place in the developed West for well over a century. The process is not complete however – there are still many aspects of the idealized description given above which have not yet fallen into place. For example, few countries, if any, could claim that they have completely effective equal opportunities in employment and promotion for all their ethnic subgroups or for women. These limitations reflect cultural assumptions regarding social status, race and gender which exist in all societies. Nonetheless, the changes occurring are in this direction, and can be seen most notably now in the Pacific Rim. For example, within the last half-century South Korea and Malaysia have established their own vehicle manufacturing industries and are treading this path, being pushed by the need for efficiency into the same technology, expertise, training, organizational structure, etc. as other developed countries.

The convergence view does not mean that the traffic is necessarily all one way, from the more developed to the less developed, although the main weight of transfer will clearly be in this direction. Contributions to effectiveness may also be passed from the less developed countries to the more developed before being incorporated into the worldwide way of doing things. For example, Japan was a late developer in the area of industrialization but the values and culture of the country enabled it to change relatively quickly. Japan put a greater priority on training workers, part of a general Japanese emphasis on education and training. Managements in the Japanese motor industry took up the ideas of the US expert, W. Edwards Deming, who was relatively neglected in his own country. Workers were trained to produce parts and vehicles to highly reliable quality standards using, among other methods, quality circles. These permitted management to draw on the shop-floor workers' knowledge of the manufacturing processes to improve product quality. Such investment paid off, giving Japan a considerable competitive edge in the market together with low rates of scrap and lower costs of reworking during manufacture. Once it had been demonstrated that such methods gave a competitive advantage the same ideas were taken seriously in the USA and the rest of the world. With the development of the total quality management movement they became part of the global management convergence.

Thus, particular management innovations will be inaugurated in cultures in which they are more likely to flourish. Then, if successful, they are adopted in some degree worldwide, even in less receptive cultures. In this way they aid the advancement of managerial convergence.

Other worldwide factors affecting management

There are five further influences on the way enterprises function across all cultures. Singly, or in conjunction, they may either foster, or hinder, convergence. They are:

1 *The size of the unit of operation*. Larger organizations will require more impersonal forms of management than smaller ones (including greater standardization of procedures and greater formalization of control mechanisms).

2 *The dependence of the organization on others in its environment.* Organizations which depend the most on others in their environment take decisions centrally and lose autonomy to, say, a controlling board or ministry. This happens because ties of ownership or contract are so important that the relevant resource decisions must be taken at the top. For example, if an enterprise purchases components from many different suppliers, decisions on each contract, including price, can be decentralized to the buying department, and some items even to junior buyers. However, a long-term commitment to another firm, which itself invests in equipment so that it can supply the major raw material, is likely to require the chief executive's personal attention, thus leading to greater centralization.

3 *The institutional environment of the enterprise.* Joint stock companies will require different styles of operation from government enterprises which, in turn, will differ from family-owned businesses (including greater centralization of authority in government and family enterprises and greater decentralization in joint stock companies).

4 *The different managerial roles*. The functional jobs that managers do (production, marketing), their level in the hierarchy (chief executive, first-line supervisor) and the training and education they have received (engineer, economist) will all produce characteristic differences in outlook everywhere.

5 *The organizational culture*. Organizations develop their own cultures and in international enterprises this will have some impact across subsidiaries in all national cultures, as is seen in the cases of ICI, Fiat, McDonald's, Mitsubishi, Nestlé and Siemens.

The above influences will be apparent across all cultures. Thus there will be important similarities as well as differences in the way organizations operate in different countries. Size of the unit of operation, dependence and the other factors listed above become key elements in the explanation of the broad features of organizations worldwide. It appears to be at least as important to know how large an organization is, who set it up and what its dependence on others in its environment is as to know the country in which it is located. Certainly, the differences between organizations within one country are greater than the average differences between countries (Pugh 1993).

Of course the pervasive influence of technology, size, dependence and so on does not mean that all organizations are inevitably becoming the same in structure. What it means is that organizations are influenced in the same way by changes in these factors. For example, growth in size increases the likelihood of greater specialization of tasks. Decline in size, however, can eventually reduce it. Thus, if organizations grow in one country but decline in another they will become ever more different; they will fail to converge. The same is relevant for dependence and centralization: if dependence is increasing so will centralization, but a reduction in dependence on others will lead to decentralization. Size and dependence are not in themselves convergence factors. Only if they change everywhere in the same direction will this be so.

Over the years, industrialization has produced larger organizations with a resulting increase in specialization and formalization of their structures. It has tied more of them into more intricate dependence upon owning parent groups, the state, suppliers and customers or clients, with a consequent greater centralization. Hence the push towards convergence. However, a decline in organizational size due to economic recession, the appearance of high-tech industries and services with small-scale units and privatization out of state ownership mean that the pressures have become more uneven, and at times are perhaps even reversed.

There will always be characteristic differences in management between, for example, large and small enterprises, government organizations and family businesses, high-tech manufacturing and retailing. The nature of these differences, however, will be the same in all cultures.

Conclusion

This chapter has concentrated on the pressures which dispose managements and organizations towards greater and greater similarity. Yet deeply cultural institutions in different societies, especially education, can be resistant. By inculcating different outlooks and training for employment in differing ways, they sustain differences in the ways that otherwise similar organizations are run. While superficialities in dress and everyday ways of speaking, or even in following technical instructions, change relatively easily – the emphasis is always on the word 'relatively' when discussing culture – the fundamental attributes of culture are relatively resistant to change.

For example, a subordinate in South America who is told to do something about which he or she is dubious is likely to carry it out in an indifferent manner rather than argue with the boss. A similar subordinate in Scandinavia or in an English-speaking country is far more likely to question the sense of it. This is due to a difference in how authority is viewed. In Asia for a superior to talk over a subordinate's personal difficulties with others in the firm is likely to be seen as well-intentioned thoughtfulness. In the West it is more likely to be seen as breaching confidence and intruding on the subordinate's private affairs. There is a difference in views on personal relationships.

The very influential research by Hofstede (1991) showed how employees in differing nations with differing cultures continued to hold distinctive attitudes to work even though all were employed by the same multinational corporation, IBM. This is not surprising when one considers the persistence over thousands of years of a minority Jewish identity in many lands, of a Gypsy identity in Europe, of an Ainu identity in northern Japan, indeed of all minority cultures, ancient and more recent, throughout the world.

It is beyond the scope of this chapter to fully examine the cultural diversity in societies around the globe which retards, even reverses, convergence. An accessible, comprehensive treatment (with exemplifying portrayals of over 20 countries) is given by Hickson and Pugh (2001). The outcome of such diversity is that no one can tell how far organizational convergence will go, or how far cultural diversity in managerial characteristics will persist undiminished.

References

Galbraith, J.K. (1978) *The New Industrial State*, revised edition, London: Penguin.

Hickson, D.J. and Pugh, D.S. (2001) *Management World-Wide: Distinctive Styles amid Globalization*, London: Penguin.

Hofstede, G. (1991) *Cultures and Organizations: Software of the Mind*, London: McGraw-Hill.

Kerr, C., Dunlop J.T., Harbison, F.H. and Myers, C.A. (1960) *Industrialism and Industrial Man*, Cambridge, MA: Harvard University Press.

Pugh, D.S. (1993) 'The convergence of international organizational behaviour', in T. Weinshall (ed.) *Culture and Management*, Berlin: De Gruyter.

Further reading

Ebster-Grosz, D. and Pugh, D. (1996) *Anglo-German Business Collaboration: Pitfalls and Potentials*, London: Macmillan.

Galbraith, J.K. (1978) *The New Industrial State*, revised edition, London: Penguin.

Hickson, D.J. (ed.) (1997) *Exploring Management Across the World*, London: Penguin.

Hickson, D.J. and McMillan, C.J. (1981) *Organization and Nation: The Aston Programme IV*, Aldershot: Gower.

Hickson, D.J. and Pugh, D.S. (2001) *Management World-Wide: Distinctive Styles amid Globalization*, London: Penguin.

Hofstede, G. (1991) *Cultures and Organizations: Software of the Mind*, London: McGraw-Hill.

Kerr, C., Dunlop J.T., Harbison, F.H. and Myers, C.A. (1960) *Industrialism and Industrial Man*, Cambridge, MA: Harvard University Press.

Luthans, F., Welsh, D.H.B. and Rosenkrantz, S.A. (1993) 'What do Russian managers really do? An observational study with comparisons to US managers', *Journal of International Business Studies* 24(4): 741–61.

Pugh, D.S. (1993) 'The convergence of international organizational behaviour', in T. Weinshall (ed.) *Culture and Management*, Berlin: De Gruyter.

Pugh, D.S. (ed.) (1998) *The Aston Programme, Vols. I, II and III*, Classic Research in Management Series, Aldershot: Ashgate.

Pugh, D.S. and Hickson, D.J. (1976) *Organizational Structure in its Context: The Aston Programme I*, Aldershot: Gower.

Chapter 3

The 'culture-free' versus 'culture-specific' management debate

Werner Braun and Malcolm Warner

Introduction

The scholarly debate on organizational convergence has been ongoing for some years now. A main prop of this discussion has been the arguments about the so-called 'industrialization' thesis (Harbison and Myers 1959, Kerr *et al.* 1960) which got under way in the post-war period. It was an intellectually bold idea in its day, if somewhat deterministic in its thrust. It had many supporters but also its critics. In any event, it led to a serious debate which has had very useful consequences for the field and which are echoed many times in this volume. We now set out below many of the arguments for and against this 'logic'. The debate itself grew out of a fertile period as far as the emergent subdisciplines of industrial sociology and organizational behaviour were concerned. In this chapter, we discuss the forces influencing organizations in perhaps often contradictory directions, generally with respect to cross-cultural management and particularly with respect to human resource management (HRM). Such influences are divided into two groups: one, 'culture-free' and the other, 'culture-specific'. We will deal with each of these in turn.

The culture-free thesis argues that a common logic of industrialization produces converging institutional frameworks and organizational solutions across nations, even against cultural constraints. According to this argument in the striving for efficiency, there is no leeway for different cultural solutions of organizational structures (Harbison and Myers 1959: 117; Kerr *et al.* 1960: 94). According to this logic, 'an oil-refinery is an oil-refinery is an oil-refinery', given its size and technology, wherever it is located across the world. In a nutshell, culture is of little importance, according to this point of view. It had a ready appeal to its adherents, as it seemed to be confirmed in common sense, as well as everyday experience and observation, at least in advanced countries. If many technocrats and technicists had not taken cultural variations into account in planning their strategies and structures, so be it. Empirical results might show similarities if researchers looked at the multinational enterprises' (MNEs') documentation and paper systems (which might look similar) rather than looking at behavioural variations on site at the plant level in specific national settings.

It is argued by a number of scholars in the field that a convergence of management structures and practices in organizations across cultures is likely to be driven by factors such as:

- the fast diffusion of management practices, for example, through international management education and activities by MNEs (Parker 1998) which could be described with normative[1] and mimetic[2] isomorphism (DiMaggio and Powell 1983)

- the 'universal language' of technology (Hickson and Pugh 1995) which deter-mines organizational structures and work processes (see also Perrow 1967; Woodward 1965).

Whereas it has been argued that certain causal relationships, such as a positive rela-tionship between the size of an organization and its needs for specialization and for-malization, have been found to be stable across different cultures (Hickson *et al.* 1974: 63), a closer look at the kind of organizational solutions as response to such universal issues shows clear cross-cultural differences (Kieser and Kubicek 1992: 254).[3]

In an interesting and relevant study of multinational banks from different coun-tries located in Hong Kong, the authors (Birnbaum and Wong 1985) could not reject their 'null hypothesis', which was that there is no statistically significant rela-tionship between employee work satisfaction and various structural organizational features. We of course know that a 'null hypothesis' is not verified if it cannot be rejected. Nevertheless, it should be mentioned that these findings stand in clear contrast to the findings of Lincoln, Hanada and Olson (1981) who found a positive association between organizational structures in congruence with particular cul-tures and employees' job satisfaction. The authors of the original study (Birnbaum and Wong 1985) have also been criticized by researchers contesting their finding, such as Ofori-Dankwa and Reddy (1999), for not having carried out a formal test of differences between the organizational structures and job characteristics before using them as independent variables. The critics argue that due to the high com-petitive environment of Hong Kong, banks might have adjusted their organiza-tional structures to the local environment. In a reanalysis of the original data, they found no statistically significant differences between the banks from different coun-tries and their organizational structure and job characteristics. So far, so good, one might say.

Comparative, now almost classic, organizational research in similarly industri-alized countries such as the UK, France and Germany, in the late 1970s and just after, however had produced evidence for structural and managerial differences between these countries' organizations on such issues as for example the cen-tralization of decision-making, the degree of supervision and the ways of co-ordination (Child and Kieser 1979; Maurice, Sorge and Warner 1980). The latter study from these researchers, sometimes referred to as the Aix (as opposed to the Aston) School looked at worksystems in specific national settings in firms in the three countries, controlling for size and technology. It found that there was something they called the 'societal effect', which suggested that there were dis-tinctive national ways of organizing. Such findings have now been taken up by a fair number of scholars as a persuasive counterbalance to the 'convergence' thesis (see chapters 4 and 5).

There was growing interest in this ongoing debate about culture and organizations at that time. Cross-cultural differences with regard to managerial behaviour were also found by such researchers as Hofstede (1982), Laurent (1983) and Hampden-Turner and Trompenaars (1993).[4] Laurent (1984) and Hampden-Turner and Trompenaars drew their sample from a pool of international managers participating in executive education programmes at two European business schools. Their samples had the advantage over Hofstede's in that they were drawn from many firms in a range of countries, rather than one MNE operating worldwide across many countries, that is the computer industry giant he called HERMES, where had been personnel director. The findings weaken the assumption that international management education has a convergence effect on cross-cultural managerial behaviour. In particular, Hofstede's

(1982) eminent work builds on a definition that culture is 'the collective programming of the mind which distinguishes the members of one human group from another' (Hofstede 1982: 21). Cross-cultural research previous to Hofstede's work had very often not offered an explicit culture definition and had rather used 'culture' as a 'trash-can' residual variable (Child 1981; Neghandi 1974; Redding 1994; Staehle 1994). The title of Hofstede's (1982) 'big book' was *Culture's Consequences* and it is now probably the best known text in its field.

Hofstede's (1982) work gains credibility through its longitudinal nature, although it was only carried out in one large MNE, a large computer-industry giant, as noted above. The use of highly standardized questionnaires as means to investigate the deeper-level cultural driving forces of managerial behaviour also appears problematic. Also Hofstede (1982) does not consider that within one culture, there is the possibility of regional variations, subcultures and individual deviations. The classification of the countries on Hofstede's (1982) four dimensions are actually based on an overall calculated mean of individual scores of respondents from different countries. Given a normal distribution of cases, it is evident that the members of a country might not correspond with this calculated mean. Thus, generalizations on the basis of Hofstede's findings are at least questionable. Also, he sees the individual in quite a passive way, in which all actions are in fact predetermined by a mental 'programme'. Yet, one may equally argue that individuals should be seen in an adaptable, learning and flexible way, as not merely passively embedded, but actively engaged with their environment. The way Hofstede (1982) backs up his culture classifications with isolated examples of historical events in a country gives further reason for doubts. The problem of 'cultural bias' of the researcher can also be mentioned for Hofstede's own work (which he tried to remedy in further research, for example, Hofstede and Bond 1984 and the Chinese Culture Connection 1987). Yet MBA students and others remain fascinated by Hofstede's work, as it has a persuasive, even perhaps grandiose, sweep to it. It has been replicated in innumerable academic papers and postgraduate dissertations. None to our knowledge has ever spoken of the 'Hofstede School' but his name is recognized around the world, mostly in business school and informed managerial circles (see Tayeb 2001).

Two perspectives have emerged in the discussion as to how how variance in organizations across different cultures is typically explained. First, the culturist perspective (with which Hofstede would be associated) links such variance to differences in belief systems; second, the institutionalist perspective stresses the impact of the institutional environment in which the organization is embedded (Wilkinson 1996). Criticism of the culturalist perspective focuses on frequent ex post conceptualization of 'culture' and its use as a residual variable (see also Child 1981; Dowling, Schuler and Welch 1994; Neghandi 1974; Staehle 1994; Wilkinson 1996). Further, it is criticized because of its gross assumptions about causal links, the danger of racism and the absence of historical understanding and neglect of institutional forces (Wilkinson 1996). Although the institutionalist perspective considers historical and political conditions, it is similarly deterministic to see organizational structures and subsequent behaviour within organizations as solely dependent on a historically grown institutional setting (Wilkinson 1996: 433). Other authors (Whittington 1992: 434; Wilkinson 1996; Child 1997) stress that an explanation of organizational variance across different cultures should also allow for 'agency' and a view that organizations are not merely passively embedded in but actively engaged with their environment.

Such is the richness of the debate on organizational convergence, as set out above. We now turn to its applicability to the realm of human resource management (HRM).

Issues arising from the cross-cultural transfer of HRM policies and practices within MNEs

In recent years, there has been a clear change in the conceptual frameworks used to understand and design MNEs (see for example Egelhoff 1999). This move reflects a shift away from the traditional contingency theories of MNE organizational designs such as the strategy–structure models (for example Daniels, Pitts and Tretter 1984; Stopford and Wells 1972) and the processes and life-cycle models (for example, Baliga and Jaeger 1985). Nowadays, the focus has been directed onto a variety of new theories about organizational design, centred on concepts such as 'transnationalism' (Bartlett and Ghoshal 1989), 'heterarchy' (Hedlund 1986) and the 'horizontal organization' (White and Poynter 1990).

Reasons for this shift may include the following new influences and issues. Traditional contingency theory views of strategy and organizational design do not adequately address the kinds of strategic complexity and levels of change that MNEs are dealing with (Bartlett and Ghoshal 1989: 197), they focus on the existing routines which are not going to be the sources of innovation and future competitive advantage. Furthermore, traditional models may be said to overemphasize the role of structure and other traditional mechanisms of co-ordination, while MNEs are held to be increasingly using different mechanisms such as informal, people-based co-ordination and control mechanisms (for example, Egelhoff 1999). As a result, we can see greater importance being given to HRM policies and practices in MNEs in order to co-ordinate and integrate their multiple affiliates (for example, Bartlett and Ghoshal 1989). Human resource management policies and practices in the organization, which would form an integral part of an input control system (Hamilton and Kashlak 1999; Snell 1992), are particularly important for MNE affiliates in locations with high culture-distance (relative to the home country of Western MNEs), high political risks and high economic volatility (Hamilton and Kashlak 1999). Such problems of tying the organizational bonds more closely together represent real challenges for the MNE in the new millenium.

Due to the high costs of people-based co-ordination and control systems (for example, Evans 1992; Martinez and Jarillo 1989), MNEs will be likely to vary the application of such a system by employee groups and will first and foremost attempt to apply it to employee groups most crucial to corporate success. Here the group of local-middle to upper management staff has to be mentioned, whose members usually happen to be the main strategy implementers (Bartlett and Ghoshal 1988; Guth and McMillan 1986) and information brokers (Bartlett and Ghoshal 1988; Hamilton and Kashlak 1999; Hedlund 1994) within the MNE affiliates.

It is not surprising that there is an upsurge in the search for 'best practice' or 'high performance' HRM systems (for example, see Huselid 1995; Pfeffer 1994; 1998; also Peters and Waterman 1982 and a critique by Guest 1992) which can be applied across cultures. Indeed, as Martin and Beaumont (1998) note, there seems to be a re-emergence of 'one-best-wayism' in the literature, perhaps most influentially expressed in the 'guru theories' associated with academics, (ex-)practitioners and management consultants (Huczynski 1993). The pressure on top managers in global firms to produce high performance results, that is, mainly vis-à-vis 'share holder value', has often become a search for the 'holy grail' of strategic people management or, in the jargon, strategic human resource management (SHRM).

On the other hand, it is known that it is the HRM function which is particularly culture-bound (Kanungo and Jaeger 1990; Laurent 1986; Poole 1990; Van Dijk 1990). Reviewing studies which both assume converging institutional frameworks and organizational solutions across nations and which assume that different cultures will maintain their specificity, Child (1981) concludes that there is evidence for both convergence and divergence. The majority of convergence studies focus on macro-level variables such as the relationship between size of organizations, technology used and structural variables. The majority of divergence studies, on the other hand, focus on micro-level variables such as the behaviour of people within organizations (Child 1981: 324). A literature survey by Adler and Bartholomew (1992) supports the view that culture has a strong impact on organizational behaviour and the individual behaviour of employees. Furthermore, it is also the HRM function which is particularly exposed to local labour regulating laws and other local stakeholders, for example, trade unions (for example, Rosenzweig and Nohria 1994). A cross-cultural transfer of HRM philosophies, policies and practices into varying economic, politico-legal and socio-cultural contexts might not only lead to organizational inefficiencies (Kanungo and Jaeger 1990)[5] but might also lead to a disruption of indigenous ways of organizing (Marsden 1991).

We can conclude that the MNE and particularly the HRM function is faced with a dilemma, or at least a puzzle. On the one hand, there are demands for using the function increasingly as the basis for the development of flexible mechanisms to co-ordinate and integrate multiple affiliates. This would necessarily involve some form of standardization of practices. On the other hand, the HRM function is probably the most culture-bound function of all management functions and is therefore more likely to resist any attempts to standardize practices across cultures, as can be seen in the debate regarding its implementation in China (see chapter 13 and Warner 1995). Indeed, Edwards, Ferner and Sisson (1996) point out that few MNEs have used global culture management techniques and HRM practices successfully to integrate their multiple affiliates. In the literature this dilemma is also referred to as the integration–differentiation puzzle (Kamoche 1996).

In the following section, we will look at the development of different HRM concepts and the way theory has responded to the above described puzzle.

Origin and development of the HRM concept

A reason for the problematic transfer of theoretical concepts cross-culturally is also seen in their own cultural origin which they often implicitly represent (Hofstede 1980; 1983; 1994; 1996). This is perhaps particularly true for HRM. In its origin HRM is a US-based concept which very much developed out of the normative, humanistic management philosophies of the human relations and behavioural sciences approaches such as for example. McGregor's Theory Y (see Guest 1990; Staehle 1988). These approaches and 'models of man' are strongly criticized for their introspection[6] and weak empirical foundation (Guest 1990; Staehle 1994).

Guest (1990: 379) goes as far as to describe HRM as a manifestation of the American Dream: 'It [HRM] is American, optimistic, apparently humanistic and also superficially simple. In short it has rediscovered elements of the American Dream'. Furthermore, it has to be seen that the newly forged bond between labour and management postulated by HRM sat rather comfortably with the deeply embedded anti-union sentiments of American managers (Guest 1990). Indeed, if one looks at the earliest Michigan HRM model, stakeholders outside the corporation are not considered (Devanna, Fombrun and Tichy 1984; Tichy, Fombrun and Devanna 1982). This model, also termed the 'hard' HRM model (Legge 1995), emphasizes a quantitative, calculative business-strategic aspect of managing people in a way as rational as for any other economic factor (Storey 1989: 8). The later developed Harvard HRM model (Beer *et al.* 1985) postulates a stakeholder perspective, however, with its basis in the human relations school; it is particularly culture-bound (Legge 1995). The difficulty of transferring the human relations heritage of HRM across cultures is further emphasized by findings of Sparrow, Schuler and Jackson (1994) who identify five country clusters which particularly diverge on such issues as promoting an empowerment culture, promoting diversity and an equality culture, emphasis on flexible work practices, emphasis on centralization and vertical hierarchy, shared benefits, risks and pay for team performance (Sparrow, Schuler and Jackson 1994: 282 ff).

Looking at concepts which deal with HRM within MNEs (i.e. strategic international HRM (SIHRM) concepts) it is interesting to note that in the early models, the culture-distance between MNE home country and affiliate host country was not specified as an independent variable. Perlmutter (1969) and Perlmutter and Heenan (1974) suggest that differentiated staffing decisions (i.e. to which degree these take place in an ethnocentric, polycentric, regiocentric or geocentric fashion) for the affiliates of MNEs depends on the attitude of the management at headquarters. The model does not specify factors which might actually influence top management attitude, nor does the concept take any other variables influencing staffing decisions into consideration. These could be, for example, industry structure, size of organization, etc.

Adler (1991) and Adler and Ghadar (1990; 1993) argue that different internationalization strategies of an MNE (expressed by different degrees of differentiation and integration) are dependent on the organization's product life cycles. Of course, the exact description of a product life cycle can only be given *post hoc* which means that such a model would only have descriptive value rather than predictive qualities. Furthermore, most MNEs have multiple products and are often strongly diversified.

The concept by Milliman, Von Glinow and Nathan (1991) extends the life-cycle model by Adler and Ghadar (1990) by looking at organizational life cycles rather than product life cycles. The criticism of being a descriptive model also applies here. Furthermore, both concepts have to be criticized for not taking further influencing independent variables into consideration.

The 1990s saw the development of a number of integrative frameworks in SIHRM. Schuler, Dowling and De Cieri (1993) integrate previous conceptual and empirical work in the area and develop a new framework which explicitly, among other factors, also considers country and regional characteristics as an exogenous independent variable influencing internationalization strategy and international HRM decisions in an MNE. The same is true for the extension of the Schuler, Dowling and De Cieri (1993) model by De Cieri and Dowling (1998). Taylor, Beechler and Napier (1996), whose model also develops out of the Schuler, Dowling and De Cieri (1993) framework, consider the culture-distance between the country of the parent company and the host country of the affiliate.

All the SIHRM concepts mentioned try to deal with the integration–differentiation puzzle. Whereas for Perlmutter and Heenan (1974) this puzzle is solved by recruiting foreign positions irrespective of nationality, Adler and Ghadar (1990) give a more detailed catalogue of suggestions regarding the different functional areas of HRM. The bottom line of their argument still remains rather superficial in that they say that MNEs have to

- recruit globally irrespective of nationality;
- make international assignments and mobility a key for advancement into top management positions;
- appraise for and reward cross-cultural adjustment skills and mobility;
- introduce global reward structures etc.

What they do not discuss, however, is *how* an MNE can introduce these standardised practices effectively while accounting for the idiosynchratic contingencies of the multiple host countries.

Schuler, Dowling and De Cieri (1993) deal with this question in a more sophisticated way. They argue that in the design of a global HRM system there are different levels of abstraction. Standardization on an HRM policy level in MNEs can take the form of defining standard global goals while the MNE still allows for context-specific local-level variations of HRM practices within the constraints set on the policy level (for example, an agreement on performance based pay on the policy level, but the possibility to introduce, for example, pay forms based on group performance versus individual performance etc.). A good example of how common goals formulated on an HRM policy level are translated to the HRM practice level allowing for context-specific variations is the 'competency approach' British Petroleum (BP) applied in the 1990s (see Bognanno and Sparrow 1995). On the basis of their 'Vision and Value' statement BP identified a range of common competencies (standardization of behavioural outcomes) required by particular employee groups to fulfil the new goals set out. Recognizing that it was not the competencies which varied across cultures but 'rather' the way in which these competencies were acted out, BP went through a long process of adjusting the behavioural indicators, which served as performance criteria of the identified competencies, to their culturally distinct employee groups abroad.

A further interesting idea is that different HRM practices vary with regard to their cross-cultural transferability (for example, Rosenzweig and Nohria 1994). It is assumed that recruitment and (technical) training are less culture-bound because they are characterized by the technical ingredients attached to various positions (Anderson 1992; Watson 1994). A production manager, for example, needs to possess a set of skills, education background and experiences independent of the country in which he or she performs. On the other hand, HRM practices such as promotion, performance appraisal and financial compensation are more distinctive from one country to another because they are induced by socio-cultural factors (Hofstede 1982).

There is some empirical evidence which supports the assumption of differences in cross-cultural transferability of HRM practices. In their sample of 65 Sino-Western joint ventures (JVs) Lu and Björkman (1997) found that recruitment and training did indeed appear to be less culture-bound than promotion, performance appraisal and financial compensation. Similarly (apart from pay), the research by Child (1994), which also focused on Sino-Western JVs, showed that the introduction of foreign approaches in appraising, promotion and career development were not very successful, whereas new approaches in payment and staffing showed a somewhat higher success rate (Child et al. 1994; Child 1991: 101). The former approaches can be deemed to be less successful because they touch sensitive fields in the social and political context of the Chinese enterprise and because they are functional areas where foreign approaches can be assumed to be furthest removed from the collective norms of Chinese tradition and socialist ideology (Child 1994: 181). Easterby-Smith, Malina and Lu (1995) see the main difference in HRM between the People's Republic of China (PRC) and the UK companies they studied in the 'softer' functional areas where relationships matter, such as appraising practices, the assessment of management potential and reward systems (Easterby-Smith, Malina and Lu 1994: 55).

Warner (1995) has highlighted the difficulties of applying an exogenous concept, like HRM, in the Chinese context. Indeed, it may be said that its extension to most Asian economies is questionable, particularly given the cultural differences which exist, say, between East and West (see chapters 11 and 12). If spreading industrialization and technological change make for similar superstructures, one would observe that national systems would move towards common HRM patterns. Globalization, in this new version of the convergence thesis, would lead to competitive pressures presenting common problems and comparable organizational solutions for enterprises wherever they were located. Deregulation and privatization would also be common and binding themes. To argue, however, that all Asian HRM systems have or are likely to converge seems to be too bold an assertion to justify at the present time, given the empirical evidence available (see chapter 13). On the surface, there may have been apparently common economic, social and political problems across the region, but the specifics have varied greatly from country to country. The devil, as always, is in the details.

In China, HRM as a academic concept was introduced by joint teaching arrangements between Chinese and foreign universities, as well as in management practice in overseas-funded firms, mainly from Japan, the USA and Europe. The translation of HRM into Chinese is *'renli ziyuan guanli'* (with the same Chinese characters as in Japanese) which means 'labour force resources management'. In fact, some people now use it misleadingly as a synonym for 'personnel management (PM)' *(renshi guanli)* and indeed treat it as such (Warner 1995). This form of older PM practice is still very common in state-owned enterprises (SOEs) and a certain conservatism continues to pervade the administration of personnel in such enterprises. It is still probably very far from the initial concept of HRM as understood in the international academic and managerial community. The term 'HRM' is in fact mostly *de rigueur* in the more prominent Sino-foreign JVs, particularly the larger ones. Even in these types of firms, management seems to be more inward looking, with a focus on issues like wages, welfare and promotion as found in the conventional personnel arrangements rather than strategic ones like long-term development normally associated with HRM

As a point of criticism, one should realize that all the above mentioned studies focus on the HRM practice level; none of the studies considered that standardization of the HRM function can also take place at a policy and a practice level. Furthermore, it is important not to see the above findings in a wholly deterministic way. Culture alone does not determine which HRM practices will or can be introduced cross-culturally. Taylor, Beechler and Napier (1996), for example, suggest that the level of standardization of HRM policies and practices varies according to the dependence structure between MNE and their foreign affiliates as well as the MNE's dependence on particular employee groups. There is rather clear empirical evidence which suggests that there is a positive association between an affiliate's dependence on the headquarters and the degree of resemblance of the HRM practices with the ones from headquarters (Beechler and Yang 1994; Hannon, Huang and Jaw 1995; Lu and Björkman 1997; Rosenzweig and Nohria 1994). This, however, might indicate more a coercive power from headquarters and does not necessarily say anything about the success or effectiveness with which such HRM practices are transferred.

The transfer of HRM policies and practices can also be seen as depending on the negotiation skills of foreign partners (Child 1991; 1994) as well as the foreign partners' bargaining power and attractiveness to varying stakeholders (Osland and Björkman 1998; Björkman and Osland 1998). Furthermore, a transfer is also dependent on existing resources within the MNE such as, for example, international management experience and the attitude of top management (for example, Taylor, Beechler and Napier 1996). We can therefore argue that with the transfer of management practices across cultures, organizations act in a 'bounded autonomy' in which they may be not only coerced into adapting to local contexts, but are also capable of using opportunities of choice within the respective environment (see, for example, Child 1997). This element of strategic choice should be emphasized, as some organizations may choose one option, whereas a similar one may not, say, in the very HRM domain we have been discussing above. Consequently, we can downplay the influence of determinism in this cross-cultural context.

Conclusion

Summing up the above debate is a more complicated matter than it would seem at first sight. In the above discussion, we have shown that cross-cultural transfer of HRM policies and practices is a highly complex issue which cannot be solved by simplistically adhering to a culture-free global 'best practice' approach. On the other hand, the realities of globalization also do not allow MNEs to completely localize this management function. Organizations need to think globally and act locally, albeit within attempts to maintain coherence in their human resource structures and practices. The hand of the head office usually weighs heavily on the subsidiaries, since organizational initiatives normally come out from the centre to the periphery. New policies in HRM appear to be no exception to this generalization.

It appears, however, that theory and research are gradually moving in the direction of solving the integration–differentiation puzzle by not seeing the HRM function as a *monolithic* block. Rather, the function is being increasingly seen as being able to apply a variety of more or less culture-bound practices. Furthermore, there are different levels of abstraction: for example, a policy level and a practice level. This could offer the opportunity to align culture-bound practices with policies which are standardized across cultures. We are, however, lacking research which is investigating such a differentiated perspective at the present time.

Theory and research also appear to be moving towards an increasingly differentiated view of the variables which influence the degree to which HRM practices can be standardized across cultures (see, for example, Schuler, Dowling and De Cieri 1993; Taylor, Beechler and Napier 1996). For instance, the framework by Taylor, Beechler and Napier (1996) considers the varying dependence on different affiliate employee groups. Of course, it would be possible to differentiate such a variable even further by, for example, taking into consideration that within a country there are a number of subcultures along such dimensions as professional education and so on. The major problem appearing from such a contingency approach is that the more variables that are added to frameworks, the less they become testable (see, for example, the critique of the Schuler, Dowling and De Cieri 1993 model in Weber *et al.* 1998); on the other hand, it is possible that frameworks are partially tested.

Finally, the creation of more complex models might actually be a truer reflection of the environmental complexity in which MNEs have to operate. We need more ambitious empirical surveys and case studies, covering a large sample of firm and national settings. Research on this complexity also needs considerable research funds, since studies have to be undertaken in many countries and this is costly. Few academic researchers have access to this level of funding these days. Collaborative work by scholars and researchers across the globe may help here. Of course, the contest between the culture-free and culture-specific theses may never be definitively resolved but greater rigour and robustness in research in this area may help us find a more intellectually satisfying and more sophisticated denouement in this debate.

Endnotes

1   Normative isomorphism is referred to by DiMaggio and Powell (1983) as resulting from professionalization.
2   Mimetic isomorphism is referred to by DiMaggio and Powell (1983) as the copying of organizational solution of other successful organizations.
3   For a critique regarding the empirical findings presented by Hickson *et al.* (1974) see also Kieser (1993: 176).
4   The two studies by Laurent (1983) and Hampden-Turner and Trompenaars (1993) are based on attitude questionnaires, answered by 'upper-middle' managers from Europe, the USA and Japan participating in management seminars in European Business schools (INSEAD Fontainebleau and CIBS Amstelveen). The findings suggest 'nationally bounded collective mental maps about organizations that seem to resist convergence effects from increased professionalization of management and intensity of international business' (Laurent 1983: 95). In a study including 160 000 employees in 40 countries administered at IBM, Hofstede (1982) identified four dimensions on which work styles differ. These are power distance, uncertainty avoidance, individualism/collectivism and masculinity/femininity.
5   An example of a problematic transfer of an organizational structural concept is the matrix structure, which is reported to have met resistance in a country like France. Laurent reports that to French managers 'the idea of reporting to two bosses was so alien . . . that mere consideration of such organising principles was an impossible, useless exercise' (Laurent 1983: 75).

Assessing a number of American management practices with behavioural implications concerning their transferability to developing countries, Jaeger comes to the conclusion that the value configurations as postulated to exist in developing countries in most cases conflict with the value configurations underlying the reviewed American management practices (Jaeger 1990: 142).

6 Guest notes that 'it is precisely because they captured the values of the vast population of middle America that they retain such a stubborn hold on the American mind' (Guest 1990: 391).

References

Adler, N.J. (1991) *International Dimensions of Organizational Behavior*, 2nd edition, Boston, MA: PWS-Kent.

Adler, N.J. and Bartholomew, S. (1992) 'Academic and professional communities of discourse: generating knowledge on transnational human resource management', *Journal of International Business Studies* 23: 551–69.

Adler, N.J. and Ghadar, F. (1990) 'Strategic human resource management: a global perspective', in R. Pieper *Human Resource Management: An International Comparison*, Berlin: De Gruyter.

Adler, N.J. and Ghadar, F. (1993) 'A strategic approach to international human resources management', in D. Wong-Rieger and F. Rieger (eds) *International Management Research*, Berlin: De Gruyter.

Anderson, G. (1992) 'Selection', in B. Towers (ed.) *Handbook of Human Resource Management*, Oxford: Blackwell.

Baliga, R. and Jaeger, A. (1985) 'Multinational corporations: control systems and delegation issues', *Journal of International Business Studies* 15: 25–40.

Bartlett, C. and Ghoshal, S. (1988) 'Organizing for worldwide effectiveness: the transnational solution', *California Management Review* 31(1): 54–75.

Bartlett, C.A. and Ghoshal, S. (1989) *Managing Across Borders: The Transnational Solution*, London: Century Business.

Beechler, S. and Yang, J.Z. (1994) 'The transfer of Japanese-style management to American subsidiaries: contingencies, constraints, and competencies', *Journal of International Business Studies* 25: 467–92.

Beer, M., Spector, B., Lawrence, P.R., Mills, D.Q. and Walton, R.E. (1985) *Human Resource Management*, New York: Free Press.

Birnbaum, P.H. and Wong, G.Y. (1985) 'Organizational structure of multinational banks in Hong Kong from a culture-free perspective', *Administrative Science Quarterly* 30(2): 262–77.

Björkman, I. and Osland, G.E. (1998) 'Multinational corporations in China: responding to government pressures', *Long Range Planning* 31(3): 436–45.

Bognanno, M. and Sparrow, P.R. (1995) 'Integrating HRM strategy using culturally defined competencies at British Petroleum', in J.M. Hiltrop and P.R. Sparrow (eds) *European Casebook on Human Resource and Change Management*. London: Prentice Hall.

Child, J. (1981) 'Culture, contingency and capitalism in the cross-national study of organizations', in L.L. Cummings and B.M. Staw (eds) *Research in Organizational Behavior*, vol. 3, Greenwich: JAI Press.

Child, J. (1991) 'A foreign perspective on the management of people in China', *International Journal of Human Resource Management* 2: 93–107.

Child, J. (1994) *Management in China During the Age of Reform*, Cambridge: Cambridge University Press.

Child, J. (1997) 'Strategic choice in the analysis of action, structure, organizations and environment: retrospect and prospect', *Organization Studies* 18: 43–76.

Child, J. and Kieser, A. (1979) 'Organization and managerial roles in British and West German companies: an examination of the culture-free thesis', in C.J. Lammers and D.J. Hickson (eds) *Organizations Alike and Unlike*, London: Routledge.

Child, J., Markoczy, L. and Cheung, T. (1994) 'Managerial adaptation in Chinese and Hungarian strategic alliances with culturally distinct foreign partners', in S. Stewart (ed.) *Advances in Chinese Industrial Studies: Joint Ventures in the People's Republic of China*, vol. 4, Greenwich: JAI Press.

Chinese Culture Connection (1987) 'Chinese values and the search for culture-free dimensions of culture', *Journal of Cross-Cultural Psychology* 18: 143–64.

Daniels, J.D., Pitts, R.A. and Tretter, M.J. (1984) 'Strategy and structure of US multinationals: an exploratory study', *Academy of Management Journal* 27(2): 292–307.

De Cieri, H. and Dowling, P.J. (1998) *The Tortuous Evolution of Strategic Human Resource Management in Multinational Enterprises*, Department of Management, Working Paper in Human Resource Management and Industrial Relations No. 5, University of Melbourne, Australia.

Devanna, M.A., Fombrun, C.J. and Tichy, N.M. (1984) 'A framework for strategic human resource management' in C.J. Fombrun, N.M. Tichy and M.A. Devanna (eds) *Strategic Human Resource Management*, New York: Wiley.

DiMaggio, P.J. and Powell, W.W. (1983) 'The iron cage revisited: institutional isomorphism and collective rationality in organizational fields', *American Sociological Review* 48: 147–60.

Dowling, P.J., Schuler, R.S. and Welch, D.E. (1994) *International Dimensions of Human Resource Management*, 2nd edition, Belmont, CA: Wadsworth.

Easterby-Smith, M., Malina, D. and Lu, Y. (1995) 'How culture-sensitive is HRM? A comparative analysis of practice in Chinese and UK companies', *International Journal of Human Resource Management* 6: 31–59.

Edwards, P.K., Ferner, A. and Sisson, K. (1996) 'The conditions for international human resource management: two case studies', *International Journal of Human Resource Management* 7(1): 20–40.

Egelhoff, W.G. (1999) 'Organizational equilibrium and organizational change: two different perspectives of the multinational enterprise', *Journal of International Management* 5: 15–33.

Evans, P. (1992) 'Management development as glue technology', *Human Resource Planning* 15(1): 85–106.

Guest, D.E. (1990) 'Human resource management and the American dream', *Journal of Management Studies*, 24: 377–97.

Guest, D. (1992) 'Right enough to be dangerously wrong: an analysis of the *In Search of Excellence phenomenon*', in G. Salaman, S. Cameron, H. Hamblin, P. Iles, C. Mabey and K. Thompson (eds) *Human Resource Strategies*, London: Sage.

Guth, W. and McMillan, I. (1986) 'Strategy implementation versus middle management self-interest', *Strategic Management Journal* July–August: 313–27.

Hamilton, R.D. and Kashlak, R.J. (1999) 'National influences on multinational corporation control system selection', *Management International Review* 39(2): 167–89.

Hampden-Turner, C. and Trompenaars, F. (1993) *The Seven Cultures of Capitalism*, London: Piatkus.

Hannon, J.M., Huang, I.-C. and Jaw, B.-S. (1995) 'International human resource strategy and its determinants: the case of subsidiaries in Taiwan' *Journal of International Business Studies* 26: 531–54.

Harbison, F. and Myers, C.A. (1959) *Management in the Industrial World*, New York: McGraw-Hill.

Hedlund, G. (1986) 'The hypermodern MNC – a heterarchy?', *Human Resource Management* 25(1): 9 ff.

Hedlund, G. (1994) 'A model of knowledge management and the N-form corporation', *Strategic Management Journal* 15: 73–90.

Hickson, D.J. and Pugh, D.S. (1995) *Management Worldwide*, Harmondsworth: Penguin.

Hickson, D.J., Hinings, C.R., McMillan, C.J. and Schwitter, J.P. (1974) 'The culture-free context of organization structure: a tri-national comparison', *Sociology* 8: 59–80.

Hofstede, G. (1980) 'Motivation, leadership, and organization: do American theories apply abroad', *Organizational Dynamics* 9: 42–63.

Hofstede, G. (1982) *Culture's Consequences – International Differences in Work-Related Values*, abridged edition, London: Sage.

Hofstede, G. (1983) 'The cultural relativity of organizational practices and theories', *Journal of International Business Studies* 14, Fall: 75–89.

Hofstede, G. (1994) 'Management scientists are human', *Management Science* 40: 4–13.

Hofstede, G. (1996) 'An American in Paris: the influence of nationality on organization theories', *Organization Studies* 17: 525–37.

Hofstede, G. and Bond, H. (1984) 'Hofstede's culture dimensions an independent validation using Rokeach's value survey', *Journal of Cross-Cultural Psychology* 15: 417–33.

Huczynski, A.A. (1993) *Management Gurus: What Makes Them and How to Become One*, London: Routledge.

Huselid, M. (1995) 'Human resource management practices and firm performance', *Academy of Management Journal* 38: 635–72.

Jaeger, A.M. (1990) 'The applicability of Western management techniques in developing countries: cultural perspective', in A.M. Jaeger and R.N. Kanungo (eds) *Management in Developing Countries*, New York: Routledge.

Kamoche, K. (1996) 'The integration–differentiation puzzle: a resource-capability perspective in international human resource management', *International Journal of Human Resource Management* 7: 230–44.

Kanungo, R.N. and Jaeger, A.M. (1990) 'Introduction: the need for indigenous management in developing countries', in A.M. Jaeger and R.N. Kanungo (eds) *Management in Developing Countries*, London: Routledge.

Kerr, C., Dunlop, J.T., Harbison, F.H. and Myers, C.A. (1960) *Industrialism and Industrial Man*, Cambridge, MA: Harvard University Press.

Kieser, A. (1993) *Organizationstheorien*, Stuttgart: Verlag W. Kohlhammer.

Kieser, A. and Kubicek, H. (1992) *Organization*, Berlin: De Gruyter.

Laurent, A. (1983) 'The cultural diversity of Western conceptions of management', *International Studies of Management and Organization*, 13: 75–96.

Laurent, A. (1986) 'The cross-cultural puzzle of international HRM', *Human Resource Management* 25: 91–102.

Legge, K. (1995) 'HRM, rhetoric, reality and hidden agendas', in J. Storey (ed.) *Human Resource Management*, London: Routledge.

Lincoln, J.R., Hanada, M. and Olson, J. (1981) 'Cultural orientations and individual reactions to organizations: a study of employees of Japanese-owned firms', *Administrative Science Quarterly* 26: 93–115.

Lu, Y. and Björkman, I. (1997) 'HRM practices in China–Western joint ventures: MNC standardization versus localization', *International Journal of Human Resource Management* 8: 614–27.

Marsden, D. (1991) 'Indigenous management', *International Journal of Human Resource Management* 2: 21–38.

Martin, G. and Beaumont, P. (1998) 'Diffusing "best practice" in multinational firms: prospects, practice and contestation', *International Journal of Human Resource Management* 9(4): 71–95.

Martinez, J.I. and Jarillo, J.C. (1989) 'The evolution of research on coordination mechanisms in multinational corporations', *Journal of International Business Studies* 20(3): 489–514.

Maurice, M., Sorge, A. and Warner, M. (1980) 'Societal differences in organizing manufacturing units: a comparison of France, West Germany, and Great Britain', *Organization Studies* 1: 58–86.

Milliman, J., Von Glinow, M.A. and Nathan, M. (1991) 'Organizational life cycles and strategic international human resource management in multinational companies: implications for congruence theory', *Academy of Management Review* 16: 318–39.

Neghandi, A.R. (1974) 'Cross-cultural management studies: too many conclusions, not enough conceptualizations', *Management International Review* 14: 59–72.

Ofori-Dankwa, J. and Reddy, J. (1999) 'Birnbaum and Wong (1985) revisited: a re-evaluation of the culture-free hypothesis', *American Business Review* 17(2): 126–34.

Osland, G.E. and Björkman, I. (1998) 'MNC–host government interaction: government pressures on MNCs in China', *European Management Journal* 16(1): 91–100.

Parker, B. (1998) *Globalization and Business Practice*, London: Sage.

Perlmutter, H.V. (1969) 'The tortuous evolution of the multinational corporation', *Columbia Journal of World Business* 4: 9–18.

Perlmutter, H.V. and Heenan, D.A. (1974) 'How multinational should your top managers be?', *Harvard Business Review* 52: 121–32.

Perrow, C. (1967) 'A framework for the comparative analysis of organizations', *American Sociological Review* 32: 194–208.

Peters, T. and Waterman, R. (1982) *In Search of Excellence*, New York: Harper & Row.

Pfeffer, J. (1994) *Competive Advantage Through People: Unleashing the Power of the Workforce*, Boston, MA: Harvard Business School Press.

Pfeffer, J. (1998) *The Human Equation*, Boston, MA: Harvard Business School Press.

Poole, M. (1990) 'Editorial: human resource management in an international perspective', *International Journal of Human Resource Management* 1: 1–15.

Redding, S.G. (1994) 'Comparative management theory: jungle, zoo or fossil bed?', *Organization Studies* 15: 323–59.

Rosenzweig, P.M. and Nohria, N. (1994) 'Influences on human resource management practices in multinational corporations', *Journal of International Business Studies* 25: 229–51.

Schuler, R.S., Dowling, P.J. and De Cieri, H. (1993) 'An integrative framework of strategic international human resource management', *International Journal of Human Resource Management* 4: 717–64.

Snell, S.A. (1992) 'Control theory in strategic human resource management: the mediating effect of administrative information', *Academy of Management* 35(2): 292–327.

Sparrow P., Schuler R.S. and Jackson S.E. (1994) 'Convergence or divergence: human resource practices and policies for competitive advantage worldwide', *International Journal of Human Resource Management* 5: 267–99.

Staehle, W. (1988) 'Human resource management (HRM)', *Zeitschrift für Betriebswirtschaftslehre (ZfB)* 58: 576–87.

Staehle, W. (1994) *Management*, 7th edition, München: Verlag Franz Vahlen.

Stopford, J. and Wells, L.T. (1972) *Managing the Multinational Enterprise*, New York: Basic Books.

Storey, J. (1989) 'Introduction: from personnel management to human resource management', in J. Storey (ed.) *New Perspectives on Human Resource Management*, London: Routledge.

Tayeb, M. (2001) 'Hofstede', in M. Warner (ed.) *IEBM Handbook of Management Thinking*, London: Thomson Learning.

Taylor, S., Beechler, S. and Napier, N. (1996) 'Towards an integrative model of strategic international human resource management', *Academy of Management Review* 21: 959–86.

Tichy, N.M.; Fombrun, C.J. and Devanna, M.A. (1982) 'Strategic human resource management', *Sloan Management Review* 23: 47–61.

Van Dijk, J.J. (1990) 'Transnational management in an evolving european context', *European Management Journal* 8: 474–9.

Warner, M. (1995) *The Management of Human Resources in Chinese Industry*, Basingstoke: Macmillan; New York: St. Martin's Press.

Watson, T. (1994) 'Recruitment and selection', in K. Sisson (ed.) *Personnel Management*, Oxford: Blackwell.

Weber, W., Festing, M., Dowling, P.J. and Schuler, R.S. (1998) *Internationales Personalmanagement*, Wiesbaden: Gabler.

White, R.E. and Poynter, T.A. (1990) 'Organizing for world-wide advantage', in C.A. Bartlett, Y. Doz and G. Hedlund (eds) *Managing the Global Firm*, London: Routledge.

Whittington, R. (1992) 'Putting Giddens into action: social systems and managerial agency', *Journal of Management Studies* 29: 693–712.

Wilkinson, B. (1996) 'Culture, institutions and business in East Asia', *Organization Studies* 17: 421–47.

Woodward, J. (1965) *Industrial Organization: Theory and Practice*, London: Oxford University Press.

Chapter 4

Theorizing about organization cross-nationally: part 1 – an introduction

John Child

Introduction

Scholars interested in cross-national aspects of organization have for many years rued the slow progress of their field. Redding (1994: 331) concluded from his 'review of the reviews' that 30 years' work had made little impression on an area of study which 'has suffered from the excessive repetition of sterile reporting, from theoretical poverty and from a lack of clear direction'. Little has happened since then to dispel this sense of frustration and crisis. The field continues to suffer from the lack of a clear focus and unifying theoretical framework. This, in turn, gives rise to conceptual and operational fragmentation.

The blurring of focus results from the fact that the field has been defined both as the cross-national study of organization *and* the study of cross-national organization. These two approaches are often distinguished respectively as the 'comparative' and 'international' study of management or organization. The first approach has been the mainstream, concentrating on the similarities and differences between features of organization that might characterize various countries or cultural regions (e.g. Hampden-Turner and Trompenaars 1993; Lammers and Hickson 1979). However, the number of organizational entities that span national boundaries is increasing rapidly. Corporations are steadily extending the scope of their international operations, and there is a burgeoning of cross-border mergers and strategic alliances. The public sector has also seen a significant increase in both cross-national and supra-national governmental agencies. A focus on corporations and other bodies that have become transnational in scope offers an alternative approach to studying organization in its international context (Ghoshal and Bartlett 1998).

Which of these options offers the more fruitful path towards understanding the relevance of nationality for organization? One possibility is to concentrate on comparing national models of organization, assuming that they are embedded within distinct systems of business, culture and innovation (Amable, Barré and Boyer 1997; Hofstede 1991; Whitley 1992a; 1992b). In addition to their intrinsic sociological interest, the national differences embodied in organization play a significant contextual role for the management of cross-national organizations. Another option is to concentrate on how organization transcends national boundaries, recognizing that in so doing it may be a powerful force for international homogeneity through the transfer of organizational and management practices (Child, Faulkner and Pitkethly 2000). At an empirical level, the subject matter of both approaches is very similar. Those who maintain that globalization is subsuming national influences within transnational forces suggest that it will become increasingly necessary to marry these two focuses within an appropriate supporting theoretical framework. The present chapter acknowledges the force of this view. It therefore considers cross-national organizational studies to embrace both the comparison of organizational forms between nations and the study of cross-national organization.

The presence of multiple theoretical frameworks further diffuses the focus of this field. As Roberts (1970) recognized 30 years ago, the difficulty of reaching agreement on the nature of the cross-national organizational beast to a large extent reflects a theoretical profusion, if not confusion. People are continuing to look at different parts of the elephant and its habitat through different theoretical lenses each with their own co-ordinates, as it were. These can range from the broad sweep of economics to the very specific focus of indigenous cultural psychology. Sometimes, scholars may even be directing their attention to the same parts of the beast and its habitat, but using the different filters supplied by apparently incompatible or non-contiguous concepts. Groups of scholars, each with their own theoretical and conceptual language, compete to define the field and their members hesitate to engage in mutual constructive discourse. It has been pointed out (Child 1997; Reed 1996) that this description applies to the current fragmentation within organizational studies as a whole. Resolution of the problem is, however, a more daunting challenge for the study of organization cross-nationally because this brings into play an additional dimension of theoretical complexity due to the diversity of contexts that have to be considered.

Theoretical fragmentation leaves a number of methodological problems unresolved. Defining the field exclusively within the ambit of a single theoretical perspective, such as national culture, discourages research designs that allow for an examination of other potential influences on organization. Thus in so-called 'cross-cultural' studies, attention to organizational variance between nations has not generally been complemented by an equivalent attention to variance within nations of the sort that might be suggested by theories of industrial economics. There has also been a long-standing and potentially confusing debate between those adopting interpretative and positivistic ontological assumptions about the possibility of achieving greater conceptual consistency and equivalence in operational measurement. Whereas economists using highly codified financial or physical data may not regard this as a serious problem, students of indigenous cultural psychology are very likely to. The dispute has particularly affected cross-national organization studies with the result that only rarely, as in the Aston Programme (Hickson and McMillan 1981), has there been any consistency in the features of organization being compared cross-nationally. This lack of conceptual and operational consistency has impeded progress on such fundamental issues as ascertaining the validity of national stereotypes of organization.

Problems such as these reflect the absence of a comprehensive and synthesizing theoretical framework to guide the design of research on organization with a cross-national focus. Theoretical pluralism has so far led to confusion and paralysis rather than to enlightenment, which leads one to ask whether the 'jungle' that confronts us can eventually be arranged into a tidy garden (Redding 1994). This chapter proceeds on the basis that some constructive arrangement is possible. Its underlying premise is that there is no problem in looking at different parts of an elephant as long as we also have an idea of how the parts fit together to describe the whole. If that is the case, we can compare black with white, blue with green elephants, or alternatively just their trunks, without forgetting that in other respects they continue to share the characteristics of being elephants. If, however, our lines of sight continue to be constrained by the fixed focal lengths of unduly bounded concepts and theories, we shall find it extremely difficult to move beyond limited and non-communicating perspectives to achieve this more holistic view.

The intention of Chapters 4 and 5 is therefore to take some small steps towards theoretical synthesis and a refocusing of the field. The term 'synthesis' is used advisedly to indicate constructive combination rather than complete integration. Chapter 4 rehearses the main perspectives that are on offer to guide the study of organization cross-nationally. Chapter 5 then explores their potential synthesis within a unifying theoretical framework. An analysis of globalization, the major contextual development for cross-national organization, demonstrates the value of the framework and assists its development.

Low- and high-context perspectives

There is a palette of theoretical perspectives relevant to cross-national organization studies. They almost all derive from Western scholarship, though contributions from anthropology and sociology have also been informed by research in other parts of the world. In fact, many of the founding fathers of Western social science adopted an internationally comparative approach in their attempts to construct general social theories and to trace the development of different civilizations.

A basic distinction can be drawn between two categories of theoretical perspective in terms of their sensitivity to nations or regions as analytically significant contexts. The first category consists of theories that are not sensitive to particular nations or regions as special contexts, but that refer instead to universal rationales. This universalism is seen to arise from ubiquitous economic and technological forces that are in turn motivated by universal human needs and drives. These generate certain operational contingencies that establish a functional imperative for organizational design and process, regardless of national setting. An extension of this perspective predicts an increasing convergence between modes of organization as countries develop industrial and post-industrial economies with similar political systems and personal lifestyles, a convergence that is seen to have accelerated under the impetus of late twentieth-century globalization. This first set of perspectives may therefore be called 'low-context' in the sense that they do not grant national context any analytical significance over and above the configuration of universals that happen to characterize a country at any point in its development.

The other category consists of theoretical perspectives that grant theoretical primacy to national cultures, or national institutional systems, when accounting for national differences in organization. Because they grant explanatory primacy to specifically national rationalities, they may be termed 'high-context' perspectives. They posit national uniqueness in organizational structures, systems and behaviours, and ascribe such uniqueness to specifically national properties of a cultural and/or institutional nature. These perspectives expect national organizational differences to persist over time regardless of economic development.

'Low-context' perspectives

A common feature of low-context perspectives is that they minimize the impact of national distinctiveness. They contain a strong presumption of eventual convergence in management and organization as nations become increasingly engaged in an increasingly efficient global economy and are increasingly subject to the impact of technological change. These perspectives imply that, as new technologies break down barriers of communication and information, and (hopefully) dire poverty is reduced, people will increasingly come to express similar demands for organization and work to be arranged in ways that meet the fundamental psychological needs and aspirations they are assumed to share. This encourages the search for new forms of organization that reconcile efficiency and human needs more effectively hitherto. Economics, technology and psychology thus figure prominently among the low-context perspectives.

Economic universalism

Economic theory centres on the allocation of scarce resources through the pursuit of utility via the market mechanism. By extension, it purports to explain the formal organization of economic activities by firms as an economically rational response to market conditions. For example, Chandler (1977) accounts for the rise of the modern 'multiunit business enterprise' by reference to the growth of markets, assisted by new production and transportation technologies, and the development of professional managers to co-ordinate activities previously conducted in the marketplace (Biggart 1997). Williamson (1985) also refers to market factors as the primary condition for hierarchically controlled and co-ordinated firms to develop. These factors include the costs of co-ordinating market transactions and maintaining market contracts, as well as risks due to opportunism by market partners when the deal entails investing in specific-use assets. Most economists assume that their market-based theories are universally applicable and can account for which forms of business organization will be effective (that is, expected to survive in the long term), wherever the national location.

The credibility of economic universalism has grown since the advent of neo-liberal economics in Western countries and the introduction of economic reform in former state-socialist or state-militarist countries. It argues that, given the growth of the global economy and common human aspirations for betterment, 'free-market' economics will eventually prevail in all societies, and present a common context for management. Thus, the editors of the Heritage Foundation/*Wall Street Journal*'s '1999 Index of Economic Freedom' state that 'freedom is the surest path to growth' (Johnson, Holmes and Kirkpatrick 1998: 14). The argument is that ultimately liberalization and financial transparency, as conditions for efficient markets, are required for sustained economic development. Institutions like the International Monetary Fund (IMF) and journals such as *The Economist* and *Wall Street Journal* praise non-intervention by governments, liberalization, transparency and freedom of capital movements.

Much economic development theory adopts the perspective of economic universalism, especially modernization theory with its late-development and catch-up variants. This posits an eventual convergence among developed countries, including their forms of organization and management (Biggart and Hamilton 1992). It is claimed that economic rationality dictates a need for professional management under world competitive conditions (Kerr *et al.* 1960). The canons of professional management include provisions that may be at variance with more traditional practices in developing nations, such as transparency of goals, rational resource allocation, systematic selection and human resource development, objective performance appraisal and reward.

The economic perspective regards the organization as a micro-level phenomenon. Economists therefore generally confine themselves to discussing broad alternative organizational phenomena, such as the choice between U- and M-form structures (Williamson 1970), the organizational internalization of markets (Buckley and Casson 1976; Williamson 1985), and models for the organization of international business (Bartlett and Ghoshal 1989; Ghoshal and Westney 1993). Economic universalism continues to hold powerful sway in much contemporary work. For example, the debate on corporate governance is powerfully informed by agency theory and by criteria for efficient resource utilization including transparency and fiduciary accountability (Hawley and Williams 1996; Shleifer and Vishny 1997).

Internal discussion in China about the restructuring of that country's leading large enterprises is today being conducted with reference not to specifically Chinese, or even socialist, principles but rather in the light of theories on transactions costs, and market forces (e.g. Qin Xiao 1999). A third example concerns one of the most far-reaching developments in cross-national organization, the internationalization of firms. The predominant line of theorizing available to account for the stages through which activities are located abroad, and the choice of forms for organizing international operations, articulates these issues in terms of general principles governing risk, managerial exigency and market opportunity (Johanson and Vahlne 1977; Kogut 1988).

Economic theory endeavours to apply principles in ways that rarely accord a positive value to national specifics. When these are taken into account, it tends to regard them as contingencies such as market imperfections that constrain economically optimum behaviour, or opportunism that generates economically dysfunctional behaviour. In other words, national conditions tend to be treated as constraints on the effective operation of the market system rather than as features that confer cultural preferences for, and differential degrees of institutional legitimacy on, particular ways of organizing.

Technology

Technological change and development has been regarded as the prime mover of capitalism (Schumpter 1943; Toffler 1971). Moreover, as Dicken (1998: 145) notes, 'technology is, without doubt, one of the most important contributory factors underlying the internationalization and globalization of economic activity'. The impact of technology extends not only to the location of productive activities but also increasingly to the ways in which these can be managed. This development is associated with the contemporary 'shift from a technology based primarily on cheap inputs of energy to one predominantly based on cheap inputs of information derived from advances in microelectronic and telecommunications technology' (Freeman 1988: 10). With the increasing importance of this 'new technology', there is a convergence between the considerations advanced for organization by information theorists and those advanced by students of technology.

Much of the literature on information and communications technologies claims that these technologies offer path-breaking new ways of handling information which have implications for the design of effective organizations (Fulk and DeSanctis 1995). It is argued, for example, that such technologies offer more effective ways of reconciling long-standing inherent organizational dilemmas such as the need for simultaneous control and flexible autonomy. Some elevate information to be the spirit of the age, and they argue that it carries a universal message for organization and management. An example is found in Applegate's (1995) writing on 'designing and managing the information age organization'. She takes the view that advances in information technology, when coupled with changes in workforce capabilities, can address the problems that previously stood in the way of transformation from bureaucratic to organic, if not virtual, organizations. Given an increasingly competitive and fast-moving world economic environment, Applegate believes that advances in information technology, and in related conceptions of information, knowledge and learning, have created an irresistible movement towards new forms of organization, a movement that she and others of a like mind indeed wish to foster.

The significance of technology for organization is, nevertheless, hotly disputed. Some have regarded technology in general, and production technology in particular, as constraining or even determining workplace organization and social relations (e.g. Hickson *et al.* 1974; Woodward 1965). The implication of their perspective for the cross-national study of organization is that, whatever the national setting, the adoption of a given technology will have the same influential consequences for the design of a viable organization and for the way that social relations at work are consequently structured (Child 1981). In other words, technological determinists argue that different production technologies determine particular organization structures and behaviours independently of the local context (Knights and Murray 1994). As Hickson and his colleagues put it, 'the technological equipment of an oil refinery requires much the same operatives and supervisors wherever it is' (Hickson *et al.* 1974: 64).

Others have, by contrast, concluded from close examination of the adoption of particular forms of technology that the decisions made at the time reflected managerial preferences for increasing control over the work process rather than any technological imperative (e.g. Noble 1977). Child and Loveridge (1990) concluded from studies of information technology (IT) in European services that it remained an open question whether the application of new technology will give rise to increasing similarities in the process of organizing across different countries. This is because there is considerable latitude in how organizational arrangements are constituted around the technology, and hence plenty of scope for their negotiation. Scarbrough (1996) argued similarly, from a study of information systems (IS) projects in six financial organizations located in Scotland, that the possibilities presented by IT for organizational redesign are worked through the social construction of different classificatory systems. In his assessment, organization is a 'contested terrain across which different classificatory systems slug it out' (ibid.: 200). Each system is fought for by interested parties whose desire is to 'promote classificatory world-views in which their own expertise is central' (ibid.: 200).

One might have expected the greater inherent flexibility of the new technology to have softened the deterministic stance. Some prophets of the new technology, however, continue to embrace a position of technological determinism even though their message may now be an optimistic one emphasizing how new technology can assist people to realize their potential (cf. Zuboff 1988), rather than the earlier pessimistic message of alienation (cf. Blauner 1964). This leads Dicken (1998: 145) to warn that 'it is all too easy to be seduced by the notion that technology "causes" a specific set of changes [and] makes particular structures and arrangements "inevitable" '.

Psychological universalism/methodological individualism
This perspective assumes that all human beings share common needs and motivational structures. The desire to satisfy common needs forms the basis for similar structures of individual motivation. In so far as such motivation drives people's behaviour in organizations, it is argued that the design of work organization as well as managerial systems for control and reward must treat this as a major exigency. Even cross-cultural psychologists who recognize that human behaviour varies across different cultural settings are primarily concerned to pursue the discipline's aim of arriving at universal generalizations. This means that they tend to regard the contextual specifics of different countries as anomalous rather than fundamental (Bond and Smith 1996). For, according to Poortinga (1992: 13), 'it is assumed that the same psychological processes are operating in all humans independent of culture'.

For the past 100 years, from scientific management through to contemporary industrial and social psychology, there has been a search for a generally applicable theory of motivation at work. Content theories attempt to identify the factors that actually motivate people, such as Maslow's (1943) hierarchy of needs model, Herzberg's (Herzberg, Mausner and Snyderman 1959) two-factor theory or McClelland's (1988) achievement motivation theory. Process theories attempt to identify the relationship among the dynamic variables that comprise motivation, and include expectancy theory (Porter and Lawler 1968), equity theory (Adams 1965), goal theory (Locke 1968) and attribution theory (Heider 1958). Cognitive social psychologists have also developed theories of chronic individual motive, emphasizing for instance uncertainty reduction (Sorrentino and Hewitt 1984), the need for structure (Neuberg and Newsom 1993) and the need for closure (Kruglanski and Freund 1983).

While these psychological theories differ in detail, they take individuals or groups as their focus, more or less in isolation from their cultural and social context. Thus people are regarded as essentially the same everywhere. They all need to eat, have security, enjoy social relations and derive some meaning from their lives. Reducing the theoretical and methodological level to the individual encourages the assumption that all people share a similar set of needs. The more basic needs are taken to be biological and physiological in nature. They are not subject to a high degree of social definition; whether you have sufficient to eat and enjoy shelter and security are to a large extent common necessities. The assumption of universal human needs has importantly informed the analysis of utility that underlies much economic theory.

Appropriate levels even of basic need fulfilment are in practice to some extent socially defined, as with acceptable levels of obesity or sexual activity. However, psychological universalism starts to run into serious problems when it addresses so-called higher-order needs that are of a cognitive rather than material nature, such as esteem and self-actualization. For these are expressed primarily through social norms and are thus subject to cultural definition. What constitutes achievement, for example, is defined for all but a few isolates in terms of cultural norms.

It is precisely because many needs are socially defined and reflect what is valued culturally that the universal applicability of psychological theories has been heavily questioned. They have been criticized for their universalism – for assuming that the same theory can be applied to all people regardless of their social origins, upbringing, education and culture. They have also been criticized for their imperialism. Hofstede (1980a) in particular has argued that these psychological theories actually reflect American cultural values, especially individualism, with their emphasis on achievement and self-actualization as the highest-level needs (see chapter 8). Some psychologists have themselves urged the need to develop theories of behaviour and motivation that are indigenous to different societies rather than universalistic in nature (e.g. Yang 1994). This critique derives, of course, from a high-context perspective, and it calls to mind Kluckhohn *et al.*'s (1951) recommendation that, even with reference to those values that express common human material or moral fundamentals, we speak about 'conditional absolutes' because they may be subject to culturally nuanced definitions. If the general applicability of current psychological work-related theories can be questioned, then their prescriptions for organizational design have to be treated with caution.

'High-context' perspectives

High-context perspectives share the strong presumption that management and organization will retain and develop their own distinct characteristics that derive from cultural preferences and embedded institutions.

Cultural theory

The cultural perspective places the previous 'low-context' theories into what it considers as their appropriate cultural context. Economic utilities, personal motivations and the ways information is interpreted and used are seen to be culture-bound. This perspective maintains that thinking and behaviour are significantly governed by cultural values. Culture therefore differentiates management across nations and other social collectivities.

The two best known cultural perspectives that have been applied to management and organization are those of Hofstede (1980b; 1991) and Trompenaars (1993). While these two Dutchmen fiercely contest the validity of their respective cultural dimensions and methodologies, they agree on the following basic assumptions.

Cultural values are deep-seated and enduring. They vary systematically between different societies. They condition what is acceptable organizational practice. And they predict intersocietal differences in economic performance (gross domestic product).

The cultural perspective has for some time provided the dominant paradigm in comparative studies of organization. It is indicative that Hickson and Pugh (1995) chose to subtitle their review of the field' *The Impact of Societal Culture on Organizations Around the Globe.* Even before Hofstede's seminal work, international studies of organization predominantly regarded culture as the key explanatory factor for cross-national differences, as reviews such as Roberts (1970) make clear. Attention to culture also has intuitive appeal to practising international managers, for whom it serves as a convenient reference for the many frustrating difficulties they can experience when working with people from other countries, the source of which they do not fully comprehend.

Despite its appeal and influence, many questions remain to be answered about the cultural perspective. The first and most fundamental concerns the theoretical status of culture. Is culture all-pervasive, as Sorge (1982) has argued, so that we need to reposition our economic and technological theories within a cultural space, as Boisot (1995) has advocated for information theory? In other words, does culture take primacy over other factors not only in terms of predictive power but also in terms of structuring the systems of meaning, and shaping the rationales, that other theorists can legitimately employ? If that is the case, then the comparative study of organization across cultural boundaries employing concepts and equivalent operational measures derived from only one culture becomes hazardous in terms of validity criteria.

Cultural relativism thus raises the question of conceptual equivalence. Indigenous psychologists argue that the meaning attached to words, and the definitions of acceptable behaviours, is particular to the members of different societies. This questions the equivalence between cultures of any comparative concept and its operational measurement. Universalistic concepts and their standardized measurement of the kind that cross-cultural scholars like Hofstede have employed become suspect on the basis of this argument. This is a problem that Hofstede has himself recognized and which encouraged Bond and he to uncover the fifth dimension of 'Confucian Dynamism' in East Asian societies (Hofstede and Bond 1988). On the other hand, standard measures such as Hofstede's appear sufficiently robust to uncover replicable differences between societies that also accord with common experience. The issue of conceptual equivalence is fundamental to our ability to undertake valid cross-national studies of organization.

Moreover, we still do not have an adequate theory on the relevance of culture for organization. Key issues remain unclear, namely which organizational features are shaped by culture, how are they so influenced and what the significance of culture is as compared to, say, economic, technological and political factors. A satisfactory theory would have to address two levels of analysis. The first concerns the independence of culture as an explanatory variable. To what extent are cultures themselves shaped by national economic, technological and political factors through the mediation of lifestyle, mass media, access to global information and government-sponsored ideology? Can culture be regarded as an independent, let alone dominant, force? The common assumption that national differences can simply be expressed in cultural terms, and that nation can be used as the unit of analysis for culture (Gannon 1994), is in reality a hypothesis that still requires testing. The second level concerns the identification of organizational attributes that are culturally specific in the sense that they vary systematically between cultures and can be shown to be impacted directly by culture.

These considerations imply that

> a test of national differences which are culturally intrinsic would require an examination of whether organizational characteristics continue to differ across nations when contingencies and economic systems are similar or controlled, and a demonstration that the remaining differences are explicable in terms of an adequate theory of national cultures.
>
> *(Child 1981: 305)*

In similar vein, one of the 'recommendations for progress' that Redding (1994: 350) offered from his review of comparative management theory is to 'enrich the current grand theory of Hofstede further by probing into the societal origins of his value clusters, and in terms of outcomes, trace more explicitly the patterns of their organizational consequences'.

Cultural information theory

Among cultural information theories, Boisot's (1986) is particularly fruitful for a comparative understanding of organizational forms. He identifies four institutionalized approaches to organizing transactions and relationships, in terms of the modes of information processing that characterize them. These modes are defined in terms of two primary dimensions of information: its codification and diffusion. Boisot named the 'space' that these create, the 'culture-space', on the basis that there are marked cultural and/or institutionalized preferences to be found in different nations for particular positions on the two dimensions. Thus the relatively open, transparent 'Anglo-Saxon' nations, with their highly codified legal and other systems, would be expected to favour a combination of high information codification and diffusion (availability). The four fundamental organizational forms to which this framework gives rise are bureaucracy, market, clan and fief. On the assumption just made, Anglo-Saxon nations should exhibit a high preference for the organization of transactions through markets, and this is undoubtedly the case.

Boisot and Child (1988; 1996) have applied this framework to a comparison of Chinese and 'Western' organizational forms. They concluded that whereas capitalist business involving private ownership and funding was significant in both societies (increasingly so even in the People's Republic of China), the mode of organizational typifying that capitalism was different. This led them to suggest that the Chinese form should be labelled 'network capitalism'. This is an example of the application of cultural information theory cross-nationally for purposes of identifying broad organizational forms.

At the group or team level, information theory adopts a quite different focus depending on whether it is sensitive to the influence of cross-national culture or not. Abstracted from culture, emphasis is likely to be placed on the effective functioning of teams as information processing units, employing procedures such as agreeing objectives, preparing briefing papers, recording the results of discussions and accumulating a relevant knowledge base. The intention is to structure team process in ways that will encourage them to transform the quality of available information, especially from tacit to explicit, and to codify that explicit knowledge so as to transform it into a property available to the organization as a whole (Nonaka and Takeuchi 1995). If, however, information theory is sensitive to cultural influences, it will recognize that accepted modes of group functioning, including the conduct of meetings, vary considerably across cultures. It will therefore pay a great deal more attention to the social composition of groups or teams within organizations, and to the processes whereby they can find a commonly acceptable way of proceeding, communicating and (eventually) sharing identity (Drummond 1997; Tjosvold 1991).

At the individual level, the cross-national sensitivity of information theory again varies. Much has focused on the cognitive capacities of individuals per se, including their ability to handle complex or incomplete information (Streufert and Swezey 1986). Other work has, however, taken account of how, for instance, interpretative models vary in different cultures, and the implications this has for information processing capabilities. An example is the contrast between factorial-analytical orientation of the Western cognitive model and the synthetic-holistic orientation of the Chinese interpretative model (Liu 1986). This type of distinction between the nationally-specific information-processing modes of individuals assumes considerable significance for organizations in two respects. First, if there are national styles of information interpretation, they will shape the preferences of organizational members for particular forms of information processing and hence transactional governance. Second, they will colour the character of whole organizations if they are strongly reflected in the decision-making and management style of leaders.

Institutional theory

This perspective emphasizes that management and business has different institutional foundations in different societies. Key institutions are the state, the legal system, the financial system and the family. Taken together, such institutions constitute the distinctive social organization of a country and its economy. The forms these institutions take and their economic role are seen to shape different 'national business systems' or varieties of capitalism (Orru, Biggart and Hamilton 1997; Whitley 1992a; 1992b). Although the institutional perspective draws on a long sociological tradition, there is still not much agreement about, or understanding of, the processes whereby institutions are formed and in turn impact on organizations (Tolbert and Zucker 1996). There is, however, much more consensus on the potential analytical power that the perspective offers.

Institutional theory implies that nations have their own logic of social and economic organization, and that theories claiming universal application may in fact betray their own specific institutional origins. Thus, neo-classical economics is most appropriate to the nineteenth-century liberal capitalism it was first developed to explain. Some institutionalists have argued that East Asian countries require their own economic theory because their dominant transactional logic is different (Biggart and Hamilton 1992). For example, in China the logic and rationale of hierarchy has been based upon the relational norms expounded by Confucius and legal codes such as those developed during the Tang Dynasty (See chapter 11). This institutionalized relational logic shapes a society whose transactional order rests on social obligation to higher authority and to the community rather than on rules oriented to protecting the individual. Chinese capitalism is seen to be intrinsically different from Western capitalism because of this contrast in institutional framing over a long period of time (Gerth and Mills 1946; Weber 1964).

Institutional theorists stress the historical embeddedness of social structures and processes. This carries two particularly significant implications for the cross-national analysis of organization. First, 'institutional theory proposes that social and economic organization is informed by historically developed logics that are only changed with difficulty' (Biggart and Guillén 1999: 742). In other words, institutions are likely to be 'sticky' in the face of economic and technological change. This means that, in so far as a country's constituent bodies (firms, public organizations and so forth) are enabled, supported and guided by national institutions, one would expect cross-national contrasts in the organizational responses to handling such change. Second, as Biggart and Guillén also note, the social organization of a country is 'a repository of useful resources or capabilities' (ibid.: 742). In other words, social organization influences a country's ability efficiently and effectively to undertake certain kinds of production or other economic activity. National institutions such as education systems and the structure of social relations can, through their impact on the degree of ascription or achievement in the society, impact on the ability of a country to base its economic wealth-creation on innovation rather than, say, mass production. Institutionalists therefore argue that the conditions of economic survival through specialization around national strengths tend to preserve nationally distinctive patterns of organization, even within a fully open and globalized competitive system.

There is, however, a problem in the weak theorization of how organizations are formed with reference to institutions as contextual analytical references (Loveridge 1998). Students of national business systems have generally confined themselves to noting aspects of congruence between forms of business organization and the nature of governmental, financial, technological, educational and community bodies, so giving rise to national or regional taxonomies. They assume that the functions performed by such bodies and the regulations or other constraints they impose upon firms substantially explain the ways that the firms are governed, the range of specialties they internalize, and their philosophies of management. This leaves unexplained the extent to which the key actors in firms can themselves determine the agendas of institutions through lobbying, co-optation, the threatened withdrawal of co-operation and so forth. This potential for social action is clearly not a trivial issue for organizational theory, because it bears directly upon the question of how much strategic choice decision-makers have for developing or maintaining their preferred organizational arrangements. It was actually a central focus of an older school of institutional analysis exemplified by Selznick's famous study of the Tennessee Valley Authority (TVA) (Selznick 1949).

Acknowledgement

This chapter is an abridged version of a paper with the same title that appeared in *Advances in International Comparative Management*, volume 13, 2000: 27–75. The author is grateful to Nicole Biggart, Andrew Brown, Joseph Cheng, Leanne Chung, Roberto Duarte, Yuan Lu, Sek Hong Ng, Suzana Rodrigues and Yanni Yan for comments made on earlier drafts.

References

Adams, J.S. (1965) 'Injustice in social exchange', in L. Berkowitz (ed.) *Advances in Experimental Social Psychology*, New York: Academic Press.

Amable, B., Barré, R. and Boyer, R. (1997) *Les Systemes d'Innovation à l'Ere de la Globalisation*, Paris: Economica.

Applegate, L.M. (1995) *Designing and Managing the Information Age Organization*, Boston, MA: Harvard Business School Press.

Bartlett, C.A. and Ghoshal, S. (1989) *Managing Across Borders: The Transnational Solution*, Boston, MA: Harvard Business School Press.

Biggart, N.W. (1997) 'Explaining Asian economic organization: toward a Weberian institutional perspective', in M. Orru. N.W. Biggart and G.G. Hamilton (eds) *The Economic Organization of East Asian Capitalism*, Thousand Oaks, CA: Sage.

Biggart, N.W. and Guillén, M.F. (1999) 'Developing difference: social organization and the rise of the auto industries of South Korea, Taiwan, Spain and Argentina', *American Sociological Review* 64: 722–47.

Biggart, N.W. and Hamilton, G.G. (1992) 'On the limits of a firm-based theory to explain business networks: the Western bias of neoclassical economics', in N. Nohria and R.G. Eccles (eds) *Networks and Organizations*, Boston, MA: Harvard Business School Press.

Blauner, R. (1964) *Alienation and Freedom*, Chicago: University of Chicago Press.

Boisot, M. (1995) *Information Space: A Framework for Learning in Organizations, Institutions and Culture*, London: Routledge.

Boisot, M. (1986) 'Markets and hierarchies in cultural perspective', *Organization Studies* 7: 135–58.

Boisot, M. and Child, J. (1988) 'The iron law of fiefs: bureaucratic failure and the problem of governance in the Chinese system reforms', *Administrative Science Quarterly* 33: 507–27.

Boisot, M. and Child, J. (1996) 'From fiefs to clans: explaining China's emerging economic order', *Administrative Science Quarterly* 41: 600–28.

Bond, M.H. and Smith, P.B. (1996) 'Cross-cultural social and organizational psychology', *Annual Review of Psychology* 47: 205–35.

Buckley, P.J. and Casson, M. (1976) *The Future of the Multinational Enterprise*, London: Macmillan.

Chandler, A.D. Jr (1977) *The Visible Hand: The Managerial Revolution in American Business*, Cambridge, MA: Harvard University Press.

Child, J. (1981) 'Culture, contingency, and capitalism in the cross-national study of organizations', *Research in Organizational Behavior* 3: 303–56.

Child, J. (1997) 'Strategic choice in the analysis of action, structure, organizations and environment: retrospect and prospect', *Organization Studies* 18: 43–76.

Child, J. and Loveridge, R. (1990) *Information Technology in European Services*, Oxford: Blackwell.

Child, J., Faulkner, D. and Pitkethly, R. (2000) 'Foreign direct investment in the UK 1985–1994: the impact on domestic management practice', *Journal of Management Studies* 37: 141–66.

Dicken, P. (1998) *Global Shift: Transforming the World Economy*, 3rd edition, London: Paul Chapman Publishing.

Drummond, A. Jr (1997) 'Enabling conditions for organizational learning: a study in international business ventures', unpublished PhD thesis, University of Cambridge.

Freeman, C. (1988) 'Introduction', in G. Dosi, C. Freeman, R. Nelson, G. Silverber and L. Soete (eds) *Technical Change and Economic Theory*, London: Pinter.

Fulk, J. and DeSanctis, G. (1995) 'Electronic communication and changing organizational forms', *Organization Science* 6: 337–49.

Gannon, M.J. (1994) *Understanding Global Cultures: Metaphorical Journeys Through 17 Countries*, Thousand Oaks, CA: Sage.

Gerth, H.H. and Mills, C.W. (eds) (1946) *From Max Weber: Essays in Sociology*, New York: Oxford University Press.

Ghoshal, S. and Bartlett, C.A. (1998) *Managing Across Borders: The Transnational Solution*, 2nd edition, Boston, MA: Harvard Business School Press.

Ghoshal, S. and Westney, E.D. (eds) (1993) *Organization Theory and the Multinational Corporation*, New York: St. Martin's Press

Hampden-Turner, C. and Trompenaars, F. (1993) *The Seven Cultures of Capitalism*, New York: Doubleday.

Hawley, J.P. and Williams, A.T. (1996) *Corporate Governance in the US: The Rise of Fiduciary Capitalism – Review of the Literature*, report to OECD, January.

Heider, F. (1958) *The Psychology of Interpersonal Relations*, New York: Wiley.

Herzberg, F., Mausner, B. and Snyderman, B.B. (1959) *The Motivation to Work*, New York: Wiley.

Hickson, D.J. and McMillan, C.J. (eds) (1981) *Organization and Nation: The Aston Programme IV*, Aldershot: Gower.

Hickson, D.J. and Pugh, D.S. (1995) *Management Worldwide: The Impact of Societal Culture on Organizations Around the Globe*, London: Penguin.

Hickson, D.J., Hinings, C.R., McMillan, C.J. and Schwitter, J.P. (1974) 'The culture-free context of organization structure: a trinational comparison', *Sociology* 8: 59–80.

Hofstede, G. (1980a) 'Motivation, leadership and organization: do American theories apply abroad?', *Organization Dynamics* Summer: 42–63.

Hofstede, G. (1980b) *Culture's Consequences: International Differences in Work-Related Values*, London: Sage.

Hofstede, G. (1991) *Cultures and Organizations: Software of the Mind*, Maidenhead: McGraw-Hill.

Hofstede, G. and Bond, M.H. (1988) 'The Confucius connection: from cultural roots to economic growth', *Organizational Dynamics* 16: 4–21.

Johanson, J. and Vahlne, J.-E. (1977) 'The internationalization process of the firm: a model of knowledge development and increasing foreign market commitments', *Journal of International Business Studies* 8: 23–32.

Johnson, B.T., Holmes, K.R. and Kirkpatrick, M. (1998) 'Freedom is the surest path to growth', *Asian Wall Street Journal* 1 December: 14.

Kerr, C., Dunlop, J.T., Harbison, F. and Myers, C.A. (1960) *Industrialism and Industrial Man*, Cambridge, MA: Harvard University Press.

Kluckhohn, C. *et al.* (1951) 'Values and value-orientations in the theory of action', in T. Parsons and E.A. Shils (eds) *Toward a General Theory of Action,* Cambridge, MA: Harvard University Press.

Knights, D. and Murray, F. (1994) *Managers Divided: Organisation Politics and Information Technology Management,* Chichester: Wiley.

Kogut, B. (1988) 'Joint ventures: theoretical and empirical perspectives', *Strategic Management Journal* 9: 319–32.

Kruglanski, A.W. and Freund, T. (1983) 'The freezing and un-freezing of lay inferences: effects on impressional primacy, ethnic stereotyping and numeric anchoring', *Journal of Experimental Social Psychology* 19: 448–68.

Lammers, C.J. and Hickson, D.J. (eds) (1979) *Organizations Alike and Unlike,* London: Routledge & Kegan Paul.

Liu, I.-M. (1986) 'Chinese cognition', in M.H. Bond (ed.) *The Psychology of the Chinese People,* Hong Kong: Oxford University Press.

Locke, E. (1968) Towards a theory of task motivation and incentives', *Organizational Behavior and Human Performance* 3: 157–89.

Loveridge, R. (1998) 'Review of "The Changing European Firm – Limits to Convergence"', *Organization Studies* 19: 1049–53.

Maslow, A.H. (1943) 'A theory of human motivation', *Psychological Review* 50: 370–96.

McClelland, D.C. (1988) *Human Motivation,* Cambridge: Cambridge University Press.

Neuberg, S.L. and Newsom, J.T (1993) 'Personal need for structure: individual differences in the desire for simple structure', *Journal of Personality and Social Structure* 65: 113–31.

Noble, D.F. (1977) *America by Design: Science, Technology, and the Rise of Corporate Capitalism,* New York: Knopf.

Nonaka, I. and Takeuchi, H. (1995) *The Knowledge Creating Company,* New York: Oxford University Press.

Orru, M., Biggart, N.W. and Hamilton, G.G. (eds) (1997) *The Economic Organization of East Asian Capitalism,* Thousand Oaks, CA: Sage.

Poortinga, Y. (1992) 'Towards a conceptualization of culture for psychology', in S. Iwawaki, Y. Kashima and K. Leung (eds) *Innovations in Cross-Cultural Psychology,* Amsterdam: Swets & Zeitlinger.

Porter, L.W. and Lawler, E.E. (1968) *Managerial Attitudes and Performance,* Homewood, IL: Irwin.

Qin Xiao (1999) 'A conceptual framework for the strategic restructuring of state-owned enterprises in China', *Chinese Management Centre Working Paper,* CMC1999-001-01, University of Hong Kong.

Redding, S.G. (1994) 'Comparative management theory: jungle, zoo or fossil bed?', *Organization Studies* 15: 323–59.

Reed, M. (1996) 'Organizational theorizing: a historical contested terrain', in S.R. Clegg, C. Hardy and W.R. Nord (eds) *Handbook of Organization Studies,* London: Sage.

Roberts, K.H. (1970) 'On looking at an elephant: an evaluation of cross-cultural research related to organizations', *Psychological Bulletin* 74: 327–50.

Scarbrough, H. (1996) 'Strategic change in financial services: the social construction of strategic IS', in W.J. Orlikowski, G. Walsham, M.R. Jones and J.I. DeGross (eds) *Information Technology and Changes in Organizational Work,* London: Chapman & Hall.

Schumpeter, J. (1943) *Capitalism, Socialism and Democracy,* London: Allen & Unwin.

Selznick, P. (1949) *The TVA and the Grass Roots,* New York: Harper & Row.

Shleifer, A. and Vishny, R.W. (1997) 'A survey of corporate governance', *Journal of Finance* 52: 737–83.

Sorge, A. (1982) 'Cultured organization', *International Studies of Management and Organization* 12: 106–35.

Sorrentino, R.M. and Hewitt, E.C. (1984) 'The uncertainty-reducing properties of achievement tasks revisited', *Journal of Personality and Social Psychology* 47: 884–99.

Streufert, S. and Swezey, R.W. (1986) *Complexity, Managers, and Organizations,* Orlando, FA: Academic Press.

Tjosvold, D. (1991) *Team Organization: An Enduring Competitive Advantage,* Chichester: Wiley.

Toffler, A. (1971) *Future Shock,* London: Pan.

Tolbert, P.S. and Zucker, L.G. (1996) 'The institutionalization of institutional theory', in S.R. Clegg, C. Hardy and W.R. Nord (eds) *Handbook of Organization Studies,* London: Sage.

Trompenaars, F. (1993) *Riding the Waves of Culture*, London: Economist Books.

Weber, M. (1964) *The Theory of Social and Economic Organization*, trans. A.M. Henderson and T. Parsons, New York: Free Press.

Whitley, R.D. (1992a) *Business Systems in East Asia*, London: Sage.

Whitley, R.D. (ed.) (1992b) *European Business Systems: Firms and Markets in their National Contexts*, London: Sage.

Williamson, O.E. (1970) *Corporate Control and Business Behavior: An Enquiry into the Effects of Organizational Form on Enterprise Behavior*, Englewood Cliffs, NJ: Prentice Hall.

Williamson, O.E. (1985) *The Economic Institutions of Capitalism: Firms, Markets, Relational Contracting*, New York: Free Press.

Woodward, J. (1965) *Industrial Organization: Theory and Practice*, London: Oxford University Press.

Yang, K.S. (1994) *Indigenous Psychological Research in Chinese Societies*, Taiwan: Kuew Guan.

Zuboff, S. (1988) *In the Age of the Smart Machine*, New York: Basic Books.

Chapter 5

Theorizing about organization cross-nationally: part 2 – towards a synthesis

John Child

Introduction

Chapter 4 illustrated how two sets of perspectives, low- and high-context, contribute in diverse ways towards the cross-national study of organization. Given the diversity of these perspectives, it is relevant to ask whether attempts to reconcile them are likely to facilitate progress in this field of study. One view is that they are rooted in incommensurable paradigms and that constructive dialogue between them is therefore not possible. This is the present de facto position in the field of cross-national organizational studies, whether by intention or by default. The alternative is to seek a bridge between the two sets of perspectives that will lead at least to greater clarification and perhaps to constructive discourse. This is the intention of the present chapter. It was, in fact, the key recommendation emerging from a commentary on the Special Research Forum appearing in the *Academy of Management Journal* in 1995 on 'International and Intercultural Management Research':

> we suggest that the field integrate its working definitions of nation and culture and create an understanding based on various facets of nations and cultures, including economic, legal, cultural, and political systems. The key to conducting quality international or intercultural research is to understand the context in which firms and individuals function and operate
>
> (*Earley and Singh 1995: 337–8*)

Low-context perspectives refer primarily to the influences on, even imperatives for, organization seen as emanating from economic and technological development. These forces are mainly *material* in nature and take effect through socially structured activities such as markets and programmes of technological innovation. By contrast, high-context perspectives identify influences on organization that are mainly *ideational* in character. The values and norms to which they refer are, however, expressed and reproduced through the medium of social institutions, some of which like legal systems and religious bodies have their own highly structured forms. Indeed, material and ideational forces are institutionally linked. In most, if not all, societies, market transactions and technological property rights are subject to institutional regulation that expresses the normative priorities of those societies.

So an institutional analysis would seem to offer an appropriate path towards synthesis.

A Weberian framework

A fruitful basis for reconciling these different perspectives, and one that is institutional in nature, has actually been on offer within social theory for many years. This is Max Weber's framework for the analysis of socio-economic development (Mommsen 1989; Schluchter 1981). Weber focused on the material and ideational forces driving social change. He used this framework to account for the emergence of the Western capitalist system as well as bureaucracy as its characteristic organizational form (Gerth and Mills 1946; Weber 1964). While Weber's two forces are not identical to low- and high-context factors as I have described them, there is quite a close correspondence.

First, according to Weber, there are dynamic material forces of an economic and technological nature that give rise to efficiency oriented rules and codified knowledge. These forces thus encourage the development of what Weber called 'formal rationality'. Formal rationality concerns literally the form of social arrangements in terms of routines, structures and so forth. As societies 'modernize' their economies and technologies, so they adopt a more complex division of labour and institutional arrangements. This increases their requirement for formal rationality. It is expressed both in legally sanctioned organizational innovations such as the joint-stock company and in more autonomous developments such as hierarchical corporate forms. Although countries vary in their level and form of economic development at any one point in time, an implication of the materialist dynamic is that the organizational structures and processes characterizing industrializing nations will become increasingly similar (Kerr *et al.* 1960). Convergence is expected to accelerate as national economic systems become part of the same global economy and as cross-border multinational corporations account for increasing shares of activity in many sectors.

Second, there is the influence of substantive values and idealism, as expressed for example in Confucianism, the Protestant ethic or political ideologies. They shape 'substantive rationality', which concerns the meaning that people give to social organization and to the processes that take place within it such as the exercise of authority. Substantive rationality is rather more far-reaching than 'culture', at least in the sense accorded to the latter by organization theory. While it is expressed by cultures, it is also conveyed in ideologies and systems of knowledge that claim an ultimate validity. Various social institutions provide vehicles for the articulation and reproduction of substantive rationality: religions, governments and business schools are among these.

Substantive rationality can impact importantly on the structural principles of organizations, as well as on how people behave and relate within them. An example is the legitimacy accorded to the stakeholder and communitarian principle of corporate governance in continental Europe resulting in measures such as the European Union's Fifth Directive on industrial participation (see chapter 9). However, one would only expect cross-national convergence in organizational substantive rationality to come about if there were a convergence of dominant ideas and principles between the institutions that frame and propagate it. This is certainly happening within the European Union, and may be replicated in other regional blocs. The increasingly popular and largely American-inspired international management education movement, centred on the MBA, is another vehicle for convergence in substantive organizational rationality (Locke 1989).

National integration within political and economic regional blocs and the rapid international growth of business education do not, however, proceed independently of materialistic forces. They are associated with economic and technological integration. In Weber's analysis, materialistic and ideational forces have the potential to impact on each other. On the one hand, the Protestant ethic laid foundations for the spirit of Western capitalism, and the Confucian ethic shaped the spirit of Chinese capitalism (Redding 1990). On the other hand, the capitalist economy itself has a significant international impact on people's values and expectations in areas such as personal achievement, lifestyle and employment. As discussed later in this chapter, the interdependence of the materialistic and the ideational is an insight of great importance for understanding the organizational impact of contemporary 'globalization'.

Weber did not adopt a wholly deterministic view of social development. He allowed for the role of 'social action', which is intentional action oriented towards others. The intention behind such action may be informed by calculation, values, emotion or tradition (Weber 1978). In other words, action may be motivated and guided by material interests, ideals or a combination of both. It is not, however, necessarily a slave to the contextual forces that express materialism or idealism. There is always a possibility for initiative and innovation on the part of those who make or influence decisions on organization. The role of social action will assume particular importance when I apply the Weberian perspective to the evolution of organization within its international context.

Figure 5.1 offers a view of organizational context that is derived from the Weberian analytical framework. Following Weber, it identifies material and ideational systems as the two primary forces in the evolution of this context, and at the same time it recognizes their interdependence. These systems are seen to imbue a nation's social institutions with both formal and substantive rationalities. Such institutions comprise the third major component of organizational context. Some institutions, chiefly the educational system, help to form organizational competencies. Others, such as the banking and insurance system, provide intermediate services, and other

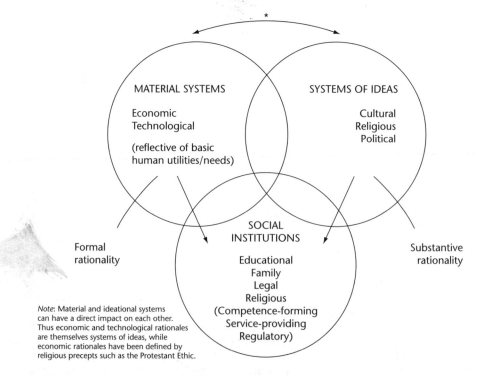

Figure: 5.1 **A Weberian interpretation of organizational context**

support services such as health care. Yet others impose legal and regulatory constraints. Governmental bodies may be involved in each of these roles.

Contributions of the framework

The integrative and comprehensive character of the Weberian framework offers two main advantages to the analysis of organizational context. It encourages a balanced appreciation of the contextual factors impacting upon organization, balanced in the sense that these are not viewed narrowly within the confines of a single theoretical lens, be this low- or high-context, idealist or materialist. I note shortly how this approach helps to unpack a major contemporary phenomenon for organization – globalization – that is often identified with the economic dimension but which actually alludes to a combination of material forces and powerful ideas. Second, the framework encourages us to take greater care in specifying the contextual location of any given organization with respect to the likely impact upon it of both material forces and the dissemination of ideas. This points to the virtue of framing propositions in future with more precise reference to the extent that an organization is affected by international material forces and value systems as opposed to local ones. An example would be the proposition that an organization will more strongly reflect the substantive rationality of its domestic national culture the more it is autonomous of both external materialist forces (such as international competition) and external values (such as those imported by a foreign partner).

Arguably the most valuable contribution of this perspective lies in the way it encourages us to reframe questions for research. It does not assume a specific national or regional context either to be inconsequential outside its relation to the world economy or, at the other extreme, to be comprehensively self-accountable in terms of culture or national institutional system. Instead, the perspective draws attention to the way organizations are situated in regard to international versus local material and ideational systems. Mainstream cross-national organizational research has notably failed to address the issue of how global and local forces, together and in relation to each other, bear upon the nature of organization.

On the material side, the question becomes how organizations are situated vis-à-vis international systems, such as international capital flows or the systematic quality benchmarking organized by the International Organization for Standardization (ISO), which are in turn stimulated by the expectations of actors in financial and product markets. To what extent do Chinese enterprises, for example, engage in the international systems of trade, finance and technology that impose common materialistic pressures, such as international competition? The general hypothesis is that the more they are incorporated into the global system, the less differentiated Chinese organization and management systems can remain from those of other similarly incorporated organizations in other parts of the world with which they are competing. In the case of China, the conditions attached to entry into the World Trade Organization (WTO) would further open the door to the impact of global economic forces (Lardy 1999; Warner 1999). It is therefore germane to ask how far the Chinese authorities are acting upon the premise that their country's long-term development needs oblige them to accept such conditions. The other side of the coin is to ask to what extent Chinese enterprises can maintain their currently preferred management and organizational practices under these circumstances, and whether some are better situated to do so than others.

Staying with the example of China, questions arise on the ideational side concerning the exposure that the members of Chinese organizations have to foreign values. If they engage in international business, does this tie them into a set of international institutional expectations and regulations on matters such as transparency of transactions and accounts? If Chinese enterprises have become affiliates or close business partners of multinational corporations, are their members likely to take on board foreign business norms and practices through the impact of strong corporate cultures and management systems? Do those local nationals who live in an urban environment with its increasingly Western lifestyles and media culture, and are connected to the Internet and other international communication media, absorb non-Chinese values to a greater extent than the members of Chinese organizations who are not so exposed? It may be hypothesized that the greater this international exposure, the more Chinese managers and other personnel will absorb foreign norms and apply them to their organizational behaviour.

These questions imply that an organization's level of autonomy from external materialistic forces and values will vary even within a single country depending on its positioning within that country: its economic sector, the size and scope of its activities, whether it is in an urban or rural location and so forth. This implication is profoundly significant for the design of comparative organizational research.

The Weberian perspective is also helpful for addressing the question of whether the impact of economic and technological forces for convergence is likely to differ according to the level of organization in question. A review of the then available literature led me to conclude that those organizational features of firms which linked closely to external institutions such as the capital market, or which were constrained by the economics of technology and scale, were more likely to show convergence (Child 1981). These are the strategic and 'macro-level' features of management and organizations, such as the structures of corporate governance and of executive management. By contrast, behavioural norms and styles of managing would be more likely to reflect cultural expectations and norms concerning how people should relate to each other and how the individual should relate to the collectivity. Interpersonal behaviours and styles are relatively insulated from the material forces in an organization's environment. International accounting criteria and performance norms are increasingly being applied to public companies, and investors, parent companies and regulators scrutinize their policies. However, the behavioural processes through which these policies are implemented are likely to be left to local discretion, and this permits some adaptation to local cultural preferences. So while it is broadly true to say that material factors and cultural values both shape organization, it is important always to specify exactly which aspects of organization constitute the focus of one's inquiry.

The Weberian approach offers useful antidotes against the temptation to ascribe explanatory primacy to any one theoretical perspective. It qualifies the current dominance that economic universalism enjoys in policy discussions by stressing the need to allow room for the influence of ideas and values. Equally, it cautions against any tendency to ascribe over-riding explanatory power to national culture. The examples just given, and other evidence, suggests that cultural theorists have assumed too much homogeneity and too much cultural 'stickiness' within national systems of management. As we all know, management philosophies and organizational practices can differ considerably within the ambit of a single national 'culture'. The question is sometimes asked in this respect whether Hewlett-Packard or General Motors is the typical US company.

The dynamic interplay between ideas and institutional forces demonstrates the fallacy of regarding culture as immutable. Cultures can themselves change under the influence of both institutional and material developments. When institutions change, people may adapt their values quite rapidly. China under the impact of the economic reform again provides an instructive example. Ralston *et al.* (1999) found large contrasts in value orientations among different generations of managers in the People's Republic of China (PRC), with the younger generation tending to demonstrate greater acceptance of 'Western' values such as individualism. The experience of

East and West Germany has shown how work-related values and behaviour can diverge substantially across two generations within the same nation due to the impact of different economic and political systems (Frese *et al.* 1996; Grabher 1995). It also appears that people can accommodate culturally to organizational and work practices which derive from different sets of values, if these are accompanied by positive material benefits such as secure employment or good rewards. An example is the positive response of workers to Japanese practices in regions of the UK that had long-established local industrial traditions (Oliver and Wilkinson 1992). Companies can also change their corporate cultures and organizational philosophies, as did many US corporations in response to the 'crisis' in American manufacturing of the 1970s and 1980s.

The broad historical sweep encompassed in the work of Weber and other fathers of sociology further suggests that the combination of materialistic and institutional features contained in the notion of 'stage of development' have their own impact upon cultural development and so, in turn, upon organizational behaviour. The virtues often lumped together as Confucian – hard work, respect for elders, strong family ties, passion for learning and knowledge – are traditional values that were probably as much a part of Victorian England as they are of Chinese communities today (Bendix 1956). While great systems of thought undoubtedly have had an impact upon the way that people think and organize, this may have been to some extent because they were 'right' for the material circumstances of the period in which they had most practical influence. Thus, in contemporary circumstances, 'empowerment' may be a quintessentially Anglo-Saxon idea but its spread to other cultural regions may be primarily to do with the pressures arising from international competition to raise productivity, to be responsive to local customer demands and to enhance employee contributions to incremental innovation.

These considerations suggest that we have to become quite subtle in our theorizing about the characteristics of organization in different countries, as well as about the organization of transnational value-chains. We have to ask specific questions about the contexts that apply to the units whose organizational forms or behaviour is the subject of study: such as the historical period, the economic sector, the nature of international economic involvement, the level of organization and which occupational and generation groups are involved. My basic contention, however, is that much of this subtlety can be provided through reference to already available theoretical perspectives that provoke the necessary questions. The challenge is to bring these together within a single framework.

Globalization: contextual analysis applying the Weberian framework

There are two reasons for attending to globalization at this point. First, it is the major contextual development bearing upon cross-national organization, and its implications cannot be ignored. Second, the analysis of globalization is quite fragmented. While it has been primarily associated with a reduction in the national barriers to the operation of economic forces, it is also being linked to profound changes in values, attitudes and personal identity (Giddens 1998; 1999). It should therefore be amenable to the form of integrative analysis concerning material and ideational systems that I am recommending.

Globalization has been variously defined, reflecting in part different disciplinary assumptions (Parker 1996). An interdisciplinary group of European scholars has recently offered a useful comprehensive definition.

'Globalization' comprises a host of facts and observations such as the accelerated growth of world trade and direct investment since the mid-80s, the global distribution of the value added chain of companies (which has been made possible through decreasing transport costs, widespread application of new information technologies and new management concepts) or the global integration of money and capital markets. Yet globalization is not only an economic phenomenon, but rather includes the contracting role of the nation-state, and the emergence of other social values and ways of life.

(Steger 1998: 1)

One may note how this definition refers both to material economic and technological forces on the one hand, and ideational ones on the other. These forces today operate primarily through the agency of transnational corporations, nation states and supra-national agencies (Dicken 1998). The liberalization of trade and of capital movements, combined with the rapid increase in information diffusion through new communication technologies, is seen to decrease market imperfections and allow competitive market forces to gain strength. This trend is supported by the pressures exerted on nation states by international institutions like the WTO towards the removal of international trade barriers and by the International Monetary Fund (IMF) towards transparency and economic rationality in financial transactions. Although these moves have clear material consequences, they are also legitimated by a dominant ideology that appeals to economic rationality and the validity of 'global standards' in matters of financial accounting and disclosure of information. The power of these ideas plays an important role in promoting moves towards globalization. The velocity of circulation of ideas and information is increasing dramatically via the Internet and the internationalization of higher education, not least management education. As a result, ideas are becoming increasingly shared, and practices transferred, between different countries (see chapter 21).

Dore (1999) notes, for example, that despite Japan's strong 'post-Confucian' communitarian organizational ethos, many Japanese are advocating a fundamental change in the country's business system to take it towards the American 'shareholder value' model which would favour shareholders rather than employees. This is being legitimated by reference to global standards of corporate governance. These global standards turn out on examination to reflect the ideology of Western business schools and the increasing influence of their graduates in Japanese industry. A shift from Japanese to American models could have profound interlocking effects on the governance structures of Japanese companies, on their internal decision processes, reward systems and work organization.

There is a widespread assumption that globalization refers to a growing national 'borderlessness' which is already well under way, and that this is leading to greater homogeniety and uniformity. It is here that a note of caution needs to be sounded, because globalization does not have a consistent social impact. Paradoxically, at the same time as transactional boundaries weaken, there is a increased awareness of cultural differences and a growing celebration of cultural diversity (Robertson 1995). The same increasingly intensive international circulation of ideas through the Internet, telecommunications and other media that promotes the dominant economic ideology seems to be strengthening cultural and subcultural identities at the same time. The technology enhances communication between the members of cultural groups and provides opportunities for their self-expression. It also appears that people's awareness of their own culture and identity is promoted by the provision of more information about other societies or communities, which enables comparisons that clarify cultural distinctiveness. The search for new business opportunities through catering for local preferences is another facet of this greater awareness and appreciation of cultural distinctiveness. Globalization may therefore be stimulating divergent as well as convergent developments in organization. On the one hand it facilitates a centralized standardization of organizational practices and products; on the other it promotes local identities which encourage decentralized organizational responses.

There is a tendency in popular discussion to assume that economic and technological forces provide the dynamic behind globalization. While they are undoubtedly of great significance, ideas also continue to play a role and we can make more sense of globalization as a phenomenon by taking account of how the ideas interface with its material aspects. Thus, the notion of 'one world' is a powerful idea per se, which undoubtedly has considerable appeal in terms of humanistic values. Nevertheless, its credibility depends on the material changes that allow for globalization, namely the lowering of economic and transportation barriers and the spread of integrative communications technologies. Equally, the diffusion of ideas about management through the medium of business schools is facilitating the adoption of new organizational forms centered around models such as 'heterarchy' (Hedlund 1986), 'hypertext' (Nonaka and Takeuchi 1995) and 'the transnational solution' (Bartlett and Ghoshal 1989). These are among the more influential examples, and it is interesting to note that they emanate from three different cultural zones – Sweden, Japan and the USA respectively. Yet the claims made for the validity of these new models are that they are adapted to emerging worldwide material conditions. That is, they meet the economic requirements of managing global value-chains and promoting innovation better than previous models.

Implications for organization cross-nationally

It follows from the previous discussion that one cannot generalize about the nature and trend of organization around the world without locating the particular case in its context (Cheng 1989; 1994). That context will be international or local to varying degrees. It will expose organizations differentially to the pressures of competition and technological change. The identity of the people living and working in the location may be strongly attached to, and defined by, local culture or it may be more multicultural in nature.

What one can do is to examine the features of organization that appear responsive to global material trends, those that appear to reflect a globalization of ideas, and those that are more susceptible to high-context local influences. This exercise will clearly demonstrate the need for a multilevel and multidimensional approach to the subject.

There are a number of identifiable organizational responses among companies to global economic and technological forces (Ghoshal and Bartlett 1998; Steger 1998). Many companies are shifting their preferred mode of organization towards forms of horizontal co-ordination such as teams, networks and partnerships. Under the pressure of competition and rapid technological advance, innovations are being introduced simultaneously rather than sequentially, so as to ensure a return on research and development (R & D) given shortening product life cycles. This is encouraging the use of integrated cross-specialist teams within firms and the formation of technological partnerships between firms. In order to reduce costs and to source where economically most advantageous, companies are dividing up their value-chains in order to place supplies and production in the most favourable locations. They may retain the ownership and management of such activities, or they may outsource them. Similarly, in order to increase market penetration through cultivation of local markets, companies are increasingly entering into distribution arrangements with local partners, sometimes before making a commitment to production. The complexity of value chains is increased as firms expand their product and geographical scope, often through merger and acquisition. These moves are usually motivated by considerations of augmenting or defending market power under intense global competition, and are moving many industries towards oligopolistic global industry structures.

The effect of these changes is to soften both the internal and external boundaries of the firms concerned. The disaggregation of value chains moves companies towards a network mode of organization (Nohria and Eccles 1992), and the use of advanced information and communication technologies permits the development of 'virtual' organization (Hedberg *et al.* 1997). External boundaries are blurred with the increasing recourse to strategic alliances and strategic partnerships with suppliers. In industries such as automobiles, pharmaceuticals and telecommunications, alliances have become the nodal points of extensive international networks. The softening of internal organizational boundaries, plus the increasing need to extend discretion and initiative to local units which are close to the situation and staffed by trained people, encourages a shift from relying on hierarchical control and direction towards 'heterarchy' (Hedlund 1986). This approach encourages local flexible modes of direct coordination and control through joint aims and targets agreed by the people concerned, rather than relying on directions from headquarters. There is also a corresponding shift from individual decision-making to group decision processes. These trends do not, however, imply an abdication of top management direction but rather a move towards less direct and more strategic control via the deployment of capital, the making of key appointments, and the fostering of a trust-based corporate culture among the core group of managers.

At the same time, a globalization of organizational ideas and practices is under way. Calori and De Woot (1994: 53) note that some of the European company directors they interviewed perceived a narrowing of the gap between American, European and Japanese management philosophies and practices, 'especially in multinational corporations which are in direct contact with the three continents'. A study of British firms acquired by companies with a range of home-base nationalities (American, British, French, German and Japanese) found that certain changes were introduced by the acquirers in the belief that they represented good practice regardless of their nationality. These included more attention to strategy and company image, more training, move towards performance-related reward systems, more open communication, team-based R & D, greater use of automation and information technology (IT), more cost control, a greater emphasis on quality, and more use of teams (Child, Faulkner and Pitkethly 2000). Lu and Björkman (1997) found among joint ventures between Chinese and transnational corporation (TNC) partners that the latter endeavoured to introduce standard international human resource management (HRM) practices into the local context, especially for selection, training and rewards. Child and Yan (2001) found that the transnational status of foreign partners was a more consistent and powerful predictor of the strategies and practices adopted by their joint ventures in China than was the national origin of those partners. The transfer of organizational practices in these ways into new national settings reflects the power of TNC organizational cultures. Although the practices may originate in response to perceived exigencies of the international economic and technological context, once they become standardized, they are essentially artefacts of corporate cultures and ideational in nature.

There is evidence, then, to support the view that globalization, both of material forces and of ideas and practices, is shaping key parameters of organization across different countries. The principal agent of this process is the TNC. Not only are TNCs introducing organizational standardization across national borders, they are themselves innovating organizational forms in the search for ways to manage transnational operations effectively. The search for a 'transnational solution' (Bartlett and Ghoshal 1989) leads directly to the thesis of convergence among TNCs, namely that 'leading corporations should gradually be losing their national characters and converging in their fundamental strategies and operations' (Pauly and Reich 1997: 1). The argument that transnational scope calls for similar novel organizational adjustments is based on the premise that 'the same challenges faced all managers everywhere as the world's increasingly linked economies sped toward the twenty-first century' (Bartlett and Ghoshal 1989: x). Or, as Ohmae has stated (1990: 94): 'country of origin does not matter. Location of headquarters does not matter. The products for which you are responsible and the company you serve have become denationalized.'

The model for the 'denationalized' TNC has increasingly become that purveyed in the large US and international business schools from which these companies draw their career managers, and at which their senior executives attend programmes on the latest thinking. An important component of the model is a long-term strategic orientation and, as indicated by Mintzberg's (1994) critique, one that has been predicated on strategic planning. Consistent with their size and with business school precepts, TNCs are expected to rely heavily on contractual arrangements and on a high level of internal formalization. Both contracts and formal systems are likely to be of a standardized nature, since TNCs seeking to benefit from global products or technologies, and having considerable ownership-specific advantages, are more likely to derive benefits from this policy than are non-TNCs.

Formalization and standardization of structures and systems are not, however, considered to be sufficient foundations by TNCs for effective cross-national management (Doz and Prahalad 1993). They also seek to achieve consistency of behaviour and process through the development of high-quality competencies among key personnel who are loyal to the corporate culture. Transnational corporations therefore attach considerable importance to training, especially managerial training. Their support for business schools and investment in corporate 'universities' stems largely from a belief that they must develop a core of highly professional executives, sharing a similar corporate culture and managerial approach, in order to maintain sufficient integration and control across their worldwide operations. These managers are likely to be deployed by TNCs into the key positions within affiliates and joint ventures in order to ensure integration with corporate policies and procedures (Edstrom and Galbraith 1977).

While the process of internationalizing organizational practices on the part of TNCs is supported by their corporate cultures, it tends to suppress the influence of national cultures. Nevertheless, many researchers see national culture as continuing to be critically important in the selection of organizational structures and methods (cf. Hampden-Turner and Trompenaars 1993; Hofstede 1991). For example, Calori, Lubatkin and Very (1994) conclude from their research that French companies prefer to exercise formal control of operations rather than informal control through teamwork in their UK acquisitions; the latter approach characterized American acquirers. Their view is that firms are liable to carry their home practices with them as they move into foreign markets. They are in this sense agents for the migration of culturally defined organizational practices. Others, like the contributors to Whitley (1992b), stress the importance of national or regional institutions and infrastructures in influencing the extent to which cross-border acquisitions actually become consolidated within the organizational systems of the foreign acquirers. The question therefore arises as to how and where, within an overall trend towards globalization, national cultures and institutions will continue to shape organizational forms and behaviour.

National differences in *cultural* values are most likely to influence matters such as personal style, desired rewards, how people relate with others and the degree of contextual structuring they seek. Contiguous organizational practices include decision-making, reward systems, the conduct of meetings, communication, trust and the structuring of jobs. These are the micro-level aspects of organization and organizational behaviour: the level of individuals and their immediate working context. This is the organizational level where the impact of national cultures is most apparent and where there can be a practical managerial reaction to it.

The cultural values held even by individuals or small groups of people can, however, have a significant impact on a macro-organizational feature such as a company's organization, if those people happen to be chief executives or boards of directors. This validly points to the need to give due weight to cultural preferences in terms of the position power that people may have to put them into effect. It does not, however, gainsay the previous conclusion that companies facing global competition and innovation may today be experiencing strengthening pressures to adapt their modes of organization away from culturally preferred approaches. The result can be considerable tension between, for example, the traditional management of family entrepreneurs and that advocated by their successors eager for international expansion (Ng 1996).

By contrast, national differences of an *institutional* nature can impact upon both micro and macro aspects of organization. A micro-level example is the way that national systems of education and training (competence-formation) affect the degree of available organizational choice in the design of jobs and allocation of responsibilities, as Sorge and Warner (1986) noted from comparisons of Germany and the UK. An example at the macro-level concerns the different national regulatory systems of company law and corporate reporting. These bear upon arrangements for corporate governance, including the structuring of stakeholder rights to participate in information and policy-making (Hawley and Williams 1996). In many developing countries, for example, government regulations mandate a sharing of corporate governance between foreign investing and local firms in the form of equity joint ventures.

Whitley's (1992a; 1992b) analyses of Asian and European business systems identify ways in which the sophistication of intermediary institutions in different countries has a bearing on the organization of firms in terms of their sources of financing (ownership), modes of control and internal specialization. The nature of a country's intermediary institutions may call for modifications in organizational practice because they impact on the availability of resources, such as working capital and specialist support services. If these are absent or inadequately provided within a country's institutional framework, then a company will have to modify its organization to provide these internally or secure them elsewhere. Similarly, the skills of available managers, technicians and employees will impinge on the internal structuring of work. These constraints may be quite significant for local firms, but rather less so for large TNCs. The latter are usually able to rectify resource or skill deficiencies themselves without any necessary disturbance to their preferred modes of internal organization. The quality of the institutional infrastructure in a particular country is thus likely to have a differential influence on organization, depending on the ability of a company to draw upon compensating resources from elsewhere.

Other institutions, however, possess a mandatory power over the organizations located within national or, as with the European Union, regional boundaries. Such institutions are usually governmental, or have the backing of law and, in some cases, organized public opinion. They may enforce certain organizational arrangements through the power of law, or via their articulation of strong social values. The latter is becoming increasingly the case with protection of the physical environment and the propagation of local community interests. These policies can come into conflict with those articulated by international companies in the name of globalization, and this typically pitches the TNC and agencies of the nation state against each other. The solutions that are negotiated will ultimately depend on the bargaining power of the respective parties and there is hence an element of indeterminacy here. In so far as the agencies prevail, they can bring national criteria to bear on the governance of organizations and the policies they can legitimately pursue.

Theorizing about organization cross-nationally therefore cannot avoid taking specific contexts into account. Every organization is located differently with respect to global and local national forces, and their material or ideational foundations. An organization's global disposition, in terms of sector, scale, spread and external networks establishes a set of contingencies that bear upon which structures and systems it can effectively adopt to assist the fundamental processes of decision-making control, co-ordination, reward and learning. These contingencies derive primarily from competitive pressures that today increasingly impinge today on public bodies such as government departments, hospitals and universities in terms of comparative performance ratings, as well as on business companies. An organization's national location at the same time brings into play institutional contingencies, not all of which TNCs can offset through their bargaining weapon of foreign direct investment (Ferner and Quintanilla 1998).

The cross-national context of organizations may be mapped in terms of the distinctions just made between (1) the global and local levels at which (2) material and ideational forces operate. Figure 5.2 does this with examples for each quadrant. While this is a static analysis, not accounting for organizational or contextual evolution, it does serve to clarify some of the key contextual configurations that impact on a given organization. In so doing, it also raises a number of pertinent questions. For example, do organizational decision-makers regard global material and ideational forces with the same sense of urgency and/or as requiring the same kind of action vis-à-vis the external constituents who are involved? Is their response therefore similar or different? When organizations are under different pressures from both global and local considerations, which set of forces will prevail and on what features of organization will they bear? Answers to questions such as these may contribute to theoretical advance because they direct our attention towards understanding how material and ideational systems at both global and local levels interact in their effect on organizations.

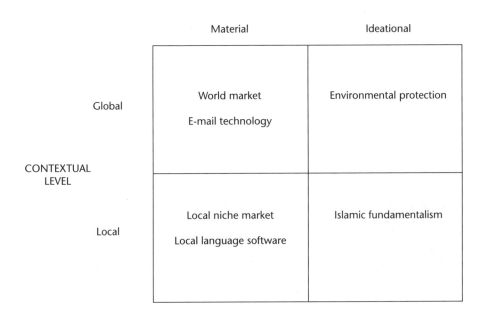

Figure: 5.2 **Cross-national organization context**

The distinctions made in Figure 5.2 are essentially comparative between countries; they are consistent with the conventional cross-national approach. However, they are also relevant to research on cross-national organizational forms. Bartlett and Ghoshal (1989) identified four types of cross-border firm: the international, multi-national (multidomestic), global and transnational. It may be hypothesized that when designing their organizations, global, and to a lesser extent international, companies will need to pay attention primarily to factors identified by low-context theories since they are situated primarily in the global/material quadrant of Figure 5.2. By contrast, multidomestic companies will find the high-context approach, and research informing it, most relevant. For research to be relevant to transnational firms, it will need to combine low- and high-context approaches, so that all the quadrants of Figure 5.2 apply more or less equally to the transnational case. By encompassing low- and high-context perspectives, global and local levels, material and ideational forces, this theoretical mapping advances our capability *both* to locate organizations in their cross-national context *and* to understand the conditions under which one form of cross-national organization may be preferred to another.

Towards synthesis

Figure 5.3 brings together the material, ideational and institutional components of organizational context with a representation of the ways, just discussed, that these have relevance for organization. There are multiple contextual domains with multiple channels of influence on organization. These reflect the theoretical insights provided by the perspectives considered earlier. In working through Figure 5.3, it is important to keep in mind that specific cases will vary in how they are situated with respect to the key components of the framework. These include the local and international context, and the nature of strategic choice exercised by organizational leaders.

Figure 5.3 depicts material and ideational systems as impacting on organization both directly as well as through the medium of institutions. Material systems have a direct impact through the economic and technological contingencies they present for the ways in which companies and other bodies can organize themselves to accomplish their tasks. They establish task contingencies for those designing and managing organization (Donaldson 1996). Systems of ideas have a direct impact on organizations through the values and normative precepts they express.

However, the members of a company or other unit, especially those exercising its managerial functions, perform an interpretative role with respect to the organizational implications posed by these material and ideational inputs. The capabilities, services and constraints arising from communal, national and international institutions provide the indirect route whereby material and ideational systems have a potential influence on organization. These inputs from institutions are also subject to interpretation by organizational members. Their interpretations, and the actions that organizational members consequently decide to take, inject an element of strategic choice into the model which is consistent with the role accorded to social action in Weberian analysis. In other words, organizational arrangements do not simply reflect the impact of external material or ideational forces, but are also the product of conscious, intentional action allows us to incorporate strategic choice into the analysis (Child 1997). The framework permits us to take into account the possibility that both the contextual location of an organization and the intentionality and understanding of its actors will have a bearing on its structure, processes and policies.

Strategic choice is also informed by the feedback of information on the performance of an organizational unit. Organizational performance is seen both as a trigger for managers to attempt to negotiate with institutional bodies, and as a

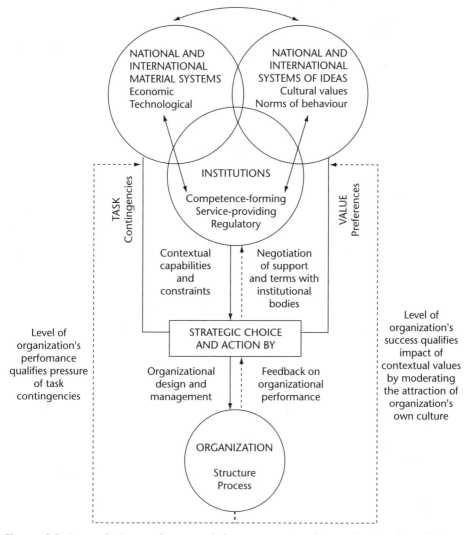

Figure: 5.3 **An evolutionary framework for cross-national organizational analysis**

factor that can moderate the direct influence of material and ideational systems. In the latter case, the level of performance achieved may qualify the pressures on organization coming from material and ideational systems respectively. If, say, a company is performing well, this should afford it some 'slack' in terms of having to respond immediately and in a predetermined way to task contingencies deriving from competitive economic and technological conditions. Success may therefore enable it to preserve certain preferred national modes of organizing, even if there are strong international conventions. Similarly, if a company is performing well and reflects this in its terms of employment, it may thereby be able to develop a commitment among its members to its own culture that qualifies the impact of national cultural norms. I have seen this take place in Sino–foreign joint ventures, where the foreign partner is a TNC seeking to introduce its own corporate culture. The feeling that the joint venture offers them a good long-term future makes local staff much more willing to accept the foreign partner's organizational cultured practices.

Thus the framework in Figure 5.3 does not depict a simple contextual determinism. Those having a significant say on the framing of organizational structures and processes are not cast in a purely reactive role vis-à-vis the context. In the light of their own ideas and preferences on organization, and informed by information concerning the performance of the units they manage, such leaders may endeavour to negotiate with external institutional bodies over the terms under which they are regulated, the opportunities they are offered, and the support they are afforded. As Peng (2000) concludes from his comparative studies of transition economies, the dynamic interaction between institutions and firms allows for strategic choices to be made, some of them concerning organization and employment, and the quality of such choices has important implications for future performance. These strategic choices include possibilities for realigning a firm's external position in regard to, say, market power, such as forming alliances with foreign firms. Alliances can themselves act as channels for the introduction of new organizational practices.

Just as the Weberian analysis on which I have drawn was concerned to account for social development and evolution, so the contribution of the framework in Figure 5.3 is not confined to the comparative-static type of research that has formed the mainstay of cross-national organizational research. The multiple feedback loops and dynamic relations it depicts, both within context and between context and organization, in fact identify conditions for both organizational and contextual evolution. Redding (2000: 100) notes how, for example, the success of business organizations operating within democratic systems in delivering 'societal purposes with wide legitimacy' has undoubtedly reinforced democratic capitalism as a set of ideals and the institutions supporting it. It is inevitable that institutions are judged and modified according to the social performance of the organizations they are intended to support and regulate, not just the other way round. In turn, the effectiveness of institutions impacts on the legitimacy of the values they express. Through the competencies educational systems develop and the regulatory frameworks set out by national and supra-national legal systems, institutions also condition the application and impact of economic and technological forces. The insertion of return arrows from institutions to material systems and systems of ideas in Figure 5.3 is intended to convey this reciprocal process. The emergence of giant global firms and business groups, having the economic and technological clout to negotiate directly with national and regional institutions, has shortened and intensified these reciprocal linkages between global systems, national and supra-national institutions, and the business firm (see chapter 21).

Concluding remarks

This chapter has been concerned with the search for an analytical framework that constructively synthesizes the present partial and sometimes narrow perspectives on the study of organization cross-nationally. It has advanced a framework that can incorporate the insights offered by the different perspectives, and that directs attention towards potential interaction between them. This framework avoids an uncritical acceptance of the primacy of any one perspective, together with its methodological or paradigmatic limitations. It also implies that one cannot reach valid conclusions about the nature and trend of organization around the world without locating the particular case in its context. Application of the framework refines our understanding of globalization by distinguishing between the features of organization that appear responsive to global material trends, those that reflect a globalization of ideas and those that are susceptible to high-context local influences.

Acknowledgement

This chapter is an abridged version of a paper with the same title that appeared in *Advances in International Comparative Management*, volume 13, 2000: 27–75. The author is grateful to Nicole Biggart, Andrew Brown, Joseph Cheng, Leanne Chung, Roberto Duarte, Yuan Lu, Sek Hong Ng, Suzana Rodrigues and Yanni Yan for comments made on earlier drafts.

References

Bartlett, C.A. and Ghoshal, S. (1989) *Managing Across Borders: The Transnational Solution*, Boston, MA: Harvard Business School Press.

Bendix, R. (1956) *Work and Authority in Industry*, Berkeley, CA: University of California Press.

Calori, R. and De Woot, P. (1994) *A European Management Model*, Hemel Hempstead: Prentice Hall.

Calori, R., Lubatkin, M. and Very, P. (1994) 'Cross-border acquisitions: an international comparison', *Organization Studies* 15: 361–99.

Cheng, J.L.C. (1989) 'Toward a contextual approach to cross-national organization research', *Advances in International Comparative Management* 4: 3–18.

Cheng, J.L.C. (1994) 'On the concept of universal knowledge in organizational science: implications for cross-national research', *Management Science* 40: 162–8.

Child, J. (1981) 'Culture, contingency, and capitalism in the cross-national study of organizations', *Research in Organizational Behavior* 3: 303–56.

Child, J. (1997) 'Strategic choice in the analysis of action, structure, organizations and environment: retrospect and prospect', *Organization Studies* 18: 43–76.

Child, J. and Yan, Y. (2001) 'National and transnational effects in international business: indications from Sino–foreign joint ventures', *Management International* Review 41: 53–75.

Child, J., Faulkner, D. and Pitkethly, R. (2000) 'Foreign direct investment in the UK 1985–1994: the impact on domestic management practice', *Journal of Management Studies* 37: 141–66.

Dicken, P. (1998) *Global Shift: Transforming the World Economy*, 3rd edition, London: Paul Chapman Publishing.

Donaldson, L. (1996) 'The normal science of structural contingency theory', in S.R. Clegg, C. Hardy and W.R. Nord (eds) *Handbook of Organization Studies*, London: Sage.

Dore, R. (1999) 'Corporate governance and Asian values: the Japanese debate', T.T. Tsui Annual Lecture in Asia Pacific Business, Hong Kong University, 3 March.

Doz, Y. and Prahalad, C.-K. (1993) 'Managing DMNCs: a search for a new paradigm', in S. Ghoshal and E.D. Westney (eds) *Organization Theory and the Multinational Corporation*, New York: St. Martin's Press.

Earley, P.C. and Singh, H. (1995) 'International and intercultural management research: what's next?', *Academy of Management Journal* 38: 327–40.

Edstrom, A. and Galbraith, J.R. (1977) 'Transfer of managers as a coordination and control strategy in multinational organizations', *Administrative Science Quarterly* 22: 248–63.

Ferner, A. and Quintanilla, J. (1998) 'Multinationals, national business systems and HRM: the enduring influence of national identity or a process of "Anglo-Saxonization"', *International Journal of Human Resource Management* 9: 710–31.

Frese, M., Kring, W., Soose, A. and Zempel, J. (1996) 'Personal initiative at work: differences between East and West Germany', *Academy of Management Journal* 39: 37–63.

Gerth, H.H. and Mills, C.W. (eds) (1946) *From Max Weber: Essays in Sociology*, New York: Oxford University Press.

Ghoshal, S. and Bartlett, C.A. (1998) *Managing Across Borders: The Transnational Solution*, 2nd edition, Boston, MA: Harvard Business School Press.

Giddens, A. (1998) *The Third Way: The Renewal of Social Democracy*, Oxford: Polity Press.

Giddens, A. (1999) *The Runaway World*, the Reith Lectures, London: British Broadcasting Corporation (http://news.bbc.co.uk/hi/english/s...events/reith_99).

Grabher, G. (1995) 'The elegance of incoherence: institutional legacies in the economic transformation in East Germany and Hungary', in E. Dittrich, G. Schmidt and R. Whitley (eds) *Industrial Transformation in Europe: Process and Contexts*, London: Sage.

Hampden-Turner, C. and Trompenaars, F. (1993) *The Seven Cultures of Capitalism*, New York: Doubleday.

Hawley, J.P. and Williams, A.T. (1996) *Corporate Governance in the US: The Rise of Fiduciary Capitalism – A Review of the Literature*, report to OECD, January.

Hedberg, B., Dahlgren, G., Hansson, J. and Olve, N.-G. (1997) *Virtual Organizations and Beyond*, Chichester: Wiley.

Hedlund, G. (1986) 'The hypermodern MNC – a heterarchy?' *Human Resource Management* 25: 9–25.

Hofstede, G. (1991) *Cultures and Organizations: Software of the Mind*, Maidenhead: McGraw-Hill.

Kerr, C., Dunlop, J.T., Harbison, F. and Myers, C.A. (1960) *Industrialism and Industrial Man*, Cambridge, MA: Harvard University Press.

Lardy, N. (1999) 'China's breathtaking WTO offer', *Asian Wall Street Journal* 19 April: 10.

Locke, R.R. (1989) *Management and Higher Education since 1940: The Influence of America and Japan on West Germany, Great Britain and France*, Cambridge: Cambridge University Press.

Lu, Y. and Björkman, I. (1997) 'HRM practices in China–Western joint ventures: MNC standardization versus localization', *International Journal of Human Resource Management* 8: 614–28.

Mintzberg, H. (1994) *The Rise and Fall of Strategic Planning*, New York: Prentice Hall.

Mommsen, W.J. (1989) 'The two dimensions of social change in Max Weber's sociological theory', in W.J. Mommsen (ed.) *The Political and Social Theory of Max Weber: Collected Essays*, Oxford: Polity Press.

Ng, D.W.N. (1996) 'Succession in the "Bamboo Network"', *Financial Times: Mastering Enterprise*, (6) 20 December: 6–7.

Nohria, N. and Eccles, R.G. (eds) (1992) *Networks and Organizations*, Boston, MA: Harvard Business School Press.

Nonaka, I. and Takeuchi, H. (1995) *The Knowledge Creating Company*, New York: Oxford University Press.

Ohmae, K. (1990) *The Borderless World: Power and Strategy in the Interlinked Economy*, New York: Free Press.

Oliver, N. and Wilkinson, B. (1992) *The Japanization of British Industry*, Oxford: Blackwell.

Parker, B. (1996) 'Evolution and revolution: from international business to globalization', in S.R. Clegg, C. Hardy and W.R. Nord (eds) *Handbook of Organization Studies*, London: Sage.

Pauly, L.W. and S. Reich (1997) 'National structures and multinational corporate behavior: enduring differences in the age of globalization', *International Organization* 51: 1–30.

Peng, M. (2000) *Business Strategies in Transition Economies*, Thousand Oaks, CA: Sage.

Ralston, D.A., Egri, C.P., Stewart, S., Terpstra, R.H. and Yu Kaicheng (1999) 'Doing business in the 21st century with the new generation of Chinese managers: a study of generational shifts in work values in China', *Journal of International Business Studies* 30: 415–27.

Redding, S.G. (1990) *The Spirit of Chinese Capitalism*, Berlin: De Gruyter.

Redding, S.G. (2000) 'Order, integration, and collaboration: progress in comparative management', *Advances in Comparative International Management* 13: 95–106.

Robertson, R. (1995) 'Glocalization: time–space and homogeneity–heterogeneity', in M. Featherstone, S. Lash and R. Robertson (eds) *Global Modernities*, London: Sage.

Schluchter, W. (1981) *The Rise of Western Rationalism: Max Weber's Developmental History*, Berkeley, CA: University of California Press.

Sorge, A. and Warner, M. (1986) *Comparative Factory Organization: An Anglo-German Comparison of Manufacturing, Management and Manpower*, Aldershot: Gower.

Steger, U. (ed.) (1998) *Discovering the New Pattern of Globalization*, Ladenburg: Gottlieb Daimler-und-Karl Benz-Stiftung.

Warner, M. (ed.) *China's Managerial Revolution*, London: Frank Cass.

Weber, M. (1964) *The Theory of Social and Economic Organization*, trans. A.M. Henderson and T. Parsons, New York: Free Press.

Weber, M. (1978) *Economy and Society*, G. Roth and C. Wittich (eds and trans.). Berkeley, CA: University of California Press.

Whitley, R.D. (1992a) *Business Systems in East Asia*, London: Sage.

Whitley, R.D. (ed.) (1992b) *European Business Systems: Firms and Markets in their National Contexts*, London: Sage.

Part II

Area studies

Chapter 6

Managing in North America

Fred Luthans and Richard Hodgetts

Overview

In the aftermath of the Second World War, management in the USA was the kind of management held in the greatest respect; in many ways it set the standard of excellence for the entire world. United States based multinational corporations dominated the international marketplace in a number of industries, from copiers and computers to industrial equipment and transportation vehicles. By the 1970s, however, this dominance had begun to fade, and during the 1980s it became clear to US managers that dramatic changes were needed. These were duly implemented, and included the use of advanced information technology, total quality management and the re-engineering of processes. United States managers also recognized the need to develop learning organizations in order to stay ahead. In order to maintain their status, to be world-class organizations, management needed to change, not simply react.

In the 1990s and now into the new millenium, management in the USA did dramatically change, and the results have been very impressive. Whereas in the previous decades US managers crossed the Pacific to learn about Japanese management, now the Japanese and others from around the world are trying to learn about US management. Going into the twenty-first century, the US economy has had sustained robust economic growth and high productivity. Much of the credit for this boom is being given to US management (see Hitt 2000; Hodgetts, Luthans and Slocum 1999)

Before looking at the recent developments in US management, this chapter will outline the traditional, time-tested approach. This discussion of classic organization design and management processes will serve as a foundation and point of departure for the examination of information technology, total quality management and re-engineering, and creative human resources management before analysing the future of management in the USA.

Classic management style

Traditionally, management in the USA has been characterized by identifiable organization design and management processes. Organization design primarily relates to the characteristics of bureaucracy and the concepts of departmentation, span of control and decentralization, while the management process involves the functions of decision-making, communication and control.

Organization design

The classic organization design used by US enterprises has its roots in bureaucracy, the ideal characteristics of which were established by the German sociologist Max Weber (see chapter 5). Weber believed organizations should be structured as follows:

1 A clear-cut division of labour.
2 A hierarchy of positions, with each lower one being controlled and supervised by the one immediately above.
3 A consistent system of abstract rules and standards to help ensure uniformity in the performance of duties and the co-ordination of tasks.
4 A spirit of formal impersonality in which duties are carried out.
5 Employment based on technical qualifications and protected from arbitrary dismissal.

These Weberian bureaucratic characteristics have traditionally formed the structural basis of most large US organizations. They are coupled with the concepts of departmentation, span of control and delegation/decentralization.

Departmentation is the process of combining jobs into groups on the basis of common characteristics. The most popular arrangement is functional departmentalization, in which work activities are grouped on the basis of the job being carried out. An example is manufacturing firms, which have traditionally been departmentalized into three major functional departments: production, marketing and finance. Another common arrangement is product departmentalization, which groups together the activities associated with a particular product line. Firms in the motor industry have long used this type of arrangement by creating divisions that focus on a specific product, such as the Buick or Chevrolet divisions of General Motors. A third common arrangement is customer departmentalization, which is designed to meet the needs of specific customer groups. For example, retail stores will have major departments for men's clothing, for women's clothing and for children's wear.

Span of control is the number of subordinates a manager directly supervises. Different factors influence this span, including the amount of time that must be spent with each subordinate, the competence and experience of subordinates and the ability of these subordinates to work on their own. While some enterprises tried to keep the span of control within a specified range, most organizations began to recognize contingency variables, such as the difficulty of the task and the personal characteristics of the manager.

Delegation is the process a manager uses in distributing work to subordinates. *Decentralization* relates to the number and importance of decisions made lower down the management hierarchy. Both delegation and decentralization represent transitionary concepts in relation to the development of organization design. For example, delegation has now evolved into empowerment, which will be discussed in the section on total quality management (TQM), while decentralization is at the forefront of today's new network and virtual organization designs.

Management processes

Alongside the classic organization design characteristics described above, management in the USA has also depended upon a process consisting primarily of decision-making, communication and control.

Decision-making is the process of choosing from among alternatives. This management function involves making rational choices by analysing situations, determining alternative courses of action, weighing the benefits and drawbacks associated with each and choosing the one that offers the best solution. Mathematical modelling and computer analysis are employed in managerial decision-making, particularly in those areas where data quantification is given high priority. Examples include economic forecasting, comparison of alternative investments, decision-tree analysis, linear programming techniques and economic value analysis.

Decision-making also relies heavily on non-quantitative or subjective analysis. For example, when making decisions that require creativity or innovation, quantitative modelling and analysis may be replaced by brainstorming, synectics or other creative problem-solving techniques. Some organizations have accomplished this by testing their employees to identify those that are heavily right brain (creative, spontaneous, intuitive) and those that are left brain (logical, sequential, rational), and creating heterogeneous teams that can draw on the analytical strengths of both types of thinkers. This approach has been widely used in advertising, design and new product development.

Communication as a management function involves the process of conveying meanings in order to spread information throughout the organization. Typical examples include: downward communication in the form of memos and reports; upward communication in the form of suggestion programmes and open-door policies that provide feedback on problem areas; and horizontal communication in the form of interdepartmental meetings and reports used to coordinate activities.

In addition to formal communication channels, there is widespread use of informal communication, represented by the so-called grapevine. While there are a variety of ways in which information can be informally passed on, the most common route is through a selective process in which some people are deliberately included on the grapevine and others excluded.

Different media are used to convey information. One of the most common is written communication, such as memos, reports, letters and organizational handbooks. Another is oral communication: face-to-face verbal orders, telephone discussions, speeches and group meetings. A third is non-verbal communication, as exemplified in the use of kinesics, proxemics and paralanguage. Kinesics deals with the use of body language, including facial expressions, gestures and posture. Proxemics deals with the way people use physical space to convey information, such as how close one person stands to another when carrying on a conversation. Paralanguage is how things are said, including the person's rate of speech, voice tension, inflection, pacing and volume level.

Today, of course, almost all communication in US organizations is done electronically – for example e-mail, Internet, intranets and extranets. This not only allows organizations to go paperless, but also has implications for organization design, management processes and human relationships.

Control is the process of evaluating performance according to plans and objectives and taking any action deemed necessary. This management function is closely related to decision-making and helps to create a closed loop between the two functions, thus ensuring continual systems feedback. As a result, all three functions in the management process – decision-making, communication and control – are in a constant state of adjustment and readjustment.

Managerial control in US firms has become quantitative through the use of accounting and information systems that provide financial and numerical feedback to decision-makers. In addition, non-quantitative information may be used for control. For example, many managers rely on anecdotal feedback from their customers regarding the quality of service and how it can be improved. In recent years there has been some rethinking and changes made in control measures. For example, while firms have traditionally determined their cost of capital and used it as a factor in evaluating performance, there has been a growing trend towards including equity capital in this calculation, thus requiring subsidiary managers to generate a profit that pays for the cost of borrowed funds as well as providing a return on invested capital. As in communication, the computer and information technology are playing an increasing role in the control process, for example electronic data interchange (EDI). Some of these developments are covered below.

Recent developments

The organization design and management processes described above have played a major role in US management over the years. However, beginning in the 1980s things began to change dramatically. United States organizations were challenged as never before, resulting in some significant alterations to the classic management approach and some entirely new ways of thinking and acting. Some of the most significant developments which affected US management starting in the 1980s included downsizing, the use of advanced information technology (IT) and now in the 2000s e-commerce.

Downsizing

By the mid-1980s, US organizations were finding themselves facing growing competitive pressure from abroad. To reduce costs and increase efficiency and productivity, a growing number of firms began to downsize. They did so by not filling the positions of those who left or retired and by eliminating jobs, first those of operating workers, then middle managers and staff personnel. In many cases high-tech equipment and computers/expert systems replaced people. The result of this downsizing (some firms began calling it 'rightsizing' to soften the blow to employees) was to flatten the organization structure and increase productivity and competitiveness in global markets (see Parker 1999).

Unfortunately, this downsizing also restructured employment and left many without jobs. Those remaining in organizations had greater responsibility and more demanding job requirements. They have become known as knowledge workers. One way that management tried to meet this new challenge was to increase the amount of training given to personnel. A second method was to cross-train personnel so they could be assigned to the growth needs of the organization and the employees themselves. A third way was by creating self-managed work teams to replace the individualism that previously dominated the work environment. Thus, as the Japanese did so successfully, US workers began to work in groups, using their cross-training combined with the new high-tech equipment and processes to dramatically increase productivity and, especially, quality. Once again they became leaders in certain industries.

These lean structures also increased the ability of companies to adapt to external conditions. For example, as the quality of goods and services started to improve, companies with bloated bureaucracies and inflexible management processes were forced either to change or to go under. Firms with flat structures found it easier to modify work processes, introduce change and incorporate quality management techniques into their operations. They also found that the flat, interfunctional structures increased their ability to respond to customer needs.

Unfortunately, there has also turned out to be a downside to this downsizing. There has been a negative impact on employee commitment and performance. The important human side of US organizations in the 1980s was slighted in the rush to beomce 'lean and mean'. These implications will be noted after the discussion of total quality.

Information technology

Along with the recent transformation in organization structure came the use of IT. Both in the form of computers and related transmission, retrieval and storage components, and in the form of telecommunications involving computers interacting with both telephone and television technology, IT greatly changed management in the USA. Many organizations began at first complementing and then replacing their large computer systems with microcomputers, most of which became networks. Management decision-making, communication and control also began incorporating other forms of IT, including fax machines, electronic organizers and cellular telephones. Many organizations were thus able to expand the horizons of their electronic office. More personnel could leave the boundaries of the traditional organization and be assigned customer-contact responsibilities, and the firm was able to communicate with them no matter where they were physically located. For example, some firms now have knowledge workers pass work off at the end of the day to other time zones around the world to, in essence, obtain a 48-hour day to help in the necessary speed needed in today's competition. Information technology also facilitated the creation of flat organization structures and played a vital role in TQM.

Information technology boosted productivity in a number of ways, one of which was by reducing the time needed to send and retrieve information. For example, by using electronic mail (e-mail), many managers were able to drastically reduce the number of inter-office memos and increase the speed with which written messages were sent and replies received. An accompanying benefit with e-mail was that everyone could communicate directly with everyone else. Thus, there was less need for the cumbersome chain of command and bureaucracy.

A second productivity-related benefit was the time savings in obtaining information. For example, Connecticut Mutual Life Insurance customer representatives now sit at IBM personal computers, where they are able to call up the necessary forms and correspondence needed to answer customer questions. As a result, the average time taken to respond to enquiries has declined from five days to two hours, 20 per cent fewer people are needed for handling customer questions and productivity has risen dramatically.

A third way in which efficiency was increased was through the use of EDI. This process allows customers, companies and suppliers to exchange information directly, computer to computer. Where customers used to place orders by filling out paper forms, a company computer can now receive an order from a customer's computer and instruct the warehouse to fill the order while also checking inventory on hand to see if more needs to be ordered from suppliers. Almost all US firms use some form of EDI.

Still another way in which computer technology has affected productivity is through the use of computer monitoring. This process is used to collect, examine and feed back information about work results. The monitoring should not be used to keep a close check on employees nor for punitive purposes, its purpose being to improve performance and help develop employees. The most effective computer monitoring systems are designed on the basis of three objectives: (1) determining the type of information that will be most useful to the employees; (2) designing a system that gathers these data and allows for useful comparisons between, and within, specific tasks; and (3) ensuring that non-relevant information is not entered into the system. A number of US firms use computer monitoring. At Hughes Aircraft Company, for example, the process has been used to facilitate integrated production and quality control strategies and to help increase productivity.

Finally, managers in the USA are now using software that allows computers to emulate management decision-making. This approach is a combination of those discussed above, but its applications are more varied. For example, many US banks have now developed expert systems which involve computer programs that allow the machine to perform a variety of functions. One such expert (or smart) system scans credit card usage for the purpose of identifying those cards that may have been stolen but not yet reported. Typical computer programs look for sudden and obvious changes in spending patterns, such as a person suddenly buying expensive clothing or jewellery or making large cash withdrawals.

To take such systems one step further, neural networks are now being developed. These are more sophisticated software packages. Applied to the credit card example, neural networks can scan transactions and more accurately spot credit fraud. This is possible because of their ability to identify those transaction patterns most likely to indicate complex fraud. For example, at the Mellon Bank's Visa and MasterCard operations in Wilmington, Delaware, neural networks keep track of 1.2 million accounts and are able to identify as many as 1000 potential defrauders a day. Other examples of the application of neural networks include optical character recognition, stock trading, property appraisal and the evaluation of machine performance.

E-commerce

In the new millenium, US firms are engaging in e-commerce. This involves more than just building a website and doing a few transactions on the Internet. For example Bill Gates, in his book *Business@the Speed of Thought* (Gates 1999) advises that he is trying to show that it is not just the transaction, but the customer service, the collaboration at a distance and the decision about what skills you need inside your company versus what things you can go out now on the web to take advantage of. Although e-commerce does involve firms marketing and selling their products directly to the consumer through their web pages, such as Internet retailers (e-tailors) Amazon.com or multichannel established retailers such as Wal-Mart, or innovative firms such as Priceline.com, by far most e-commerce is business-to-business or intra-business on the Internet. For example, Cisco Systems has become a virtual organization by connecting through the Internet its various functions with other business partners. This business-to-business e-commerce is expected to grow to well over a trillion dollars in the next few years. United States firms have found that e-commerce not only has an impact on revenue but also can greatly reduce costs and adjust quickly to changing customer needs.

From total quality to learning organizations

Traditionally, US management concentrated on quantity – how much could be produced at the lowest cost. However, starting in the 1990s it became clear that in order to compete in world markets, quality must assume greater importance. At first the emphasis on quality was a direct reflection of successful Japanese management practices and procedures. Some of the techniques, such as quality circles, were copied directly, but when this did not work, US management began to develop their own approach. Quality management involved both the development of an overall philosophy and perspective of total quality as well as the application of specific techniques such as empowerment and benchmarking best practices.

Philosophy and perspective of total quality

The philosophy of quality management in the USA is grounded in ten core values. These values are reflected in the overall approach taken. They serve as the basis for planning, implementing and controlling total quality efforts.

1 *Customer-driven focus*. All methods, processes and procedures are designed to meet both internal and external customer expectations.
2 *Leadership*. Management understands what total quality entails and fully supports the organization's efforts to achieve it.
3 *Full participation*. Everyone in the organization is provided with TQM training and is actively involved in implementing these ideas.
4 *Reward system*. A reward system is developed to motivate personnel and ensure continual support for the overall effort.
5 *Reduced cycle time*. Great effort is made to reduce the amount of time needed to deliver output by continually analysing work procedures and workflows and eliminating or streamlining the process.

6 *Prevention not detection.* The focus of all quality efforts is on preventing mistakes and errors from occurring, rather than detecting and correcting them later on; the guideline is, 'do it right the first time'.

7 *Management by fact.* Feedback on TQM efforts are databased and often quantitative, with minimum attention given to anecdotal references, intuition and gut feeling.

8 *Long-range outlook.* There is continual monitoring of the external environment in order to answer the question: what level of quality or service will have to be provided to our customers over the next 12 to 36 months and how can this goal be attained?

9 *Partnership development.* A co-operative network system is created between organizations and their customers and vendors, thus developing a process for helping improve quality and keep costs down.

10 *Social responsibility.* Corporate citizenship and responsibility are fostered through the sharing of quality-related information with other organizations that can profit from these ideas, and by working to reduce negative impacts on the community by eliminating product waste generation and product defects or recalls.

Empowerment

Empowerment is the delegation of authority to employees in order for them to take control and make decisions. The objective of empowerment is to encourage employees to become more personally involved in their jobs and to use their authority to get things done and deliver quality to (meet the expectations of) internal and external customers. Empowerment is becoming increasingly recognized and used by management in the USA (see chapter 9). For example, at the Ritz-Carlton hotel chain, the only hotel firm to win the national quality award the Baldrige and the only firm to win it twice, employees are authorized to spend up to $2000 to handle problems, such as mailing a suit to a customer who checked out and left it in his room, sending a pot of herbal tea and aspirin to a guest who has just checked in and has a cold, or renting a television monitor and video cassette recorder because all of the hotel's units are in use and a client needs this equipment for a meeting scheduled to start immediately. At AT&T Universal Card Services, employees are allowed to authorize whatever expenditures are necessary to reduce cost and improve customer service, such as sending out a replacement card by overnight delivery to a customer whose card has been lost and who needs a new one as soon as possible.

Empowerment is typically tied to training. Empowered employees are trained so they are aware of how to do their jobs correctly and can then take action that will help deliver quality service to customers. At Motorola, for example, employees are trained in both hard (technical, engineering) and soft (interpersonal relations, customer service) skills. As a result, each Motorola employee learns how to handle their own quality and productivity, create production schedules and job assignments, manage material supplies, set up equipment and conduct routine maintenance, provide input to both product and process design, design the workplace, develop and manage budgets, generate input for hiring decisions, provide information for peer-performance reviews and train new employees.

Empowerment is also closely tied to work improvement systems. For example, at Zytec the empowerment plan includes an element known as the implemented improvement system (IIS), a Japanese-style suggestion system that places major emphasis on employee involvement with the goal of generating new ideas for increased productivity. There are three stages to IIS:

1 The organization encourages employees to examine their jobs and work areas, think of ways of improving them and make small developments.

2 Employees are educated and developed so that they are better equipped to analyse problems, devise ideal solutions and undertake more ambitious improvements.
3 The organization encourages employees to pursue major improvements to achieve significant financial benefits.

At the heart of this system is the concept of continuous improvement. Continuous or constant improvement focuses on never being satisfied with the status quo, always striving to improve quality to customers. Innovation, characterized by improvements in the creation and delivery of quality goods or services, plays a key role. Most firms stress constant improvement as reflected by ongoing, small, incremental gains. In contrast to the dramatic gains that can result from highly innovative approaches, constant improvement provides more long-term gains because of its ongoing nature. In addition, constant improvement places the emphasis on people, both employees and customers, not just technology, and promotes group effort (in contrast to individualism).

Today, many US managers recognize that continuous improvement is necessary but not sufficient. Now discontinuous leaps in improvement are necessary to compete in the hypercompetitive global economy.

Benchmarking and best practices

Another dimension of total quality is benchmarking and best practices, a process of comparing current performance and practices with those judged to be the very best. There are two ways in which this can be used to manage quality: (1) by studying the best processes and practices used internally and seeing how these can be employed by the group conducting the best practices effort; and (2) by studying best practices for the purpose of picking up new ideas which can be copied or modified for use. In the case of IBM Rochester, which designed and built the successful AS/400 mini-computer, the group benchmarked both in-house and outside firms. In-house the group learned how other IBM divisions successfully handled defect prevention, hardware process documentation and resource manufacturing capability. Outside they learned about quality improvement techniques from Motorola, about resource manufacturing planning capability from 3M, about the effective use of service representatives from Hewlett-Packard, about improved secretarial performance planning from Honeywell and about just-in-time (JIT) inventory from Japanese firms.

Learning organizations

Although the total quality approach has dramatically changed US management in the 1990s, it is now recognized that this is just the starting point for managing successfully in the twenty-first century. In particular, US management is attempting to move towards becoming learning organizations. These new paradigm organizations incorporate total quality but go beyond it (Luthans, Hodgetts and Lee 1994). For example, while total quality depends on single-loop and adaptive learning, learning organizations move towards double-loop and generative learning. Similarly, while the total quality approach continually adapts strategies to resolve problems and meet challenges, learning organizations anticipate change and analyse the causes of problems, thus preventing their recurrence.

Learning organizations have a number of common characteristics and values. One is an intense desire to learn how to prevent problems. This is commonly done by carefully analysing mistakes and failures to determine how their recurrence can be prevented. A second is a strong commitment to the generation and transfer of new knowledge and technology. This commitment typically encompasses information-gathering and training programmes for personnel. A third characteristic is that of continuously scanning the external environment, learning of new developments and incorporating this information into all relevant aspects of the operation. A fourth feature is the use of shared vision and systems thinking to evoke a personal commitment from all participants. Systems thinking is also used to understand the interrelationships between causes and effects and thus avoid the use of short-term solutions that lead to long-term problems.

Other characteristics of learning organizations can be seen in the contrast between the traditional resource-based enterprises and emerging knowledge-based organizations (see Senge 1993). Such differences include the way in which shared vision is created, the formulation and implementation of ideas, the nature of organizational thinking, conflict resolution and the role of leadership.

In traditional resource-based enterprises, vision was created by top management. In the new, knowledge-based learning organization, vision can emerge from anywhere, although top management remains responsible for the existence of such a vision and for promoting it through organizational processes. In the same way, in a resource-based enterprise formulation occurs at the upper levels and implementation is at the lower levels. In the knowledge-based learning organization, both formulation and implementation are carried out at all levels. It is in such situations that total quality techniques, such as empowerment, apply to learning organizations: empowered employees at any level can formulate the ideas and then implement them to get the job done right the first time and meet customer expectations at any cost.

The nature of organizational thinking differs between the two types of organizations in that employees in resource-based organizations understand their specialized jobs and what is expected of them. However, little attention is paid to how these jobs interrelate with others. The flow of authority and the focus of attention tends to be in a vertical, downward hierarchy. In contrast, in learning organizations employees are taught to understand how their jobs and actions influence those of others in the enterprise, and vice versa. An example is provided by Hanover Insurance, a medium-sized property and liability insurer. This firm steadily increased local control of regional operations, promoting a greater sense of ownership among personnel. The company also developed a claims management learning laboratory to help local managers better understand how individual decisions interact. As a result of this learning, Hanover managers discovered that some well-accepted practices used in the industry were contributing to problems, such as escalating costs and premiums. By rethinking the ways in which settlement costs were handled, the company was able to reduce payouts.

Conflict resolution is also handled in different ways. In the traditional approach, disputes tend to be mediated politically. Learning organizations approach conflict management differently, operating under the premise that, frequently, conflicts cannot be solved through the sheer use of power or hierarchical influence. Effective solutions often require input from an array of organizational personnel throughout the enterprise. Collaborative learning and the integration of diverse viewpoints are encouraged. For example, the product development departments of learning organizations may create competing teams that develop different approaches to the same project. These teams will then debate the advantages and disadvantages of the approaches. Under the guidance of team leaders, the groups eventually develop a common agreement as to the best approach.

The role of leadership is still another critical difference between traditional and learning organizations. In the resource-based organization, the leader sets the direction. In the learning organization, leaders are responsible for the processes of building a shared vision. One of the most commonly cited examples of this contrast is the way in which leaders motivate their people. In resource-based enterprises, rewards and recognition as well as punishment are used, while in learning organizations the personnel are empowered and inspired towards full commitment. While the resource-based organization relies on external tools and techniques designed to control local actions, learning enterprises work at creating an internally motivated workforce that is willing to use its increased authority and training to get things done.

Since learning organizations are future oriented, they also make use of techniques such as scenario analysis. This involves the formulation of future plans based on responses to possible situations that could develop in the future. While future environmental conditions are not totally predictable, the use of scenario analysis helps learning organizations predict likely developments and develop plans for addressing these conditions. This allows managers to stay ahead, not merely to adapt and react to changing environments.

The future: world-class organizations

The most recent development in US management with significant implications for the future is the move beyond learning organizations to become what could be called world-class organizations (see Parker 1999). These enterprises are recognized as global leaders in their respective industries; they dominate their markets. World-class organizations are additive in the sense of incorporating both total quality and learning organizations, but they extend beyond this. In particular, US managers of world-class organizations realize that change is not only desirable but necessary to compete successfully in an anywhere–anytime–anyplace twenty-first century environment. Today, US managers of world-class organizations continually monitor their environment and assess new technological developments not as threats but as opportunities. They realize that their present stakeholders (customers, owners, employees, suppliers and communities) and their current state of technology can be limiting or inhibiting to their future action (see Hodgetts, Luthans and Slocum 1999). As a famous US manager said as his company was coming off another record year in 1999, 'We have to reinvent ourselves!', and as Rosabeth Kanter (1999: 10) declares, 'the best way to predict the future is to create it'. There are several support pillars that can be used to characterize world-class organizations: (1) customer focus; (2) continuous improvement; (3) flexibility; (4) creative programmes for managing human resources; (5) an egalitarian climate; and (6) technological support (see Luthans, Hodgetts and Lee 1994). Once again, these are quite similar to what has been discussed under both total quality and learning organizations. Although the pillars use the same familiar terms, such as customer focus and continuous improvement, they are more comprehensive. Much of the following summary of the pillars, including the examples, has been suggested by Sang M. Lee and is drawn from Luthans, Hodgetts and Lee (1994).

Perhaps the most important pillar of the world-class organization is *its customer focus*. The organization puts the customer at the centre of its strategy, and all systems and personnel are organized to serve the customer. One way in which this is done is by flattening the structure and reducing the distance between the customer and the organizational personnel most directly serving customers. This type of structure can better gather information about customers' current and future needs. Organizations not only meet customer needs but also create new demand for their goods and services. For example, Pitney-Bowes, long known for its innovativeness in the postage meter/franking machine business, has continually developed creative products that have made it indispensable to the US Postal Service, as well as to a wide array of domestic and international customers, by expanding its focus from the postal business to the entire mailing business for its customers. The firm thus created both new product and service demand.

A second pillar is the need for *continuous improvement* as reflected by the way world-class organizations learn to be faster and more effective than competitors. Large enterprises partly accomplish this by sharing information on a worldwide basis. For example, IBM research scientists are in constant online contact with each other. Research and development personnel in Europe and Asia know what their colleagues in US laboratories are doing, and vice versa. This practice is used by all major functional groups, thus ensuring global learning throughout the enterprise. Another approach is the use of process engineering to create virtual offices at home or at customer premises. Most US managers now have laptop computers and cellular phones. This allows them to set up virtual offices everywhere and, in the process, reduce employee working space and allow personnel to spend more time with ustomers. Emerging IT tools such as Dell's Premier Pages (small web pages linked to large customers' intranets, that let approved employees configure their personal computers online, pay for them and track the delivery status) not only cut costs and improve quality (ordering errors), but also led to improved selling and customer service from freed-up Dell representatives.

The third pillar of world-class organizations is *flexibility*, the use of flexible arrangements that allow enterprises to respond quickly, decisively and correctly to changes in the environment. These enterprises become what is called a virtual corporation, which is a firm that acts just like a corporation but is organized through a network of partners and alliances (Davidow and Malone 1992). For example, while the virtual corporation produces goods and services and continually generates new offerings for the marketplace, many of these activities are often performed through an outside sourcing arrangement or the formation of temporary alliances with other companies. For example, Corning Inc. uses 23 strategic alliances to compete in a variety of high-tech markets. In this way, world-class companies are able to reduce costs and share risks with other firms.

Another example of flexibility is the way in which world-class organizations use JIT inventory systems and multiskilled personnel. For example, Kawasaki Manufacturing USA, in Lincoln, Nebraska, produces several models of motorcycles, all-terrain vehicles and jet skis. Relying heavily on its ability to switch production from one product to another, the company is able to achieve rapid set-up time, low-cost and high-quality output. Some of the characteristics of this flexibility pillar include the use of modular or matrix organizations, the use of multifunctional teams, the simultaneous processing of ideas, multiskilled workers, empowered teams; cross-training and job rotation of workers, and innovative approaches to cycle-time reduction.

Creative human resource management programmes represent the fourth pillar. Most US managers today recognize what has become known as high-performance work practices or HPWPs. Although there is not a single agreed-upon definition of HPWPs, a recent comprehensive review of the definitions and research literature concluded that the best definition is 'an organization system that continually aligns its strategy, goals, objectives and internal operations with the demands of its external environment to maximize organizational performance' (Kirkman, Lowe and Young 1999). The HPWPs can be operationalized as specific techniques such as multisource or 360-degree feedback, pay for performance, self-managed work teams and employee involvement/participation (Luthans *et al.* 2000).

Creative human resource management techniques have considerable research support linking them to organizational performance (Faris and Varma 1998). Yet in actual practice, only the world-class organizations fully utilize them. Pfeffer (1998) notes that only about half US organizations and their managers believe in the strong relationship between creative human resources techniques and bottom-line success. Of the half that do believe, only about half of them implement HPWPs, and then only half of the remaining one-fourth stick with these creative human resource management techniques long enough to reap the benefits of retention of the best people, productivity improvement and increased profit and growth. Pfeffer (1998) has documented that these one-eighth firms (1/2 × 1/2 × 1/2) are world-class organizations such as Southwest Airlnes, GE, Gallup, Norwest Bank and Microsoft.

Another pillar is the existence of an *egalitarian climate* in which the organization and its participants value and respect one another. This philosophy also extends to those whom the organization serves: customers, owners, suppliers and the community. At Wal-Mart, for example, all employees are called associates, and store managers have weekly meetings during which they hold open discussions with the associates for the purpose of reviewing operations and freely discussing new ideas for improving customer service. Some of the most important features of this pillar are open communication between all parties, a friendly environment, a mentoring, coaching and 'buddy' system, active employee involvement and participation in all phases of operations, and sponsored community, health and family programmes.

The final pillar supporting world-class organizations is technological support. Many of the creative, innovative or productive approaches of these organizations are made possible because of advances in technologies, such as computer-aided design, computer-aided manufacturing, telecommunications, expert systems, distributed database systems, intra-, inter- and extra-organizational information systems, multimedia systems and executive information systems. This technological support helps the enterprise use speed, information knowledge and differentiation to gain competitive advantages. An example is provided by American Express's company AmeriTax, which provides electronic tax filing by creating an electronic linkage between the Internal Revenue Service (IRS) and tax preparation firms. Through this interorganizational information system, AmeriTax offers a tax-return preparation service to its customers, while also developing a conduit for a larger set of financial products and services. The key elements of the technological support pillar include technology–human interface, modern information/telecommunication systems, distributed information/database systems, shared ownership of information knowledge and intelligence, decentralization of decision-making to the lowest level possible and continuous technical education and training.

Conclusion

United States management has a strong foundation in classic organization design and management processes, but has undergone dramatic change of late. To some extent Japanese management techniques and competitive battles stimulated US managers to abandon the classical approach about 15 years ago but, as has been discussed here, some changes are unique to the USA. In particular, there has been, and will probably continue to be, a great deal of focus on adjusting to the external technical and global environment. Customer service, quality management, reduced time to market, continuous improvement, outsourcing of goods and services, and creative human resource management programmes are all key factors in US management efforts to attain and maintain world-class levels of goods and services.

Not all US organizations have achieved world-class levels, but, even to survive, they know they need to continually improve to fend off competitors and maintain local markets. The concepts of total quality, learning and world-class organizations are increasingly being adopted by US managers in order to sustain and strengthen their position in the domestic economy, and now the reality of the global economy.

References

Davidow, W.H. and Malone, M.S. (1992) *The Virtual Corporation*, New York: HarperCollins.
Faris, G. and Varma, A. (1998) 'High performance work systems: what we know and what we need to know', *Human Resource Planning* 21(2): 50–5.

Hitt, M.A. (2000) 'The new frontier: transformation of management for the new millenium', *Organizational Dynamics* 28(3): 7–17.

Hodgetts, R.M., Luthans, F. and Slocum, J.W. Jr (1999) 'Strategy and HRM initiatives for the '00s environment: redefining roles and boundaries linking competencies and resources', *Organizational Dynamics* 28(2): 7–21.

Kanter, R.M. (1999) 'Change is everyone's job: managing the extended enterprise in a globally connected world', *Organizational Dynamics* 28(1): 7–23.

Kirkman, B.L., Lowe, K.B. and Young, P.D. (1999) *High Performance Work Organizations*, Greensboro, NC: Center for Creative Leadership.

Luthans, F., Hodgetts, R.M. and Lee, S.M. (1994) 'New paradigm organizations: from total quality to learning to world-class', *Organizational Dynamics* 22(3): 5–19.

Luthans, F., Luthans, K.W., Hodgetts, R.M. and Luthans, B.C. (2000) 'Can HPWPs (high performance work practices) help in the former Soviet Union? A cross-cultural fit analysis', *Business Horizons* September–October: 15–25.

Parker, B. (1999) *Globalization and Business Practice*, Thousand Oaks, CA, and London: Sage.

Pfeffer, J. (1998) *The Human Equation*, Boston, MA: Harvard Business School Press.

Senge, P.M. (1993) 'Transforming the practice of management', *Human Resource Development Quarterly* 4(1): 5–32.

Further reading

Bowen, D.E. and Lawler, E.E., III (1992) 'The empowerment of service workers: what, why, how, and when', *Sloan Management Review* 33(3): 31–9.

Davidow, W.H. and Malone, M.S. (1992) *The Virtual Corporation*, New York: HarperCollins.

Dixon, N.M. (1992) 'Organizational learning: a review of the literature with implications for HRD professionals', *Human Resource Development Quarterly* 3(1): 29–49.

Faris, G. and Varma, A. (1998) 'High performance work systems: what we know and what we need to know', *Human Resource Planning* 21(2): 50–5.

Fulmer, R.M. and Gibbs, P. (1998) 'The second generation learning organizations: new tools for sustaining competitive advantage', *Organizational Dynamics* 21(1): 7–20.

Gates, W. (1999) *Business@the Speed of Thought*, London: Penguin.

Glanz, E.F. and Dailey, L.K. (1993) 'Benchmarking', *Human Resource Management* 32(1/2): 9–20.

Hammer, M. and Champy, J. (1993) *Reengineering the Corporation*, New York: Harper Business.

Hitt, M.A. (2000) 'The new frontier: transformation of management for the new millenium', *Organizational Dynamics* 28(3): 7–17.

Hodgetts, R.M., Luthans, F. and Slocum, J.W. Jr (1999) 'Strategy and HRM initiatives for the '00s environment: redefining roles and boundaries linking competencies and resources', *Organizational Dynamics* 28(2): 7–21.

Howard, R. and Haas, R.D. (eds) (1993) *Learning Imperative: Managing People for Continuous Innovation*, Boston, MA: Harvard Business School Press.

Kanter, R.M. (1999) 'Change is everyone's job: managing the extended enterprise in a globally connected world', *Organizational Dynamics* 28(1): 7–23.

Kirkman, B.L., Lowe, K.B. and Young, P.D. (1999) *High Performance Work Organizations*, Greensboro, NC: Center for Creative Leadership.

Luthans, F., Hodgetts, R.M. and Lee, S.M. (1994) 'New paradigm organizations: from total quality to learning to world-class', *Organizational Dynamics* 22(3): 5–19.

Luthans, F., Luthans, K.W., Hodgetts, R.M. and Luthans, B.C. (2000) 'Can HPWPs (high performance work practices) help in the former Soviet Union? A cross-cultural fit analysis', *Business Horizons* September–October: 15–25.

McGill, M.E., Slocum, J.W. Jr and Lei, D. (1992) 'Management practices in learning organizations', *Organizational Dynamics* 21(1): 5–17.

Parker, B. (1999) *Globalization and Business Practice*, Thousand Oaks, CA, and London: Sage.

Pfeffer, J. (1998) *The Human Equation*, Boston, MA: Harvard Business School Press.

Rogers, C.S. (1993) 'The flexible workplace: what have we learned?', *Human Resource Management* 31(3): 183–9.

Schonberger, R.J. (1992) 'Is strategy strategic? Impact of total quality management on strategy', *Academy of Management Executive* 6(3): 80–7.

Senge, P.M. (1993) 'Transforming the practice of management', *Human Resource Development Quarterly* 4(1): 5–32.
Tully, S. (1993) 'The modular corporation', *Fortune* 127(3): 106–15.
Warner, M. (ed.) (1997) *Comparative Management*, 4 volumes, London: Routledge.

Chapter 7

Managerial decision-making: an Anglo-Brazilian comparison

Carlos Alberto Arruda and David J. Hickson

Introduction

Although calls for more, and more carefully thought out, cross-societal cross-culture research continue to be justified, during the last quarter of a century work of this nature has expanded apace. It has progressed from a stage when there was a mere handful of publications to survey, to a stage where sophisticated syntheses and appraisals become not only possible but necessary. Those by Boyacigiller and Adler (1991), Triandis (1982–3), Lachman, Nedd and Hinings (1994), Redding (1994) and Smith (1992) all testify to this, in themselves and in the substantial lists of references they encompass.

The reasons are both practical and theoretical. The advent of the jet engine made travel easy and, for those in richer lands, affordable. Hence more Westerners could study other Westerners and more Westerners could study non-Westerners, the latter a virtual one-way flow due not only to the ability to pay the air fare but perhaps also to less affinity by some non-Westerners with Western research methods and thought ways. A second practical stimulus was the economic rise of Japan and subsequently of other nations of the Asian Pacific rim, which drew to itself the attention of Westerners generally and Americans especially.

Theoretically, some conceptual commonality was needed which, even thought disputed – as it properly should be – offered a point of departure for research. Here the vital impetus was given by the work of a single Dutch individual, Hofstede (1980; 1991). Until he brought into organizational analysis four sociologically derived concepts of 'work-related values' there was no widely recognized conceptual means of comparison across societies. Like them or not like them, these concepts – power distance, individualism-collectivism, uncertainty-avoidance, mascuinity-femininity (and a fifth added later, 'confucian dynamism' [Hofstede and Bond 1988] or long-term-short-term), showed how necessary it is to have concepts of culture pertinent to this field of research that run across societies. Others have tried to follow Hofstede's lead (e.g. Trompenaars 1993 – see Chapter 8).

The point has been reached where it is even becoming possible to attempt to portray worldwide the cultural linkages with management and organization. 'Worldwide' is the term used by Hickson and Pugh (2001) for their series of succinct portrayals of the approaches to management which typify the Anglos, the Latins, the Northern Europeans, the East-Central Europeans, the Asians, the Arabs and developing countries generally. Though sometimes the evidence is thin and the portrayals precarious, such an attempt exemplifies the current rapid widening of perspective to encompass the many 'mindscapes of management' (Maruyama 1994).

It is an enthralling perspective, partly because it reveals so many conceptual puzzles. It shows how the cultures of societies enter unevenly into features of management and organization. Management and organization-relevant characteristics of societal cultures make more of an impression in some directions in some societies, in other directions in other societies. This is well illustrated by Tayeb:

> Take three colectivist nations – Japan, India and Iran, for example. These societies are characterized by, among others, a strong sense of the group and the community. A typical Japanese, Indian or Iranian person is very loyal to his or her own group or team and places the interest of the group before his or her own interests. On the face of it, one would expect to see this characteristic – collectivism – carried over into their work organizations in the form of, for instance, hard work and a high degree of commitment, dedication and emotional attachment to the company. However, a close examination of societal cultures, employees' attitudes and values and the management structure of work organizations in these countries (Tayeb, 1979; 1988; 1990) reveals that it is only in Japan where the collectivism of Japanese culture has been carried over into its companies. The Iranians and Indians as employees are as detached from their work organizations and have as individualistic a relationship with their work places as any individualistic nation. There are, of course, several cultural and non-cultural reasons for this, but the reasons will reveal themselves only through a careful and detailed study of these nations and their organizations.
>
> *(Tayeb 1994: 38)*

The puzzle is, into which features of management and organization do societal cultures enter most? In other words, how uneven is organizational culture-sensitivity? This is a question put in a different way by Redding (1994: 341) when he asks the seventh of seven questions about 'cross-cultural OB': 'Which aspects of organizing and managing may be said to be universal and which are most affected by culture (that is, if there is such a construct as managing which can be disembedded at all)?'

Cases in point: Brazil and England

This puzzle was brought out by a comparison of top management decision-making in Brazil and England. Decision-making at this level involves a number of individuals, sometimes just a few, sometimes many and the weighing of the interests involved, which again may be few or many (across 150 British cases reported by Hickson *et al.* (1986) the number of interests ranged from two to twenty, a mean of almost seven). It is a socio-political process, of a kind which a priori would be thought to be highly susceptible to the influence of societal culture.

It was decided to compare such processes among Brazilian and English managers because of the sharp contrast between a Latin New-World culture and an Anglo Old-World culture. The lead given by Tayeb (1987; 1988; 1994) was followed as far as possible. Cross-national research had been criticized both for failing to separate clearly the characteristics of a culture from those of management and organization that they were supposed to explain and, even more, for retrospective explanation – that is, for finding differences between organizations in different societies and attributing them to 'cultural effects' with no direct evidence for that (for example, Child 1981). In response, Tayeb (1987; 1988) gave a remarkable demonstration of how societal cultures could be defined and operationalized separately from and before studying organization structural and behavioural features, and only then interrelating the two.

To operationalize cultures, she used published sociological research results, histories and literatures together with an original questionnaire administered personally by her to other respondents outside the work situation. Our time and funding did not permit the latter, but prior to defining and operationalizing the variables of decision-making on which managements in Brazil and England were to be compared, portrayals of each culture were independently composed from sociological, historical and literary sources (for example, for Brazil: Azevedo 1963; Da Matta 1983; Faoro 1975; Hollanda 1969; Marshall 1966. For England: Commager 1974; Gorer 1955; Lytton 1833; Orwell 1947; Priestley 1973; Tayeb 1988; Terry 1979). In addition, unstructured interviews, which concluded with the completion of questionnaire scales largely taken from Terry (1979), were conducted with six Brazilian (English speaking) managers working in England and six English (Portuguese speaking) managers who had worked in Brazil and/or with Brazilian managers. These interviews explored the experience each had of the other and their views of the other, as a small but separate verification. The results accorded closely, indeed perfectly, with the cultural portrayals that had been built up (Oliveira 1992).

Management is society and it is culture, of course. The one is part of the other. But they can be separated analytically for explanatory purposes and this is what is done here.

Throughout this research and this chapter we again follow (Tayeb 1987; 1988) in referring specifically to England and the English, not to Britain and the British. All published research deals only with the English, not with the Scottish, Welsh or Irish nations within the United Kingdom and we make no presumptions concerning them.

In brief, the composite cultural portrayals of the Brazilians and the English depicted them as follows:

The Brazilians

The culture of the Brazilians is influenced by a rural plantation past and by recent urbanization and industrialization. This society, which in 1940 found 60 per cent of its population in rural areas, now finds 76 per cent of it in urban centres with several cities of over one million inhabitants each. So its culture is made up of a blend of rural traits, colonial in origin, with urban values. For most sociologists and anthropologists (Azevedo 1963; Da Matta 1983; Faoro 1975; Hollanda 1969) two of the most representative features are legacies from long ago rural Brazil: a strong respect for authority, from the old patriarchal family structures and *personalism* from a highly collectivist rural society. Respect for authority is, quite possibly, the most traditional trait. Brazilian history is rife with examples: the long incumbency of a Portuguese as the first Brazilian ruler, the great number of military coups, two long periods of authoritarian rule and, in all matters, the importance of the paternalistic family in the make-up of society.

Personalism, which means relating to other people by means of personal knowledge of them rather than in terms of impersonal rights and duties, is accompanied by other characteristics such as informality and cordiality. Thus, extensive networks of people who know each other involve almost all Brazilians (Da Matta 1983). These networks limit the privacy and outcomes of individuals and shape their personal development. This emphasis on direct informal relationships has as an attractive consequence the cordiality which is one of the most positive features of these people, in the opinion of both Brazilians and of foreigners visiting the country (Hollanda 1969; Marshall 1966).

Other less traditional, but not less significant, characteristics are immediacy and peacefulness. Brazilian immediacy has been observed by several authors (Amado and Brasil 1991; Faoro 1975; Hollanda 1969; Marshall 1966) who, while perceiving Brazil as the country of the future, find Brazilians mainly concerned with the here and now. Things are needed now and ought to be done now. This is the most criticized feature of this culture since it tends to overcome consideration of future consequences. It may be an escape from uncertainty. It comes together with a propensity for the multification of rules and decrees which, according to Hofstede (1980), create a façade of apparent certainty.

Brazil is seen as a peaceful society, non-aggressive and non-assertive. There is an aversion to violent situations and a strong belief in the efficacy of mediating interventions, of personal negotiations, of the quest for a common solution which will benefit all.

The interviews with Brazilian and English executives reinforced this profile. They saw Brazilians as characterized by a personalized emotional involvement with work and, at the same time, flexibility. Brazilian executives tended to perceive themselves as open to argument and discussion through having a strong respect for all in positions of authority. However, English executives discussing Brazilians, perceived them as capable of taking risks to the extent of daring, but inefficient in transforming decisions into action.

Table 7.1 summarizes this picture in terms which are relative to the English, as in the English portrayal relative to the Brazilian. It uses the expressions 'power distance' and 'uncertainty avoidance' as they are used by Hofstede (1980; 1991).

The English

Historically, being English meant being at the apex of an empire on which it was said the sun never set. And many of the English, secure on their island, still think in this manner. England was the country where the Industrial Revolution began, where capitalism has its deepest roots and where tradition plays an important role. It is the land of time honoured unwritten law, where class differences are still carefully preserved. Visually, it is the land of ancient ceremony, historical buildings, gardens and parks. It is a land where leisure and life beyond work are important in the lives of every citizen.

English society has been studied over and over by many authors from different angles. Social investigators (Gorer 1955; Terry 1979; Tayeb 1988) as well as novelists and travellers (Commager 1974; Lytton 1983; Priestley 1973; Orwell 1947; Santayana 1922) have written numerous books about this society and its people. In a few words, being English means being a member of a society where due respect for authority is nevery misunderstood as submission; where the future is not controlled by written laws and rules but by caution, by the belief that changes are a part of a natural and continuous, not abrupt, process. Where relatively reserved behaviour and individual autonomy, together with a law-abiding honesty, and personal development and liberalism are taken as the basic rules of life. But also where the ego can prevail over the social and aggressive assertiveness is a component of daily life.

These aspects are not exclusively English, but this is a particular combination which can be summed up, in Hofstedian terms, as low power distance, low uncertainty avoidance and high individualism associated with personal assertiveness and conservatism under the rule of law. When interviewed, the Brazilian and English executives agreed with these characteristics. Both said that English managers and executives are much too inflexible. Brazilians emphasized their conservative and

Table 7.1: **Brazilian culture profile (in relative terms)**

Broad traits	Some associated characteristics
High power distance	Political authoritarianism, autocracies
	Need for strong leadership
Medium uncertainty avoidance	Need for formalized rules
Immediacy	Risk-taking capacity
Personalism	Strong interpersonal networks
	Informality and cordiality
Peacefulness	Low assertiveness

cautious ways, their slowness in decisions, the lack of emotivity in their business relationships and their arrogance. English executives added that English society is still too tied to traditional class structures with low mobility at the higest levels.

Table 7.2 sums up these characteristics.

Sample and data collection

Equipped in advance with these cultural portrayals, of which the above are just a summary of salient aspects, the research then moved on to the empirical comparison of managerial decision making to investigate how far it might accord with them and be held to be explained by them.

In both countries, the chief executives of organizations selected from business directories and/or business association lists were approached by letter and by phone, beginning with those most easily accessible geographically. Co-operation was far harder to obtain in England than in Brazil. In England managements are now besieged by researchers and students, whereas they are still a relative curiosity in Brazil, much as the second author recalls they were in England in the 1960s. In a neat demonstration of Brazilian immediacy and the English longer (gradualist) conception of time, when phoned for an appointment two or three weeks ahead Brazilians often laughed and asked to be contacted a few days beforehand, whereas the English routinely fixed dates many weeks or even months in advance.

The English sample, listed in Table 7.3, was built up first and it was hoped to match the Brazilians as closely as possible to it. This ideally required matching of both organizations and decisions, that is, finding similar organizations in which similar decisions had recently been or were being taken. That ideal was a very stringent requirement and was achieved in only three pairs of organizations, two universities, two textile firms and two newspapers (these are examined later in this chapter). One obstacle was that the range of business organizations is less varied in Brazil than in England so there were not many to choose from to effect matching. But irrespective of that, the chances of happening upon a similar decision in a similar organization were low.

The Brazilian sample is listed in Table 7.4. In all there are 20 Brazilian cases and 20 English, a total of 40. The decisions to be studied were chosen during the preliminary interview or conversation with the chief executive or other senior director, choosing those that were major in relation to the organization and recent enough or current so that memory would be fresh. There is not alternative to relying on memory if more than perhaps one case is to be studied, for the observations of the entirety of even a single decision-making process is impossible and this cannot even be attempted on larger numbers. In this kind of research, memories of the main happenings are surprisingly clear and mutually corroborating, for as Cray *et al.* (1988: 23)

Table 7.2: **English culture profile (in relative terms)**

Broad traits	Some associated characteristics
Low power distance in a finely layered society	Political liberalism
	Deference in accepting authority
Low uncertainty avoidance	Low formalization (fewer written rules)
Conservatism	Less risk-taking capacity
	Gradualism
Individualism	Reserved behaviour
	Less emotional involvement in the work organization
Assertiveness	Greater personal competitiveness

Table 7.3: **English sample of organizations and decisions**

| Code | Decision | Activity | Organizations' Main Characteristics | | |
			Size (Employees)	Ownership	Number of informants
E1	Rationalization of expenditure	Retailing	3000	Co-operative	3
E2	Introduction of franchises	Dairy Company	5500	Private	1
E3	Rationalization and reorganization	Food Manufacturer	2500	Private	2
E4	Re-equipment	Textile	2000	Private	2
E5	Diversification	Textile	1500	Private	1
E6	New presses	Daily Newspapers*	1200	Private	2
E7	Computerization	Daily Newspapers*	1200	Private	2
E8	Rationalization of expenditures	University*	430	Public	5
E9	Disposal of division	Construction	3250	Private	1
E10	Reorganization	Chemical*	1740	Private	3
E11	Budget	University*	430	Public	2
E12	Merger	Chemical*	1740	Private	3
E13	Acquisition in the Netherlands	Games Manufacturer	4200	Private	1
E14	New divisions in the USA	Road Transporter	1600	Private	2
E15	New service	Finance	3450	Building Society	2
E16	Acquisition of competitors	Construction	1300	Private	1
E17	Closure of division	Textile	4800	Private	1
E18	Re-equipment	Textile	900	Private	1
E19	Budget	University	1050	Public	2
E20	Move the company's headquarters	Retailing	3500	Co-operative	1

Note: *Organizations with two decisions studied

found from the experience of 150 cases in 30 organizations, 'the difference between shorter recall in concurrent cases and the longer recall taped in interviews is that the story becomes les cluttered and relatively simpler, not that it changes'.

Tables 7.3 and 7.4 show that the 20 English cases of decisions occurred in 17 organizations (one each in 14 organizations, two each in 3 organizations), the 20 Brazilian decisions in 16 organizations (one each in 12 organizations, two each in 4 organizations). Though there is no claim to exact matching, the organizations overall are not unlike in their broad diversity. The English include 13 manufacturing, 7 service, the Brazilians respectively 10 and 10. The English include 17 privately owned, 3 governmental, the Brazilians respectively 15 and 5. At first sight there is a sharp disparity in mean size, the English 2264 employees and the Brazilians 5426 and this does seem to represent a difference in economies, the older British economy having more middle-sized firms, whereas in Brazil there is a greater gap between small businesses and newer large corporations superimposed, so to speak, by recent industrialization. However, if three exceptionally large units are removed from the Brazilian calculation – the nationalized steel busines (13 400) and two huge constructions firms – sustained partly by lucrative state contracts (24 300 and 21 900) – then the remaining organizations average out on a par with the English at 2220 employees.

Table 7.4: **Brazilian sample of organizations and decisions**

| Code | Decision | Organizations' Main Characteristics | | | Number of informants |
		Activity	Size (Employees)	Ownership	
B1	Modify existing structure	Retailing*	1700	Private	2
B2	New branch in Brasilia	Retailing*	1700	Private	2
B3	New presses	Daily News-papers	1110	Private	2
B4	Merger	Transporter	1650	Private	2
B5	Modify and rationalize structure	Steel Industry*	13 400	Public	4
B6	Divisionalization/ professionalization	Retailing	2100	Private	3
B7	Computerization	Daily News-papers	900	Private	3
B8	Budget	University*	2880	Public	1
B9	Increase in the number of staff	University*	2880	Public	2
B10	New division	Retailing*	1700	Private	1
B11	Closure of division	Retailing*	1700	Private	1
B12	Divisionalization	Construction	24 300	Private	1
B13	New furnace technology	Steel Industry	1300	Private	1
B14	Introduction of information technology	University	4600	Public	1
B15	Merger	Construction	2200	Private	2
B16	New line of products	Steel Industry*	13 400	Public	2
B17	Re-equipment	Textile	1800	Private	1
B18	New image	Banking	2700	Private	1
B19	Takeover bid	Textile	4600	Private	1
B20	Takeover a Portuguese firm	Construction	21 900	Private	2

Note: *Organizations with two decisions studied

The tables show that there were one, two or three informants per case (and four in one of the Brazilian cases). There is no question that more would have been desirable, had they been available and had time and funding been available. The practical issue is how great the marginal addition to data would have been. These are informants, giving information about when a decision was reached (the authorized go-ahead for implementation), the kinds of information used, the main interests involved and so on, not respondents talking about details of who had said what or about their own feelings (though they may do so) or psychological processes. This study confirmed again the experience of Hickson *et al.* (1986), reported also by Cray *et al.* (1988), that a second or third informant added remarkably little to what a single centrally involved informant could recount. In any case, employees below the top echelon, even those immediately below, know little of what took place in the making of major decisions, so the number of useful informants is a handful at most.

The means of comparison

More than a decade of basic research in England, known as the Bradford Studies since it was (and continues still to be) based at Bradford Management Centre, provided the conceptual and operational means for the research reported here. This is the second cross-national extension of this work, the first having been in Sweden (Axelsson *et al.* 1991). There is no known previous Brazilian/English study because variables of decision-making which could be used for comparison were not available and no data collection experience on relatively large numbers of cases had accumulated, until the publications by Hickson *et al.* (1986) and Cray *et al.* (1988; 1991).

Interviews followed what these precursors had done by being a mixture of narrative case histories, open questions and rating scales (here 5-point scales), so numeral (rating) answers could be understood in the context of case knowledge. Oliveira (1992) contains full results, forty case histories, the interview schedule in English and in Portuguese.

The schedule was designed and tested first in English, guided by that used by Hickson *et al.* (1986). It was then translated into Portuguese by another Brazilian but in co-operation with the Brazilian author of this chapter, Arruda de Oliveira, then independently translated back by a Portuguese speaking Englishman and finally minor discrepancies of meaning were reconciled by all three together.

The salient variables are defined in Table 7.5. They are taken from those devised by Hickson *et al.* (1986), in some instances with improved definitions, except for Meanering Meetings, Meetings Completion, Informal Interaction Off Job, Interpersonal Facilitation and Organizational Innovativeness. These were added to extend the coverage of managerial decision making appropriate to the Brazilian setting. Since the variables used by Hickson *et al.* (1986) had been formulated in

Table 7.5: **Definitions of variables**

Influence in favour, influence ratings of those who are favourable to the decision, from (1) a little to (5) a very great deal.

Number of active interests, the number of individuals, or groups (e.g. departments, committees, other organizations) who have influence on the process, not including any participant who although involved had not actively influenced the course of the decision.

Information diversity, a count of the variety of sources of information used (e.g. plans, internal documents, personal knowledge).

Meandering meetings, how far meetings meandered before becoming decisive, from never (1) to very often (5).

Meetings' completion, how far meetings finished the agenda, from never (1) to very often (5).

Overall informal interaction, how much discussion and toing and froing took place, in addition to pre-arranged meetings, from little (1) to a very great deal (5).

Informal interaction in breaks, how far people continued chatting about the decision during breaks in the working day, from never (1) to very often (5).

Informal interaction off the job, how far people continued chatting about the decision after normal working hours, from never (1) to very often (5).

Interpersonal facilitation, how far the right people knowing each other personally beforehand helped in coming to a decision, from not at all (1) to a great deal (5).

Negotiation scope, how much negotiation and compromise there was during the process, from little (1) to a very great deal (5).

Duration, the length of time from the first identiable action which began movement towards a decision, to the moment when implementation was authorized or, in some cases, when the implementation began.

Perceived pace, how rushed was the decision, from not at all (1) to a great deal (5).

Organizational innovativeness, the extent to which decisions, in general, in the organization are novel, from not at all (1) to a great deal (5).

---

the English setting, it was recognized that they would include neither all the characteristics of interest in Brazil nor, therefore, all those pertinent to the comparison. The additional variables were defined so as to detect any reflection in decision making of the Brazilian cultural propensities for sociable personal relationships and for taking risks. Working within a single society, Hickson *et al.* (1986) had had no thought of covering these aspects. If they had not been included in this study the chances of revealing different culture effects would have been markedly lessened. Conversely, their inclusion added some bias towards detecting such effects.

Culture-linked contrasts

Before any fieldwork had commenced, the two culture portrayals were used to predict what the Brazilian and English positions would be on every variable of decision making, assuming every variable to be highly, and to a similar degree, culture-sensitive. In a few words, predictions from the more leader-seeking, at times authoritarian, cordial, immediatist, optimistically risk-taking, Brazilian culture were that managerial decision making processes would be comparatively centralized, even autocratic, interpersonally interactive, fast and receptive to novel proposals. Whereas predictions from the deferential yet participative, personally reserved, gradualist, cautious English culture were that decision making would be comparatively less centralized, impersonal, slow and wary of innovation.

The main results are given in Tables 7.6 and 7.7. It must be stressed that in these tables and in the text, all results are relative. That is, indications of magnitude, of more or of less, are of Brazilian managements by reference to the English, of the English by reference to the Brazilian.

Table 7.6 contains those variables in which the strongest differences were found between the two societies. The impact of their cultures is plain to see.

First, there is a marked difference in how authority is used. Forty 'control graphs' were drawn from the influence ratings given to those actively involved, excluding those opposed, following Tannenbaum (1968). All are reproduced in Oliveira (1992),

Table 7.6: **Cuture-linked contrasts in decision-making**

	BRAZIL*	ENGLAND*	One Way: F	Sig.
Authority				
Influence in favour:	Hierarchical (smooth) slope	Participative (layered) slope	–	–
Active interests permitted:	5.5 (2.5)	6.8 (2.1)	2.9	087
Information diversity admitted:	3.0 (1.6)	4.6 (1.5)	11.3	001
Interpersonal Interaction				
Meandering meetings:	4.4 (0.9)	3.2 (1.1)	11.8	002
Meetings completion:	3.6 (1.1)	4.2 (0.5)	3.6	067
Informal interaction off job:	3.7 (1.7)	2.7 (1.6)	4.9	034
Interpersonal facilitation:	3.8 (1.7)	2.7 (1.6)	4.0	052
Temporal				
Duration (months):	8.2 (9.3)	12.2 (11.0)	1.5	ns.
Innovation				
Organizational innovativeness	3.9 (1.4)	2.9 (1.1)	5.1	030

Note: *Mean scores, standard deviations in parentheses

Table 7.7: **Common managerialism**

In making major decisions, both Brazilian managements and English managements:
Confine the process, to the top élite.
Squeeze out opposition.
Interact and negotiate informally among themselves, on the job, about the matter on hand.
At least prepared to handle internal reorganization decisions.

together with their grouping in terms of angle and smoothness of slope. At the extremes, there were six Brazilian cases of steep, unbroken hierarchical slope, that is, dominant chief executive influence unrivalled by any other. There were no such English cases. But there were nine English cases of a 'double-zed' type, that is, a layered slope with successive Z shapes in which each layer or step represents influence by others, lesser influence but nevertheless strong influence. There were fewer Brazilian examples of this, namely five. Overall, Brazilian cases inclined towards the more hierarchical slope, English cases towards the more layered slope.

Figure 7.1 shows contrasting examples. Brazilian Case 2 is a typically opportunistic fast president-only decision (president's influence 5) to launch a retail chain cross-country out of its accustomed regional market into the capital Brasilia. Only the corporation's bank manager (influence 3) and a consultant acquaintance of the president (1) figured at all. Whereas the English decision, by coincidence also numbered Case 2, involved a series of others. It switched retail doorstep distribution from employees to a franchise form of operation, involving the managing director (president), operations director and production director, all of whom had an equal say (all

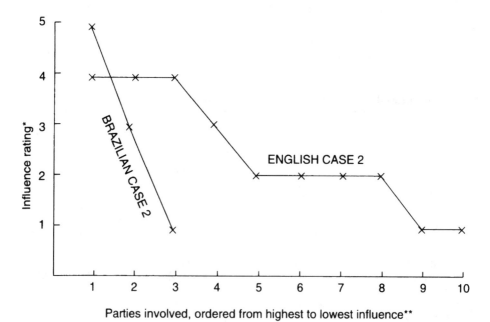

* from 1 = little to 5 = a very great deal
** informants were allowed to name whomever they perceived as being involved: individuals, departments, other organizations, etc.

Figure 7.1: **Patterns of influence among the élites**

influence 4), the sales director (3), the marketing director, with his deputy and staff, the finance director with his deputy and staff (all 2), and holding company's chairman and a colleague director (1). During interviews, many Brazilian managers remarked that this was 'the President's decision', whereas the English cases did not identify a single pre-eminent personage.

The two cases in Figure 7.1 also illustrate vividly the difference in the number of active interests drawn in that appears in Table 7.6. The short sharp Brazilian slope encompasses only three, whereas the way in which authority is used in the English cases involves more – and more diverse – in this instance ten. The diversity extends, also, to the diversity of sources of information used. The less authority-focused, more involving, English processes draw on more sources.

The greater Brazilian readiness to exploit personal relationships and face to face contacts, in a cordial manner, compared to which English social inhibitions produce an aloof façade, shows plainly in the variables grouped in Table 7.6 under Interpersonal Interaction. In Brazilian decision-making, meetings are more inclined to meander on to other subjects, including personal matters, whereas the English more often stick to the point. In consequence, whereas the English are likely to complete the agenda, the Brazilians are more likely to leave matters unfinished and, one of the most distinctive differences, to talk things over after work or in sociable situations at weekends, such as barbecues. To the English, sullying the social scene by 'talking shop' is, as another English expression has it, 'not done'. At the end of the working day, Brazilian executives could be found chatting over coffee in designated lounge corners: not so the English, who went home with a bulging briefcase or worked on at a solitary desk. Not surprisingly, the English more impersonal style pays less attention to knowing the right people (interpersonal facilitation), whereas the well-known *jeitinho brasileiro*, the Brazilian little way, uses contacts to find a way around.

The difficulty of interpreting statistical significance arises with duration, the time taken to reach a decision (counting from the first identifiable action which set off the overt process, for example, discussions leading to placing the matter on an agenda, a presidential phone call, the preparation of a report). The spread of times taken by both Brazilian and English cases is wide. Either can take a long time or be quick. The difference between them is not numerically significant. Yet five Brazilian decisions were accomplished in only a month, under the impulse of presidential direction, as in the example in Figure 7.1, while no English decision was that fast. Table 7.6 shows an English mean of 12.2 months, which is extraordinarily close to the 12.4 and 12.5 obtained at different times from different samples by Hickson *et al.* (1986) and Mallory (1987), as also is the distribution (a finding which tends to validate the methods used). By comparison, the Brazilian mean is less, just over eight months, as would be expected. So Hickson *et al.*'s (1986) presumption that strategic decisions most often take around a year would seem to have been culturebound. As is Eisenhardt's (1989) finding of fast decision-making, which must be accelerated by the American cultural setting as well as by its occurring in small electronic firms.

Did Brazilians feel stampeded, rushed off their feet? Did the English feel impatient? Not at all. If anything, the inclination was the other way around. Few Brazilians suggested that they felt hurried along, whereas many English managers felt there should have been more time to consider information, with less pressure from competitors, customers or shareholders. Hence an intriguing contrast. Where the Brazilians and the English differed in this respect, the immediatists felt their shorter time had been enough, the gradualists felt their longer time had rushed them!

Finally, in Table 7.6, the English saw themselves as running organizations less receptive to novel decisions. The Brazilians more often saw theirs as innovations. Other interview data implies that Brazilian managers see risk in a lack of information rather than in innovation itself and are willing to accept that risk and welcome an innovative disposition in their organizations. The English however, whilst they may well innovate no less than Brazilians when they have to, do so more as a necessity and are less inclined to regard innovativeness as attractive in itself.

The contrasts in Table 7.6 therefore bear out predictions of culture effects. Here is societal culture at work within work. In these respects, managerial decision making is culture-sensitive. Brazilian élites are relatively authority-centred, personal and sociable, wanting to get a move on and open to innovation. Not so the English. Their élites are relatively receptive to wider influences, impersonal with a clear separation of work and play, patiently slow-moving, cautious about innovating.

Common managerialism

Table 7.7 shows the opposite to Table 7.6. It presents those ingredients of managerial decision making in which there are no noticable differences between the way the Brazilians go about it and the way the English do. In these managerial ingredients they are, more or less, the same.

In organizations in both societies, the major decisions are taken above the heads of those below. Mostly they are unaware of what is going on, certainly of exactly what is being discussed among the élite and of how that discussion, if there is much discussion, is going. This means that those fully in the know are a topmost group of just a few, maybe up to a dozen or so, but hardly more. Analysis of what happened in the Brazilian and English cases to those who did get to know and did not like what they heard, shows that they were in all instances effectively squeezed out. These were occasional middle managers, technical or financial staff, unions and shareholders. Their unfavourable views were of little effect, their influence minimal. In two Brazilian and three English cases where one of the élite (a director) disagreed, the consequences for him and usually his department were adverse. Either the individual subsequently lost his job or his future prospects deteriorated.

For example, in Brazilian Case 1, the commercial director opposed a decision to reorganize the management structure, following a proposal by American consultants to decentralize retail operations. During two difficult years the atmosphere in the executive suite worsened, until the commercial director realized he had to go. This he did, at an emotional meeting. He was succeeded by one of the president's sons. It may be wondered how this proposal stemming from American values may have been carried out in so Brazilian an organization.

In English Case 3, opposition to a decision to drastically rationalize the traditional varieties produced by a biscuit (cookie) manufacturer led to a diminution of the responsibilities of the sales director and his department. Loyal to longstanding customer retailers who had always had custom-designed lines, they resisted the change, but lost out and lost position.

In the organizations in both societies, the most immediate effect of such opposition was usually an increase in discussion and negotiation, as might be expected.

In any case, informal interaction and negotiation, in the sense of talks in the corridors or, more likely, the offices of power, was the norm for both Brazilian and English managers, over and above anything that took place in arranged meetings of committees or task groups. This is task-oriented talking with not, for the English, the degree of sociability woven in by the Brazilians.

Table 7.7 indicates that the inherent complexity of whatever is being decided also transcends societies. Both in Brazil and in England, decisions over internal reorganizations or external mergers and takeovers were experienced as the most complex, that is in essence most unusual, radical and serious. Decisions about new products or services and especially on budgets or personnel questions, were less so. In these latter decisions, managers (irrespective of whether they were Brazilian or English) appeared to know what they were about, whereas with reorganizations, either internal or external, they faced the indefinable. These were decisions the dimensions of which were not quantifiable, nor the consequences calculable.

Indeed, these unknowable matters could have strange effects. In some respects they seemed even to reverse the usual culture-imbued contrasts. Faced with such an issue, Brazilians seemed to become more cautious, using more information and taking longer over the decision, English style. Conversely, the English case histories contained more instances of off-the-job getting together and inconclusive meetings on-the-job, as if they coped by adding some interaction Brazilian style.

Here then is the kernel of a common managerialism in the handling of major decisions which is little, if at all, sensitive to differing societal cultures. It cuts across them, the way of the world managerially speaking, which Brazilians and English share equally. It is the mutually most readily recognizable content of what transpires. Each would take for granted, and be right to take for granted, that this kind of decision making by the other would be an élite process within the highest two echelons, reaching beyond or below only for information inputs, brushing doubters aside, continually alive in talks around the office desk in addition to any committee work (brief and limited though this may sometimes be in a Brazilian hierarchy), groping with the unfathomable when the issue is changing the organization itself. In these respects, it would be a process just like their own.

Testing the results

It will be recalled that these results are from samples that are not exactly matched. This defect can be partly overcome by making comparisons of decisions in organizations of as near as possible equivalent sizes, purposes and ownership.

First, two subsamples in the same size bands were compared: eight decisions each in Brazilian and English organizations from 1050 to 1800 employees, plus five Brazilian and six English decisions in organizations from 2000 to 3500. Second, decisions were compared in service organizations (ten Brazilian, seven English) and in manufacturing organizations (ten Brazilian, thirteen English). This included some degree of simultaneous control for size, services in both countries being smaller and manufacturers larger. Third, private owner-managed firms were compared (thirteen and seven respectively) and government owned undertakings (five and three).

The outcomes were overwhelmingly and reassuringly the same as on the full samples. There were two variations, most probably showing common organizational effects.

In the largest organizations, especially manufacturers, the number of interests involved in the Brazilian cases reached English levels and this, together with the greater numbers of senior colleagues, placed more restraints upon the preident as impersonalism began to intrude.

In the public sector universities, English informal interaction and decision times were close to the Brazilian. These speedy English decisions, around six months in duration, supported the finding by Hickson *et al.* (1986) within their British sample that university decision making is not unduly slow, as often averred, something which they attributed to smooth flow-through committee systems. Decision making in universities, as in other public services, has been found to be more concerned with process than with resources, relative to manufacturers (Rodrigues and Hickson 1995).

These tighter tests compare kinds of organization, but still do not compare like with like in decisions. For this, the three matching pairs mentioned earlier were used. These were two regional newspapers, the managements of both of which had decided to re-equip with new computer-controlled presses, two textile manufacturers where it had been decided to expand and modernize production capacity and the corporate budget and business plan decisions of the universities (cases B3 and E6, B17 and E18, B8 and E19 in Tables 7.3 and 7.4).

Comparison of these cases feature by feature, combining numerically expressed variables and narrative case histories, was both the most stringent and most exhaustively detailed test. It too accorded with the results given so far in this chapter. In summary, the Brazilians were again seen to have taken more risks in more of a crisis atmosphere, interacting in a smaller clique around the president, failing to finish within meetings and continuing outside working hours, off the job. Once more the English appeared more cautiously defensive, but kept matters within working hours despite involving more participants. Both had in common the same holding of the interactive process within the bounds of the top echelons alone.

There was one exception to the accordance with the results from the full samples. The chairman of the English textile firm took things into his own hands and pushed the decision through quickly, in a manner that could be described as Brazilian-style. For some time the production and marketing directors had been pressing for new equipment, anxious about requests from their main customers for improved quality to equal that obtainable from competitor suppliers. Once capital became available, the chairman short-circuited the proper procedure laid down for an investment decision which required double scrutiny, from a steering committee and from an implementation committee both specially constituted. He himself acted alone in the capacity of 'steering committee' to approve the detailed proposal drawn up by the implementation committee, and ensured its rapid rubber stamping by the main board. In such ways do organizational imperatives for survival, faced in common by managements everywhere, override what may be the more accustomed approach.

Conclusions

How far can this study by construed not only to have posed the puzzle 'into which features of management and organization do societal cultures enter most', but to have fashioned a part of the solution?

Certainly, managements in a variety of organizations in Brazil and in England have been shown to differ sharply relative to one another in how they take major, indeed strategic, decisions. These differences have been attributed to differences in societal cultures, the more confidently because those cultures were portrayed prior to collecting data on decision making and predictions made of what differences they would make to it so that cultural explanations could not be put down to *ex post facto* wishful thinking. These cultures themselves originate in Latinesque Portuguese colonization of a New World still expansive and spacious and in the Anglo-Saxon takeover a thousand years earlier of an island where even then Old World traditions were taking shape.

So, in making decisions the Brazilians weave patterns of effusive interaction around dominating authority figures, ever hopeful but unwilling to wait long for a future that in an unsettled continent may not come. The English move coolly and cautiously, respecting but not over-needful of an authoritative lead, in time which for them stretches from a long settled past into an equally lng future so that, as they say, patience is a virtue. Of course, these are stereotypical summaries. Not every Brazilian manager, not every English manager, is like this in all things all the time. There is widespread variation and these are, in effect, statements of differing central tendencies.

They are central tendencies which envelope but do not suppress a common managerialism that belongs to both. A managerialism at the top, moving decisions through an élite coterie who talk them over again and again inside meetings and out. What else is to be expected? Only the chief executive sees an organization whole, whole as far as the view downwards can scan and only his (there was no her in this study, anyway) nearest colleague can see enough from their more partial perspectives, to talk with him and each other about matters so weighty. Others have neither the authority nor the outlook at that level to be able to take part in the same way. Once a pyramidal purposive organization has been set up, this is its effect on decision making whatever the society and whatever the politico-economic system.

Which then has the greater consequences, cultural difference or common managerialism? On the face of it, Table 7.6, which concerns the former, has more variables than Table 7.7 which concerns the latter. But counting variables must be nonsense. They and their effects cannot be added and weighed. Yet taken together, these tables and their elaboration in the text, could be interpreted to mean that those aspects of management which are interpersonal (that is, the use made of authority over others and of personal relationships with them) and philosophical (that is, the view taken of time and of change) are the most susceptible to cultural variation. How each deals with and responds to their fellow humankind and conceives of the temporal situation of humankind, are at the heart of societal culture. Fundamentally they define the nature and progression of life. Small wonder, the, that they imbue managerial behaviour and distinguish by it the organizations of one society from those of another. Ultimately, the decision making that is at the core of management is itself 'social reprsentation' (Laroche 1995).

Whereas the more formal structural features of organization design, in those aspects which are everywhere much the same, engender the same structure-linked responses everywhere. They give rise to internally interactive élite processes. It may be some part of the solution to the puzzle as to which managerial and organizational features are most and least societal culture-sensitive. It is, however, derived from a Brazilian–English comparison only, of decision making processes only.

References

Amado, G. and Brasil, H.V. (1991) 'Organizational behaviors and cultural context: the Brazilian "jeitinho"', *International Studies of Management and Organization*, 21(3): 38–61.

Axelsson, R., Cray, D., Mallory, G.R. and Wilson, D.C. (1991) 'Decision style in British and Swedish organizations', *British Journal of Management*, 2: 67–79.

Azevedo, T. (1963) *Social Change in Brazil*, Gainesville, FL: University of Florida Press.

Boyacigiller, N. and Adler, N.J. (1991) 'The parochial dinosaur: organizational science in a global context', *Academy of Management Review*, 16(2): 262–90.

Child, J. (1981) 'Culture, contingency and capitalism in the cross-national study of organizations', in L.L. Cummings and B.M. Staw (eds) *Research in Organizational Behavior*, Greenwich, CT: JAI Press.

Commager, H. (1974) 'English traits one hundred years later', in H. Commager (ed.) *Britain Through American Eyes*, Oxford: Blackwell.

Cray, D., Mallory, G.R., Butler, R.J., Hickson, D.J. and Wilson, D.C. (1988) 'Sporadic, fluid and constricted processes: three types of strategic decision-making in organizations', *Journal of Management Studies* 25(1): 13–40.

Da Matta, R. (1983) *Carnavales, Malandras y Héroes*, Rio de Janeiro: Zahar.

Eisenhardt, K. (1989) 'Making decisions in high-velocity environments', *Academy of Management Journal* 32(3): 543–76.

Faoro, R. (1975) *Os Donos do Power*, Rio de Janeiro: Globo.

Gorer, G. (1955) *Exploring the English Character*, Crosset Press.

Hickson, D.J., Butler, R.J., Cray, D., Mallory, G.R. and Wilson, D.C. (1986) *Top Decisions: Strategic Decision Making in Organizations*, San Francisco: Jossey-Bass.

Hickson, D.J. and Pugh, D.S. (2001) *Management Worldwide: The Impact of Societal Culture on Organizations Around the Globe*, Harmondsworth: Penguin.

Hofstede, G. (1980) 'Culture's consequences: international differences in work-related values, (summarized in D.S. Pugh and D.J. Hickson *Writers on Organizations*, 4th edition, Harmondsworth: Penguin, 1989).

Hofstede, G. (1991) *Cultures and Organizations: Software of the Mind*, London: McGraw-Hill.

Hofstede, G. and Bond, M.H. (1988) 'The Confucius connection', *Organizational Dynamics* 16(4): 4–21.

Hollanda, S.B. (1969) *Raíces del Brasil*, Rio de Janeiro: José Olympio.

Lachman, R., Nedd, A. and Hinings, R. (1994) 'Analysing cross-national management and organizations: a theoretical framework', *Management Science* 40(1): 40–55.

Laroche, H. (1995) 'From decision to action in organizations: decision-making as a social representation', *Organization Science* 6(1): 62–75.

Lytton, Edward (1833) *England and the English*, London: Berkley.

Mallory, G.R. (1987) 'The speed of strategic decision-making', PhD thesis, University of Bradford.

Marshall, A. (1966) *Brazil*, London: Thames and Hudson.

Maruyama, M. (1994) *Mindscapes in Management: The Use of Individual Differences in Multi-Cultural Management*, Aldershot: Dartmouth.

Oliveira, C.A.A. (1992) 'Societal culture and managerial decision making: the Brazilians and the English', PhD thesis, University of Bradford.

Orwell, G. (1947) *The English People*, London: Collins.

Priestley, J.B. (1973) *The English*, London: Heinemann.

Redding, S.G. (1994) 'Comparative management theory: jungle, zoo or fossil bed?', *Organization Studies* 15(3): 323–59.

Santayana, G. (1922) *Soliloquies in England and Later Soliloquies*, London: Constable.

Smith, P.B. (1992) 'Organizational behaviour and national cultures', *British Journal of Management* 3: 39–51.

Tannenbaum, A.S. (1968) *Control in Organizations*, New York: McGraw-Hill.

Tayeb, M. (1979) 'Cultural determinants of organizational response to environmental demands: an empirical study in Iran', M. Litt. thesis, Oxford.

Tayeb, M. (1987) 'Contingency and culture: a study of matched English and Indian manufacturing firms', *Oganization Studies* 8(3): 241–61.

Tayeb, M. (1988) *Organizations and National Culture: A Comparative Analysis*, London: Sage.

Tayeb, M. (1990) 'Japanese management style', in *Organisational Behaviour*, London: Pitman.

Tayeb, M. (1994) 'Organizations and national culture: methodology considered', *Organization Studies* 15(3): 429–46.

Terry, P.T. (1979) 'An investigation of some cultural determinants of English organization behaviour', PhD thesis, University of Bath.

Triandis, H.C. (1982/3) 'Dimensions of cultural variation as parameters of organizational theories', *International Studies of Management and Organization* Winter: 139–69.

Trompenaars, F. (1993) *Riding the Waves of Culture: Understanding Cultural Diversity in Business*, London: Economist Books.

Chapter 8

Images of Europe: past, present and future[1]

Geert Hofstede

Introduction

Once upon a time, not so long ago, in a pub at the Vrijthof in Maastricht three women and four men were discussing Europe. The women were a historian, a lawyer and a medical doctor. The first three men were a geographer, a politician and an economist. The fourth man was the owner of the pub.

'Europe,' said the geographer, 'is a peninsula of the Asian continent. It would objectively merit the name "West Asia" as much as we talk about "East Asia" for China, Japan and Korea. The population of West Asia is less than that of East or South Asia, but for the time being it is still the wealthiest of the three, although it will probably soon be passed in wealth by East Asia. The land borders between Asia and its Western peninsula are arbitrary; the Urals are not much of a mountain range; if one takes the train from here to China one doesn't meet any real obstacles until near the Mongolian border.'

'That is why Central Asian invaders had such an easy passage in past ages,' said the historian. But the distinction between Europe, Asia and Africa existed already at the time of Herodotus, that is the fifth century BC.

'Does the word "Europe" mean anything?' asked the pub owner.

'The name' said the historian 'is supposed to have been derived from a Phoenician word *ereb* meaning "darkness" or "sunset".[2] The Phoenicians were the great sailors of the millennium before Christ and they came from the present Lebanon, so for them Europe was in the West, where the sun goes down. Herodotus, by the way, also wondered why three different names were used for Asia, Africa and Europe which were really one continent.'[3]

'Nice to know that Herodotus agreed with me,' muttered the geographer. 'I would accept Africa as a separate continent, but the distinction between Europe and Asia is irrelevant, geographically and politically. The major border states, Russia and Turkey, cover both continents. I believe the reason why our ancestors treated the West-Asian peninsula as a separate continent and called it "Europe" was that it allowed them to move the centre of the world this way: it inflated their self-image. The Chinese do the same. They do not refer to their part of the world as East something: They call their country "the Middle Empire", the centre of the world. We made Europe the centre; when the American continents were discovered, they were marginalized by calling them "the New World" allowing us to be the old world. Nonsense of course, all continents are equally old.'

'The Old World included Asia and Africa,' corrected the historian. 'Anyway, Asia had the oldest civilizations. It seems that civilizations have followed the introduction of agriculture with a delay of some millennia. Agriculture has been introduced in Europe by gradual migration from South-East to North-West, starting in Anatolia, that is Asia.[4] European civilizations have moved the same way, starting with the Greeks, followed by the Romans. After the Romans Europe had little civilization at all for about a thousand years: it really deserved to be called the land of darkness, compared to other parts of the world like the Muslim countries and China.'

'But then the Europeans went out to discover the world,' interrupted the geographer.

'Civilizations have often expanded by traveling,' said the historian. 'The new voyages of discovery started in the fifteenth century and soon developed into a competition among several European nations, first the Portuguese and later the Spaniards, the Dutch, the English and the French. Then they gradually developed what you called their inflated self-image of Europe as the centre of world civilization and progress. It reached its apex in the nineteenth century when they tried to divide the whole world into European colonies.'

'And in the meantime the Europeans fought each other,' said the politician, entering the discussion. 'Europe has been a very murderous place during these centuries, which doesn't make its claim at civilization too credible. I wonder whether Europe would still hold its leading position in the world if its countries had cooperated more? Now it lost out to North America in the twentieth century, and more recently it is losing out to East Asia.'

'I don't like this talking about leading positions and losing out,' said the geographer. The world is round and no part of it is more leading than another. Europe's inflated self-image should be over; Europe is just one part of the world and not its centre. To people living in or around the Pacific Basin – like in Hawaii or Samoa – Europe is not a very relevant place at all.'

'Present-day Europe,' said the politician, 'nevertheless got something that no other part of the world has got. I mean the European Union (EU), an attempt at voluntary economic and political integration of a number of nation states without the dominant power of a leading country. As I said these nation states have all fought each other, some quite recently. Shouldn't we be proud of the EU, certainly in this town of Maastricht where the 1991 Treaty was concluded?'

'I don't know whether there is much to be proud of' – this was the economist. 'The European integration hasn't been making much headway since Maastricht. It is moving from one disaster into the other. Also don't forget that the EU only covers half of Europe – 350 million people – with some 400 million Europeans still standing by the side.'

'It is never easy to make fundamental changes,' protested the politician. 'It is pilgrim's progress: two steps ahead and one step back. When the step back is taken, people forget the two steps ahead. It is very unlikely that EU countries will evermore go to war against each other. Shouldn't we see the European Union as a laboratory for the world? If one realizes the size of the problems mankind has to cope with: overpopulation, exhaustion of resources, a wise use of nuclear and genetic engineering, national and religious fanaticisms, incurable diseases, there is no other way to survival than international co-operation. If only for that reason, the EU merits our commitment and our pride.'

'At one time,' said the lawyer, clearing her throat, 'I believed the EU meant that Europe would grow to a common legal and judicial system. But what we have learned since is that a written law does not necessarily mean the same thing in different countries. Take the problems in implementing the 1985 Schengen Agreement about the opening of the internal borders and the control of the external borders. Like the French government not wanting to move ahead with Schengen because of the Dutch way of handling drug addiction. It makes you realize that besides the written laws there are unwritten "living laws" in the minds of the people that differ from country to country and that you cannot harmonize by formal agreement. Besides, the institutions that have to implement them differ; the German police, for example, does not report to the civil authorities, the burgomasters, like in our country. And even more fundamentally, the mutual roles of the citizens and the authorities differ. There is more mutual trust between police and citizens in the Netherlands than in Belgium. Therefore in our country the police can rely more upon the help of the citizens in a crisis situation, and the citizens upon the police, than in Belgium.'

'The mutual roles of patients and doctors are also different from country to country,' said the doctor. 'A dissertation at Maastricht University in 1990 studied sickness absences from work in Belgium, Germany and the Netherlands. Controlling for all kinds of compounding factors, time lost from work in Belgium was 3 per cent, in Germany 5 per cent, and in the Netherlands 8 per cent: two and a half times as much as in Belgium (Prins 1990). I think the decisive cause is the attitude of the medical officers who have to certify these absences. We Dutch doctors are treating our patients more kindly, and give more weight to their opinions. There is no evidence of real differences in health between the countries. Life expectancy at birth is about the same all over the EU, between 74 and 77 years.[5] We see the same patient-oriented attitude in the Dutch position towards euthanasia, and in our treatment of hard drug addicts to which you already referred.'

'You are really suggesting that our medical and our legal differences have common roots,' said the lawyer.

'And very old roots at that,' resumed the historian. Countries have remained separate precisely because there existed fundamental differences in thinking and feeling between them. Why do you think the Belgians revolted against the Dutch in 1830? The border between Belgium and the Netherlands revives the border between the Roman Empire and the barbaric Germanic tribes, which has been fixed in its present position in about the fourth century AD. The other national border close by here, the border between Germany and the Netherlands, follows the division of Charlemagne's empire among his three sons at his death in AD 814. Since, the Netherlands have turned towards the sea and the German states have turned inland, which has resulted in quite different mentalities.'

'There seem to be as many mentalities as there are countries,' reflected the doctor. Take the attribution of the causes of sickness. If they don't feel well, Germans – doctors and patients alike – tend to blame their hearts, French their liver, and Brits their lack of self-control (Payer 1989). No wonder they cannot agree on the EU either.'

'Which is a great pity,' said the economist with a sigh, 'For Europe is an enormous market. It potentially represents a tremendous economic power. Why does economic co-ordination meet such irrational barriers? With the present recession even the EU can hardly withhold governments from attempting the old pernicious national protectionism again, which can only make the recession worse as everybody should know. And why do the British resist a common Social Charter? And why are the Danes so difficult? And the problems are not only on the government level. Cross-border mergers of private firms and other forms of inter-business co-operation often run into trouble. Germany is the biggest trade partner of the Netherlands and yet several mergers between firms from the two countries have been dramatic failures. And this is only the EU. Include Eastern Europe and the irrationality becomes complete. Apart from being barbaric, the wars in the former Yugoslavia are ruining the economies of those countries for the next half-century or more. Why would anybody want to do that?'

'Yes, it is horrible,' said the politician uneasily, 'it is returning to the Middle Ages but with modern weapons. But still I think that without the European Union things would be even worse, much worse. And to what extent are we responsible for Eastern Europe? Shouldn't they resolve their own problems first, like we should resolve ours? Some countries like Czechia and Hungary are already setting the example. In a decade or so, they may be ready to join the EU. Maybe the other former communist countries should first bundle their forces in a new common market of their own. Something like a neo-Comecon. Then they would be in a much better negotiating position than all those unstable old and new countries.'

'If I hear you all speak about Europe,' said the historian, 'you confirm a truth that has existed for 25 centuries: Europe is a social construction.'[6]

'That may be so,' said the pub owner. 'But to me Europe has become a reality because I am from here. It was real luck that we got the EU Ministers' conference here in December 1991. I don't know what will happen to the Treaty, but everybody in Europe knows the name Maastricht now. Europe may be a social construction, but I feel no longer only a Mestreechter, a Limburger and a Dutch citizen, but also a European.'

Mental programming in five dimensions

The consensus of the discussion was that the way people think, feel, and act in many different kinds of situation is somehow affected by the country they are from rather than by their being European. The country is of course not the only factor: In the discussion it was evident, for example, that among the seven participants the *profession* of the speaker affected her or his viewpoint and feelings. On top of that people's social class, education, generation, gender, working place and other collective characteristics also influence their thinking, feeling and acting. I have called these influences metaphorically 'collective mental programming'. Maybe 'preprogramming' is an even better term, because the programming is only partial: It is up to the individual what he or she does with it. The seven people in the pub called it 'different mentalities'. A fashionable term in sociology is 'habitus', a word introduced by the Frenchman Pierre Bourdieu.[7]

For an explanation of the country influence on people's habitus we have to turn to social anthropology: the science of the functioning of human societies. Anthropology teaches us that all human societies, both traditional and modern ones, face some of the same basic problems; but the answers differ from one society to the next. What these problems are is a matter of empirical research. It has been one of the main purposes of my own research efforts over the past 30 years (Hofstede 1991; 2001). Many of you will know that I found four, and later five, universal problems to which people from different countries tend to give different answers. These explain differences in collective behaviour in many different spheres of life: in the family, at school, at work, in politics and in the cherishing of ideas.

The first question deals with the inequality between people in any society. I expressed this in the term 'Power Distance'. The answers to the inequality questions reach from: 'inequality is a normal and desirable thing', which means large Power Distance, to 'inequality should be avoided as much as possible', which means small Power Distance.

The second question deals with the relationship between individuals within a society. The answers to this question reach from 'everybody for him or herself', which is called Individualism, to 'people should remain attached to tight groups throughout life', which is called Collectivism.

The third question deals with the social roles in a society related to being born as a boy or as a girl. The answers to this question reach from 'social gender roles should be maximally different', which is called Masculinity, to 'social gender roles should be maximally overlapping', which is called Femininity. A large difference between gender roles leads to a 'tough' society; a large overlap to a 'tender' society.

The fourth question deals with the level of anxiety in a society when it is confronted with the unknown. I expressed this in the term 'Uncertainty Avoidance' The answers to this question reach from fear, which means strong Uncertainty Avoidance, to curiosity, which means weak Uncertainty Avoidance.

The fifth question deals with the time perspective in a society for the gratification of people's needs. This runs from long, like a lifetime, to short, focusing on gratifying needs 'here and now'. I have labelled the range of answers to this question: Long-Term versus Short-Term Orientation. Long-Term Orientation implies a stress on virtuous living in this world, with Thrift and Persistence as key virtues. Short-Term Orientation implies seeking immediate gratification.

In my research I have considered these five questions as *dimensions* of national mental programmes. For each dimension I have developed a yardstick allowing to quantify, that is express in a number, the position of a country on that dimension relative to other countries. Quantification is a common way of simplifying complex information. Professors do it when they allocate grades to students on the basis of their answers on tests. Consumer organizations do it when they compare the performance of different products. In the case of dominant national mental programming I constructed the numbers for more than 50 countries on the basis of the answers on survey questions by large samples of similar employees from the multinational corporation IBM around 1970.

A key question for any type of quantitative scores is their *reliability*, that is, the extent to which different observers arrive at the same results. The reliability of research results can be determined by independent replications of the research. In social science independent replications are essential to make research respectable.

The most extensive replication of my research so far has been done by Michael Hoppe from North Carolina (Hoppe 1990: 133).[8] His data were collected from alumni of the Salzburg Seminar in Salzburg, Austria. Salzburg Seminar participants are élites, 'current and future leaders in their respective countries. They include, among others, Chief Executive Officers of prestigious national and international companies, top-level administrators of national and international governments, diplomats, chancellors and deans of universities or colleges, supreme court justices, and artists.' (see Hoppe 1990: 23). Hoppe obtained survey results from more than 1500 Salzburg alumni from 19, mainly European countries, in 1984, that is some 14 years after my research data were collected. His research is therefore really independent from mine.

The differences in mental programmes he found between these élites were quite similar to what I had measured before and, allowing a margin of measurement error in both mine and his data, supported my quantifications. Limitations to the Salzburg sample are its smaller size (1500 versus over 100 000 for the IBM data) and the fact that the selection process of Salzburg participants is not necessarily matched from one country to the next. The respondent groups differ in composition across professions and political affiliations, and for some countries this reduces the comparability of the answers to other countries.

As this chapter deals exclusively with European countries, I can use Hoppe's (1990) more recent country scores for differences between national mental programmes, rather than my own IBM-based scores. I will limit myself to the first four dimensions, because for the fifth dimension, Long-Term Orientation, data are so far available for only five European countries.

While I was working on this Chapter, Europe was very much in the news, mostly bad news, like the failure of the European Monetary System and the inability to take effective joint action in the former Yugoslavia. At times I regretted the choice of my topic. It is not easy to be reflective while the house is on fire. On the other hand it may be more than ever needed.

Are Europeans special?

A first issue is whether Europeans are collectively different from other world citizens. Do they give similar answers to the problems of inequality, individualism, gender roles and uncertainty?

Figure 8.1 is based on data from 16 European countries: Austria, Belgium, Britain, Denmark, Finland, France, Germany, Greece, Ireland, Italy, the Netherlands, Norway, Portugal, Spain, Sweden and Switzerland; no East-European countries were included. It shows the difference between the highest and the lowest scores on each dimension among the 16 countries, compared to the maximum difference found in the entire world. The entire world means more than 50 countries.

The diagram shows that, for example, on Power Distance the scores for these European countries in the 1970 IBM study fell in the lower 61 per cent of the world range, and in the 1984 élites study they fell in the lower 75 per cent of the world range. For Individualism the scores fell in the upper 75 per cent, etc. So, in both studies European countries varied strongly in the answers their citizens gave to questions related to the same basic problems of human societies. The extremes not found among these 16 European countries are very large Power Distances, very low Individualism, that is, strong Collectivism, and very strong Masculinity. But the differences are still large enough to consider Europe a small-scale model of the world in terms of variety in mental programming.

Latin versus Germanic minds

In the pub discussion the historian said that the border between Belgium and the Netherlands near Maastricht revives the border between the Roman empire and the barbaric Germanic tribes. In fact, the inheritance of the Roman empire cuts through the middle of the European Union (EU). On the Latin side we find Belgium, France,

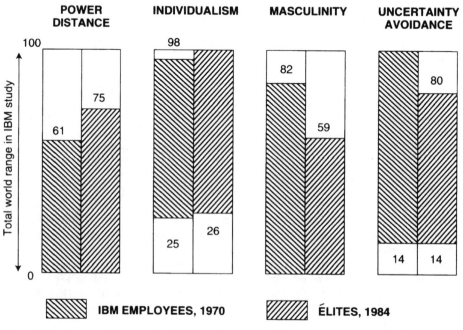

Figure 8.1: **Range of scores for 16 European countries**

Italy, Portugal and Spain, all countries speaking a Romance language, plus Greece; on the Germanic side Britain, Denmark, Germany, Ireland, Luxemburg and the Netherlands, all countries speaking a Germanic language. Although parts of some of the Germanic countries have also been under Rome for some time – like Southern Germany and Britain – the Roman civilization has not settled there. Flanders is the only Germanic-speaking region that acquired a Latin mentality, because it was dominated by French-speaking overlords.

The Roman empire – the first large empire in the heart of Europe – was characterized by a single power centre (implying large Power Distances) and a uniform system of laws (implying strong Uncertainty Avoidance). In Figure 8.2 I have plotted the scores on Power Distance and Uncertainty Avoidance for 11 countries from the EU (all except Luxembourg for which I have no data).

Figure 8.2 is based on Hoppe's Salzburg study of élites in 1984. Power Distance scores are plotted horizontally from left to right, Uncertainty Avoidance scores vertically from top to bottom. In comparison to the 1970 IBM study the 1984 Salzburg study scores are most different for Portugal and Spain: the élites indicate much smaller Power Distances and weaker Uncertainty Avoidance. Spain and Portugal both went from dictatorships to democracies in this period. The Salzburg Seminar is likely to have selected the elites who stood for democracy, not the ones who stood for dictatorship. The IBM data have not selected respondents on this criterium so they were probably more representative of the thinking of the total population.

The points representing the 11 countries are all close to the top left to bottom right diagonal of the diagram. This means that for these EU countries, Power Distance and Uncertainty Avoidance vary together. This is a peculiarity of this group of countries which not necessarily applies to other countries.

The Latin countries present medium to large Power Distances and medium to strong Uncertainty Avoidance, the Germanic countries smaller Power Distances

DEN = Denmark, NET = Netherlands, POR = Portugal, GBR = Great Britain, IRE = Ireland, SPA = Spain
GER = Germany, ITA = Italy, FRA = France, GRE = Greece, BEL = Belgium

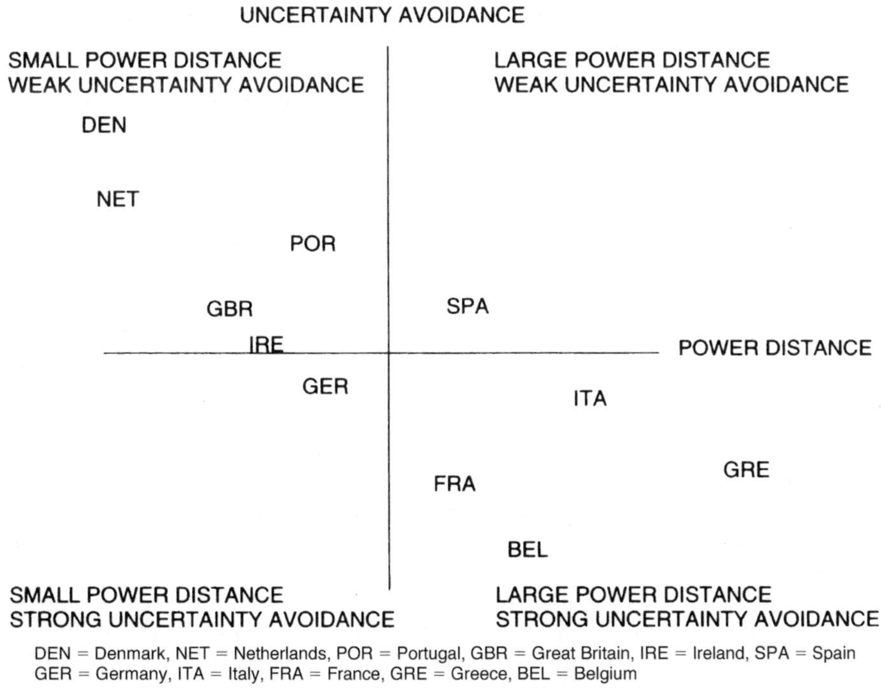

Figure 8.2: **Power distance versus uncertainty avoidance for 11 EU countries**

and weak to medium Uncertainty Avoidance. In fact Figure 8.2 looks somewhat like the map of Europe, with Greece in the South-East and Denmark and the Netherlands in the North-West, but the plot was not based on geographical data but on mental programmes. The inheritance of the Roman empire survives in the minds of the populations of the Latin countries. The long shadow of Emperor Augustus shows in this diagram. The Germanic countries never knew the same centralization of power, nor a universal system of laws, implying greater equality and tolerance for uncertainty.

On the Germanic side the extreme country is Denmark; this was also the case in the 1970 IBM study. The Danes are characterized by very small Power Distances and very weak Uncertainty Avoidance. This fact explains the hesitation of the Danish voters in ratifying the Maastricht Treaty. The small population of Denmark – 5 million out of 350 million for the whole EU – has a strong sense of equality; thus a referendum on the Treaty was inescapable. The Danish voters are critical about transferring part of their government power to Brussels, which will increase its distance. They are also critical about receiving more EU directives for which they may feel no need.

Surprisingly, Denmark among these 12 EU countries has the best record of application of EU directives in its national legislation. Belgium, on the opposite side of the Power Distance and Uncertainty Avoidance scales has the worst record. The need for, or the rejection of, rules as a function of Uncertainty Avoidance is emotional, not instrumental; so if there is a strong need for rules, this does not mean that the rules established will also be followed. In Denmark the feeling is that rules should only be established when really needed, but then they should also be followed.

In both the IBM and the Salzburg study, Germany occupies a middle position in Figure 8.2 with small Power Distance but medium Uncertainty Avoidance. Britain and Ireland are close to Germany in this diagram, but they produced lower scores on both dimensions in the IBM study: they were in between Denmark and the Netherlands. German Uncertainty Avoidance stands for clear rules; because Power Distances are small, indicating a sense of equality, these rules apply irrespective of persons. To Dutch observers in the different cross-border studies I have been involved in, German mental programming is legalistic.

A joint PhD research project between Maastricht University and the Rheinisch-Westfälische Technische Hochschule Aachen has been investigating why German-Dutch mergers of business companies had such a poor success record. In one case of a failed merger the new international corporation, on the advice of a famous consultancy firm, introduced a product-based divisional structure. This new structure cut right across the legal structure of the corporation, which still followed national lines. It turned out that the Dutch were able to work within this set-up; the Germans were not (Olie 1996).

In another recent project a team from IRIC, the Institute for Research on Intercultural Co-operation of which I have been the founding director, studied cross-border cooperation between the police forces of Belgium, Germany and the Netherlands; for this project IRIC collaborated with METRO, the research institute of the Law department of Maastricht University. One difference between Germany on the one side and the Benelux countries on the other is the amount of discretion left to a police officer to report or not to report infringements of the law. Both in the Netherlands and in Belgium the 'principle of expediency' applies, which means that the police officer may decide whether or not to report a law infringement. In Germany the 'principle of legality' applies, which means that every law infringement should be reported. The police officer has no discretion in this respect. In practice reporting every infringement is not always possible, but this is something German police officers do not like to talk about: to them it would mean confessing that they have acted illegally.

In my books I have showed that Uncertainty Avoidance is negatively associated with 'citizen competence', that is the extent to which citizens believe they can effectively participate in local political decisions: whether they feel they can get the local political system to move on issues important to them, or whether they feel helpless in front of that system (like the personalities in Kafka's novels; see Hofstede 2001: 171, 194). The rank order of the three border countries on Uncertainty Avoidance, both in the 1970 IBM study and in the 1984 Salzburg alumni study, is: Belgium very high, Germany medium, Netherlands lowest. The same order is reflected in the two areas mentioned in the pub discussion: sickness absence and relationship between police and citizens. In both cases Belgium and the Netherlands are far apart, in spite of having been neighbours for ever and shaped by the same historical events, sharing a common language, collaborating in the Benelux Union since 1960 and being indistinguishable to travellers from overseas. I found no other case in the world of two neighbouring countries having so much in common and still showing such differences in their mental programming.

Lone versus together and tender versus tough minds

In Figure 8.3 I have plotted the scores for the same eleven countries on the two remaining dimensions: Individualism and Masculinity. The diagram is again based on Hoppe's Salzburg study of élites. Individualism scores are plotted vertically from top to bottom, Masculinity scores horizontally from left to right. Again the Salzburg study scores are most different from the IBM scores for Portugal and Spain: the élites from Portugal score more masculine, and those from Spain more individualist and more feminine.

On Individualism the extreme countries are Britain which scores very individualist in both studies, and Greece which scores collectivist. The problems of the ratification of the Maastricht Treaty by Britain are well known. The British – like the

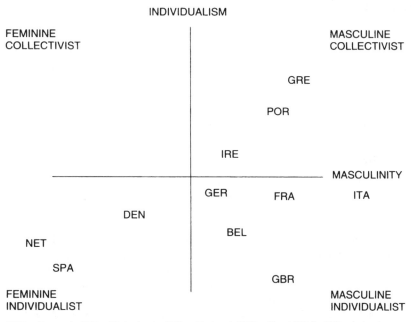

DEN = Denmark, NET = Netherlands, POR = Portugal, GBR = Great Britain, IRE = Ireland, SPA = Spain, GER = Germany, ITA = Italy, FRA = France, GRE = Greece, BEL = Belgium

Figure 8.3: **Masculinity versus Individualism scores for 11 EU countries**

Danes – have acquired several exception clauses. The most sensitive issue for Britain is the Social Paragraph. This sets minimum standards for working conditions in the member states. British individualism implies a strong belief in the market, and in Britain this includes the labour market. Working conditions are supposed to be a topic for negotiation between employers and labour unions. Governments should not interfere in this process. The argument that labour, as the weaker party, should be protected by laws does not appeal to the fairly masculine British mentality which leaves little sympathy for anything weak. The 12-year regime of Prime Minister Margaret Thatcher has strongly manifested both individualism and masculinity. It has stressed those individualist values on which Britain differs most from other EU members.

In the case of Greece the EU has hurt itself against Greek nationalism in the recognition of the former Yugoslav state of Macedonia as an independent country. Greece combines strong Uncertainty Avoidance (as we saw in Figure 8.2) with Collectivism. Uncertainty Avoidance stands for intolerance of what is different, Collectivism for loyalty to one's own group and hostility to other groups. Collectivism is at the root of ethnic conflicts anywhere in the world. The Greeks have argued that allowing a country to call itself Macedonia represents a threat to Greek sovereignty because Northern Greece is also called Macedonia. Imagine the Dutch refusing Belgium the right to call its North-Eastern province Limburg, because this means a threat to the Dutch province of Limburg which they will probably want to annex. In individualist Netherlands such an argument would be ridiculous, in collectivist Greece it is not.

The Netherlands, both in the Salzburg study and in the IBM study, figures as among the more feminine of the EU countries. The Dutch have a strong sympathy for the underdog and the anti-hero, which within the EU they share with the Danes. In this respect they differ from both neighbours Germany and Belgium; the difference shows, among other things, in the tender approach of the Dutch to sickness absence and drug addiction.

On behalf of the EU Commission, IRIC is involved in research on the public acceptance of biotechnology. Biotechnology and genetic engineering are areas of great innovative promise, but they raise questions about ethical acceptability, environmental risks, and the need for government control. Public opinions about biotechnology have been measured within the EU, and they differ strongly between countries for reasons not evident at first sight. In the first phase of our research we have shown that a combination of Masculinity and large Power Distance characterizes countries in which the population has a 'great expectations, no problems, no nonsense' attitude towards biotechnology. The opposite, Femininity and small Power Distance, characterize countries where expectations are mixed, the awareness of risks is high, and the call for government control is strong.

Eastern Europe

The last part of this chapter will be devoted to Eastern Europe. The classification of countries into East- and West-European was imposed by the former Iron Curtain, but it is historically unfounded. Now that the Curtain has been lifted we can start to look behind it. We find an extremely diverse collection of nations, some with homogeneous and some with heterogeneous populations, some industrially developed and some agrarian, some relatively rich and some extremely poor. The only thing these nations share is the experience of communist rule but this experience has been relatively short, historically speaking: for most of them some 45 years only.

Communism was an attempt to stop history and to make it obey new rules; to clean people's minds of their historically developed programmes and to reprogramme them. This was an arrogant claim; an attempt by political leaders to play God. It has bitterly failed. History resumes according to the old rules where it was interrupted.

Now, however, a similar arrogance can be noticed in the claims of those Western economists and politicians who believe that after the failure of communism they can turn the people of the East-European nations into free-market capitalists. They do not know history, and they seem to ignore that there is such a thing as collective mental programming.

Communism was closer to the mental programmes of many East-European peoples than is free-market capitalism. In the eyes of many people in Eastern Europe, the communist period was not all that bad. To quite a few it was better than anything they had known before. The French anthropologist Emmanuel Todd (1985) has argued that the ideology of communism fits the traditional family structures in those countries. I think he oversimplified; he overlooked other influences and he did not take account of the fact that only in Russia was communism a native development; in the other East-European countries it was imposed by military force. But at least Todd pointed to a source of mental programmes that politicians cannot change. In my research it shows up as Collectivism. Americans sometimes use the word 'collectivism' for 'state collectivism', as a synonym for 'communism'. This is not what I mean; I use the word in the sense of group collectivism; but the group collectivist mind is also more prone to accept state collectivism.

Free-market capitalism presumes an individualist mentality, which is exactly the opposite. Everyone for him- or herself, and the invisible hand of enlightened self-interest will lead us all to the common good. This ideology stems from Adam Smith who was a Scot; it is most actively practised and preached in the UK and the USA. No country of continental Western Europe has ever fully embraced it. In my research I have shown a statistical relationship between the degree of Individualism of countries and their national wealth. However, the arrow of causality is not from individualism to wealth, but from wealth to individualism (Hofstede 1991: 75–6): a country becomes more individualist after it has increased in wealth, but not necessarily wealthier after it has become more individualist. This means that free-market capitalism is more suitable for wealthy countries than for poor ones, and unlikely to make poor countries wealthy as quite a few economists seem to believe.

Relatively well-to-do Eastern European countries are Czechia, Poland, Hungary, Slovenia and Estonia. In these a certain measure of capitalism has the best chances, but it should still be capitalism European style, say German style; not American or British style.

In the poorer East-European countries the demise of communism has not eased the way for capitalism. The only visible alternative to communism in these countries is militant nationalism; we can find daily testimonies of it in our newspapers. Like communism, nationalism is based on group collectivism: 'It is them or us.' Collectivism combined with strong uncertainty avoidance produces an explosive mixture: strong Uncertainty Avoidance stands for intolerance of others, of 'What is different, is dangerous'. This mixture exists in the case of Greece, but mitigated by the fact that Greece is a relatively prosperous country which therefore undergoes individualist influences.

The Hungarian political philosopher István Bibó has written about the 'national materialism' of the East-European countries, a state of mind which the Western Europeans cannot understand. It has grown out of the daily fight for mere survival. One citation:

One of the most characteristic features of the soul that has been tortured by fear and feelings of insecurity and major historical traumata and injuries is, that *it does not want to make a living out of its own existence* but it takes the position that it has a lot to *demand* from life, from history and from the others. In this state of mind the individual loses his sense of moral obligations and responsibilities towards the community. *He uses every moral rule to prove his own demands.*

(Bibó 1986: 238, quoted in Varga 1993)

This, I am afraid, brings us to what is happening in Yugoslavia, where people have reached a state of mind that Western Europeans cannot understand at all, and where the endless so-called peace conferences only seem to be a forum to repeat each party's demands on history. The IBM study contains data from a Yugoslav agent of IBM. In 1993 I went back to the data, which were collected in 1971, and split them into Slovenia, Croatia and Serbia; the company did not have sufficient employees in the other republics. The results are shown in Figure 8.4, together with the scores for the highest and lowest EU country on each dimension.

What strikes us first is the similarity among the three Yugoslav republics. In all three republics of the former Yugoslavia the 1971 scores showed large Power Distances, Collectivism, and strong Uncertainty Avoidance. Slovenia scored feminine, the other two republics medium on Masculinity. Serbia manifested a significantly larger Power Distance than the two other republics; it was also slightly more uncertainty-avoiding and Collectivist. Twenty years before Serbians started the Yugoslav civil war their compatriots within the IBM agency gave evidence of the state of mind conducive to explosive nationalism; and their two sister republics produced only slightly different answers.

The Serbian data from 1971 show a combination of large Power Distance plus strong Uncertainty Avoidance unequalled anywhere in my research in Europe. In 1988, before the breakdown of communism, my French co-author Daniel Bollinger administered the IBM questions to a group of engineers, more or less matched with the IBM employees, in Russia.[9] They produced scores for Power Distance and Uncertainty Avoidance almost equally high as the Serbs did. From the original IBM data the European country that comes closest is Greece.

About the only countries at present where the population sympathizes with the Serbians are Greece and Russia. It appears that the three share a common mental programming: it is the Latin pattern of large Power Distance plus strong Uncertainty Avoidance – like Hoppe found in France, Belgium and Italy – but taken to the

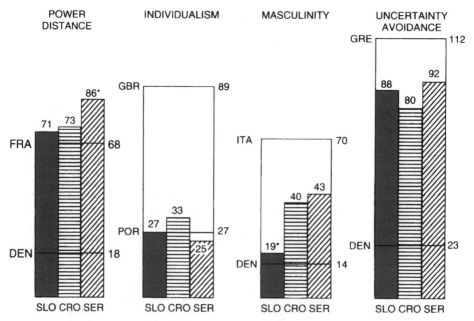

* significantly different from other 2 republics at .05 level
DEN = Denmark, FRA = France, GBR = Great Britain, GRE = Greece, ITA = Italy,
POR= Portugal, SLO = Slovenia, CRO = Croatia, SER = Serbia

Figure 8.4: **Scores for Yugoslav republics versus EC countries**

extreme. With a sense of history we can identify it as a Byzantine pattern, the inheritance of the offspring of the Roman empire that lasted another thousand years in Byzantium after Rome fell, and that presently survives in Eastern Orthodox Christianity.

Greece and Russia scored collectivist, but not as much as Serbia, which makes them less explosive. But signs of militant nationalist and racist currents in these two countries are regularly in our news. Such currents are a potential threat to peace, especially if economic conditions deteriorate.

Concluding remarks

Regardless whether one considers free-market capitalism desirable for Eastern Europe, one should face the fact that in most countries concerned the population's mental programming does not allow it. For the same reasons the poorer East-European countries will also have to do without democracy, at least for the foreseeable future, let us say the next 50 years or so. Democracy presumes at least a minimum level of individualism: 'one man one vote' is an individualist principle. We also saw that individualism presupposes a minimum amount of wealth. Therefore democracy is for the wealthy or moderately wealthy countries only.[10] This is unfair, but I cannot change it. It is as unfair as the law of Jesus Christ according to Saint Matthew: 'He who has, to him shall more be given.'[11]

You may consider me a pessimist, or taking a static view of societies. I only try to be realistic. Mental programmes do change, but slowly and not according to anyone's master plan. Changes take decades, if not centuries. If the inheritance of the Roman empire still separates Belgium from the Netherlands, two countries in intimate contact for over 2000 years, one should not believe one can change the minds of Serbs, Russians or Albanians within a few years. In planning, we better take mental programmes as given facts.

Endnotes

1 This chapter is based upon the author's valedictory address to the Department of Economics and Business Administration, Maastricht University, the Netherlands, October 1993.

2 The Phoenician word *ereb* has the same root as the Arab word *Maghreb* which also means 'The West'. The similarity of the name to Europa, the beautiful princess abducted by god Zeus (who for the occasion had disguised himself as a bull) is therefore accidental, except that in the legend Europa was a *Phoenician* princess. Herodotus wrote: 'As for Europe, nobody knows if it is surrounded by sea, or where it got its name from, or who gave it, unless we are to say that it came from Europa, the Tyrian woman, and before that was nameless like the rest. This, however, is unlikely; for Europa was an Asiatic and never visited the country which we now call Europe, but only sailed from Phoenicia to Crete and from Crete to Lycia.' (Herodotus 1972: 285). Herodotus evidently did not know Phoenician.

3 Herodotus commented: 'Another thing that puzzles me is why three distinct women's names should have been given to what is really a single land-mass' (ibid.: 285).

4 This is reflected in the results of recent research into the frequency distribution of human genes in Europe (Cavalli-Sforza and Piazza 1993).

5 World Bank (1992: table 1). The figures are 77 years for the Netherlands versus 76 for Belgium and Germany.

6 Inspired by Berger and Luckmann (1966). The title of this lecture 'Images of Europe' was inspired by Morgan (1986).

7 Bourdieu's definition of *habitus* can be translated as 'a system of permanent and transferable dispositions'; it 'functions as the basis for practices and images . . . which can be collectively orchestrated without an actual conductor'; see Bourdieu (1980: 88–9); translations by Geert Hofstede.

8 Since this was written, several other large-scale replications were published. See Hofstede (2001).

9 This study was part of a consulting project of CEGOS-Co-operation, Paris, France. The number of responses was 55, but not all were ethnic Russians; the group contained some Baltic and some Armenian members. The scores were Power Distance 93, Individualism 47, Masculinity −1, Uncertainty Avoidance 75.
10 The reverse is not true: wealth is possible without democracy, as Singapore and Hong Kong show.
11 From the New Testament, Matthew 13:12.

References

Berger, P. and Luckmann, T. (1966) *The Social Construction of Reality*, Harmondsworth: Penguin.

Bibó, I. (1986) 'The misery of the Eastern European small states', in *Selected Studies Vol. II*, Budapest: Magvetô. (In Hungarian; originally published 1946.)

Bourdieu, P. (1980) *Le sens pratique*, Paris: Éditions de Minuit.

Cavalli-Sforza, L.L. and Piazza, A. (1993) 'Human genomic diversity in Europe: a summary of recent research and prospects for the future', *European Journal of Human Genetics*, 1: 3–18.

Herodotus (1972) *The Histories, Book Four*, trans. A. de Sélincourt and A.R. Burn, Harmondsworth: Penguin.

Hofstede, G. (1991) *Cultures and Organizations: Software of the Mind*, London: McGraw Hill.

Hofstede, G. (2001) *Culture's Consequences: Comparing Values, Behaviors, Institutions and Organizations across Nations*, 2nd and revised edition, Thousand Oaks, CA: Sage.

Hoppe, M.H. (1990) 'A comparative study of country elites: international differences in work-related values and learning and their implications for management training and development, PhD dissertation, University of North Carolina at Chapel Hill, NC.

Morgan G. (1986) *Images of Organization*, Newbury Park, CA: Sage.

Olie, R.L. (1996) 'European transnational mergers', PhD dissertation, Maastricht University.

Payer, L. (1989) *Medicine and Culture: Notions of Health and Sickness in Britain, the U.S., France and West Germany*, London: Gollancz.

Prins, R. (1990) 'Sickness absence in Belgium, Germany (FR) and the Netherlands: a comparative study', PhD dissertation, Maastricht University.

Todd, E. (1985) *The Explanation of Ideology: Family Structures and Social Systems*, Oxford: Blackwell.

Varga, K. (1993) 'Either Them, or Us': National Materialism in Central Eastern Europe', Conference on Conflict Management, Houthalen, Belgium.

World Bank (1992) *World Development Report 1992*, New York: Oxford University Press.

Chapter 9

Empowering Europe: empowerment, national culture and cultural congruence

Lena Zander

Introduction

An important question in leadership is how much employees should be involved in decision-making. Early attempts to encourage participation by workers in decision-making received more attention and local support in Europe than in the USA (Scott 1992). Not surprisingly a group of European researchers launched the Industrial Democracy in Europe (IDE) project in 1970s with follow-up replications in the 1980s. The aim of the project was to assess the impact of the formal legally prescribed systems of participation on the actual patterns of involvement and influence in organizations. The main finding of the IDE research group was that a high level of employee participation in decision-making was related to both managerial attitudes and the national laws or collective bargaining systems. The authors emphasized that these variables were stronger predictors of participation than 'objective' variables such as organizational size or levels of automation (i.e. so-called technological or structural variables). Before the 1980s, indirect forms of participation, such as work councils and co-determination, were in focus. The change in focus from indirect to direct forms of participation have resulted in increased employee participation through delegation of responsibility as well as authority for decision-making to the subordinates (Gill 2000). A wide diversity across Europe both in types and levels of participation was identified by the IDE researchers and later in a study of diffusion of participation in new technology by Gill and Krieger (1992). The intra-European differences relate to not only managers and employees but also to policy-makers and legislators' attitudes and behaviour. As a result Europeans have for quite some time intensively debated the most appropriate forms of employee participation in decision-making (Gill 2000).

Participatory management practices such as participation in decision-making but also management by objectives (MBO) and self-managing teams has from the 1970s received increased attention from academics. The resulting employee-oriented management theories have been advocated as motivating for the employees and beneficial for the company's bottom line. They have been presented as universal theories applicable anywhere in the world without concern about the cultural context. Critical voices have been raised against these assumptions but seem to receive only limited consideration by academics, practitioners politicians.

An early and very illustrative example of the consequences of the cultural relativity of theories was presented by Hofstede in 1980 (see chapter 8). This has been followed by a series of well-argued articles (see, e.g., Boyacigiller and Adler 1991; Hofstede 1996; Redding 1994), but judging from the persistent stream of articles explicitly or implicitly assuming that participatory management theories are applicable worldwide many remain unconvinced. One reason could be that in most of the research displaying across-country differences regarding participation in decision-making, the relationship between the participatory practices and culture is discussed and hypothesized, but not shown. Similarly in the research on cultural dimensions, the influence of these dimensions on managerial practices are discussed and hypothesized, but not displayed. In other words, the relationship between national cultural differences, and management and leadership practices has most often been theoretically discussed but not empirically ascertained. Studies leave the reader with an assumed relationship between management and culture that has not been empirically established.

In an attempt to cast light on the relationship between employees' preferences regarding interpersonal leadership and national cultural dimensions, Zander (1997) examined data from more than 17 000 respondents in 18 countries. Interpersonal leadership was defined by Zander as leadership that is characterized by an interpersonal nature and a hierarchical relationship. The interpersonal nature implies that the focus is not on 'leading' organizations, but *leading people* through interpersonal communication and interaction. In a hierarchical relationship the leader, the person at the higher level in the relationship, has authority. This authority can be exercised, shared or delegated at the 'leader's' discretion to the person who is the subordinate. Thus, even if the hierarchical relationship becomes less hierarchical, it remains a key characteristic of interpersonal leadership. The seven identified elements of interpersonal leadership included: 'empowering', 'coaching', directing in the form of both 'supervising' and 'reviewing' as well as communication in the form of 'general communication', 'personal communication' and 'feedback-based communication'. Zander displayed how employees' preferences regarding interpersonal leadership are related to national cultural dimensions in 18 countries.

In this chapter, the relationship between national culture and employees' preferences for empowering in 12 European countries is analysed and discussed. After establishing the relationship between culture and participatory management practices, the question whether cultural congruence is necessary for empowering is raised. This issue is approached by examining whether the gap between the empowering that employees' would prefer and the empowering that they currently experience is related to employees' satisfaction. In particular, it is of interest how satisfied the employees are with their work duties and with their managers' delegation of responsibility. The chapter concludes with a discussion of the implications for research and practice.

Earlier research on participation in decision-making and national cultural dimensions

In the brief review presented below, earlier research on multicountry comparative studies of participatory management practices is examined with the purpose of identifying measures of participation in decision-making as well as any across-country variation (see Zander 1997 for a more in-depth review). Research where cultural dimensions are defined and discussed was reviewed with the purpose of identifying cultural dimensions that are assumed to be related to participatory management practices (for a more in-depth review see Janson[1] 1992; Zander 1997; 2001).

Participation in decision-making in earlier multicountry comparative studies

A majority of the more than 7500 studies of leadership that have been conducted since the beginning of the last century were carried out in the context of one country (see Bass and Stogdill 1990 for an extensive review). Some across-country comparative studies have been conducted on managers' and subordinates' needs, sources of motivation, work goals, and other individual-related issues. However, only a limited number of multicountry studies with a focus on interpersonal leadership, such as participation in decision-making, have been carried out. Zander (1997) conducted an in-depth review and observed that the earlier studies on participatory management could be divided into three groups: the early studies with a bipolar view of participation in decision-making, the studies measuring a continuum of participation in decision-making and the more recent studies of context-dependent participatory management practices.

A few overarching observations can be made regarding the *early studies with a bipolar view of participation in decision-making* by Haire, Ghiselli and Porter (1966), Tannenbaum and Rozgonyi (1986), Tannenbaum *et al.* (1974), Redding and Casey (1976), Bass *et al.* (1979) and Badawy (1980). First, these studies tended to focus on authoritarian-directive as opposed to democratic-participative managerial styles. Hence, the bipolar view on leadership suggests that participation in decision-making represents the opposite of authoritarian decision-making. In these studies, questions were asked about authority and influence, participation in decision-making as well as managers' assumptions about people's capacity for initiative and need for direction. Second, some of the research findings were contradictory in that participatory preferences were identified on some questions, and autocratic tendencies on others. In other words, it was not possible to ascertain a preference by managers or employees for only autocratic-directive or only democratic-participative managerial practices. Second, in the work by Tannenbaum *et al.* it was clear that what they refer to as 'interpersonal participation', i.e. managers soliciting opinions and suggestions from subordinates, existed in organisations not characterised by high degrees of participation in decision-making and vice versa. Consequently, the bipolar view, representing an underlying assumption that autocratic or authoritarian managers do not endorse participative managerial practices and vice versa, could not be empirically validated. Third, a suspicion was formulated that positive attitudes in general towards participation in decision-making could be an example of socially desired responses, since attitudes towards participation in decision-making did not always correspond to attitudes concerning people's capacity. In other words, managers would argue the merits of participation in decision-making while at the same time declaring that their employees did not have the skills and abilities to participate. Finally, the bipolar studies indicated that across-country differences existed. These differences were most often assumed to be due to culture, but this was not analysed.

A few observations can also be made regarding the *studies measuring a continuum of participation in decision-making* by IDE (1976; 1979; 1993), Schaupp (1978), Heller and Wilpert (1981) and Bottger, Hallein and Yetton (1985). First, the continua consisted of four to six different decision-making methods with varying degree of subordinate participation. The use of the continua facilitated the interpretations of participation in decision-making. Instead of discussing a score somewhere in between participative and directive as in earlier studies, it became possible to identify different types of methods, such as consultative or joint decision-making. Second, in all studies, except Schaupp's, specific decision-making situations were described instead of referring to participation in decision-making in general. Describing situations assisted in establishing a common reference point for respondents that facilitated the interpretation of the data as well as the comparative component of the analysis. One of the imperative findings from studies differing between types of decisions was that participation in decision-making was perceived to be higher in short-term work-oriented decisions than in long-term strategic-oriented issues. Finally, all studies reported differences across countries. In these studies, the authors were more explicit about their cultural assumptions and hypotheses. However, they often emphasized that their study was not a study of culture and, consequently, they refrained from conducting cultural analysis. Some cross-national context analysis was carried out, which compared the influence of historical, social, economic and political issues on participation.

A number of observations can be made concerning the more recent studies on *context-dependent participatory management practices* (Ah Chong and Thomas 1997[2]; Al-Jafary and Hollingsworth 1983; Peterson, Smith and Tayeb, 1993; Redding and Richardson 1986; Smith, Misumi, Tayeb, Peterson and Bond 1989; Smith, Peterson, Misumi and Bond 1992; Tayeb 1995). The earliest of these studies were conducted with a research instrument developed by Likert (1967) in the USA, which was tested in other areas of the world. The rest of the studies were carried out with a research instrument developed by Misumi (1985) in Japan, which was tested in the West.[3] Likert's and Misumi's view on leadership is that it is not bipolar as the early studies, nor continuums of participation as in the second group of studies. They both work with the notion of leadership as context dependent. In the case of Likert's instrument, the organizational climate is measured as the context. Each of Likert's four systems includes a specific leadership style and a specific climate. Misumi, on the other hand, argues that some of the managers' behaviour is comparable across different cultural contexts and can be measured with the same questions across varying cultural, industrial and firm-specific contexts. However, other managerial behaviours are context dependent and special questions need to be formulated for each context. Differences across countries were identified in all studies, and although the group of researchers did not explore these further in terms of cultural explanations, they discussed how the specific managerial behaviours were related to culture. The studies in the late 1980s and early 1990s display a cultural awareness quite different from that found in earlier comparative multicountry studies of interpersonal leadership. In the earlier studies, the assumption often seemed to be that any differences across countries would be cultural, while in later studies the researchers are more sophisticated in their way of acknowledging culture. Al-Jafary and Hollingsworth, and Redding and Richardson present an explanation of why there would be cultural similarities between the countries they are studying. Misumi constructed a theory of both general and culture-specific managerial behaviour. However, there still seems to be very limited attempts, if at all, to empirically test whether the differences in participation in decision-making across countries are related to national cultural dimensions.

Some *concluding reflections* on the review of comparative across-country studies of participatory management practices will be presented. The first group of studies included participation in decision-making, but it was only during the 1970s and early 1980s that participatory management practices received an increased interest. This resulted in a number of studies with a focus on the degree of participation in decision-making, the decision-making methods in use, and the degrees of industrial democracy measured in terms of influence and involvement in decision-making. Studies differentiated between participation in decision-making and 'interpersonal participation' as well as between the degree of involvement in short-term versus long-term decisions. In later context-dependent leadership studies, participation in decision-making was seen as a 'part of the parcel' of a management system or style.

Studying the phrasing of the questions used in the studies discussed suggests that they are time as well as context dependent. The discourse in the 1960s and 1970s seemed to view 'persuasion' and 'influence' as words that suggested using less authority, and describing a tendency towards participative beliefs and behaviour. In the 1990s, to 'influence or persuade' somebody had rather negative connotations and was probably more associated with the use of authority than with participative practices. Consequently, the understanding of what a particular construct attempts to measure, based on the label of the construct as well as the items included in the construct, could vary across time as well as across various contexts such as countries and disciplines. Thus, the phrasing of the items used to measure 'participation in decision-making and interpersonal participation' will be detailed in this chapter to facilitate readers' understanding of what is measured, analysed and discussed.

In earlier research, across-country differences in managers' and well as employees' behaviour and attitudes regarding participation in decision-making have been displayed. Most often these behaviours and attitudes were assumed to be related to cultural differences. Within cross-cultural management, cultural dimensions have been measured, discussed and often hypothesized to be related to management and organization. The cultural dimensions argued to be related to participatory management practices will be introduced below.

National cultural dimensions measured in earlier studies

A small group of researchers like Hofstede (1980/4), Laurent (1983), Trompenaars (1993), Schwartz (1994) and Maznevski et al. (1997) have attempted to quantitatively measure cultural dimensions in a large number of countries. Hofstede based his work on data from 40 countries, which have later been increased to about 50 countries. Schwartz has hitherto gathered data for 41 cultural groups in 38 nations. Trompenaars has databases including around 50 countries (see chapter 12). Laurent has data from ten countries and Maznevski et al. have hitherto measured the Kluckhohn and Strodtbeck value orientations for 10 nationalities. With the exception of Schwartz, these researchers have all discussed how the cultural dimensions influence participatory management practices. Their hypotheses were used to formulate the predictions that are examined and discussed in this chapter.

The in-depth theoretical review of national cultural frameworks by Zander (1997; 2001) includes 31 cultural dimensions from the above mentioned five cultural frameworks. It is highlighted that some of the cultural dimensions seem to capture different aspects of the same elements of culture. Five dimensions concerned beliefs about status differentiation and approached the topic of authority allocation from different perspectives. Zander grouped them together and labelled them 'status allocation'. Sully de Luque and Sommer (2000) group similar cultural dimensions together into a 'cultural syndrome', which they label 'status identity'. They draw upon Triandis (1996) who suggests that a 'syndrome' can be constructed when the cultural dimensions can be shown to be conceptually similar. Earley (1997) also used this approach and identified 'syndromes' of existing cultural dimensions when studying culture's effect on 'face'-related issues.

Zander's 'status allocation' includes three dimensions that address status allocation in terms of hierarchical differentiation, i.e. Maznevski's 'hierarchical orientation of relationships', Hofstede's 'power distance' and Schwartz' 'hierarchy'. Two further dimensions are concerned with the allocation of authority. Trompenaars' 'achievement versus ascription' dimension measures beliefs of how authority should be accorded. Laurent's 'authority systems' dimension differentiates between authority believed to be related to a person or to the position the person holds.

'*Hierarchical relationship*' is one of three orientations of the relationship dimension identified by Kluckhohn and Strodtbeck (1961) and measured by Maznevski et al. (1997). The relationship dimension is concerned with what responsibility one has for others. 'Hierarchical' societies are characterized by groups that are nested in a hierarchical order (e.g. aristocracy and caste systems). This is an arrangement were those higher in the hierarchy have responsibility for those lower in the hierarchy, and the nestings are assumed stable over time. Values about relationships are hypothesized by Lane, DiStefano and Maznevski (1997) to have a strong impact on managers' basis for authority and decision-making procedures. It is also argued that people's perception of the differentiation between levels in the organisation is influenced by this dimension, where the hierarchical form emphasizes the vertical differentiation in organizations. Thus, the hierarchical relationship dimension is hypothesized by Lane, DiStefano and Maznevski (1997) to influence management practices such as participation in decision-making.

'*Power distance*' is defined by Hofstede (1991: 28) as 'the extent to which the less powerful members of institutions and organisations within a country expect and accept that power is distributed unequally'. He argues that the power distance country scores indicate the dependence relationship between subordinates and managers in a country. In a low power-distance country, there is limited dependence of subordinates on the bosses. In high power-distance countries, there is a strong dependence on an autocratic or paternalistic boss. In exchange for subordinates' loyalty and obedience, managers provide support and take care of them. According to Hofstede, power distance is supposed to influence the relationship between manager and subordinate in such a way that in a high power-distance country, subordinates are expected to be supervised by their managers, and MBO will not work. In a low power-distance country, subordinates see managers as accessible as well as democratic and subordinates expect to be consulted before their managers make decisions. In his early work, Hofstede emphasized the relationship between power distance and employees' values about participation in decision-making, while in his later work the focus is more on power distance and autocratic versus democratic leadership general.

Schwartz' (1994) development of the *hierarchy* dimension is to some extent based on Rokeach's (1968) work on values as guiding principles in life. The legitimacy of hierarchical roles and a preference for hierarchical treatment of people and resources is captured by the hierarchy dimension. The values used to measure hierarchy include authority, being influential, wanting social power, desiring wealth and being humble. That Schwartz's hierarchy dimension does not correlate with Hofstede's power distance was attributed by Schwartz to the fact that hierarchical differences in society are not compatible with power differences in manager–employee relationships as is argued by Hofstede. Schwartz has not hypothesized any relationship between hierarchy and management. However, based on the definition of hierarchy, a prediction of a negative relationship between espoused hierarchy values and participatory management practices is formulated.

The '*achievement versus ascription*' dimension identified by Parsons and Shils (1951) and measured by Trompenaars (1993) deals with the basis for the attribution of status. In some societies, status is based on achievement, while in others it is based on ascribed characteristics such as age, class, gender and education. Status is consequently based on 'what you do' in achievement-oriented cultures, while in ascription-oriented cultures status is based on 'who you are'. Trompenaars emphasizes that managers in achievement-oriented cultures can use MBO techniques and that their decisions are challenged on functional grounds. In ascriptive-oriented culture decisions are challenged only by people with higher authority, and MBO techniques are less effective and difficult to apply. An important point when discussing the influence of this value orientation on participatory management practices is that a manager's position within an ascriptive-oriented culture is interrelated with both the superiors and the subordinates in a strict and well observed rank ordering. Consequently, no changes in status will occur at one level without repercussions at the other levels. Delegating decision-making authority to employees' would affect the whole status rank system. Thus, the 'achievement–ascription' dimension is expected by Trompenaars to have an influence on the use of employee participatory management techniques such as management by objectives.

Laurent's dimension '*organisations as authority systems*' is intended to measure whether the manager's authority is viewed as personal or instrumental. The perception of authority as personal is a more social concept of authority regulating relationships among individuals in the organization. Consequently, authority is in this case, according to Laurent, a property of the individual. Instrumental leadership, on the other hand, is seen as a more rational view that regulates the interaction among tasks and functions, and authority is seen as an attribute of a role or function. Thus, 'organizations as authority systems' are seen by Laurent as influencing how authority is viewed and most probably how participatory management practices such as delegation of authority to make decisions would be perceived.

In sum, three dimensions address status allocation in terms of hierarchical differentiation (Maznevski's hierarchical orientation of relationships, Hofstede's power distance and Schwartz' hierarchy). These dimensions measure values and beliefs about the degree of hierarchical differentiation in societies and are suggested to be related to preferences regarding participatory management practices. Two dimensions reflect status allocation in terms of how authority should be accorded (Trompenaars's achievement versus ascription dimension and Laurent's authority systems dimension). Preferences regarding participatory management practices are seen as related to whether status and authority are allocated based on achievement or ascription or whether they are believed to be related to a person or to the position of the person. Consequently, these five cultural dimensions all capture different beliefs about *status allocation*. These dimensions were hypothesized by most of the researchers who measured them to be related to participatory management practices such as MBO and/or participation in decision-making. These hypotheses are used to formulate the predictions regarding the relationship between empowering and national culture that are examined in this chapter.

The study: research design, sample, measuring empowering and formulating research predictions[4]

The purpose of the empirical study presented in this chapter is to examine the relationship between national culture and employees' preferences regarding empowering in 12 European countries. The research design involves a main analysis of the data collected from one company, Pharmacia (before the merger with Up-John), and then repeating the analysis in a hold-out sample consisting of data collected from companies in the food, candy, brewery and tobacco industries. Hence, any identified relationship between empowering preferences and national cultural dimensions will hold across several companies and industries in each country. Furthermore, to avoid that the analysed country means are based on only one group of employees, the data was collected from respondents working at different departments, in different work positions, of different age groups and different gender. The country means were adjusted accordingly.

First, a multivariate analysis of variance (MANOVA) was conducted to examine whether employees' preferences regarding empowering *vary across countries*. Second, the *relationship* between the collected data on empowering and dimensions of national culture measured in earlier research was examined by Spearman's rank correlation analysis using adjusted country means.

The database of specially formulated and translated questions was collected during a quantitative survey conducted at the end of 1992 and during 1993. The sample consisted of more than 17 000 managers and employees working for 28 companies owned by the large Swedish multinational conglomerate, Procordia, active in different types of industries in 18 countries. Data from the following 12 European countries are analysed in the study presented in this chapter: Austria, Belgium, Denmark, Finland, France, Germany, the Netherlands, Norway, Spain, Sweden, Switzerland and the UK.[5] These 12 countries include more than 11 000

Table 9.1: **The sample: number of respondents by country and company**

COUNTRY	MAIN SAMPLE* Kabi-Pharmacia	Bio-Tech	Swedish Match	Other Companies**	Total hold-out	SAMPLE IN USE*	TOTAL SAMPLE
			HOLD-OUT SAMPLE*				
Austria	45	9	4	Felix 99	112	157	172
Belgium	72	19	126	Procordia EuroCentre 9	154	226	285
Denmark	41	29		Beauvais 158, Anjo 6,	598	639	679
Finland	34	7		Abba 405, Abba Felix 67,			
				Ahlgrens 19	93	127	129
France	183	27	141		168	351	301
Germany	321	86	43	Abba 9, Swedish Tobacco 10	148	469	446
Netherlands	137	27	125		152	289	273
Norway	200	23	6	Hansa 362, Abba Felix 29	420	620	582
Spain	361	8	1		9	370	313
Sweden	2362	910	277	Abba 425, Ahlgrens 210, Ekströms 119, Falken 246, Felix 827, Flavoring 56, Pripps 1829, Procordia 215, Ramlösa 85, Sofiero 45, Svensk Snabbmat 110, Österberg & Lofqvist 56, Önus 250	5660	8022	8795
Switzerland	39	14	17		31	70	98
United Kingdom	144		273	Lighthouse of Scotland 39	312	456	498
Total	3939				7857	11 796	12 983

Notes: * The respondents' nationality is determined by a question asking whether the respondent is working in the country that they are from, in this way the respondents themselves decide whether they feel as part of a certain country, rather than legal criteria such as citizenship. Respondents who have answered no to the aforementioned question are omitted from the sample used for the analysis presented in this paper. Respondents who had answered that their immediate manager was not from the country that they worked in were also omitted from the sample. Due to the unbalanced sample sizes in each country only 350 randomly selected respondents from Denmark, Germany, Norway, Sweden and United Kingdom were included in the within country analysis.
** Other companies owned by Procordia that were included in the survey are included in this column of the table (see Zander 1997 for details).

respondents, constituting a 70 per cent average response rate. To avoid that the analysis was influenced by non-local employees; the respondents who themselves or whose managers were not from the country that they were working were omitted from the sample (see Table 9.1).

After conducting an in-depth review of earlier comparative multicountry studies of participatory management practices, a few observations were pertinent for the formulation of the items used to measure participation in decision-making. Amid the important findings from these studies was the observation that when participatory management was measured as a part of a bipolar leadership the results were inconclusive since both the autocratic and the democratic poles were scored on different questions. The results from the more recent studies were not inconclusive, but they were 'all-inclusive' since participatory management practice were a 'part of a parcel' of the generated management systems or styles. However, the use of a continuum of participation in decision-making had several advantages for studying participation in decision-making. Their usefulness includes establishing a common reference point by describing the decision-making situations, and achieving precision in the measurement by differentiating between various decision-making methods. None of this was feasible in the design of the questionnaire presented in this chapter due to space limitation, and the restriction of a standardized response format.[6] The solution was to capture three different types of decision-making methods by phrasing the items as follows (see Table 9.2 for the exact phrasing of items): to what extent the immediate manager should *discuss company strategies* with the respondent, should *share decision-making* with the respondent, and should *delegate responsibility* to the respondent. Consequently, these three questions can be regarded as similar to what is often referred to as 'consultative decision-making', 'joint decision-making' and 'delegation'. Thus, on continuums of 'participation in decision-making' with five methods of participation, the three items mentioned above would be comparable to the three methods that are 'closest' to subordinate participation on the continuum. In the two methods furthest from subordinate participation in most continua, the manager makes the decisions, and then informs or explains the decision to the subordinates. It has been shown in earlier research that these two methods are rarely the preferred choice of subordinates. However, in the current study the respondents have the option of scoring 'not at all' if they think that it is the manager who should make all the decisions.

Another important finding in earlier research was that attitudes and behaviour regarding 'participation in decision-making' did not necessarily have to correspond with attitudes and behaviour in form of soliciting suggestions, i.e. 'interpersonal participation'. Consequently, it was decided to operationalize the following two items for interpersonal participation: to what extent the immediate manager should *take advice* from the respondent, and to what extent the immediate manager should *appreciate that the respondent takes the initiative* (see Table 9.2 for an exact phrasing of the items). The first mentioned item is stronger than 'soliciting ideas and suggestions', which is the phrasing most often used in earlier research. The formulation of the question of 'taking advice' is a result of informal interviews with managers who have been working abroad for longer time spans in several continents. In their experience, soliciting ideas and suggestions could be carried out for a variety of reasons and did not necessarily entail interpersonal participation. However, one of the notable differences across countries, in their experience, was whether managers took advice from their subordinates. Listening to and taking advice from the subordinates were seen as a type of participation. The second mentioned item 'appreciating initiative' is a broader concept than those used in earlier research, and it includes both ideas generated by employees and work conducted resulting from employees'

Table 9.2: **Items used to measure 'participation in decision-making and interpersonal participation', i.e. empowering***

To what extent does your immediate manager . . .**	To what extent should your immediate manager . . .**
. . . delegate responsibility to you?	. . . delegate responsibility to you?
. . . share decision-making with you?	. . . share decision-making with you?
. . . discuss company strategies with you?	. . . discuss company strategies with you?
. . . take advice from you?	. . . take advice from you?
. . . appreciate your taking initiative?	. . . appreciate your taking initiative

Notes: * The five-point Likert scale varies from 'not at all' to 'a very large extent'.
** The questions were translated into local languages after a back translation process (see Zander 1997 for details).

initiative. These two items also attempt to capture the flavour of contemporary work psychology and organizational behaviour research such as 'self-managing employees' and 'self-managing teams'. Consequently, five items were used to measure 'participation in decision-making and interpersonal participation' (see Table 9.2).

Finally, in the research of the applicability of Misumi's performance maintenance theory it was ascertained that certain questions would refer to something general and valid in all studied countries, while other questions needed to be specifically phrased for each cultural context. This strongly emphasizes the need to analyse the *interrelationship between the items* measuring 'participation in decision-making and interpersonal participation' *within each country*. This must be done to ensure that they relate to each other in a similar way within each studied country before comparing them across countries. Zander (1997) also argues the importance of *testing the reliability* of a construct *in each individual country* before using it any comparative analysis.

The pattern of interrelationship between the five items measuring 'participation in decision-making and interpersonal participation' was similar in all 18 countries in Zander's study. This has two implications. First, the earlier finding of a difference between participation in decision-making and interpersonal participation was not replicated in this study. Second, it was possible to add the items together to create a construct. The construct was labelled *empowering* since the measured items represent the idea of enabling and empowering employees. Empowerment is carried out by *delegating responsibility* to the employees and by giving them the possibility of *discussing strategies* and *sharing decision-making* processes. In order for this to work, employees also need to be enabled, which is done by supporting their development by *appreciating their initiatives* and *taking their advice*. The construct was internally consistent and strongly reliable in the studied countries with Cronbach alphas for empowering all above .74 (see Nunnally, 1967; 1978 for a discussion of reliability measures).

During the review of the cultural dimensions that measured status allocation it became clear that the researchers who had measured them had also hypothesized how they would influence participatory management practices such as participation in decision-making. Thus, employees' preferences regarding empowering were at the onset expected to be related to beliefs about status allocation. This general prediction was specified as follows: (1) in cultures where there is a belief in hierarchical allocation, employees are predicted to have a low preference for empowering (−*Maznevski's hierarchical relationships,* −*Hofstede's power distance* and −*Schwartz's hierarchy*); (2) if promotion and status are accorded by achievement, employees are expected to have a higher preference for empowering than if promotions are based on ascription (+*Trompenaars' achievement*); (3) if authority is perceived as a social property that is present both inside and outside organizations, employees are not expected to have a high preference for empowering (−*Laurent's authority systems*). These predictions were analysed with Spearman's rank correlation analysis and the results are presented and discussed below.

Is there a relationship between employees' preferences regarding empowering and national culture?

First, employees' preferences regarding empowering across countries was examined by a MANOVA. The results displayed that employees' preferences regarding empowering varied across countries (F-value 3.94, at the 1 per cent significance level). Second, the predictions that the across-country differences in employees' preferences for empowering were related to beliefs about status allocation were examined with Spearman's rank correlation analysis. In the correlation analysis, all the 31 cultural dimensions reviewed in Zander (1997; 2001) were included. Employees' preferences regarding empowering in both the main and the hold-out analysis correlated *as predicted* with two of the five cultural dimensions regarding beliefs about status allocation: achievement orientation and authority systems. In addition, empowering in both samples also correlated significantly with an unpredicted cultural dimension: Trompenaars' universalistic versus particularistic value orientation. The predictions and the results concerning employees' preferences in both the main sample and the hold-out sample are shown in Table 9.3.

Status allocation and participation in decision-making

It was predicted that employees will have a higher preference for empowering if status and promotion are based on *achievement* rather than ascription. Trompenaars has measured the achievement versus ascription orientation in the 12 European countries included in the main analysis. These are labelled according to Internet addresses country suffices in Figure 9.1 as follows: Austria (AT), Belgium (BE), Denmark (DK), Finland (FI), France (FR), Germany (DE), Netherlands (NL), Norway (NO), Spain (ES), Sweden (SE), Switzerland (CH) and the United Kingdom (UK). Norway, Denmark, and the UK score high on achievement while Spain, Belgium and France score low, that is displaying an ascriptive-orientation. Employees in the achievement-oriented countries have higher preference for empowering than those who work in ascriptive-oriented countries (see Figure 9.1). Austria is an exception in that the country scores are low on achievement, while employees have a high preference for empowering. However, the Austrian employees had a lower preference for empowering in the hold-out sample.

It was also predicted that employees who work in countries where *authority* is seen as instrumental and connected to a specific work position have a higher preference for empowering than employees who work in countries where authority is seen as personal, i.e. that authority is connected to the person who holds the work position. Laurent has calculated the scores on the authority dimension for eight European countries included in the main sample labelled in Figure 9.2 as follows: Belgium (BE), Denmark (DK), France (FR), Germany (DE), Netherlands (NL), Sweden (SE), Switzerland (CH) and the United Kingdom (UK). The European countries with the lowest

Table 9.3: **Empowering, predictions and outcome**

Cultural Dimensions	n[1]	n[2]	PREDICTED[3] Relationship with empowering	OUTCOME[4] Main analysis	OUTCOME Hold-out analysis
Status allocation:					
Hierarchical relationships (Maznevski)	5	3	−hier	−.70*	−.50
Power distance (Hofstede)	16	15	−pdi	−.61**	−.05
Hierarchy (Schwartz)	10	9	−hier	.29	−.59**
Achievement/ascription (Trompenaars)	16	14	+ach	.45**	.44*
Authority systems (Laurent)	9	9	−aut	−.78***	−.53*
Unpredicted cultural dimensions:					
Universalism/particularism (Trompenaars)	16	15		.62**	.64**
Mastery (Schwartz)	10	9		.40	.72***

Notes: [1] The number of countries included in the Spearman rank correlation analysis of the main sample in Zander (1997).

[2] The number of countries included in the Spearman rank correlation analysis of the hold-out sample in Zander (1997).

[3] Predicted positive correlation is denoted with '+' and a negative with a '−'. When no relationship is predicted, this is denoted with '.'. Abbreviations for the name of the dimensions are used as clarifications.

[4] Spearman's rank correlation significant at the .10 level*, .05 level**, .01 level*** (one-tailed test for predicted relationships and two-tailed tests for the others).

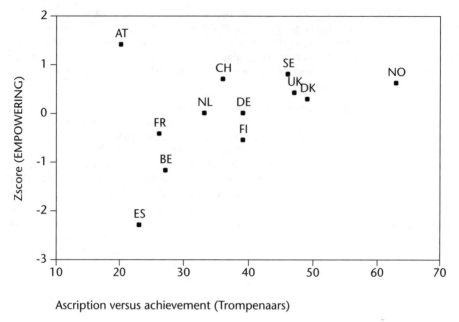

Ascription versus achievement (Trompenaars)

Scale: ascription (low) and achievement (high).

Figure 9.1: **Empowering and achievement**

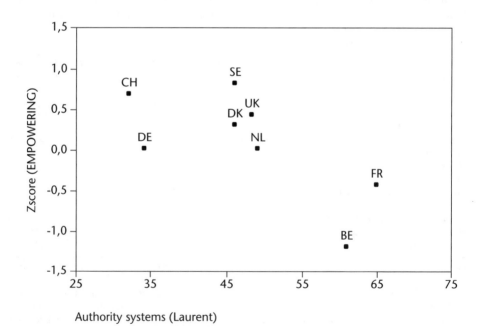

Authority systems (Laurent)

Scale: authority based on position (low) on person (high).

Figure 9.2: **Empowering and authority systems**

preferences for empowering include Belgium and France where authority is seen as personal, as opposed to Switzerland and Germany where authority is seen as instrumental and where employees have a higher preference for empowering (see Figure 9.2).

Empowering and universalism versus particularism

The relationship between *universalistic* orientation and preferences regarding empowering was unpredicted. Trompenaars argues that an universalistic orientation will have an influence on structures and policies. In a universalistic country, there is an adherence to rules and formalized structures as well as consistent and uniform procedures. On the other hand, in a country characterized by a particularistic orientation, there is a preference for taking each situation and relationship into account when deciding if rules and procedures should be followed. Hence, it is possible that employees who work in a country where rules and formalized policies should be universally followed feel comfortable with assuming delegated responsibility, shared decision-making and discussion of strategies. They also like to take their own initiatives and to supply their immediate manager with advice. On the other hand, in a particularistic-oriented country the relationship between subordinate and manager is characterized by commitment, in everything from security to socio-emotional support, as Trompenaars expresses it. This does to some extent resemble what is often referred to as a 'paternalistic' type of management. Particularistic managers are authoritarian in their decision-making style, which is often seen as not compatible with empowering. Thus, the positive correlation between empowering and a universalistic orientation could be the result of employees in universalistic-oriented countries wanting more empowering as they feel comfortable in assuming a more empowered role, while the employees in the particularistic-oriented countries do not want to be empowered to any large extent since they view their manager as the authority who should take decisions.

Trompenaars has measured the universalistic versus particularistic orientation in the 12 European countries included in the main sample. These are labelled in Figure 9.3 as follows: Austria (AT), Belgium (BE), Denmark (DK), Finland (FI), France (FR), Germany (DE), Netherlands (NL), Spain (ES), Switzerland (CH) and the United Kingdom (UK). Sweden and Norway have the same universalistic value but differ slightly in their preferences for empowering where Sweden is represented by a standardised adjusted country mean of 0.83 and Norway by 0.65. For clarity in the graph, Sweden and Norway are represented by one point only labelled with 'SE/NO'. Switzerland, Sweden and Norway are among the countries that score high on universalistic values and the employees in these countries have high preferences for empowering. Spain, Belgium and France score towards the particularistic orientation and have lower preferences for empowering. Again, Austria is an outlayer in this case with high preferences for empowering while endorsing more particularistic-oriented scores. However, the outlayer pattern is not repeated in the hold-out sample.

In sum, first the results of the MANOVA clearly indicate that employees' preferences regarding empowering vary across countries. Second, the correlation analysis both in the main sample and the hold-out sample display that empowering preferences are strongly and significantly related to national culture. Trompenaars' achievement versus ascription dimension, Laurent's authority system dimension as well as Trompenaars' universalistic versus particularistic dimension are related to levels of participation. In the light of these results, the relationship between empowering and national culture will be discussed more in detail.

Empowering and national culture

Employees who are empowered by their managers participate in decision-making and strategy discussions, and responsibility is delegated to them. Empowering also means that managers appreciate their employees taking initiative and giving them

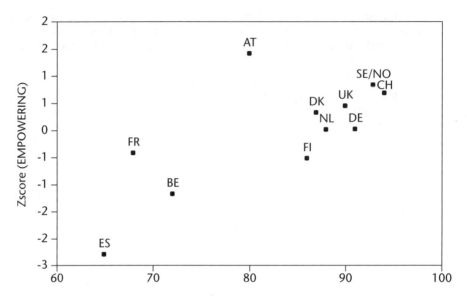

Particularism versus universalism (Trompenaars)

Scale: particularism (low) and universalism (high).

Figure 9.3: **Empowering and universalism**

advice. The relationship between employees' preferences regarding empowering and cultural dimensions was predicted to be related to beliefs about how status and authority are accorded. This was partly confirmed by the results. In contradiction to hypotheses in previous research, the results show that hierarchical differentiation is *not* related to empowering. Lane, DiStefano and Maznevski (1997) suggested that the degree of hierarchical differentiation would be related to the forms of decision-making used in an organization. Hofstede has argued that the degree of employee participation in decision-making is highly dependent on how equally power is distributed (Hofstede 1980/4). In societies that are characterized by equal distribution of power and correspondingly flat hierarchies, employees would have a higher preference for empowering than in societies characterized by multilevel hierarchies. Schwartz did not hypothesize a relationship between hierarchy and empowering, although the definition of his dimension is in line with Maznevski's hierarchical relationships and Hofstede's power distance. The results clearly display that the predicted negative relationship between hierarchical differentiation and empowering did not receive any support, suggesting that empowering preferences are not related to the de facto distribution of power nor to a hierarchical-based status allocation. However, the lack of a significant relationship between Maznevski's hierarchical relationship and employees' empowering preferences can be viewed as tentative since the sample of countries is still small.

A low preference for empowering is displayed by employees in cultures where status is accorded on ascriptive criteria such as seniority or family ties, and authority is related to the person that holds the position, and not the position per se. Correspondingly, a high preference for empowering was identified as related to status being accorded on achievement and authority based on the position that a person holds. It should also be mentioned that there was a significant positive correlation with Schwartz' mastery values in the hold-out sample and a strong, but not significant, correlation coefficient of .40 in the main sample. Schwartz' mastery values includes 'independence', 'ambitious', 'capable', 'daring' and 'choosing own goals' as guiding values in life. It is perhaps not surprising that employees working in countries where these values are espoused have high preferences for empowering. However, it is to be observed that Hofstede's masculinity dimension, which measures beliefs about assertiveness and success, does not correlate with preferences for empowering. In addition, the preference for empowering was unexpectedly identified as related to whether principles and rules should be universally followed or particularly treated. Hence, in environments where principles and policies are universal, employees' prefer to be empowered to a higher degree than in particularistic-oriented environments where the managerial role is most often more authoritarian.

In sum, employees' preferences for empowering are related to value orientations where status or authority is based on work and achievement, and on beliefs that policies and principles should be universally followed. Empowering preferences are not related to the hierarchical differentiation in the cultural environment where the employees work. The fact that employees' empowering preferences are related to national culture raises the question whether cultural congruence regarding empowering is important for employees' satisfaction with their work duties and with the experienced delegation of responsibility.

Empowering and cultural congruence – does it matter?
Employees' preferences regarding empowering have been identified as related to national cultural dimensions. This highlights the question whether it is important that managers adhere to employees' preferences. In other words, is it important that the practised empowering is congruent with national cultural values? Wright and Mischel (1987) argue that management practices that are congruent with national cultural values will yield predictable behaviour and according to Earley (1994) will result in high performance. The results of Newman and Nollen's (1996: 755) study clearly support that congruent management practices lead to better business performance. The authors' phrase this as follows: national culture is a

> central organizing principle of employees' understanding of work, their approach to it, and the way in which they expect to be treated, and when management practices are inconsistent with cultural values, employees are likely to feel dissatisfied, distracted, uncomfortable and uncommitted.
>
> (*Ibid.*)

In the empirical study presented in this chapter, employees were asked not only to answer questions on what their immediate manager *should do*, but also on what their immediate manager *does*. In addition, *satisfaction* questions regarding employees' present duties as well as whether their managers need to improve delegation of responsibility were also included in the survey. Hence, it is possible to calculate the size of the gap between what the managers should do and what they currently do, and analyse whether it corresponds to the degree of employee satisfaction. In other words, are employees who experience that there is a big gap less satisfied with their duties and consider improvement to be needed and vice versa.

The proposition that cultural congruence regarding empowering in Europe is related to employees' work satisfaction was examined with a Spearman's rank correlation analysis using both the main sample and the hold-out sample. This analysis was *conducted within each country using the individual level data,* and not at the country level using country means. Employees' satisfaction with their work duties was measured by adding five of the items measuring present duties. These were exactly phrased as follows: what do you think of your present duties as regards (1) utilizing your skills and abilities, (2) offering variety, (3) offering opportunities for responsibility, (4) providing the chance to influence/design your job content and (5) appreciation of ideas and initiative. Employees were asked to respond on the following scale: very satisfied today, fairly satisfied today, some improvement needed, much improvement needed and very much improvement needed. The construct 'satisfaction with present duties' was strongly reliable in the main sample with Cronbach alphas of more than .80 in all countries except one with an alpha of .68. In the hold-out sample, alphas were also above .80 in all countries but one country where it was .79. In addition, one question was asked specifically about delegation of responsibility and it was phrased as follows: 'How do you feel about your immediate superior as regards delegating responsibility'. The same satisfaction-improvement scale as described above was used.

In both the main analysis and the hold-out analysis it was clear that the size of the gap between what the immediate managers should do and what they were perceived as doing is significantly correlated with satisfaction as regards both present duties and the delegation of responsibility in almost all the studied European countries (see Table 9.4). Consequently, in countries were employees experience a larger gap between what is done and what should be done they are less satisfied and consider that there is a need for improvement regarding their present duties as well as delegation of responsibility.

These results suggest that cultural congruence regarding empowering is important in order to ensure employee satisfaction. However, it should be mentioned that several decades of research have failed to demonstrate a clear relation between worker satisfaction and productivity (Scott 1992). On the other hand, according to Scott critics call these attempts 'cow sociology' alluding to that the happier the cow is the more milk she produces, and argue that worker satisfaction is an end in itself. Here it should be emphasized that most of the studies of the relationship between work satisfaction and productivity have been conducted within one country, the USA. It is possible that work satisfaction is an important motivator and driver for productivity in countries other than the USA. It is also possible that work satisfaction regarding empowering is important for efficiency, creativity and competitiveness, which

Table 9.4: **The cultural congruence results**[1]

		MAIN SAMPLE			HOLD-OUT SAMPLE	
COUNTRY	n^3	Empowering Gap and Duties	Empowering Gap and Delegation	n^3	Empowering Gap and Duties	Empowering Gap and Delegation
Austria	44	.62***	.55***	105	.31***	.24***
Belgium	53	.22	.48***	118	.21***	.55***
Denmark	32	.51***	.13	551	.50***	.46***
Finland	34	.16	−.21	92	.43***	.40***
France	168	.54***	.58***	133	.43***	.48***
Germany	321	.52***	.50***	125	.43***	.58***
Netherlands	128	.52***	.55***	145	.40***	.47***
Norway	175	.52***	.46***	407	.48***	.48***
Spain[2]	307	.36***	.38***	6	n.a.	n.a.
Sweden	2137	.55***	.52***	5243	.48***	.50***
Switzerland[2]	39	.62***	.46***	18	n.a.	n.a.
United Kingdom	125	.42***	.41***	299	.29***	.41***
Total n	4112			10 170		

Notes: [1] The correlation analyses were conducted within each country. Correlation significant at the .10 level*, .05 level**, and .01 level***.
[2] The sample sizes in the hold-out samples were too small and correlation analyses were not conducted in Spain and Switzerland.
[3] The sample sizes after omitting employees who consider that they themselves and/or their managers do not come from the country that they are working in.

have not been studied to the same extent. The findings from the European Foundation for the Improvement for Living and Working Conditions (1997) study of direct participation in 15 European countries displayed that participation in decision-making was in particular present in organizations competing in the international market. In addition, advanced forms of participation existed in firms that produced value-added high-quality goods. Furthermore, participative initiatives were seen as strategic and as important for enhancing competitiveness. Finally, according to Gill (2000) indirect more collective forms (work councils, etc.), and direct more individualistic forms of participation (e.g. authority to take decisions delegated to individuals) were found to be complementary. Examples from the Gill (2000) study suggest that successful organizations had integrated both forms of participation into their employment policies.

Empowering Europe: implications for research and practice

From the early discussions of worker participation, through various forms of participation in decision-making to the current focus on self-management, the concepts and theories have been assumed culture-free. Empowering was seen as a universal blessing to practitioners and a theoretical challenge to the instrumental view of the firm. The results in this chapter not only refute the taken-for-granted universality, but it also displays how employees' preferences are related to national culture. In earlier culture research there is a hypothesized relationship between hierarchical differences in society as defined and measured by Hofstede (1980/4), Schwartz (1994) and Maznevski *et al.* (1997), and preferences for participatory management practices. This hypothesis was not supported, which raises two questions that need to be addressed in culture theory. The first question is whether it is possible that hierarchical relationships, power distance and espoused hierarchy values are only related to status allocation in structures, e.g. organizational forms, levels of hierarchy, rather than to management practices. The second question is whether status allocation based on hierarchical variation is company or industry sensitive since the relationship was significant in one of the two samples included in the study.

The findings presented in this chapter do not only eradicate assumed universality but also an often proposed regional application of management theory and methods. A significant variation in empowering preferences was ascertained in this study of 12 European countries. These results corroborate current research on 'outstanding leadership attributes' within Europe. Brodbeck *et al.* (2000) could clearly identify differences in the 'attributes evaluated as facilitating outstanding leadership' by middle managers in 22 European countries. The data collected as a part of the GLOBE project included a 'participative' scale as one of the 21 leadership prototypicality scales. The across-Europe variation in middle managers' view of 'participative' as facilitating outstanding leadership mirrors the empowering preferences based on the sample of employees with different work positions at different levels in the organization in different age-groups and of different gender presented in this chapter. The theoretical implications of the findings from the GLOBE study and the findings presented in this chapter include not only the geographical limitation of participatory management theories, but also the need for leadership theory development in general to incorporate cultural context dependence as a possibility until proven otherwise.

For practitioners, a number of implications could be outlined. One of the common questions is the need for cultural congruence in management, e.g. when sending an expatriate manager to a position in a new country. In this chapter, it has been shown that the lack of cultural fit regarding empowering will have an effect on employees' satisfaction with their work duties as well as their satisfaction regarding manager's attempts to delegate responsibility. These results were mapped for local managers but the need for cultural congruence would most probably increase with expatriate managers. It is still an open question whether work satisfaction is related to productivity, efficiency and creativity. However, there is some evidence that culturally congruent management results in higher and better business performance as well as increased competitiveness within international markets.

In Europe and in particular within the European Union, the degree of culturally diverse workforces due to larger international labour mobility and the continuous growth of globally spanning organizations will pose a challenge for managers who manage and lead multicultural teams. The team members could carry different assumptions regarding status allocation and, consequently, different expectations regarding empowering with them into the team. According to Maznevski and Zander (2001: 158) this could lead to 'a situation in which the leader and one or more members differ strongly from each other in their preferences regarding the ideal distribution of power in decision-making in such a way the preferences are mutually incompatible'. They refer to this as the 'power paradox'. Empirical evidence has shown that the power paradox creates conflict and tension that is very difficult to handle even in teams that successfully develop synergistic approaches to manage cultural differences. The power paradox will surface when there are members who consider that decision-making authority should be allocated based on achievements and would prefer high degrees of empowering, while the leader endorses authoritarian values and wishes to take the decisions him- or herself. The leader may have the power, but members who want to be empowered will not view the leader as powerful if they are not empowered. Instead, members will be frustrated and seriously question the leader's competence and authority, refusing to be led by the leader. Thus, caught in a power paradox the leader may 'have the power', but does not in reality have the power since she or he is not given the licence to lead by the team members and as soon as the leader 'takes power' it disappears through his or her fingers.

Finally, one overarching question is whether Europe is becoming empowered or whether this is yet another management fad that is redressed every decade in the latest wording, becomes the 'talk of town', and fades into ignorance without influencing the work life of employees. Perhaps it is still only an appealing and politically correct rhetoric that managers 'pay lip-service' to but never intend to implement, as it was argued by Haire, Ghiselli and Porter already in the 1960s. Evidence hitherto however paints another picture. According to Gill (2000: 103) 'a strong institutional basis for indirect participation stimulates the emergence of direct forms [of participation]'. These are research results that echo the findings of the IDE research in the 1980 and the 1990s that political and other group- initiated rhetoric results in laws and regulations that are followed by action in organizations. The findings of the empirical study presented in this chapter indicate that employees' preferences regarding empowering in Europe clearly exceed the perceived current levels of empowering. Although, the variation in preferences varies across Europe, employees' work satisfaction are related to how culturally congruent managers are when empowering them. Most probably, Europe is still to be more empowered in the future.

Acknowledgements

The author would like to express her gratitude to ASKUS AB, in particular Göran Larsson and Gunilla Wredenberg, for their enthusiasm for cross-cultural research that made the complex and time-consuming questionnaire development and data collection possible. The author would also like to thank all the respondents at Procordia, Kabi-Pharmacia, Swedish Match and the other Procordia-owned companies. In particular, comments and feedback from Rolf Björsne, Jacques Vernet and Hans Carlson were valuable. Financial support was generously supplied by the Jan Wallander and Tom Hedelius foundation (Stiftelsen för samhällsvetenskaplig forskning). The author would especially like to thank Bengt Björck and Ulla Beau at the Jan Wallander and Tom Hedelius foundation. Finally, financial support from the Swedish Environment Work Council is gratefully acknowledged.

Endnotes

1 Janson was Zander's maiden name.
2 See also Peterson and Misumi (1985); Peterson (1988); Peterson, Peng and Smith (1999); Smith, Peterson, Misumi and Tayeb (1989a); Smith, Tayeb and Peterson (1989); Smith, Peterson, Misumi and Tayeb (1989b); Smith, Peterson, Misumi and Sugiman (1990); Smith, Tayeb, Sinha and Bennett (1990); Smith, Peterson, Bond and Misumi (1992) for further discussions of the research on the application of the PM theory in the West.
3 A systematic interdisciplinary research programme has been conducted for 30 years in Japan (Peterson and Misumi 1985). The programme, was inspired by the early Lewin, Lippitt and White studies in 1939, and numerous experimental and field studies, cross-sectional as well as longitudinal studies, have been conducted and led to the development of the PM theory. According to Misumi and Peterson (1985) there were reasons to believe that conclusions from the PM research in Japan may be applicable in the West. This task was undertaken by an international group of researchers.
4 For an in-depth discussion of research design, sample, questionnaire development and design, as well as the development of reliability measures see Zander (1997).
5 Spain and Switzerland are only analysed in the main sample since the sample size in the hold-out sample is too small to be included in the statistical analysis.
6 The conglomerate, Procordia, was exceedingly generous in supplying the opportunity to add questions to their own internal survey. Thus, the space and format restrictions were seen as a challenge (rather than a problem) to the research design.

References

Ah Chong, L.M. and Thomas, D.C. (1997) 'Leadership perceptions in cross-cultural context: Pakeha and Pacific Islanders in New Zealand', *Leadership Quarterly* 8(3): 275–93.

Al-Jafary, A. and Hollingsworth, A.T. (1983) 'An exploratory study of managerial practices in the Arabian Gulf region', *Journal of International Business* 14(2): 143–52.

Badawy, M.K. (1980) 'Styles of Mid-Eastern managers', *California Management Review* 22: 51–8.

Bass, B.M. and Stogdill, R.M. (1990) *Bass & Stogdill's Handbook of Leadership: Theory, Research, and Managerial Applications*, 3rd edition, New York: Free Press.

Bass, B.M., Burger, P.C., Doktor, R. and Barrett, G.V. (1979) *Assessment of Managers: An International Comparison*, New York: Free Press.

Bottger, P.C., Hallein, I.H. and Yetton P.W. (1985) 'A cross-national study of leadership: participation as a function of problem structure and leader power', *Journal of Management Studies* 22(4): 358–68.

Boyacigiller, N.A. and Adler N.J. (1991) 'The parochial dinosaur: organizational science in a global context', *Academy of Management Review* 16(2): 262–90.

Brodbeck, F.C., Frese, M., Akerblom, S., Audia, G., Bakacsi, G., Bendova, H., Bodega, D., Bodur, D., Booth, S., Brenk, K., Castel, P., Den Hartog, D., Donnelly-Cox, G., Gratchev, M.V., Holmberg, I., Jarmuz, S., Jesuino, J.C., Jorbenadse, R., Kabasakal, H.E., Keating, M., Kipiani, G., Konrad, E., Koopman, P., Kurc, A., Leeds, C., Lindell, M., Maczynski, J., Martin, G.S., O'Connell, J., Papalexandris, A., Papalexandris, N., Prieto, J., Rakitski, B., Reber, G., Sabadin, S., Schramm-Nielsen, J., Schulz, M., Sigfrids, C., Szabo, E., Thierry, H., Vondrysova, M., Weibler, J., Wilderom, C., Wikkowski, S. and Wunderer R. (2000) 'Cultural variation of leadership prototypes across 22 European countries', *Journal of Occupational and Organizational Psychology* 73: 1–29.

Earley, P.C. (1994) 'Self or group? Cultural effects of training on self-efficacy and performance', *Administrative Science Quarterly* 39: 89–117.

Earley, P.C. (1997) *Face, Harmony and Social Structure*, New York: Oxford University Press.

European Foundation for the Improvement of Living and Working Conditions (1997) *New Forms of Work Organisation: Can Europe Realise its Potential?: Results of Survey of Direct Participation in Europe*, Dublin: EFILWC.

Gill, C. (2000) 'Industrial relations in Europe', in M. Warner (ed.) *Management in Europe, Regional Encyclopaedia of Business and Management*, London: Business Press, Thomson Learning

Gill, C. and Krieger H. (1992) 'The diffusion of participation in new information technology in Europe: survey results', *Economic and Industrial Democracy*, 13(3): 331–59.

Haire, M., Ghiselli, E.E. and Porter, L.W. (1966) *Managerial Thinking: An International Study*, New York: Wiley.

Heller, F.A. and Wilpert, B. (1981) *Competence and Power in Managerial Decision-Making*, Chichester: Wiley.

Hofstede, G. (1980) 'Motivation, leadership and organization: do American theories apply abroad', *Organizational Dynamics* Summer: 42–63.

Hofstede, G. (1980/4) *Culture's Consequences: International Differences in Work-Related Values*, Newbury Park, CA: Sage.

Hofstede, G. (1991) *Cultures and Organizations: Software of the Mind*, London: McGraw-Hill

Hofstede, G. (1996) 'An American in Paris: the influence of nationality on organization theories', *Organization Studies* 17(3): 525–37.

Industrial Democracy in Europe (IDE) (1976) 'Industrial democracy in Europe: an international comparative study', *Social Science Information* 15, February: 177–203.

Industrial Democracy in Europe (IDE) (1979) 'Industrial democracy in Europe: participation, formal rules, influence and involvement', *Industrial Relations* 18: 273–94.

Industrial Democracy in Europe (IDE) (1993) *Industrial Democracy in Europe Revisited*, Oxford: Oxford University Press.

Janson, L. (1992) 'Culture's influence on leadership – Hofstede's four dimensions re-explored', in A. Sjögren and L. Janson (eds) *Culture and Management: In the Field of Ethnology and Business Administration*, Stockholm: Swedish Immigration Institute and Museum and Institute of International Business.

Kluckhohn, F.R. and Strodtbeck F.L. (1961) *Variations in Value Orientations*, New York: Row, Peterson.

Lane, H.W., DiStefano, J.J. and Maznevski, M.L. (1997) *International Management Behavior*, 3rd edition, Cambridge MA: Blackwell.

Laurent, A. (1983) 'The cultural diversity of Western conceptions of management', *International Studies of Management and Organization* 13(1–2): 75–96.

Lewin, K., Lippitt, R. and White, R.K. (1939) 'Patterns of aggressive behaviour in experimentally created social climates', *Journal of Social Psychology* 10: 271–99.

Likert, R. (1967) *The Human Organisation*, New York: McGraw-Hill.

Maznevski, M.L. and Zander, L. (2001) 'Leading global teams: overcoming the challenge of the power paradox', in M.E. Medenhall, T.M. Kuhlmann and G.K. Stahl (eds) *Developing Global Leaders: Policies, Processes, and Innovations*, London: Quorum.

Maznevski, M.L., DiStefano, J.J., Gomez, C.B., Noorderhaven, N.G. and Wu, P. (1997) 'The cultural orientations framework and international management research', paper presented at Academy of International Business Annual Meeting.

Misumi, J. (1985) *The Behavioral Science of Leadership*, Ann Arbor, MI: University of Michigan Press.

Misumi, J. and Peterson, M. F. (1985) 'The performance-maintenance (PM) theory of leadership: review of a Japanese research program', *Administrative Science Quarterly* 30: 198–223.

Newman, K.L. and Nollen, S.D. (1996) 'Culture and congruence: the fit between management practices and national culture', *Journal of International Business Studies*, fourth quarter: 753–59.

Nunally, J.C. (1967) *Psychometric Theory*, New York: McGraw-Hill.

Nunally, J.C. (1978) *Psychometric Theory*, 2nd edition, New York: McGraw-Hill.

Parsons, T. and Shils, E.A. (1951) *Toward a General Theory of Action*, Cambridge, MA: Harvard University Press.

Peterson, M. (1988) 'PM theory in Japan and China: what's in it for the United States?', *Organizational Dynamics*, 16(4) Spring: 22–38.

Peterson, M.F., Peng T.K. and Smith P.B. (1999) 'Using expatriate supervisors to promote cross-border management practice transfer: the experience of a Japanese electronics company', in J.K. Liker, W.M. Fruin and P.S. Adler (eds) *Remade in America: Transplanting and Transforming Japanese Productions Systems*, Oxford: University Press.

Peterson, M., Smith, P.B. and Tayeb, M.H. (1993) 'Development and use of English versions of Japanese PM leadership measures in electronics plants', *Journal of Organizational Behavior* 14: 251–67.

Redding, G.S. (1994) 'Comparative management theory: jungle, zoo or fossil bed?', *Organisation Studies* 15(3): 323–59.

Redding, S.G. and Casey, T.W. (1976) 'Managerial beliefs among Asian managers', *Proceedings of the Academy of Management*, New Orleans, LA: 351–5.

Redding, S.G. and Richardson, S. (1986) 'Participative management and its varying relevance in Hong Kong and Singapore', *Asia Pacific Journal of Management* 3: 76–98.

Rokeach, M. (1968) *Beliefs Attitudes and Values: A Theory of Organization and Change*, San Francisco: Jossey-Bass.

Schaupp, D.L. (1978) *Cross-Cultural Study of a Multinational Company: Attitudinal Responses to Participative Management*, New York: Praeger.

Schwartz, S.H. (1994) 'Beyond individualism/collectivism: new cultural dimensions of values', in U. Kim, H.C. Triandis, C. Kagitcibasi, S.-C. Choi and G. Yoon (eds) *Individualism and Collectivism: Theory, Method, and Applications*, London: Sage.

Scott, R. (1992) *Organizations: Rational, Natural and Open Systems*, Englewood Cliffs, NJ: Prentice-Hall.

Smith, P.B., Misumi, J., Tayeb, M., Peterson, M. and Bond, M. (1989) 'On the generality of leadership style measures across cultures', *Journal of Occupational Psychology* 62(1): 97–109.

Smith, P.B., Peterson, M.F., Bond, M.H. and Misumi, J. (1992) 'Leader style and leader behaviour across cultures', in S. Iwawaki, Y. Kashima and K. Leung (eds) *Innovations in Cross-Cultural Psychology*, Amsterdam: Swets and Zeitlinger.

Smith, P.B., Peterson, M.F., Misumi, J. and Bond, M. (1992) 'A cross-cultural test of the Japanese PM leadership theory', *Applied Psychology: An International Review* 41(1): 5–19.

Smith, P.B., Peterson, M.F., Misumi, J. and Sugiman, T. (1990) 'Cross-cultural tests of P-M leadership theory: East meets West', *Japanese Journal of Experimental Social Psychology* 29: 53–64.

Smith, P.B., Peterson, M.F., Misumi, J. and Tayeb, M. (1989a) 'The cultural context of leadership action', in D.M. Keats, D. Munro and L. Mann (eds) *Heterogeneity in Cross-Cultural Psychology*, Amsterdam: Swets and Zeitlinger.

Smith, P.B., Peterson, M.F, Misumi, J. and Tayeb, M. (1989b) 'Testing leadership theory cross-culturally', in J.P. Forgas and J.M. Innes (eds) *Recent Advances in Social Psychology: An International Perspective*, Amsterdam: Elsevier.

Smith, P.B., Tayeb, M. and Peterson, M.F. (1989) 'The cultural context of leadership actions: a cross-cultural analysis', in J. Davies, M. Easterby-Smith, S. Mann and M. Tanton (eds) *The Challenge to Western Management Development: International Alternatives*, London: Routledge.

Smith, P.B., Tayeb, M., Sinha, J. and Bennett, B. (1990) 'Leader style and leader behavior across cultures: the case of the 9,9 manager', *International Human Resources Management Review* 1: 141–52.

Sully de Luque, M.F. and Sommer, S.M. (2000) 'The impact of culture on feedback-seeking behavior: an integrated model and propositions', *Academy of Management Review* 25(4): 829–49.

Tannenbaum, A.S. and Rozgonyi, T. (eds) (1986) *Authority and Reward in Organizations: An International Research*, Ann Arbor, MI: Institute of Social Research, University of Michigan.

Tannenbaum, A.S., Kavcic, B., Rosner, M., Vianello, M. and Wieser, G. (1974) *Hierarchy in Organizations*, San Francisco: Jossey-Bass.

Tayeb, M. (1995) *Supervisory Styles and Cultural Contexts: A Comparative Study*, Oxford: Elsevier Science.

Triandis, H.C. (1996) 'The psychological measurement of cultural syndromes', *American Psychologist* 51: 407–15.

Trompenaars, F. (1993) *Riding the Waves of Culture: Understanding Cultural Diversity in Business*, Bath: Bath Press.

Wright, J.C. and Mischel, W. (1987) 'A conditional approach to dispositional constructs: the local predictability of social behavior', *Journal of Personality and Social Psychology* 53: 1159–77.

Zander, L. (1997) *The Licence to Lead: An 18 Country Study of the Relationship between Employees' Preferences Regarding Interpersonal Leadership and National Culture'*, Stockholm: Institute of International Business, Stockholm School of Economics.

Zander, L. (2001) 'A review of quantitatively measured national cultural dimensions', *JIBS Web Literature Reviews*, forthcoming.

Chapter 10

Managerial evolution in Central and Eastern Europe: the impact of cultural resources and constraints

Vincent Edwards

Managers in Central and Eastern Europe (CEE) and the former Soviet Union (FSU) have undergone a process of extensive change since 1989. The collapse of the communist regimes of CEE was the forerunner (represented both literally and metaphorically by the opening of the Berlin Wall in November 1989) of a historically unprecedented system change as the countries of the region rejected communism as an ideology and a system for organizing political, social and economic activities. A highly structured and closed system of social organization was accordingly discarded and attempts were initiated that would transform societies, creating political democracies and market economies. In the Soviet Union, too, a movement to reform the communist system in the latter part of the 1980s, with its slogans of *glasnost* (openness) and *perestroika* (restructuring), succeeded only in retarding the collapse. Discussions of the need for fundamental reforms tended to highlight the inherent weaknesses and contradictions of the system and in 1992 the Soviet Union was finally dissolved.

Such momentous and far-reaching events could not but have a substantial impact on managers in CEE and the FSU. Although we will primarily deal with the issues facing managers, the changes affected individuals not only in their professional roles but also in their social and political roles. The communist system had been highly structured, leaving only limited scope for individual discretion. However, it was also a system of considerable clarity and certainty, in a way obviating the need for individual discretion. Some of these certainties included the supremacy of the Soviet Union and the Communist Party, employment for all a guaranteed basic standard of living, and widespread provision of social facilities (e.g. education, health care and housing). Although life under communism was controlled and in many respects dull, communism did provide a basic level of security.

The general characteristics of the communist system were also reflected in the management culture of communist enterprises.[1] Enterprises were state-owned hierarchical organizations in which 'top-down' management predominated. Furthermore, enterprises were part of a broader 'command' structure. Enterprises were responsible to ministries which passed on orders (or targets) derived from the national economic plan agreed by the Communist Party. Orders were passed down from the Party to the ministries and from them to enterprises. The role of enterprises (and their managers) was to achieve the specified plan targets.

Reflecting the hierarchical structure of the economic system, the style of management tended to be largely autocratic, although there were variations between countries (Kieżun 1991). Superiors gave orders to subordinates; in the event of difficulties subordinates referred problems back to their superiors. It was generally considered wiser to avoid assuming individual responsibility and taking decisions which might turn out to be politically incorrect. As a consequence the system tended to react slowly to difficulties.

Pressure to ensure political compliance and conformity was manifested in numerous ways, including a consensual approach to decision-making within enterprises. Decision-making bodies included representatives of the Communist Party and trades unions as well as enterprise managers. A consensual approach was also used by managers in dealing with employees. As the latter were guaranteed employment and the working class was ideologically regarded as the leading class in society, it was on the whole difficult for managers to coerce the workforce. Even means of motivation tended to be limited and managers were often caught between the twin pressure of the party (pressing for plan fulfilment) and the reluctance of workers to submit themselves to the system ('workers pretended to work and enterprises pretended to pay them'). In practice managers under communism enjoyed only very limited discretion and, not surprisingly, often displayed 'servility and a heads-down mentality' (Kornai 1992: 121).

At least two other features of the system are worth noting. First, enterprises as portrayed above were not autonomous entities (with strategic decision-making responsibilities). They were largely production units with the role of achieving plan targets. The concern of managers was largely on the production function and on activities which affected production directly such as purchasing. Enterprises did not normally get involved in sales and marketing. Accordingly, managers tended to be preoccupied with, and specialists in, production. Many managers were, in fact, engineering graduates or graduates of engineering-related subjects such as chemical engineering or shipbuilding.

Second, and reinforcing the enterprise's lack of autonomy, enterprises were not expected to operate according to what, in market economies, are regarded as strict financial criteria but were subject to 'soft budget' constraints (Kornai 1992). Enterprises' budgets did exist, but they were negotiable. Senior managers expended considerable energies in obtaining budget concessions which would make life easier for both management and workforce. In order to obtain such concessions managers had to resort to considerable lobbying of their political superiors. Both Party membership and political contacts were thus of great significance to senior managers in communist enterprises.

The system change inaugurated by the opening of the Berlin Wall ushered in a period of major change which overturned the certainties of many of the practices of the communist system. The macro-environment in which companies operated was transformed virtually overnight. The state and the government assumed new roles, most importantly, relinquishing direct involvement in the management of companies. Communist governments generally gave way to democratic governments intent on dismantling rapidly the structures of communism. In this process state-owned assets were privatized and companies became privately owned, independent legal entities. The transformation of the economic system included the development of markets, not only for goods and services, but also for labour and capital. With markets came competition, often in the shape of foreign competitors, skilled and proven in the rules of the market economy. A major feature of the transformation was the opening of the economies of CEE and FSU to the global economy. The vast majority of these states had been members of the Council for Mutual Economic Asistance (COMECON). However, COMECON too became a victim of the transformation as the states rejected old relationships and sought to establish new ones. The countries of CEE now looked to the European Union (EU) for support and future membership and their political and economic relationships tended to be reoriented in this direction. In general, there was a massive redirection of trade (both exports and imports) from the Soviet Union and other COMECON members towards the EU.

Looking back over the first decade of the transformation, the nature and scale of system change are manifest. However, what is also evident is that in practice the process of change has been uneven and inconsistent. One explanation of this uneven and inconsistent process of transformation has been that the countries of CEE and FSU did not enjoy in 1989 and the early 1990s the same conditions for transformation and that accordingly the transformation in individual countries was 'path dependent' (Peng 2000). Hungary provides an illustration of this path dependency. Already in the 1980s Hungarian managers were attempting to reconcile the conflicting pressures of hierarchical and market relationships induced by the implementation of the guided-market model of economic management (Bőgel, Edwards and Wax 1997). As a consequence Hungarian managers were described as being 'Janus-faced' because of their need to reconcile both sets of forces (Balaton 1998: 36, quoting Dobák). Peng (2000) moreover comments that while the transformation has had a substantial impact on formal institutional constraints, informal institutional constraints have been left largely untouched. In a situation of a new formal institutional framework and the persistence of traditional informal institutional practices, opportunistic behaviour, for example, bribery and personal enrichment, has flourished.

Culture clash

The transformation from a communist system of economic management to a market economy may be conceptualized as a clash of cultures. The collapse of the communist regimes did not eradicate overnight the influence of 45 years of communism in CEE and of 75 years of communism in the FSU, even though it was possible to create new formal institutions relatively quickly.

The transformation therefore involves the interaction of two competing cultures, one of which, the culture of the market economy, may be considered dominant since 1989. This interaction is, however, complex and identifying possible explanatory variables for the distinctive evolution of individual countries difficult, especially with regard to investigating the impact of beliefs, values and so-called 'hidden assumptions' which permit cultures to manage the relationships within societies and with the external environment (Schneider and Barsoux 1997).

Kraybill and Nolt (1995) have investigated the relationship of a community living within a dominant culture in their study of Amish entrepreneurship in the USA, focusing on the way cultural resources have been utilized to both bolster and restrain economic activity. Kraybill and Nolt (1995: 16) develop an interactive model of culture and entrepreneurship which posits that 'A cultural heritage carries both *resources* and *restraints* for the development of entrepreneurial activity'. The cultural resources and restraints interact to provide negotiated outcomes which in their turn have an impact on the society's cultural resources and restraints. The model is thus dynamic and particular cultural factors may function as either a resource or a constraint, depending on the outcome. The process of cultural change (or adaptation) thus involves both facilitation and resistance and the emergence of cultural revisions as the community seeks an accommodation with the dominant culture (Kraybill and Nolt 1995: 17–19).

The national and managerial cultures of CEE and the FSU, strongly influenced by the legacy of communism, are now seeking an accommodation with the dominant culture of liberal democracy and the market economy, Following Kraybill and Nolt's model, it is argued that features of national cultures can act both as resources for and constraints on transformation in terms of the dominant culture. Cultural factors regarded historically as strengths (resources) may under the new circumstances become a constraint on transformation. To take just one example at this stage, namely from the Czech Republic (Edwards and Lawrence 2000), a centuries-long experience of resistance to foreign occupation has fostered a tradition of quiet resistance and self-sufficiency, coupled with the development of a social consensus. These 'strengths' can however turn into a feeling that there is nothing to be learned from expertise and practice in other countries and that foreigners are incapable of understanding the situation in the country. Resources that served the nation during centuries of foreign domination (including communism especially after 1969) may become a restraint on transformation.

Dimensions of the management culture

In this section we will examine certain dimensions of the management culture in CEE and Russia. As well as with specific managerial aspects, the section will also discuss issues relating to the organizational and broader social context.

Strategic thinking

One characteristic of managerial practice which has distinguished management in communist enterprises from those in market economies has been the significance and extent of strategic thinking and decision-making. Although Bőgel and Huszty (1999) have argued that some Hungarian enterprises undertook corporate strategic thinking from the late 1970s, communist enterprises, as previously noted, were on the whole production units concerned with operational decisions of meeting plan targets (Edwards and Lawrence 1994). Under communism the strategic elements of enterprise activity were largely the preserve of the central planners, the leading organs of the Communist Party and the various industrial ministries.

With the change of system, however, companies themselves have had to deal with strategic issues as companies have sought to survive and prosper in the new competitive environment. Strategic thinking has developed in terms of product–market relationships, product selection and development and overall issues of investment and examples of such activities can be found in Edwards and Lawrence (1994), Bőgel, Edwards and Wax (1997) and Edwards, Polonsky and Polonsky (2000).

It would be wrong to assume, however, that strategic thinking and behaviour is necessarily becoming the norm across the region as examples of strategic behaviour are matched by evidence of short-term opportunistic behaviour (e.g. personal enrichment to the detriment of the company) and the exploitation of informal practices to mitigate market forces. In Romania, moreover, the propensity to undertake strategic thinking is hampered by a time horizon focused predominantly on the present and a reluctance to take decisions (Catana and Catana 1999). Procrastination is regarded as a management characteristic. Moreover, 'Long-run planning is limited to a process of creating "daydream scenarios" which are unlikely to materialize' (Catana, Catana and Finlay 1999: 152).

Organizational structure

The change of economic system has had a profound impact on companies and, consequently, on the managers who work within them. From being components of a highly integrated system with limited discretion and scope, companies became responsible for their own decision-making and survival. Companies reoriented themselves, with varying degrees of success, from being largely concerned with production and introduced sales, marketing and finance departments. Before 1989 enterprises had been structured predominantly along functional lines, although some Hungarian enterprises had experimented with non-functional organizational structures under communism (Dobák and Tari 1996). After 1989 the pressures of privatization and marketization encouraged companies to downsize, largely by shedding surplus labour, but also by focusing on a restricted range of products (Edwards and Lawrence 1994).

Moreover, this shift in functional emphasis from production to sales and marketing, was not always straightforward. In some countries the shift was constrained by cultural values. According to Lascu, Ahmed and Vatasescu (1997) Romanian managers regard marketing and sales as enjoying low status. In Bulgaria the development of a service culture is impeded by a perception that offers of service place individuals under an obligation to reciprocate (Reeves-Ellington 1998). Holden, Cooper and Carr (1998: 152–3) mention an 'innate Russian bashfulness, which does not make Russians into natural salesmen', although Liuhto (2001: 120) notes that 'a sales background is becoming more frequent'.

The process of organizational restructuring was evident as managers sought to restructure their companies into what they considered to be appropriate for the market economy. The new body of shareholders (in many cases managers and employees) hoped to extract personal benefits from the restructuring process, either in the form of dividends or salaries or by diverting company assets into private sources of wealth (Edwards, Polonsky and Polonsky 2000). In many countries and companies there was only limited separation of ownership and control. Many former directors and senior managers were transformed and in some cases transformed themselves into the new owners of formerly state-owned enterprises. In the case of Russia privatization may have actually impeded the cause of company restructuring, with dominant shareholders seeming to work against the long-term interests of the company (Polonsky and Iviozian 2000).

The process of organization restructuring in Slovenia has been clearly analysed by Pučko *et al.* (Edwards and Lawrence 2000). By the end of the 1990s privatized firms in Slovenia were reporting increasing returns on equity following a three-stage restructuring process. The first phase (early 1990s) was characterized by enterprise retrenchment which had a negative impact on output and the size of the labour force. The second phase (mid-1990s) was largely involved with enterprise privatization. The third phase saw privatized companies beginning to pay greater attention to issues of total quality management, in particular management and workforce quality.

Organizational change

Many observers have been struck by the slow pace of change within organizations. Although there had been a considerable turnover of managers in Hungary in the early 1990s, actual organizational change appeared somewhat limited (Whitley and Czaban 1998). Kelemen (1999) found that at most 10 per cent of companies in Romania had begun economic restructuring of any significance. Rożański and Sikorski (1996) identified no significant changes in Polish companies' behaviour in the early 1990s and attributed this fact to the reluctance of company directors to change and accept risk. By the mid-1990s, however, Polish organizations and their managers were being forced to embrace change as a result of the increasing influence of environmental forces. Boerner (1998) relates the process of change to increasing societal 'openness' brought about by the political and economic changes. Boerner also notes, however, that increasing 'openness' has brought with it demands for measures which provide a certain degree of stability and security.

With regard to Poland Kostera, Proppé and Szatkowski (Kostera 1995; Kostera, Proppé and Szatkowski 1995) have noted that traditional communist practices (e.g. political lobbying) have persisted and many managers, even though using the discourse of Western management, still behave as if the economic system had not changed. The persistence of such practices and behaviours is by no means restricted to Poland and is a characteristic of managerial behaviour in the region.

Autocracy and hierarchy

Numerous writers have commented on the persistence of autocratic styles of management and strongly hierarchical relationships between superiors and subordinates. Maly and Dedina (1997), writing about the new firms which have emerged in the Czech Republic in the post-communist period, describe how traditional hierarchies have been re-established and top managements are characterized by inflexible attitudes and behaviours. According to Rychetnik (1996) one manifestation of an authoritarian management style has been the tightening of employee discipline within the overall framework of a Taylorist-Fordist approach. The typical Czech manager is described as a 'dominant and superior male' who regards non-managers as 'impractical and lazy people' (Pavlica and Thorpe 1998). Other writers (e.g. Clark and Soulsby 1999) identify a temporal consistency in the paternalism/authoritarianism of Czech management as well as a continuity of the managerial group as evidenced by the dominant presence of former Communist Party members in companies.

Similar observations are made in Romania, where an autocratic style of management is widespread and strict hierarchical relationships between superiors and subordinates prevail. Hierarchy and autocracy appear even stronger in privatized companies than in state-owned enterprises, because managing directors often double as owners and can assert their personal power and authority (Catana and Catana 1996). Accordingly, decision-making is very much top-down, with managers mistrusting their subordinates and demanding exhaustive knowledge of subordinates' activities and strict control (Kelemen 1999). Such a style of management is very much in tune with Romanian culture with its 'careful observance of hierarchical niceties' and 'strong differences of status between superiors and subordinates' (Campbell 2000).

Michailova (1996) also notes that the system change did not transform the traditionally hierarchical and autocratic style of management in Bulgaria. A number of authors (Koparanova 1998; Michailova 1996; Todeva 1996) exemplify the management style by reference to managers' views and use of information. Information was regarded by managers as a source of power and status and was as a consequence monopolized by them. This style of management finds acceptance among employees as it reduces the uncertainty of working in the new business environment. Younger employees, however, aspired to a more consultative and consensual approach, which is some indication that attitudes are evolving (Reeves-Ellington 1998).

Edwards, Polonsky and Polonsky (2000) found that in Russia the introduction of new organizational structures was hampered by the persistence of hierarchical flows of communication. Most communication flows were vertical, with only limited evidence of horizontal exchanges of information between departments. The authors also found that the management style continued to be autocratic and paternalistic, a situation reinforced by a general unwillingness on the part of employees to accept personal responsibility.

Management learning

As a result of the change of economic system in CEE and the FSU, managers experienced an enormous need to acquire new knowledge and skills, because they lacked much of the knowledge and many of the skills needed for successful operation in a market economy. The main deficiencies were in areas such as sales and marketing, strategic management, human resource management and financial management. Throughout the region managers responded to the challenge by attending courses and seminars (both at home and abroad), by periods of exposure to management in foreign companies and by self-tuition (Bőgel, Edwards and Wax 1997; Edwards and Lawrence 1994; Edwards, Polonsky and Polonsky 2000).

This acquisition of new knowledge and skills, however, did not necessarily translate into more effective managerial behaviour and enhanced company performance. There is also evidence of considerable resistance to change. Catana, Catana and Finlay (1999) found in Romania considerable resistance to change and a marked desire to retain the status quo among the senior managers they surveyed. This resistance was fuelled by a number of factors, for example, feelings of incompetence, a general fear of change, the stress of working in the new circumstances and perceived threats to the managers' personal image. Dumitrescu's (1997) study found, however, that there was some evidence of change, notably in companies with foreign ownership, although Romanian managers continued to value knowledge more highly than skills. All in all, throughout CEE and the FSU, even though managers had made considerable strides in equipping themselves for the demands of working in the market economy, they often lacked the experience and conviction for translating learning into practice and continued to resort to modes of behaviour which were redolent more of the former system than the market economy.

Management prerogative

In spite of the reservations expressed in the previous section about the transformation of individuals into market-economy managers, there is little doubt that managers have been among the main beneficiaries of the system change and have been able to assert their so-called 'managerial prerogative'. Under communism managers had to operate within a framework in which decisions were made on a consensual basis with the Party and trades union. The system change tended to destroy the power of the Communist Party and trade unions within the workplace.

The power of managers is further strengthened by the relative lack of separation of ownership and control throughout the region. Managers are often shareholders, senior managers are often majority shareholders. Transformation of state property into private property has on occasions happened quickly and covertly (although not necessarily illegally). With legislation relating to privatization and corporate governance embryonic and evolving, there have been numerous opportunities for directors and managers of former state-owned enterprises to seize the initiative and gain control of new privatized companies. Management buyouts have been particularly prevalent in a number of countries, for instance, Slovakia, where the former communist élite has sought to retain its influence by gaining control of the economic sphere. Within Slovak companies, moreover, managers exert close control over the workforce by using a range of bureaucratic procedures (Letiche 1998). The lack of separation between ownership and control has been described by Martin (1999) as managerial capitalism.

The broader cultural context

The discussion of the issues explored previously can furthermore be broadened to encompass factors of a wider social significance. One such issue is the extent to which the societies of CEE and the FSU can be regarded as predominantly individualist or collectivist (Hofstede 1980), as these factors have considerable implications for the organization and management of work as well as for individuals' attitudes. Societies in the region characterized by individualism include Hungary (Edwards and Lawrence 2000) and Poland (Podgórecki 1993). Hungarians' inclination to individualism has been proposed as one of the underlying drives to carry out economic innovation and change. The Hungarian experience of communism was marked by attempts to implement 'market mechanisms' in the economy from the late 1960s, which encouraged enterprises to pay greater attention to consumer demands, efficiency and the achievement of profits. In the 1980s, moreover, the establishment of

Enterprise Economic Work Partnerships was sanctioned. In practice this permitted employees to set up their own small businesses to carry out subcontracted work for their enterprise (Bőgel, Edwards and Wax 1997).

Podgórecki (1993) stresses the significance of individualism in Poland, dwelling also on the negative manifestations of this factor. Individualism allied to the lack of an entrepreneurial tradition in Polish society (Sikorski 1998) was not in itself a strong basis for economic change after 1989. However, the tradition of individualism did reflect certain cultural resources which could be exploited by individuals wishing to take advantage of the new circumstances and since 1989 a new class of often young entrepreneurs has emerged in Poland.

In many countries of CEE and the FSU, on the other hand, society has been characterized by collectivist modes of behaviour. A quintessential example of a collectivist society is Russia (Smith 1976). The collectivist roots of Russian society were in many respects strengthened by the experience of 75 years of communism. The organization of economic activities since the collapse of communism has continued to reflect these collectivist influences. In their study of Volgograd (Edwards, Polonsky and Polonsky 2000) the authors found that company ownership and control were often in the hands of a closely knit group of family members and friends. Company owners tended furthermore to develop close links with the local administration. Companies were run predominantly on a paternalistic and autocratic basis, with senior managers displaying both a strongly autocratic management style and a feeling of genuine responsibility towards their employees, even though this did not exclude redundancies. The experience of redundancy, however, appeared traumatic for employees and certainly was not relished by employers, and there is some evidence that employers sought to make as few employees as possible redundant.

Collectivism is also typical of social organization in other countries such as Romania and Serbia (Edwards and Lawrence 2000). The change of economic system has promoted economic and social goals and aspirations which are largely of an individualistic nature. Kelemen and Gardiner (1999) identify a tension between traditional collectivist values and the economic criteria introduced since the collapse of communism. Even though economic criteria such as efficiency and profitability have come to the fore, Romanians may feel reluctant to dismiss economically redundant employees and may also feel obliged to find positions for members of their family.

These cultural differences are deep-rooted in the fabric of different societies, extending to influence a wide range of factors, attitudes and behaviours. One of the themes identified in a seven-country study of managers in CEE (Edwards and Lawrence 2000) was differing and disparate attitudes to the relationship between work and leisure. While in some countries, the dividing line between work and leisure is blurred, in other countries, for example Romania (Catana and Catana 1999), a clear distinction is drawn between home and work, reflecting the high regard for communal and family values.

Managers and management typologies

Numerous writers have generalized on the evolution of managerial practice in CEE and the FSU. There is a common consensus that many older managers, brought up and accustomed to working under the former system, found it extremely difficult to change attitudes and behaviours. Many were unable to transform themselves to meet the new circumstances and ceased to work. Others continued to work as if nothing had changed. However, such a generalization obscures the detail of the situation and there is considerable variation between countries. Even though the younger generation has shown itself more adaptable to change and embracing the values of the market economy, by no means all new entrepreneurs have been young. There is considerable evidence of many former Communist Party officials seizing the opportunity of the change of system to gain positions of economic power. Such individuals were often described as 'wrynecks' (or turncoats) in view of their rapid transformation from communists to capitalists (Edwards and Lawrence 1994).

Other authors have attempted more analytical approaches to the changing nature of management. Hoffmann *et al.* (1996) present a typology of Czech managers which comprises four archetypes: manager-entrepreneur, manager-professional, manager-passenger and manager-speculator. Manager-entrepreneurs represent the new driving force of the economy, while manager-professionals provide the knowledge and skills to run organizations effectively and efficiently. Taken together these two archetypes represent positive forces in the transformation process. Manager-passengers and manager-speculators, on the other hand, represent a barrier to a positive outcome to the transformation, either by lack of involvement or by seeking purely personal gain (often illegal or barely legal). As to older managers Hoffmann *et al.* comment that those who remained in employment after 1989 are making a positive contribution (although between a quarter and a third of managers took retirement for various reasons because of the change of system). All in all, the authors express the view that manager-entrepreneurs and manager-professionals are becoming the dominant archetypes in the Czech Republic.

Rogovsky, Grachev and Bertocchi (1997) developed a typology of Russian managers, also with four archetypes which, however, differ from those of Hoffmann *et al.*, so that a straightforward comparison is not possible although the typological differences are in themselves illuminating. The authors identify four archetypes: socialist managers, pragmatic managers, predatory managers and socially responsible managers. Rogovsky, Grachev and Bertocchi's archetypes of pragmatic and predatory managers are similar to Hoffmann *et al.*'s manager-professionals and manager-speculators. The socialist manager archetype reflects the persistence of traditional modes of economic behaviour in Russia, with many managers continuing to work according to the codes of practice of the former system. Socially responsible managers seek to combine economic objectives with social and national goals. In a survey conducted in Moscow in 1993 Rogovsky, Grachev and Bertocchi found that the dominant archetype was that of the predatory manager. Compared to, for example, the Czech Republic, Russian management has undergone less and slower change.

Some countries in CEE also exhibit a considerable degree of resistance to change, with relatively limited evidence of organizational restructuring and individual development (Edwards and Lawrence 2000). Where there is change, it is often in companies with foreign involvement. For example, Dumitrescu (1997) studied managers employed in the Bucharest subsidiaries of foreign corporations and found evidence that, although the traditional business culture was still evident in many respects, the Romanian managers had to adapt their behaviour to meet at least in part the expectations of their foreign employers. Similarly in Bulgaria, Todeva (2000) found only limited change among managers of state-owned enterprises. In privatized companies, on the other hand, managers had begun to display more entrepreneurial attitudes and behaviour.

The evolution of management in CEE and the FSU shows considerable variation between countries in terms of both the rate and nature of change. An explanation based solely on economic criteria would, however, be misleading as there is evidence of differences even between the more advanced economies of CEE. A study of the business élite in the Czech Republic, Hungary and Poland (*ACE Quarterly* 2000) found significant differences between the three countries which were exemplified by different attitudes to accession to the EU. Among the reasons cited for the differences were means of privatization and ownership structures, with foreign capital regarded as a source of introducing new business cultures.

Virtuous and vicious circles: Kraybill and Nolt's model revisited

Kraybill and Nolt's (1995) interactive model of culture and entrepreneurship postulated that socially negotiated outcomes were the result of the interaction of a society's cultural resources and restraints. Moreover, the negotiated outcomes themselves impacted on a society's existing cultural resources and restraints to create a new constellation of resources and restraints (cultural revisions) and consequently a new set of interrelationships. In the context of managerial evolution in CEE and the FSU it is manifest that in the years since the collapse of communism negotiated outcomes have varied considerably between countries. The pace and nature of change in the economic sphere have varied to such an extent that it is not a difficult task to identify winners and losers of the system change.

With specific regard to managers and the management of economic organizations some countries (e.g. the first-wave group of aspirants to EU membership) have made faster progress towards achieving outcomes that reflect a positive transformation from a command to a market economy. Measures such as per capita gross domestic product give eloquent testimony to the continuing divide between the economically more and less successful countries in CEE and the FSU. In terms of the model some countries have used cultural resources and overcome cultural restraints in order to achieve on the whole positive outcomes. These positive outcomes are related to economic restructuring and the establishment of working market institutions. In other countries cultural restraints appear to act as an effective brake on developments. As a consequence the economies of these countries appear to be clinging to the mould of the former system, with limited restructuring and managers continuing to prefer traditional modes of behaviour.

Cultural revisions can have either positive or negative consequences. The emphasis on individual (rather than collective) decision-making and responsibility has the potential to release the individual initiative which was to a large degree stifled by the former system. Many individuals seized upon this individualism to set up new businesses and to manage in a more proactive manner. The change of system in Hungary, for example, encouraged the existing predisposition to individualism and entrepreneurship and stimulated the process of economic transformation. Similar developments took place in Poland which witnessed the emergence of a new class of entrepreneurs. Of course, these domestic cultural resources were enriched by their contact with ideas, practices and also finance from other countries. Significantly, however, these 'imported' ideas and practices found a fertile ground in which to develop, with managers generally keen to acquire new knowledge and skills.

In other countries, however, this new emphasis on individualism manifested itself in various forms of opportunistic behaviour in which individuals sought to enrich themselves and a close circle of family and friends. In many instances members of the former political élite exchanged political power for economic power and were able to achieve their particular economic goals with limited interference from the new political and legal institutions. In such cases the outcomes actually impacted negatively on the transformation process as managers (especially when coterminous with owners of former state-owned enterprises) sought to maintain the status quo to further their own interests. Although not unreceptive to new knowledge and skills, many managers in these countries attempted to persist with traditional modes of management, running their companies as if nothing or little had changed and demonstrating in general considerable resistance to change.

It would be wrong, however, to impute resistance to change solely to the desire of managers to maintain the status quo for purposes of personal enrichment. As mentioned earlier in examples from Bulgaria, Romania and Russia relating to service, sales and marketing, there may be deep-rooted cultural values which inhibit the adoption of certain attitudes and practices which are taken for granted elsewhere.

Such deep-rooted cultural values may be in conflict with the professed values of advanced market economies and create difficulties in relations with foreign investors. Furthermore, such values may be difficult to change, especially in the short term.

Two patterns of managerial evolution thus seem to be emerging in CEE and the FSU. In one set of countries there appears to be a virtuous circle of cultural resources supporting the transformation process, creating negotiated outcomes which in their turn further strengthen the resources of society which support transformation. Cultural restraints may slow down or amend the achievement of outcomes but on the whole resources predominate over restraints.

In another set of countries the reverse is overwhelmingly the case. Cultural resources are often dysfunctional under the new circumstances. Cultural restraints have a powerful influence. As a consequence negotiated outcomes are often unsatisfactory in terms of the transformation process. Furthermore, the cultural revisions engendered by the outcomes often tend to reinforce the cultural restraints. A vicious circle of unsatisfactory outcomes and negative revisions ensue. The only hope that remains is that a new generation of managers will eventually emerge. This hope is not without its foundations. However, it requires the passage of a considerable period of time. In the meantime the populations of these countries remain stuck in a 'valley of tears' (Peng 2000).

Conclusion

Since the collapse of communism managers in CEE and the FSU have had to adapt to a systemic shift in the formal institutional context of managing companies and conducting business. The extent of this adaptation has varied considerably between countries although there is substantial evidence of what Kraybill and Nolt (1995) call signs of modernity (e.g. efficiency, rationality and individualism). The practice of management in some countries is becoming more and more similar to that in Western Europe and North America. Traditional values and attitudes have, however, also shown considerable durability and in other countries a distinctive model of management may be emerging.

Endnote

1 The discussion in this chapter will focus on Russia and the countries in CEE considered part of the former Soviet bloc. For the former Yugoslavia see Edwards (2000) and Edwards and Lawrence (2000).

References

ACE Quarterly (2000) 'The business elite of central Europe', *Ace Quarterly* 15: 6–7.

Balaton, K. (1998) 'The role of management executives in the transformation process in Hungary', in R. Lang (ed.) *Management Executives in the East European Transformation Process*, Munich and Mering: Rainer Hampp Verlag.

Boerner, S. (1998) 'Transformation als Führung in die offene Gesellschaft – Ergebnisse einer empirischen Untersuchung in polnischen Betrieben', in R. Lang (ed.) *Management Executives in the East European Transformation Process*, Munich and Mering: Rainer Hampp Verlag.

Bőgel, G. and Huszty, A. (1999) 'Strategy-making in Hungary', in V. Edwards (ed.) *Proceedings of the Fifth Annual Conference on the Impact of Transformation on Individuals, Organizations, Society*, Chalfont St Giles: CREEB.

Bőgel, G., Edwards, V. and Wax, M. (1997) *Hungary since Communism: The Transformation of Business*, Basingstoke and London: Macmillan.

Campbell, A. (2000) 'Management in Romania', in M. Warner (ed.) *IEBM Regional Encyclopaedia of Business & Management: Management in Europe*, London: Thomson Learning.

Catana, A. and Catana, D. (1999) 'Romanian cultural background and its relevance for cross-cultural management', *Journal for East European Management Studies* 4(3): 252–8.

Catana, D. and Catana, A. (1996) 'Aspects of transformation of corporate cultures in Romania', in R. Lang (ed.) *Wandel von Unternehmenskulturen in Ostdeutschland und Osteuropa*, Munich and Mering: Rainer Hampp Verlag.

Catana, D., Catana, A. and Finlay, J. (1999) 'Managerial resistance to change: Romania's quest for a market economy', *Journal for East European Management Studies* 4(2): 149–64.

Clark, E. and Soulsby, A. (1999) *Organizational Change in Post-Communist Europe, Management and Transformation in the Czech Republic*, London and New York: Routledge.

Dóbak, M. and Tari, E. (1996) 'Evolution of organizational forms in the transition period of Hungary', *Journal for East European Management Studies* 1(2): 7–35.

Dumitrescu, M.-F. (1997) 'Attitudes of Romanian managers towards business, as reflected by the Romanian national culture. A foreign enterprise perspective', unpublished MA dissertation, Chalfont St Giles, Buckinghamshire College of Higher Education/Brunel University.

Edwards, V. (2000) 'Management in the former Yugoslavia', in M. Warner (ed.) *IEBM Regional Encyclopaedia of Business & Manaaement: Management in Europe*, London: Thomson Learning.

Edwards, V. and Lawrence, P. (1994) *Management Change in East Germany*, London: Routledge.

Edwards, V. and Lawrence, P. (2000) *Management in Eastern Europe*, Basingstoke: Palgrave.

Edwards, V., Polonsky, G. and Polonsky, A. (2000) *The Russian Province after Communism, Enterprise Continuity and Change*, Basingstoke and London: Macmillan.

Hoffmann, V., Jirásek, J., Kubr, M. and Pitra, Z. (1996) *Czech Manager in the Process of Transformation*, Prague: National Training Fund.

Hofstede, G. (1980) *Culture's Consequences*, Beverly Hills, CA: Sage.

Holden, N., Cooper, C. and Carr, J. (1998) *Dealing with the New Russia*, Chichester: Wiley.

Kelemen, M. (1999) 'The myth of restructuring: "competent" managers and the transition to a market economy: a Romanian tale', *British Journal of Management* 10: 199–208.

Kelemen, M. and Gardiner, K. (1999) 'Paradoxes of managerial work: the case of Ghana and Romania', in V. Edwards (ed.) *Proceedings of the Fifth Annual Conference on the Impact of Transformation on Individuals, Organizations, Society*, Chalfont St Giles: CREEB.

Kieżun, W. (1991) *Management in Socialist Countries, USSR and Central Europe*, Berlin and New York: De Gruyter.

Koparanova, M. (1998) 'Danone-Serdika JS Co', *East European Economics* 36(4): 27–39.

Kornai, J. (1992). *The Socialist System: The Political Economy of Communism*, Princeton, NJ: Princeton University Press.

Kostera, M. (1995) 'Differing managerial responses to change in Poland', *Organization Studies*, 16(4): 673–97.

Kostera, M., Proppé, M. and Szatkowski, M. (1995) 'Staging the new romantic hero in the old cynical theatre: on managers, roles and change in Poland', *Journal of Organizational Behavior* 16: 631–46.

Kraybill, D. and Nolt, S. (1995) *Amish Enterprise*, Baltimore and London: John Hopkins University Press.

Lascu, D.-N., Ahmed, Z. and Vatasescu, M. (1997) 'Applications of the marketing concept philosophy in Romania', in L. Stan (ed.) *Romania in Transition*, Aldershot: Dartmouth.

Letiche, H. (1998) 'Transition and human resources in Slovakia', *Personnel Review*, 27(3): 213–26.

Liuhto, K. (2001) 'Ex-Soviet enterprises and their managers facing the challenges of the 21st century', *Studies in Industrial Engineering and Management* 12, Lappeenranta: Lappeenranta University of Technology.

Maly, M. and Dedina, J. (1997) 'Veränderungen im Management tschechischer Betriebe', in *Journal for East European Management Studies*, 2(1): 8–21.

Martin, R. (1999) *Transforming Management in Central and Eastern Europe*, Oxford: Oxford University Press.

Michailova, S. (1996) 'Approaching the macro–micro interface in transitional societies: evidence from Bulgaria', *Journal for East European Management Studies* 1(1): 43–70.

Pavlica, K. and Thorpe, R. (1998) 'Managers' perceptions of their identity: a comparative study between the Czech Republic and Britain', *British Journal of Management* 9: 133–49.

Peng, M. (2000) *Business Strategies in Transition Economies*, Thousand Oaks, CA: Sage.

Podgórecki, A. (1993) 'Polish traditions and perspectives of post-socialist reforms', in M. Mayurama (ed.) *Management Reform in Eastern and Central and Eastern Europe: Use of Pre-Communist Cultures*, Aldershot: Dartmouth.

Polonsky, G. and Iviozian, Z. (2000) 'Restructuring of Russian industries – is it really possible?', *Post-Communist Economics* 12(2): 229–40.

Reeves-Ellington, R. (1998) 'Cooperative learning for business change: a Bulgarian example', in V. Edwards (ed.) *Proceedings of the Fourth Annual Conference on Convergence or Divergence: Aspirations and Reality in Central and Eastern Europe and Russia*, Chalfont St Giles: CREEB.

Rogovsky, N., Grachev, M. and Bertocchi, S. (1997) 'Social exclusion and business initiatives in the economies in transition: the case of Russia', *New Partnership for Social Cohesion Working Paper Series* No. 6, Copenhagen: Danish National Institute of Social Research (Socialforskningsinstituttet).

Rożański, J. and Sikorski, A. (1996) 'Polnische Unternehmen und ihre Führungskräfte im kulturellen Wandel zur Zeit der wirtschaftlichen Transformation in Polen', in R. Lang (ed.) *Wandel von Unternehmenskulturen in Ostdeutschland und Osteuropa*, Munich and Mering: Rainer Hampp Verlag.

Rychetnik, L. (1996) 'The management of labour: a way to an economic miracle? The case of medium-sized Czech firms', *Emergo* 3(1): 75–91.

Schneider, S. and Barsoux, J.-L. (1997) *Managing Across Cultures*, Hemel Hempstead: Prentice Hall.

Sikorski, R. (1998) *The Polish House: An Intimate History of Poland*, London: Orion.

Smith, H. (1976) *The Russians*, London: Sphere.

Todeva, E. (1996) 'Dynamics of management practices in Eastern Europe: the case of Bulgaria', *Journal for East European Management Studies* 1(4): 47–63.

Todeva, E. (2000) 'Management in Bulgaria', in M. Warner (ed.) *IEBM Regional Encyclopaedia of Business & Management: Management in Europe*, London: Thomson Learning.

Whitley, R. and Czaban, L. (1998) 'Institutional transformation and enterprise change in an emergent capitalist economy: the case of Hungary', *Organization Studies* 19(2): 259–80.

Chapter 11

Managing in Asia: cross-cultural dimensions[1]

Rosalie L. Tung

Overview

In recent decades, many countries in East Asia have experienced some of the world's highest economic growth rates. Despite the financial crises that erupted among several Asian economies in late 1997, leading to speculations among some about an Asian economic 'meltdown', many believe that the restructuring required to deal with the crises can indeed contribute to further growth in these countries. Investors from the industrialized West continue to express confidence in the economic future of these countries. In order to take advantage of the economic opportunities in this region and to co-operate and compete effectively with East Asians, it is imperative to understand the mindset which lies behind their business dealings. This mindset influences both approaches to competition and co-operation, and the formulation and execution of business strategies.

In general, business people from Japan, Korea, China, Hong Kong and Taiwan tend to draw their inspiration in the formulation and execution of business strategies from several ancient works, widely disseminated and read in East Asia but little known in the West. These works include Sun Tzu's *The Art of War* and Miyamoto Musashi's *The Book of Five Rings*, which are known to some extent in the West, and the lesser-known *The Three Kingdoms* and *The Thirty-Six Stratagems*. A synopsis of each of these four works is presented below.

This chapter examines the important themes which underlie these works and analyses how they affect East Asia's overall approach to business co-operation and the formulation, reformulation and implementation of general business strategies.

Sources of East Asian strategy

The Art of War

The Art of War (or *Bingfa*) was purportedly written by Sun Tzu (also spelt Sun Zi), a Chinese military strategist who lived some 2500 years ago. Sun Tzu identified six major components to success in military warfare. These are (1) the moral cause, (2) leadership, (3) temporal conditions, including the four seasons and the changes in weather, wind and tidal conditions, (4) the terrain, (5) organization and discipline and (6) use of espionage.

The Book of Five Rings

Miyamoto Musashi, a samurai in the late sixteenth to early seventeenth century, purportedly wrote a book entitled *The Book of Five Rings*. In his later life, Musashi became a devoted student of Zen philosophy and sought to unravel the relationship between swordsmanship and Zen. Zen is not a religion in the Judaeo-Christian tradition; rather it is a way of life. In the book, Musashi contemplates his path of enlightenment and identifies several major tenets to success: (1) to grasp relationships between matters and to view situations from multiple perspectives, (2) to seek knowledge and information, (3) to be patient, (4) to train and discipline oneself, (5) to disguise one's emotions and true intentions, (6) to possess flexibility, (7) to use diversion as an attack strategy, (8) to divide and conquer and (9) to assess the terrain.

The Three Kingdoms

The Three Kingdoms (or *Romance of the Three Kingdoms*) was written by fourteenth-century Chinese novelist, Lo Kuan-chung. It is a semi-fictional historical account of the struggle for power among the leaders of three fiefdoms for the control of China after the collapse of the Han dynasty (206 BC–AD 220), China's longest-running and mightiest dynasty. The novel details the intrigues, strategies, ploys and alliances used by the leaders of these three kingdoms and their advisers to gain control over China.

The Thirty-Six Stratagems

The Thirty-Six Stratagems is based on principles contained in *The Book of Changes* (or *I Ching*) and military strategies contained in 24 volumes of Chinese historical chronicles and literary classics, including *The Three Kingdoms*. Each stratagem has widespread applicability in military and non-military settings, including business and interpersonal relationships.

Principles guiding the East Asian approach to business

Based on a comprehensive analysis of these significant writings, there appear to be 12 common themes or principles which underlie the knowledge advanced in these collective works. They are listed in detail below.

The importance of strategies

According to Sun Tzu, the highest form of victory is to conquer by strategy. To wage a protracted war against one's adversaries, even if it culminates in a final victory, is costly and inefficient, whereas a brilliantly conceived strategy that can accomplish the same objective is both swift and efficient. From the East Asian perspective, there is a hierarchical ordering of preferred methods (from most to least desired) to gain the upper hand in any type of confrontation:

1 The formulation of a brilliant strategy to deal a swift and fatal blow to one's adversary/competitor.
2 Resorting to diplomatic means (such as negotiations, mutual discussions and intermediaries) to resolve a confrontation.
3 Resorting to non-diplomatic means (such as open warfare or litigation) to resolve a confrontation.
4 Besieging a fortified city, that is, to wage war against a well-established opponent.

The significance assigned to strategy formulation has resulted in the East Asian disposition to engage in 'mind games', that is, to ferret out the hidden message in any type of communication (written, verbal or silent) and, subsequently, to formulate a strategy to counteract the perceived message sent by the other party. In the West, there is usually a negative connotation associated with 'game playing'. In China and East Asia, by contrast, game playing is considered to be an asset. Consequently, Westerners who seek to do business with East Asians have to be aware of this tendency and should try to fathom the hidden message or meaning associated with certain actions by their East Asian partners.

Transforming an adversary's strength into weakness

Sun Tzu's *Bingfa* calls for exhausting one's opponent through false alarms so that when it comes time for the real battle, they will be drained. This is the stratagem of 'relax while the enemy exhausts himself'. Several other stratagems also address this theme. One of these stratagems was entitled 'chain together the enemy's warships'. In *The Three Kingdoms*, two opposing armies were preparing for a battle on water. The troops from the fiefdom in the north were far stronger but were prone to motion sickness. At the advice of their strategist, the warships in their fleet were chained together to provide greater stability. The opposing side, however, took advantage of this situation and changes in wind directions (temporal conditions) and set the warships on fire. The chains, while providing greater stability against the tide and wind (therefore, a strength), became a liability because it was difficult to disengage the ships in the fleet once a vessel caught fire.

Of course, transforming an adversary/competitor's strength into a weakness can also be used in reverse, namely, to transform one's own weakness into a strength. For example, from the ruins of the Second World War, Japan was able to rebuild the country by importing technology from the West, and thus leapfrog the process of technological development, to establish a modern industrial base from which it could compete with the USA.

The moral of this principle is that one should not be complacent about one's strength nor abject over one's liabilities since fortunes or misfortunes can be reversed. East Asian philosophy believes that all events occur in cyclical patterns, whereas the West tends to perceive matters in discrete phases. The themes of non-complacency, reversal of fortunes, saving over spending and contradictions pervade the East Asian approach to business and are echoed through the other principles discussed below.

Engaging in deception to gain a strategic advantage

Many of the stratagems entail the use of some deceptive tactics or devices, such as creating an illusion that an attack will be launched from the east when the real offensive is to occur from the west, and pretending to be greater than one really is or have more than one really has, as exemplified by the stratagem 'deck the tree with bogus blossoms'.

In the West, because of the Judaeo-Christian influence, deception is considered as immoral and wrong. In East Asia, however, where there is no indigenous religion akin to Judaism or Christianity, deception has a neutral connotation, and should be engaged in if it brings about a greater good. From the East Asian perspective, the 'greater good' embraces the nation state, the clan (that is, geographic region from which one's ancestors originate), the extended family, the nucleus family, the corporation for which one works and oneself. The hierarchical ordering of the aforementioned entities, in terms of importance, do vary across East Asian countries, however.

Three stratagems, 'pretend to be a pig in order to eat the tiger', 'play dumb while remaining smart', and 'inflict injury on oneself to win the enemy's trust', have specific implications for Westerners who seek to do business in East Asia. All three stratagems call for the aggressor to play the fool, including self-infliction of physical injury, so that the other party can become complacent. Through arrogance and complacency, when the opponent lets his guard down, the aggressor can launch an attack and thus emerge victorious.

Understanding contradictions

A principal tenet of Taoism, a major school of thought in China with worldwide followers, is the *yin/yang* principle which, on the one hand, emphasizes the contradictions and opposites inherent in all matters, and, on the other, stresses the unity of opposites. *Yin* represents the passive, negative, dark and female elements; *yang* represents the active, positive, bright and male elements. While opposites, *yin* and *yang* must coexist before there can be life, and in order for life to continue. Following the principles of contradiction and duality, a perceived weakness can become a strength and vice versa.

An understanding of the contradictions and duality inherent in all matters can thus be put to one's advantage. An illustration of this principle is the oak tree versus a blade of grass. An oak tree is strong and mighty while a blade of grass is small and fragile. However, in a storm, the oak tree may collapse under the force of the wind, whereas the blade of grass can yield to the blowing wind and hence stand firm under such adverse conditions.

Compromise

Confucius preached the importance of moderation in all undertakings, and Musashi advocated the adoption of a 'middle-of-the-road' attitude. In other words, East Asian philosophy is guided by the premise that in order to attain the desired outcome, one has to compromise. At least three of the 36 stratagems call for the need for compromise and for baiting one's opponent with a small gain in order to obtain a greater prize. Consequently, gift-giving, lavish entertainment and the use of bribes to facilitate a desired outcome are common practice in East Asian societies.

Striving for total victory

While emphasizing compromise, East Asian philosophy also stresses the need to strive for total victory. Two of the 36 stratagems address this principle. 'Shut the door to catch the thief' and 'pull the ladder after the ascent' are strategies to cut off all escape routes for one's opponents/competitors so that they cannot regain strength and thus resurface as a threat in the future.

There are two important implications associated with this principle. First, do not be complacent or careless during good times and, second, think about the long-term consequences/implications of one's actions.

Taking advantage of misfortunes of an adversary/competitor

Since East Asians believe that fortunes and misfortunes occur in cyclical patterns, one should make the best use of what one has for the moment. Consequently, if an adversary/competitor is down, try to seize that opportunity to eliminate the former altogether, so that they cannot be a potential threat at a later time.

East Asian philosophy essentially espouses a pragmatic approach to life. The Chinese, in particular. emphasize pragmatism more than their counterparts in Japan and Korea. This Chinese emphasis on pragmatisim has led to the formulation of the last, but considered by many to be the most important, of the 36 strategems: 'run away'. When faced with imminent defeat, the Chinese believe it is best to escape from the situation rather than commit suicide or be killed. With escape, there is always a chance of regaining one's strength and position. The Japanese, however, believe that to face death is the brave thing to do. Some people have attributed this difference in attitude between the Chinese and Japanese to the size (land mass) and natural resource endowment of the respective countries. In the case of China, the extensive land mass and vast natural resources have led its people to believe that there is always the opportunity of escape and regaining strength: hence, escape is preferred. In the case of Japan, however, the limited land mass and absence of natural resources have fostered a mentality among its people that since there is no escape, death is preferred.

Flexibility

According to Sun Tzu, one must 'know when to fight and when not to fight . . . . The laws of military operations are like water . . . . Consequently, just as water ceaselessly changes its flow, there are no constant methods of directing military operations'. In other words, it is important to maintain flexibility and adapt to changing conditions and fortunes.

This emphasis on flexibility accounts, in part, for the East Asian perspective of written legal contracts as organic documents which can be altered as the circumstances change.

Gathering intelligence and information

Both Sun Tzu and Miyamoto Musashi strongly emphasized the importance of gathering information and intelligence about one's opponents/competitors in order to gain the upper hand in a confrontation. Such information can be obtained through a variety of sources, including the use of spies. In the business context, industrial espionage has become common practice. Other means of information gathering include entering into alliances with local partners, and the employment of local nationals. The principle of gathering intelligence also involves the intentional spreading of erroneous information to one's opponents/competitors to contaminate their plans and foil their decision-making efforts.

In the East Asian context, knowledge entails not only the gathering of technical information but also intelligence about the key players. An accurate assessment about human nature can only be made after an extended period of time, however. Consequently, a lot of attention is directed towards developing relationships with business counterparts to discover their true intentions.

Grasping the interdependent relationships among matters/situations

The *yin/yang* principle outlined earlier emphasizes the duality and contradictions inherent in all matters. Since such duality and contradictions may not always be apparent, it is important to try to unravel such relationships so that they can be put to good use. The use of spiral and non-linear logic is common in East Asia.

Patience

Experienced Westerners who have had successful dealings in East Asia will readily concede that patience is a major requisite to success in conducting business in that region of the world. Several factors have accounted for the relatively slow pace at which actions occur in East Asia. First, the East Asians like to focus on the long-term implications of actions. Second, they assign importance to developing and nurturing human relationships. Finally, they believe that everything occurs in cyclical patterns. Hence, one should wait for the opportune time.

Avoiding strong emotions

Confucius cautioned against taking extreme positions on all matters. Sun Tzu warned that a military commander should never fly into a rage. Since strong emotions can confuse or distort logical thinking and action, this principle can be used against one's opponents/competitors to bring about their downfall. Two stratagems specifically address this principle. The first is entitled 'provoke strong emotions', and the second 'use a woman to ensnare a man', which explains why women and other forms of sensual entertainment are used often in Japan and Korea to enhance the chances of attaining desired outcome in business transactions.

Again, there are differences across countries as far as public display of emotions are concerned. In Japan, for example, it is considered to be bad form for a widow to cry incessantly during her husband's funeral, whereas in Korea, the converse would be true if a person did not cry loudly at even a distant cousin's funeral.

Conclusion

These 12 underlying themes identified and briefly explained here can be manifested in munificent ways. Each can be used in isolation, in the reverse, and/or combined with one or several others to produce an almost infinite array of stratagems.

While business people from Japan, Korea, China, Hong Kong and Taiwan may derive their inspiration from a common source, there can be important differences in how these are interpreted and applied in specific situations. Reference was made to two of these differences: escape versus death and public display of emotions. These cross-country differences are further compounded by foreign religious influences, education at universities abroad, overseas travel and social and business contacts with foreigners. Consequently, while it is erroneous to assume that East Asians are just like Westerners, it is equally fallacious to stereotype them as a homogeneous group.

Endnote

1 This is an abridged version of R.L. Tung (1994) 'Strategic management thought in east Asia', *Organizational Dynamics* Spring: 55–65. Reprinted with permission.

Further reading

Chan, M.W.L. and Chen, B.F. (1989) *Sunzi on the Art of War and its General Application to Business*, Shanghai: Fudan University Press.

Chu, C.N. (1988) *The Chinese Mind Game*, Beaverton, OR: AMC.

Hall, E.T. and Hall, M.R. (1987) *Hidden Differences: Doing Business with the Japanese*, Garden City, NY: Anchor Press.

Kang, T.W. (1989) *Is Korea the Next Japan?*, New York: Free Press.

Lasserre, P. and Schutte, H. (1999) *Strategies for Asia Pacific: Beyond the Crisis*, London: Macmillan Business Press.

Luo, Y. (1999) *Entry and Cooperative Strategies in International Business Expansion*, Westport, CT: Quorum.

Seligman, S. (1999) '*Guanxi*: grease for the wheels of China', *China Business Review* 26(5): 34–8.

Tung, R.L. (1991) 'Handshakes across the sea: cross-cultural negotiating for business success', *Organizational Dynamics* 14(3): 30–40.

Yeung, I.Y.M. and Tung, R.L. (1996) 'Achieving business success in Confucian societies: the impact of *guanxi* connections', *Organizational Dynamics* 24(3): 54–65.

Yuan, G. (1991) *Lure the Tiger out of the Mountains: The Thirty-Six Stratagems of Ancient China*, New York: Simon & Schuster.

Chapter 12

A mirror-image world: doing business in Asia

Charles M. Hampden-Turner and Fons Trompenaars

Introduction

Approaches to values and to moral reasoning differ markedly among nations: (Hofstede 1980; Hall 1976). The view taken here is that while virtually all members of the human race engaged in enterprise face the same problems or dilemmas, their responses to these vary widely (Hampden-Turner 1994).

All human beings have a logical, sense-making view of the world which works for them, after a fashion. In the case of Singapore or Taiwan it obviously works *very* well in certain fields, while remaining strange to westerners. In the case of China, it has resulted in 8.0–10.0 per cent annual growth rate averaged over two decades. That happens to be faster than any nation has *ever* grown in the history of capitalism.

In the industrial revolution in Britain and North America, GNP annual growth rarely topped 3 per cent. Around 0.5 per cent to 1.0 per cent was the norm (Dobbs 1951). The rest of the world was not growing at all and the technologies had to be pioneered which the Chinese have only to borrow. Nevertheless, 9 per cent growth per annum for 1.2 billion people is going to change everything. The centre of gravity for world economic development is going to swing decisively eastwards. That a country still officially communist has beaten all capitalist growth records is, to say the least, ironic. Despite East Asia's recent financial crisis growth rates are once again impressive, with the exception of Japan's long recession and Indonesia's political turmoil.

Dilemma methodology

Our methodology (Trompenaars and Hampden-Turner 1997; Hampden-Turner and Trompenaars 1994) assumes that everyone in the world is alike in certain key respects, but are almost opposite and mirror images in other respects. For example, books published in East Asian languages start at what is for us, 'the back' and end at 'the beginning'. Instead of eyes scanning left to right like Westerners, their eyes scan right to left. It is as if we held a mirror up to our culture and saw a looking-glass world beyond. We are all alike in the fact that we face key dilemmas. All of us have to reconcile communities with individuals, rules with exceptions, wholes with atoms or parts, ideas within us with developments outside us, time passing with timeliness, equality with hierarchy. Conflicts between these elements constitute dilemmas and dilemmas are as old as recorded civilization. We encounter dilemma in The Garden of Eden and on the road to Thebes when Oedipus confronted the riddle of the Sphinx. Those who cannot solve riddles and dilemmas may be destroyed by them. Cultures try to pass on the answers to future generations and where they cannot, they pass on the problem for future generations to ponder, as in Herman Melville. Sphinx would eat you if you could not solve the riddle, much as people who cannot solve dilemmas are destroyed today. But where people of the world differ is in the horn of the dilemma with which they start the work of reconciliation. Some cultures put the individual before the community. They argue, for example, that if each person were taken care of, the good society would follow. Some cultures put the community before the individual. If the community is taken care of, then individuals will find their fulfilment and happiness in this responsibility. So cultures are very different, indeed they are opposite, in the priorities they set. Yet we are all united by the same issues. Somehow, some way individuals must be joined to their community. We seek the same ends; we employ different means.

The meaning of culture

Culture means 'to work upon'. Hence agriculture works upon crops; horticulture works upon plants; aquaculture works upon the water; culture works upon human environments. Cultures say 'the rule comes before the exception' or vice versa. Cultures are not right or wrong, they simply have orientations to issues. They say 'this is the way you set about to solve this problem ...' Why must they agree on this? Because there would be chaos unless they did so. Everyone must stop at red lights and go on at green ones. If half the population had a different preference, driving would be a lot more hazardous than it is already. Similarly, if half the population was taught to be selfish and half unselfish, the first half would exploit the second half and there would be furious recrimination. You have to 'work upon' your environment in similar ways if civic order is to be maintained; expectations must be shared.

Seven cultural bifurification

Trompenaars and Hampden-Turner (1997) identified seven important dimensions on which cultures disagree. Faced with an existential question or basic dilemma of being, they go opposite ways. The seven dilemmas are as follows:

Universalism vs. particularism
When no code, rule or law seems to quite cover an exceptional case, should the most relevant rule be imposed, however imperfectly, on that case, or should the case be considered on its unique merits, regardless of the rule? At stake here is the relative salience of *rules* (universal) or *exceptions* (particulars).

Analysed specifics vs. integrated wholes
Are we more effective as managers when we analyse phenomena into *specifics*, i.e. parts, facts, targets, tasks, numbers, units, points, or when we integrate and configure such details into diffuse patterns, relationships and wider contexts? At stake here is the relative salience of *analysed* specifics vs. *integrated wholes*.

Individualism vs. communitarianism
Is it more important to focus upon the enhancement of each individual, his or her rights, motivations, rewards, capacities, attitudes, or should more attention be paid to the advancement of the corporation as a community, which all its members are pledged to serve?

Inner-directed vs. outer-directed orientation

Which are the more important guides to action, our inner-directed judgements, decisions and commitments, or the signals, demands and trends in the outside world to which we must adjust? At stake here is whether virtue and right direction is located *within* us or *outside* us.

Time as sequence vs. time as synchronization

Is it more important to do things fast, in the shortest possible sequence of passing time, or to synchronize all efforts, just-in-time, so that completion is co-ordinated? At stake is *time-as-a-race* vs. *time-as-a-dance*.

Achieved status vs. ascribed

Should the status of employees depend on what they have achieved and how they have performed, or on some other characteristic important to the corporation, i.e. age, seniority, gender, education, potential, strategic role? At stake is *judging by results* vs. *a priori judgements*.

Equality vs. hierarchy

Is it more important that we treat employees as equals so as to elicit from them the best they have to give, or to emphasize the judgement and authority of the hierarchy that is coaching and evaluating them? At stake is the *equality of process* vs. *the authority of judging and sponsoring* the contest itself.

To say that cultures 'differ' on the relative importance of these values is an understatement: often such issues are loaded with ideological fervour. How often have we heard colleagues call for more 'law and order' (universalism) and less indulgence towards suspected wrongdoers (particularism). Some managers demand 'the facts' and 'the bottom line' (analysis) and regard all attempts to put these into context (integration) as mere window dressing. If there are problems in the organization, they look for specific persons or 'troublemakers' to blame (individualism) for a 'rotten apple in the barrel'. In their view, there is nothing wrong with the organization (communitarianism) that cannot be cured by 'kicking asses and taking names'.

Everyone should be a 'self-starter' (inner-directed) and must beware of 'group think' and running with the herd (outer-directed). Employees must realize that 'time is money' and efficiency the key (sequential time). Workers must get on with the job and not talk all the time (synchronize their efforts). For ten years our manager has been 'busting his gut' to succeed in a job he was given (status by achievement) but now some wise guy has 'moved the goal posts' (altered the kinds of work to which status is ascribed). All he ever wanted was 'an even break' (equality) but the people 'up there' (hierarchy) were not interested.

We can see from these examples that values clash, misunderstandings are rife and getting values to harmonize in ways that create wealth is not an easy task. Foreigners are seen as subversive of what we believe in. Let us take these dilemmas one by one.

Universalism vs. particularism

How can we measure the relative enthusiasm a culture has for making rules (universalism) vs. discovering exceptions (particularism). Our methodology consists of dilemmas. Here is one:

The mirror image complementarity of Western and East Asian values is illustrated in Figure 12.1, although the looking-glass writing makes it awkward to read. UNiversalisim—PArticularism (dimension 1) has been reversed, as has INdividualism—COmmunitarianism (dimension 3) and SPecific analysis—DIffuse holism (dimension 2). The values have had their priorities reversed, yet the essential complementarity remains. Let us now turn to measurement.

Figure 12.1: **Culture as a mirror image**

You are riding in a car driven by a close friend. He hits a pedestrian. You know he was going at least 35 miles per hour in an area of the city where the maximum allowed speed is 20 miles per hour. There are no witnesses. His lawyer says that if you testify under oath that he was only driving 20 miles per hour it may save him from serious consequences. What right has your friend to expect you to protect him?

(a) My friend has a definite right as a friend to expect me to testify to the lower figure.
(b) He has some right as a friend to expect me to testify to the lower figure.
(c) He has no right as a friend to expect me to testify to the lower figure.

Here is how the different nations scored:

Table 12.1: **Responses to Question 1**

Univeralism 'no right'										... Particularism 'some or definite right'	
CAN	USA	GER	UK	NL	FRA	JP	SIN	THAI	HK	CHI	SK
96	95	90	90	88	68	67	67	63	56	48	26

Why does Canada, and for that matter America, score so consistently high in Universalism? One reason is that they all share a British heritage in which the rule of law looms large, but in addition to this they are all *immigrant nations*, which causes them to score even higher than the UK. Why should immigration matter? Because under immigration *you have to teach new rules to adults*. You cannot rely on nearly everyone having been taught what is right at their mother's knee, and 'mother's knee' is probably the chief source of particularism. You cherish those with whom you have special relationships, wives, children, husbands, relations, friends (Lipset 1974).

There is also a consistent Protestant background to nations high in universalism. The Protestants believed that the written word of God in the newly-translated bible was the universal code all people should live by. Catholics offered you many special relationships with the saints of your choice. Note the sizeable jump from Protestant Netherlands to Catholic France although both countries are contiguous geographically. The Roman Catholic confessional in which your particular relationship with the priest is secret, cannot easily be generalized from. The six Asian countries in Table 12.1 – Japan, Singapore, Hong Kong, China, Thailand and South Korea – are, on the whole, even more particularistic, The USA and Canada are consistently the more universalistic cultures on earth (Bellah 1985).

Or consider another question:

You are a doctor for an insurance company. You examine a close friend who needs more insurance. You find that he is in pretty good shape, but you are doubtful on one or two minor points which are difficult to diagnose. What right does your friend have to expect you to shade the doubts in his favour?

A   My friend would have a definite right as a friend to expect me to shade the doubts in his favour.
B   He would have some right as a friend to expect me to shade the doubts in his favour.
C   He would have no right as a friend to expect me to shade the doubts in his favour.

Here is how the different nations answered to Choice C:

Table 12.2: **Responses to Question 2**

CAN	UK	US	FR	NL	GER	JP	SIN	CHI	IDO	HK	SK
79	70	69	62	59	59	54	52	48	48	42	24

Or consider a third dilemma:

You have just come from a secret meeting of the board of directors of a company. You have a close friend who will be ruined unless he can get out of the market before the board's decision becomes known. You happen to be having dinner at the friend's home this evening. What right does your friend have to expect you to tip him off?

A   He has a definite right as a friend to expect me to tip him off.
B   He has some right as a friend to expect me to tip him off.
C   He has no right as a friend to expect me to tip him off.

Here is how the different nations scored on Choice C:

Table 12.3: **Responses to Question 3**

JP	CAN	US	GER	UK	NL	THAI	FR	CHI	HK	SIN	SK
87	84	83	66	65	62	56	56	53	47	43	31

Consider the implications for a life insurance industry seeking to expand into SE Asia?

The first implication is that 'the letter of the law', the requirement that the insured and his/her doctor follow universal rules of truthful witness in making out the application form, is not going to stir up much enthusiasm in SE Asia. In reality, 74 per cent of South Koreans would perjure themselves in a court of law to help their best friend; 52 per cent of mainland Chinese would do so; 58 per cent of the managers in Hong Kong, and we are speaking of the *middle class*, would side with their friend, were they a doctor, examining a patient under contract to an insurer. These are not legal-rational cultures. Just as they have difficulties with the idea of 'human rights' as an abstract Western concept, so they have difficulties with putting abstract codes ahead of living people all together.

If a person cannot help his/her best friend, what is law worth? Your friend pleads with you. You put an abstract principle ahead of your friend, and it is not just SE Asia. It is much of Latin Europe. In our sample, we had a French female executive from Air France. She waved her hand – 'What happened to the pedestrian?' she wanted to know. 'The pedestrian died . . .' we said, '. . . does it matter?' 'Of course it matters!' she said. 'If the pedestrian died I would side with my friend! After all, what can I do for the pedestrian now?' And she had a good point. Only universalists laugh; to a particularist, there are particular people to be helped.

Does this mean that essentially SE Asians, not to mention the French, have no morals to speak of? Not at all. Their moral view is simply different. The particular relationship, in these cases friendship, are seen as stronger in their obligations, than are rules. Confucius, for example, said: 'the son must hide the father's crime. The father must lean towards his son's advantage.' It is clear from this passage that particularism is strongly to be preferred for children and is to be given moderate priority by parents in matters involving their children.

In 1980, attempts by the government to insure bicycles in China had to be abandoned in the face of floods of claims, all with police certificates attached. As of last year you could insure yourself against AIDS for three years, for 90 yen, roughly US$12. In order to make insurance work in most of SE Asia, friends must sell to friends and false information of false claims must be detectable by the friendship network and must be inconsistent with the maintenance of that friendship network. If claims are subtracted from premiums in every friendship network, so that the seller and the claimant, although strongly related, have an opposite balance of interests, then Asian particularisms will balance out as a bargain.

We have to realize that for these cultures, laws are not unimportant, but they originate in friendship. We must therefore design the system so that friendship, *not* abstract principle, monitors and controls the process. Do not assume that third parties, like doctors, will be neutral. The doctor must be a friend of the local agent or representatives, or he may sign up people after their cancer has been diagnosed. Readers may feel we are libelling particularist cultures, but this is not so. In our view, rules are breaking down in the West on a massive scale because the particular relationships within the family are breaking down. Law and order must be supported by the networks of friendship and family in a culture. The Chinese concept of *guanxi*, 'bond between people' and the Japanese advocacy of *'wan'* or harmony in relationships are values that underpin morality and will, in most cases, support the law of the land as well (see chapter 11). These and 'the spirit of the law' and laws may not survive their absence. Perhaps the clue to understanding Universalism vs. Particularism is to see that they are interdependent views upon the human condition. You can only make better rules if you heed all exceptions. You only appreciate unique exceptions if you are aware of the rules. Each potentially enhances the other so:

The spiral (Figure 12.2) illustrates the concept that people generalize from fortunate experiences during socialization and derive from these particular experiences universal legal and moral principals (see Hampden-Turner 1994).

Analysed specifics vs. integrated wholes

Here the question is what a culture does when faced with a complex phenomenon. Should we immediately analyse it to specific 'points' or atoms, making 'bullet statements', or should we search for the pattern and structure that integrates the whole?

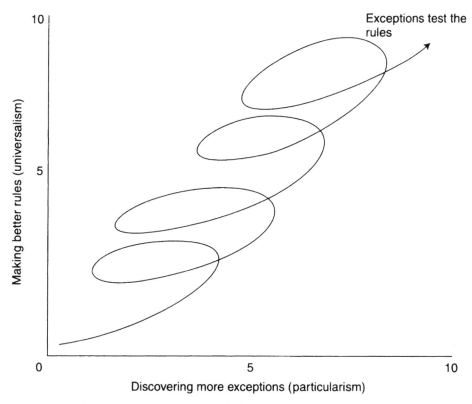

Figure 12.2: **Universalism versus particularism**

Consider, for example, the definition of 'a good manager':

A   Some argue that a good manager is a person who gets the job done. He takes care of the information, people and equipment needed for the execution of the tasks. He leaves his subordinates free to do their part of the job and intervenes only if necessary.

B   Others argue that a good manager is a person who gets his group of subordinates working well together. He knows the right answer to most of the questions arising at work. He guides his subordinates continuously and helps them solve various problems, ranging from work-related problems. He is a kind of father.

Question:
Which one of these two descriptions do you think best represents a good manager, A or B?

This question poses a choice between a set of discrete and specific entities, 'gets the job done', 'takes care of people', 'provided information and equipment', 'lets the subordinates do their parts'. All these are specific units or atoms.

The alternative description, however, is irreducible to parts, 'gets subordinates working well together', 'guides subordinates continuously and helps them solve various problems'. Finally a familial metaphor is used. It all speaks of wholeness and integration. Various cultures scored as follows on endorsing A – 'gets on with the job'.

Table 12.4: **Responses to Question 4**

CAN	FRA	GER	USA	NL	UK	JP	THAI	MAL	CHI	HK	SIN
95	89	87	85	81	78	69	67	63	57	45	38

Here we see that Asian countries Japan, Thailand, Malaysia, China, Hong Kong and Singapore all tend toward the holistic end.

Or consider a second dilemma:

A meeting is called to take a decision about the dismissal of an employee. He has worked 15 years for the company and performed his job in a satisfactory way. For various reasons last year, the results of his work dropped to an unsatisfactory level. There are no reasons to believe that this situation will improve.

The members of the meeting are divided into two parties and come up with the following arguments:

A One part of the group says that the job performance should remain the criterion for the dismissal, regardless of the age of the person and his previous record.

B The other part of the group argued that one cannot disregard the 15 years the employee has been working for the company. One has to take into account the company's responsibility for his life.

Question:

Which one of these two ways of reasoning do you think is usually best in these cases, A or B?

Here we have a choice of narrowing down the discussion to a specific, a single indisputable fact, the employee's work is unsatisfactory, as of now. He is not fulfilling his contract. He is not doing a good job.

Is this the only consideration or must we look at it in context? What about his 15 years with the company, the effect on the morale of other employees, management's responsibility for not supervising him better – does none of this matter? A lot of clarity and precision comes to our thinking, only by excluding several considerations. Here is how the various cultures scored on Choice A:

Table 12.5: **Responses to Question 5**

CAN	USA	CHI	HK	UK	THAI	JP	GER	NL	FRA	SIN	IND
59	52	48	47	41	38	37	37	36	28	20	13

Here China scores remarkably high. Perhaps the recent legal changes modifying lifetime employment in Warner (1999) give us a clue.

A major element of specific vs. diffuse thinking is the number of mental divisions you make. The Dutch feel they can criticize your work as 'crazy' and this does not insult you. The Italians stormed out of a meeting with Dutch engineers because to call the work of Italian designers crazy is to insult the designers. Their work and their persons are an indivisible whole. Is your boss in charge of your work life only, or is he your boss in all things? Some cultures have a diffuse sense of authority, some a narrow, specific sense of authority (see chapter 8).

When, for example, one is invited to speak at a North American University one can be 'Professor' at the lectern, but Charles in the bar, or worse Chuck or Chuckles at a late night drink, or down at the bowling alley, 'Hey buddy, get outa the way'! In France, Monsieur Le Directeur carries his status with him even in his bathing trunks. In Germany, a wife would be 'Frau Professor' even in the supermarket. Your status spreads around you like ripples in a pond.

We posed the following dilemma to pick up this aspect of specific diffuse:

A boss asks a subordinate to help him paint his house. The subordinate, who did not feel like doing it, discusses the issue with a colleague:

A The colleague argues: 'You don't have to paint if you don't feel like it. He is your boss in the company. Outside the company he has little authority'.

B   The subordinate argues: 'Despite the fact that I don't feel like it, I will paint anyway. He is my boss, and you cannot ignore it outside your work either'.

Question:
Which of the two arguments do you think is usually best in these cases, A or B? The scores were as follows for Choice A:

Table 12.6: **Responses to Question 6**

Refuse to paint

NL	FRA	UK	GER	CAN	JP	HK	MAL	THAI	SIN	IDO	CHI
93	93	93	89	84	83	66	64	60	56	48	28

We see China at the most diffuse end on this issue. Around 72 per cent would paint their boss's house at the weekend even when they didn't want to. We asked several of my Chinese friends why this was. Curiously it has to do with learning which spreads out through diffuse relationships. The maxim is: If a person is your teacher for even one day, he is a lifetime father'. Just as your boss's teaching spreads through your whole life, so must his influence.

Perils of negotiating

Regarding parts or wholes as the starting point occasions massive misunderstandings. When Americans or the British go abroad they tend to 'get to the point'. They say 'Here is my proposition', 'This is the deal', 'Here is my product', 'Let's get down to brass tacks', 'Don't beat about the bush'. We do this to save time and to zero in on 'the target'. After all, there are hundreds of people whom it would be nice to have tea with, but only one or two are likely to do a deal with us. It makes sense therefore to get to know the person *after* we have talked turkey to him or her. That's common sense surely? Here are the two styles:

The Anglo-Saxons tend to start in the middle of the spiral on the left and then to circle from specific to more general. The Japanese, Asians generally, but also Southern Europeans and in the American Deep South, there is a tendency to start at the outside of the spiral on the right, talk all around the point for several minutes or even hours and get to the point at the end.

Is this all time-wasting nonsense? Not if you think that the real scarcity is good relationships as opposed to tempting propositions; if you hope that this relationship can last two decades at least; if your biggest nightmare is a relationship that fails five years from now after you have poured your time and money into it. After all, it is easy for A to con B about a profitable deal. It is virtually impossible for A to con B about a broad-ranging discussion that touches on mutual friends and mutual tastes,

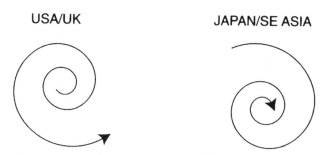

USA/UK   JAPAN/SE ASIA

Figure 12.3: **Circling round or getting straight to the point**

so the Japanese find that it saves them time and money to simulate, early on, all the variations a durable relationship is likely to encounter. *All cultures are logical.* They simply start from different premises.

Westerners often have difficulty in SE Asia with the idea of contracts. For most of us in the West a contract is what it says, no more, no less. If you don't read the small print the judge will. But in much of SE Asia the general intention of the parties and the fund of goodwill they have for each other is the prime consideration. If circumstances change, they will expect their insurance cover or pension fund to change along with their lives. We are beginning to do this in the West, but these are small departures from the idea of fixity. The Chinese don't have the notion of fixity to begin with. The *Tao*, the *Yin* and *Yang* are eternally ebbing and flowing like the tide – we accommodate each other.

A few years ago the Japanese got into a dispute with Australian sugar exporters. When the world price of sugar fell by $10 the Japanese asked to renegotiate. Was not mutuality the main thing? For the Australians the contract said it all. Get a better lawyer next time! The 'small print' in our contracts is not decisive for most SE Asians. The Chinese way is to get a local wise person to arbitrate, to try and settle disputes amicably and keep the relationship. This can only work if the company's interests are represented at local level. One reason Confucianism is so popular today in China is that Mao tried to suppress it. He failed. The universal communist system with its specific codes could not prevail against the ever shifting tides of personal relationships. As Confucius said: 'If your friend gives you a peach, you give him a plum'. In other words, give him something different, particularly personal, not specified in advance.

An observation of the Japanese is that they do not look at a business relationship as a lot of profitable deals added up. They are often prepared to make seeming losses in the early stages. We say 'seeming' because what is really happening is that you give your partner or customer *more* than was contracted, but your customer must then reciprocate *more* than he was given. He may even go broke if you do not return even more. Many Asian relationships have escalating obligations of this kind. You cannot give away the store, because those you give it to are busy shovelling it back at you. Mutual gratitude and obligations are the cement of these cultures. Once again, Analysing Specifics vs. Integrating Wholes is a reconcilable dilemma, see below. The other side of the world knows the other side of truth.

Individualism vs. communitarianism

Is it more important to focus on the enhancement of each individual, or should more attention be paid to the advancement of groups in which many individuals have membership? 'We believe in the dignity, indeed the sacredness of the individual', wrote Robert Bellah (1985) in *Habits of the Heart*. 'Anything that would violate our right to think for ourselves, judge for ourselves, make our own decisions, live our lives as we see fit, is not only morally wrong, it is sacrilegious'. Americans and Canadians are easily the most individualistic nations on earth, as our research shows. We asked our samples the following question:

In the case one gets promoted, two of the following issues can be emphasized:

A   The new group of people with whom one will work.
B   The bigger responsibility of the work and the higher income.

Question:
Which one of these two issues would you emphasize more strongly in case of a promotion, A or B?

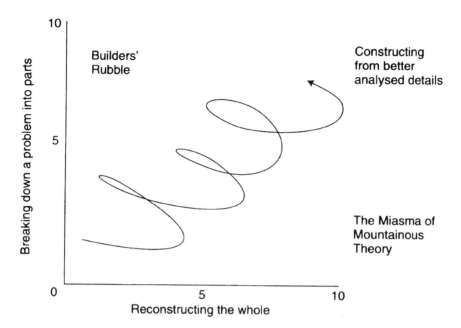

Figure 12.4: **Analysing versus synthesizing**

The answers were as follows for Choice B:

Table 12.7: **Responses to Question 7**

Bigger responsibilities and income

CAN	THAI	UK	USA	NL	FRA	JP	CHI	SIN	HK	MAL	KOR
77	71	69	66	64	61	61	54	50	47	38	32

Clearly Canadians and surprisingly the Thais, go for bigger personal responsibility and personal income. The Chinese, Singaporeans, Hong Kong, Malaysian and Korean managers are all more concerned with the new group of people with whom they will be working. Presumably an independent person would want to find his/her own house and locate his/her own property and would not expect the company or community to provide this. So we asked:

Different people have different opinions about the responsibility a company carries for the housing of its employees:

A   Some people think a company is usually responsible for the housing of its employees. Therefore, a company has to assist an employee in finding a housing facility.

B   Other people think the responsibility for housing should be carried by the employee himself. It is so much to the good if a company helps.

Question:
Do you think the responsibility of a company for housing is best represented by A or B?
The results from our sample of cultures were as follows to Choice B:

Table 12.8: **Responses to Question 8**

USA	NL	UK	HK	FR	CAN	GER	MAL	THAI	SIN	JP	IDO	CHI
86	83	83	82	81	77	76	76	76	72	45	26	18

In this case Malaysia, Thailand, Singapore and Hong Kong all side with the West. But 55 per cent of Japanese managers, 74 per cent of Indonesian managers and 82 per cent of Chinese managers expected the company to provide housing. This is a massive responsibility. If you want to fire the employee you must either evict the whole family or have a malcontent on your property. In practice, most employees in Communitarian countries stay put.

We next compared two motives for working:

Two persons were discussing ways in which one could improve the quality of life:

A   One said: it is obvious that if one has as much freedom as possible and the maximum opportunity to develop oneself, the quality of one's life would improve as a result.
B   Another said: if the individual is continuously taking care of his fellow men the quality of life of us all will improve, even if it obstructs individual freedom and individual development.

Question:
Which of the two ways of reasoning do you think is usually best, A or B?

The scores were as follows for Choice A:

Table 12.9: **Responses to Question 9**

CAN	USA	IDO	NL	HK	UK	CHI	JP	GER	SIN	THAI	SK	FR
79	79	71	69	69	66	64	60	59	50	50	49	48

Here the surprise is how high some nations of SE Asia score. Indonesia is up there with the Netherlands. China is only marginally below the UK with Japan at 60 per cent. We took these results to Chinese colleagues. 'See' we said, 'only the French are still enamoured with dedication to their fellow man'. 'No, you *don't* see', they told us, 'freedom in this context does not mean freedom of the individual but of the *group* to serve the rest of society in the way it chooses. Freedom of the individual from the group hardly exists in China. One person cannot grow rice – it takes at least 12 to 20'. In Japan, for example, the word for individual is 'person-among-others'. You can say 'person-on-their-own' but the expression is one of sadness and regret as you say it – the implication is of an outcast.

North America tends to celebrate 'Man Alone'. Han Solo of *Star Wars*, Rick the hard-boiled cynical saloon keeper in *Casablanca*. Such individuals are symbolized by Lone Ranger, Lone Eagles, innovative seagulls, hard-bitten detectives, mountain men, mavericks, lovable bank robbers, pool-sharks, con men, junk bond salesmen, even Colonel Oliver North. TV series' end routinely with the hero riding off alone into the next episode. Extraordinary invention goes into justifying their aloneness, for example, a medical condition in which you turn green and burst out of your shirt.

The point is not that these individuals think of only themselves. Great Britain owes Andrew Carnegie much of its public library system. Individualism properly understood leaves you free to be selfish and selfless. The point is that this is the heroes' choice. Thus, in *Star Wars* Han Solo rushes to the rescue of Luke Skywalker and Rick in *Casablanca* joins the battle against fascism at the cost of his love life.

What distinguishes individualism from communitarianism is not the individual's *motive*, which may be social but where value is seen to accrue. Even in Salem Village, Alcoholics Anonymous or Mothers against Drunk Driving value accrues to the freely associating individual who formed the covenant with others. In Bunyan's *Pilgrims Progress*, Christian literally shakes off his wife and child, shouting 'Salvation, I will have salvation!' He then treks off alone in search of the Celestial City and of his family we hear no more. Once he gets to the city one assumes community will be restored to him. In the meantime and for the whole story, he walks alone amid fiends and flatterers. It is a Protestant way of thinking.

One reason for the headlong Chinese growth rates is their savings rate of 37 per cent. This in turn is part of Buddhism. You are likely to be reincarnated at least twice and since no one can remember their previous life, this is the first go round. It follows that you should invest in the environment to which you will return and the more you invest the higher is the station to which you will return. Chinese levels of investment are far too high to be motivated simply by a personal desire for profit. Money is pouring into China from Hong Kong, Singapore, Taiwan, Malaysia and overseas Chinese populations in towns like Vancouver. These people see their ancient country arising like a Phoenix and they want to be part of its collective expression.

Ever since a Scottish tutor called Adam Smith taught us that an Invisible Hand would turn our selfishness into public service, we have assumed that this is the only way the equation works. SE Asia has turned Adam Smith upside down. These cultures argue in exactly the opposite sequence, from concern for customers and the community will come the self interest of all concerned. We call this 'The writing hands', a motif we have borrowed from M.C. Escher. If you turn the page upside down then interest in your community rises to the top and advantage to yourself becomes the consequence. The larger truth is the whole cycle rather than the two arcs. It is illustrated in Figure 12.5.

There is a fair amount of mystification about individualism in the West. We know from psychological research about individuals who refuse to conform (Milgram 1963), refuse to torture a fake assistant in a learning experiment. Refuseniks are *well* socialized, not badly socialized. When you stand alone, all those who ever loved you stand ghost-like by your side.

Let us now turn to our fourth diversion.

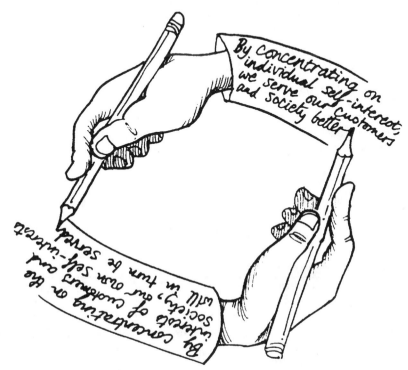

Figure 12.5: **The writing hands**

Inner-directed vs. outer-directed

By which moral compass should we steer, by *inner* convictions and beliefs or by the ebb and flow of forces in the *external universe*?

Americans, Britons and Canadians are not just individualists in valuing the individual above the group, they believe that the origins of all important social and physical forces lie within the protean person. It is possible to be thoroughly individualistic, as are the Dutch, and still believe your environment has more powers than you have. The Dutch have learned in their long battle with the sea that huge powers are located in the environment.

We administered the following questions:

A Without the right breaks one cannot be an effective leader.

B Capable people who fail to become leaders have not taken advantage of their opportunities.

Clearly the second option is inner-directed and the first is outer-directed. Here is how cultures scored on Choice B:

Table 12.10: **Responses to Question 10**

MAL	US	CAN	SIN	THAI	UK	GER	HK	JP	FR	NL	CHI	IND
82	80	71	70	67	66	52	51	51	50	48	39	36

Note that Malaysia is the most inner-directed of all, although we need to be cautious because most of these results are from one star Motorola plant in Penang. Singaporeans are inner-directed, but Chinese and Indonesians are outer-directed. The scores vary when we vary the questions:

A I have often found what is going to happen will happen.

B Trusting to fate has never turned out as well for me as making a decision to take a definite course of action.

Table 12.11: **Responses to Question 11**

CAN	GER	MAL	US	UK	FR	CHI	NL	THAI	HK	JP	SIN
88	83	82	80	73	72	71	68	65	64	49	32

Canadians are especially down on 'trusting to fate'. Singaporeans and Japanese are attracted to this but not the Chinese. One reason we were told is that if you work hard the fates are supposed to respond. You do not trust them, you push them. Small differences in wording make all the difference. Consider:

A Becoming a success is a matter of hard work, luck has little or nothing to do with it.

B Getting a job depends mainly on being in the right place at the right time.

Table 12.12: **Responses to Question 12**

MAL	CAN	US	CHI	FR	IND	GER	UK	HK	NL	SIN	THAI	JP
82	72	69	59	57	56	55	50	47	46	44	40	39

The Chinese are decidedly on the side of hard work with luck obliging. But five nations from Hong Kong to Japan feel that being in the right place at the right time is the most important, even the British divide evenly.

A   Most people don't realize the extent to which their lives are controlled by acci-
    dental happenings.
B   There is really no such thing as 'luck'.

Table 12.13: **Responses to Question 13**

There is no such thing as 'luck'

MAL	CAN	FR	US	GER	HK	NL	THAI	UK	SIN	IND	CHI	JP
59	42	39	38	36	31	27	27	25	19	18	14	13

But ask the Chinese to deny the role of luck in their lives and they refuse by a
larger percentage, 86 per cent. So what is going on here? Are outer-directed people
merely the tellers of hard luck stories? Surely what we are encountering here is a form
of moral inferiority, people who decline to take responsibility for their own lives, fail
to carry enough insurance and so on.

If that is how it seems then this is because our questionnaires originated in the
West and we failed to tap the logic behind outer-directness. In much of SE Asia being
stronger or better than your environment is not admired. What is idealized is *wa*, or
harmony, that is, being harnessed to your environment. A Japanese axiom states
'Man alone is weak, but harnessed to nature he is strong'. Martial arts like judo and
aikido use the strength and momentum of opponents.

Moreover, religions like Shinto or Buddhism are partly nature worship. You should
be as serene as the lily pond, fierce as the fire, swift as the wind. Westerners complain
when Asians 'follow fast' and catch us up, but that is what outer-directedness is all
about. You jump on the back of a new technology invented in the West and domes-
ticate it like a wild horse. You even get to market sooner with a product for customers
because, of course, the outer-directed are more customer orientated.

The Japanese comic book hero is not Superman, but Monkey. The way of Monkey
is to spring on the backs of stronger creatures and be borne along in directions he
too wishes to travel. There are free rides after all if you understand nature.

If we cross-correlate Individualism-Communitarianism with Inner-direction/
Outer-direction we get some interesting combinations. See Figure 12.6.

In Canada, managers see themselves ascending a staircase or career ladder by dint
of individual effort. In France the ethos is Communitarian, every worthwhile reform
having been achieved by an angry group, but it is also *inner-directed*. Injustices ignite
the consciences of organized people. The Netherlands and Sweden show a pattern of
outer-directed individualism. Here the little Dutch boy put his finger into the dike to
save everyone. Finally the Japanese, Chinese, Koreans, etc. show a pattern of Communitarian outer-directedness. We have caught this with the image of the White

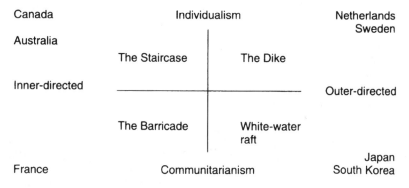

Figure 12.6: **Two-way matrix**

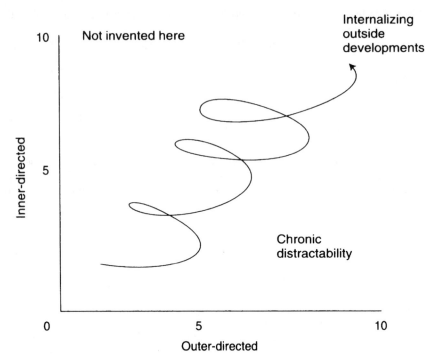

Figure 12.7: **Inner versus outer-directed**

Water Raft, something that carries you along but which you adapt to, by hanging in there together. In fact Japanese top managers often refer to themselves as 'white water groups'.

Once again the ideal is reconciliation. The right direction is both inside us *and* outside us. We have to *internalize outside developments*, so:

Once again we have to avoid the extremes of Not Invented Here and Chronic Distractibility (Figure 12.7) by circling progressively toward synergy.

Time as sequential vs. time as synchronous

Should we see time as a *race* in which we must beat an adversary toward a 'finishing post' or is time more like a *dance*, in which steps are timely and elegantly co-ordinated? Edward T. Hall (1976).

The American view of time is time as a race. As the chorus sings in a Broadway musical:

> *When you're racing with the Clock*
> *The second hand doesn't understand*
> *That your back's all ache*
> *And your fingers break*
> *And your constitution isn't made of rock.*

This view of time believes in speeding up the assembly line as products are worked on one by one. The synchronous view does as much as possible in parallel processes and joins these. We measured the managers' conception of time by presenting our respondents with three circles drawn on a half sheet of paper representing past present and future. This is known as a projective test and was designed by Tom Cottle (1968). When we give this test two extreme reactions are possible, see Figure 12.8.

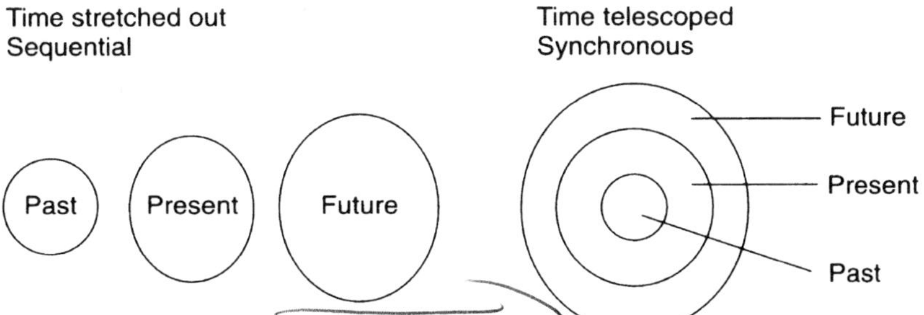

Figure 12.8: **Two models of time**

Sequential thinkers put past, present and future in a straight line, time stretched out and synchronous thinkers telescope time. In practice, few managers put the circles inside each other, although nearly one-third of Japanese, Chinese, South Korean and Singaporean managers did. The range is between those who overlap the circles while maintaining direction and those who separate them. How various nations score is set out in Figure 12.9.

Sequential and synchronous styles vary as follows:

Sequential Managers

Try to do one thing at a time

Concentrate on the job

Regard appointments and time commitments seriously

Accustomed to a series of short-term relationships, quickly broken and quickly reformed

Managers are responsible for present performance

Time is real and objective which means that only the present is really knowable, the past and the future are remote from us

Rationality is fault-free, provided future events follow immediately on present action like striking billiard balls

Planning has to do with forecasting and extrapolating trends.

Products are regarded as young, mature and dying

The future is far away. The discounted present value of a future income stream is usually small.

Synchronous Managers

Try to do many things simultaneously

Are easily distracted

Regard appointments as modifiable, time as elastic

Accustomed to durable relationships with friendships periodically renewed and sustained

Managers are responsible for how they used the past to advance the future

All time is only *ideas* of time. The past and the future are both fused in the present

Reasonableness is encompassing and synchronizing past events with imagined futures

Planning has to do with scenarios where alternative futures are considered.

Products have genes which pass to future generations.

The future is in the room with us now. Start to create it and discover information.

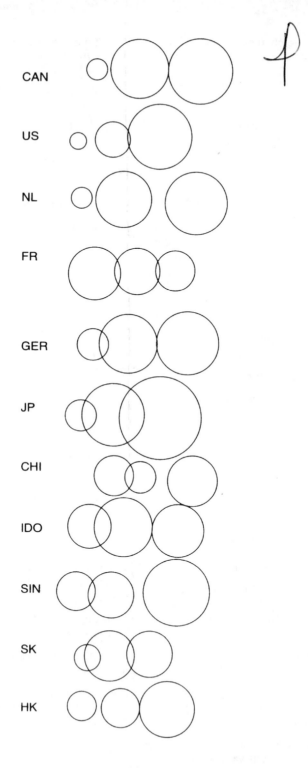

Figure 12.9: **A positive test of time-orientation**

Various nations conceived of time as follows:

Notice that the Japanese and Germans, two of the world's most successful economies, are highly overlapped but without losing a sense of direction. Our hypothesis is that harmonizing these two senses of time is most effective. Americans are stronger on sequential time than synchronous time, along with most English-speaking economies. For synchronous cultures, time is an old friend who keeps calling your age. He is not a grim reaper hovering near by. Old age is revered. Chinese grandparents play with their grandchildren almost as a cultural ritual.

Buddhist immortality is living through your children, falling like leaves from a tree to fertilize the ground. Life is not over when you die. You are likely not simply to be reincarnated but watch silently over the welfare of children as an ancestral spirit. In Japanese Buddhism you enter the womb of great-granddaughter to be born again, but always you have watched over her. Products, too, pass on their 'genes', like a strand of DNA is passed on for ever to enrich the generations. Products procreate like families passing on genetic information.

Once again there is a culture of cultures.

Achievement vs. ascription of status

Should all status be *achieved* by what the manager succeeds in accomplishing, or should at least part of it be *ascribed* a priori?

Achievement is close to being the cultural bedrock on which Britain and the USA are founded. It is surely in the interest of any organization that the best employees should rise in their influence and the mediocre or poor should move elsewhere. Employment contracts offer payment in exchange for work. What could be fairer than to pay more for better work and confer recognition and status commensurate with what the organization has received? It partakes of natural justice. Achievement provides feedback on how well the organization and the achiever is faring. By moving resources towards achieving groups you invest in success and amplify ability.

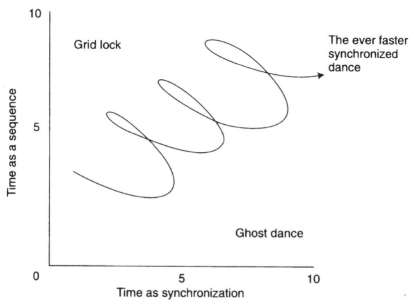

Figure 12.10: **Time as sequence and synchronization**

Status by achievement is pragmatism applied to progress, rewarding best who or what works best. Achievement is the reality test of human potential . . .

If we have gone over the top in extolling achievement it is only to show how self-evidently right cultural beliefs are to those who hold them.

We asked our samples the following question:

The most important thing in life is to think and act in the ways that best suit the way you really are, even if you don't get things done.

This was rejected in the following proportions:

Table 12.14: **Responses to Question 14**

US	CAN	UK	GER	SIN	NL	HK	JP	SK	IND	CHI	FR
55	53	47	39	34	33	29	28	28	27	26	26

Of the Chinese 74 per cent endorse being 'the way you are' because this is consistent with Tao. You harmonize with nature. You discover yourself as you discover the environment. The letter 'O' in Japanese means 'the way of'. Hence Bushido – the way of the sword, Shinto – the way of gods. To be 'the way you are' is thus admirable, more so than achieving if this violates your nature.

We asked three more questions about achieved vs. ascribed nature and lumped together the answers:

Older people should be more respected than younger people.

B It is important for a manager that he is older than most of his sub-ordinates.
C Becoming successful and respected is a matter of hard work.

The first two were rejected by pro-achievement managers. The last was accepted. Here are the scores vis-à-vis Choice C:

Table 12.15: **Responses to Question 15**

US	CAN	UK	GER	FR	NL	SIN	HK	JP	SK	CHI	IDO
63	62	60	58	57	50	44	43	42	37	34	31

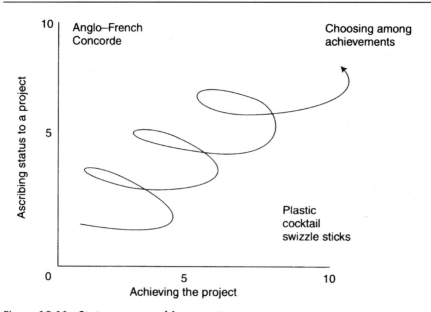

Figure 12.11: **Status versus achievement**

The mystery to many of us is how SE Asia can develop so fast without putting achievement motivation before anything else. Is the world economy really being changed not by movers and shakers but by people who defer to age and are searching for their own true nature?

What makes ascribed status potentially dynamic are two factors often overlooked. First, if you pay more for older people you have to train them or they simply lumber you with dead wood. Hence investment in human resources is massive in economies like Japan. If you are stuck with people for life you have to develop them. Secondly, status by achievement tends to look backwards towards what you did in the past. Only ascribed status can look to the future, calling something important because you want that project to succeed. Stated differently, to ascribe status to a person, project or technology makes it more likely it will be achieved. It is a self-fulfilling prophecy. For it is surely an advantage to make a product which your culture has long admired, as the British admire theatre, the Japanese miniaturization. In other words, status is first ascribed to particular activities and then they are made to world-class standards. Achieving and ascribing are thus reconcilable. We choose our achievements.

Equality vs. hierarchy

Is equality of process more or less important than the hierarchy of judgements that sponsors and judges the contest?

All societies need to encourage participants to give their best. Unless their contributions are weighted *equally* they may be seriously discouraged, yet someone has to choose the contest itself and someone not competing in that contest has to evaluate those taking part. This cannot be achieved without hierarchy.

We showed managers various hierarchical shapes, see Figure 12.12.

How different nations of the world chose flat or steep hierarchies is revealed in the same figure.

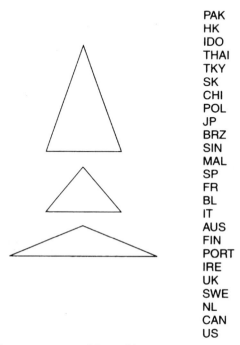

PAK
HK
IDO
THAI
TKY
SK
CHI
POL
JP
BRZ
SIN
MAL
SP
FR
BL
IT
AUS
FIN
PORT
IRE
UK
SWE
NL
CAN
US

Figure 12.12: **Flat versus steep hierarchies**

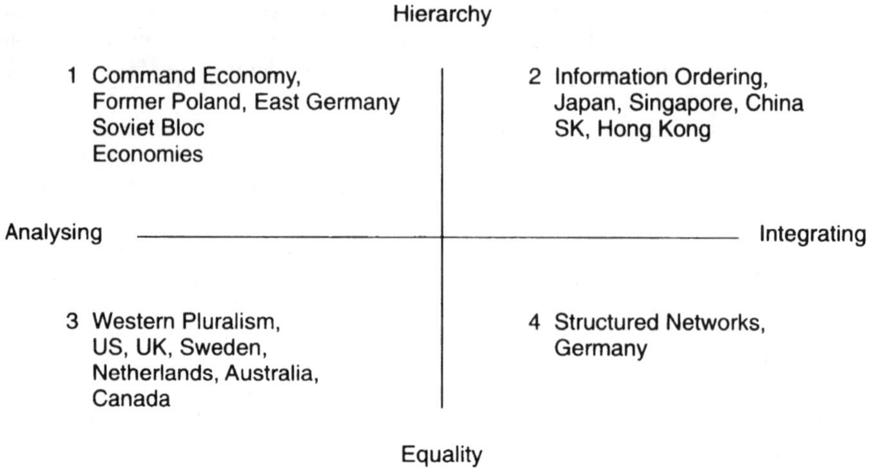

Hierarchy

1 Command Economy,
   Former Poland, East Germany
   Soviet Bloc
   Economies
	2 Information Ordering,
	   Japan, Singapore, China
	   SK, Hong Kong

Analysing ———————————————————— Integrating

3 Western Pluralism,
   US, UK, Sweden,
   Netherlands, Australia,
   Canada
	4 Structured Networks,
	   Germany

Equality

NB At the top left we have Command Economies; they are hierarchical **and** give specific orders.

Figure 12.13: **A four-way model**

What is puzzling about these results is how well some hierarchical nations are doing economically, even in fairly complex fields like electronics. All North American tradition suggests that a steep hierarchy will cripple you. You will not get desperately needed information from the field to the top of the organization, so why isn't Japan crippled? Why doesn't Singapore and South Korea rigidify and grow stupid?

Because the degree of hierarchy is not the only variable, there is also the Analysing-Integrating, our second dimension:

At the top left we have Command Economies: they are hierarchical *and* give specific orders. This fails. It is a disaster. At bottom left Western Pluralism has a lot of ideas jostling each other and contending in a roughly equal marketplace. At bottom right we have Germany with its highly integrated structural networks of businesses and its decentralized federalism. But most interesting and least familiar is Information Ordering. This is hierarchical but socially intimate and close like a family. Because holism is high status, the people at the top have the theories and the concepts and the people lower down the data. These cannot give orders to each other, rather they have to meet and match up their contributions. The Japanese hierarchy *mimics the hierarchical ordering of information itself,* with theories and laws at the top, general propositions in the middle and data at the bottom. All levels need to integrate with each other. This may be the future of all knowledge-intensive organizations. They are in the business of creating knowledge from seas of data.

A new questionnaire: transcultural competency

Over time we have become dissatisfied with our old questionnaire which forces managers to choose one value *over* the other, despite the fact that many prefer integrity and reconciliation. Is it possible to measure reconciliation itself? Does this reveal the dynamics of wealth creation? We believe so. Consider the case of the traffic accident cited earlier. Here there were two polarized choices, 'uphold the law' (universalism) or 'help your friend' (particularism). But in the new questionnaire there are five choices, of which two are reconciliation.

(a)   There is a general obligation to tell the truth as a witness. I will not perjure myself before the court. Nor should any real friend expect this from me.

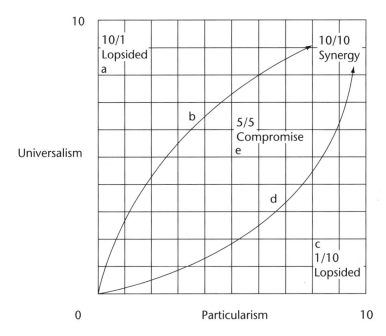

Figure 12.14: **Dual-axis map showing range of responses**

(b) There is a general obligation to tell the truth in court, and I will do so, but I owe my friend an explanation and all the social and financial support I can organize.

(c) My friend in trouble always comes first. I am not going to desert him before a court of strangers based on some abstract principle.

(d) My friend in trouble gets my support, whatever his testimony, yet I would urge him to find in our friendship the strength that allows us both to tell the truth.

(e) I will testify that my friend was going a little faster than the allowed speed and say that it was difficult to read the speedometer.

Figure 12.14 is a dual-axis map that graphs the range of responses.

(a) (10/1) is a polarized response in which the the law is affirmed but the friend is rejected (universalism excludes particularism).

(b) (10/10) is an integrated response in which the rule is first affirmed and then everything possible is done for the friend (universalism joins with particularism).

(c) (1/10) is a polarized response in which the friend is affirmed as an exception to the rule, which is then rejected (particular excludes universalism).

(d) (10/10) is an integrated response in which exceptional friendship is affirmed and then joined to the rule of law (particularism joins with universalism).

(e) (5/5) is a stand-off or fudge, in which both the rule of law and loyalty to friends is blunted (universalism comprises with particularism).

Our calculation is as follows:

• Integrated responses b and d show more transcultural competence than do polarized responses a and c, and compromised responses e.

- While American managers will typically put universalism first, and East Asian/southern European managers will typically particuarism first, each can integrate his or her priority with its opposite.
- From which it follows that there are at least two paths to integrity, not 'one best way'.

To date, 3000 managers have filled in the transcultural competence (TC) questionnaire and the findings are all in the predicted direction. High TC managers are more likely to volunteer for foreign postings and to do better in those postings. Those winning a strategy simulation game are higher in TC. Those promoted in the last three years in Bombardier, a French-Canadian aeronautics company, are significantly higher in TC than those laterally transferred or not promoted. Finally in *21 Leaders for the 21st Century* (Trompenaars and Hampden-Turner 2001) our 'outstanding leaders' outscored the rest of the database by wide margins.

Conclusion

We have seen that China and much of SE Asia is both a mirror and a mirror image of traditional Western management culture. Yet these economies are now developing fast, faster in most cases than the West's own 'catch-up' economies.

Our main conclusion is that the values at stake are complementary, an insight contained within Taoist traditions, but less developed in the West where 'the market place of ideas' is adversarial. For example, Universalism (or the rules) are not genuinely opposed to Particularism (or exceptions). Rather the rule *needs* the exception. This is true whether your aim is to improve rules by studying exceptions, or whether you aim to celebrate the unique and the exceptional by transcending the present rules. In either case, each value is definable only in contrast with the other.

This applies to all the bifurcations discussed. A good community requires that its individual members vouch for its qualities. Those extolling individualism must test their enthusiasm by inquiring into what 'fulfilled individuals' have done for the common good.

We suggest, therefore, that what all cultures share, everywhere, are certain key dilemmas. All need to analyse and synthesize, to attribute values and achieve these, to take streams of passing time and co-ordinate these 'just in time'. We are different in our *logical priorities*, in 'what comes first' but these, however shocking and bewildering, are really disputes about 'where a circle starts'. The larger truths are circular. Exceptions improve rules which in turn enhance exceptions. Communities nurture individuals who enhance communities in original ways. Problems are analysed so as to be better synthesized, so that all details can be examined, including qualities of the whole not present in the parts. It causes us anxiety, sometimes suspicion to be thrown in among people who reverse our favourite axioms, but they are describing the other half of key cultural experiences. We have everything to learn from them. The capacity to reconcile dilemmas is called transcultural competency, a capacity present in outstanding contempory leaders, as well as those with successful international experience.

References

Bellah, R.N. (1985) *Habits of the Heart*, Berkeley, CA: University of California Press.
Cottle, T.J. (1968) 'The location of experience: a manifest time orientation', *Acta Psychologica* **28** . 129–49.
Dobbs, C. (1951) *Studies in Capitalism*, London: Longman.
Hall, E.T. (1976) *Beyond Culture*, New York: Doubleday.
Hampden-Turner, C.M. (1994) *Corporate Culture: Vicious and Virtuous Circles*, London: Piatkus.

Hampden-Turner, C.M. and Trompenaars, F. (1994) *The Seven Cultures of Capitalism*, London: Piatkus.

Hampden-Turner, C.M. and Trompenaars, A. (2000) *Building Cross-Cultural Competence*, Chichester: John Wiley, and New Haven, CT: Yale University Press.

Hofstede, G. (1991) *Cultures and Organisations: Software of the Mind*, London: McGraw-Hill.

Lipset, S.M. (1974) *The First New Nation*, New York: Doubleday.

Melville, H. (1981) *Moby Dick*, New York: New American Library.

Melville, H. (1981) *Billy Budd: Foretopman*, New York: New American Library.

Milgram, S.L. (1963) 'Behavioral study of obedience', *Journal of Abnormal and Social Psychology* **67**.

Trompenaars, A. and Hampden-Turner, C.M. (1997) *Riding the Waves of Culture*, London: Nicholas Brealey.

Trompenaars, A. and Hampden-Turner, C.M. (2001) *21 Leaders for the 21st Century*, Oxford: Capston, and Chicago: McGraw-Hill..

Warner, M. (ed.) (1999) *China's Managerial Revolution*, London: Frank Cass.

Chapter 13

Implementing China's people-management reforms

Malcolm Warner, Keith Goodall and Daniel Z. Ding

Introduction

The People's Republic of China (PRC) celebrated its fiftieth birthday anniversary in 1999. China today is almost another country from the one in which Mao lived and died. It no longer has a planned economy like the Soviet model it tried to copy but one more closely geared to the market. Organizations in this economy are now experiencing successive waves of reforms. In turn, its managers have had to adapt their 'mindsets' to these new challenges. Nowhere is this is most relevant than in the domain of its people management.

China has indeed undergone many far-reaching changes since Deng Xiaoping introduced the 'Four Modernizations' (of Agriculture, Industry, Science and Technology, and Defence) and 'Open Door' policies at the end of the 1970s. After Mao Zedong's death, Deng initiated the move from a 'command' towards a 'socialist market' economy, albeit 'with Chinese characteristics' (Naughton 1996: 2).

State-owned enterprises (SOEs) once dominated industrial production. Such work units (*danwei*), as they were called, embodied the so-called 'iron rice bowl' (*tie fan wan*) which ensured 'jobs for life' and 'cradle to grave' welfare for mostly urban industrial SOE employees (Lu and Perry 1997). Now, a wider range of ownership has been introduced, most notably joint venture firms (JVs) whereby state enterprises have linked up with foreign business partners. Joint venture collaborations were introduced from the early 1980s in order for China to obtain the transfer of both technical 'hardware' and managerial 'software'. Deng believed such firms would also produce goods on a substantial scale for export (Naughton 1996).

Foreign investment has transformed the face of Chinese business and management. The PRC has received a vast flood of inward investment after 1979; China had, by the end of the 1990s, over 315 000 agreed foreign investments, of which about half had been implemented. State firms, having contributed two-thirds of China's industrial production, now account for less than a third (Lardy 1998). A central feature of the reforms has been the development of equity joint ventures, although many fully foreign-funded enterprises have been set up (Vanhonacker 1997). The country has been the largest recipient of such funds among developing countries. Some joint ventures have involved taking over existing state-owned plant and equipment, while others have been developed on 'greenfield sites' (Tsang 1998). China has increasingly opened its door to foreign funds (and continues to do so), although this has mostly been in manufacturing. Only recently, service industries have been opened up to foreign investors. However, a disproportionate amount of investment has gone to the coastal areas and much less inland. Multinational corporations from the West and Japan have been prominent in setting up the larger JVs and have in important ways facilitated 'hard' technology transfer. Many of the wholly owned foreign-funded enterprises (FFEs), on the other hand, have been on a smaller scale, and mainly founded by Overseas Chinese investors, especially from Hong Kong and Taiwan. Above all, the JVs and FFEs were intended to foster 'soft' technology transfer, such as the introduction of Western (and Japanese) modern management methods. The goal was to have 'role-model' enterprises for Chinese management in SOEs to emulate. State-of-the-art JVs and FFEs would provide 'benchmark' exemplars. Reform of SOE human resource management was a major aim of this exercise, and this contribution attempts to see how far significant change has been achieved.

The enterprise reforms that occurred in the 1980s and early 1990s were aimed at phasing out the 'iron rice bowl'. Managers were given more autonomy, particularly to hire and fire, and decision-making was decentralized not only with regard to personnel, but also marketing and purchasing issues (Child 1994). Many, though not all, JVs had already incorporated such practices in their management systems (Goodall and Warner 1997). Personnel reforms involving the introduction of labour contracts, performance-related rewards systems and contributory social insurance were also introduced (see Ng and Warner 1998). Initially, separate sets of government regulations governed the JVs and FFEs, but later reforms applied to both state and non-state enterprises.

We have attempted in this investigation to see what the differential effects of ownership forms have been on changes in labour management in industrial enterprises. If the general thrust of the government's reforms was to use foreign firms as exemplars, then we would expect the effects of the reforms to have been most visible in JVs rather than SOEs, since many of the management reforms were first implemented in the former rather than in the latter.

Methodology

This study basically adopted a case study approach for data collection. Semi-structured interviews were conducted in 62 Chinese firms, both JVs and SOEs, with managers, technicians, trade union representatives and workers. A semi-structured questionnaire was used during the interview for gathering both quantitative and qualitative information (see Goodall and Warner 1998). The sample firms were located in seven major Chinese cities: Beijing, Dalian, Jin'an, Nanjing, Shanghai, Guangzhou, and Zhongqing. These cities are located in the North and North East, the Central East coast areas, the South, and also the Inland regions, approximating, therefore, to a nationwide coverage. The firms can be broadly classified into five industrial sectors: engineering, electrical engineering, electronics, chemicals and pharmaceuticals. The size of the firms ranges from small to medium to very large. In each location, we attempted, whenever possible, to match JVs with corresponding SOEs in the same industry. This effort was constrained by the distribution of firms in each sector, and difficulties of access to Chinese firms. The degree of matching was thus relative rather than absolute. The major characteristics of the firms are summarized in Table 13.1.

Major findings

The employment system

The reform of the employment system in SOEs is focused on attempts to break the so-called 'iron rice bowl', a system of unified job allocation, guaranteed lifelong employment, and cradle-to-grave welfare (Warner 1996; Yip 1996). This rigid

Table 13.1: **Characteristics of Chinese enterprises sampled**

	Number of JVs	Number of SOEs
Location:		
Dalian	6	5
Beijing	3	3
Jinan	6	6
Shanghai	10	12
Guangzhou	5	6
Number of employees:		
Less than 200	2	0
200–499	12	4
500–1499	10	6
Above 1500	6	22
Turnover in 1996:		
Less than 10 m (RMB yuan)	1	0
10 m–100 m	11	7
100 m–1000 m	12	16
Above 1000 m	4	5

Note: Cases of missing data due to confidentaility of responses in limited instances.

employment system existed for several decades before economic reform, and resulted in low productivity and the need for dramatic reductions in staffing. In the early 1980s, a labour contract system emerged and was tried on an experimental basis in eight regions, representing a major departure from the traditional centralized allocation of labour (Korzec 1992; Zhuang 1994). During this experimental phase increasing numbers of SOEs were granted greater degrees of autonomy in running business operations, and were also held accountable for their own profits or losses. The 1994 Labour Law, which came into effect on 1 January 1995, eventually formalized the labour contract system. The new law required all employees, regardless of the types of ownership of their employers, to be hired on labour contracts. Thus, a formerly centrally planned employment system has been gradually transformed into a more market-oriented, extensive labour contract system.

Foreign-invested enterprises were allowed to operate in a market-oriented fashion after China opened its door to foreign investment in 1978. However, although they were free to determine the size of their staff and recruit workers and senior managerial personnel according to their business needs, their employment practices were constrained by the emergent nature of the labour market and the organizational inheritance of practices from their Chinese JV partners.

Our study investigated the differences in recruitment practices and employment contracts used by JVs vis-à-vis SOEs. As illustrated in Table 13.2, a larger number of JVs adopted market-oriented recruitment than SOEs, while the majority of SOEs adopted 'hybrid' practices in recruiting new employees. Individual contracts were much more extensively used in JVs than collective contracts. Interviews with senior managers and personnel directors in the firms studied revealed that, in JVs companies, the external labour market (for example, various job fairs), advertising in the local media, and campus recruiting for university and college graduates are the three most frequently used channels in recruiting new employees. A preliminary labour market has emerged in China in recent years, which offers JVs a greater degree of freedom in choosing production workers. Advertisements by reputable JVs, especially prestigious multinational corporations attract numerous applicants.

Table 13.2: **HRM practices in Chinese enterprises**

	Number of JVs	Number of SOEs
Recruitment:		
Old	2	2
Hybrid	8	18
Market-oriented	19	11
Employment contract:		
Individual contract	20	17
Collective contract	9	15
Average monthly wage (RMB yuan):		
Less than 500	2	6
501–750	6	14
751–1000	13	6
1001–1500	5	3
1501–2500	3	1
Social insurance:		
Old	0	0
Hybrid	7	18
Market-oriented	23	14
Role of personnel manager:		
Old	5	27
Hybrid	25	5
Labour turnover:		
Less than 1%	3	7
1–3%	12	17
3.3–5%	5	5
5.1–10%	7	2
Above 10%	4	1
Union participation:		
Less than 25%	8	3
26–50%	0	0
50–75%	0	0
75–95%	2	4
Above 95%	20	25
Workers' Congress:		
0 = do not meet	6	2
1 = meet once yearly	6	9
2 = meet twice yearly	8	12
3 = meet thrice yearly	0	7
4 = meet more often	0	2

Note: Cases of missing data due to confidentiality of cases in limited number of firms.

Graduates from leading universities and colleges are seen as the best candidates for JVs in high-tech industries. University-based recruiting has become increasingly popular. Few JVs simply took employees transferred from their Chinese partner's parent company, or accepted new ones assigned by labour bureaux (Goodall and Warner 1998).

Our study found that recruitment practices were clearly less market-oriented in SOEs compared with JVs. The two major sources of new employees for SOEs in the sample are workers recommended by the labour bureau, and recruits from company-affiliated vocational schools. Since the beginning of the labour reforms, the role of labour bureaux has gradually changed from directly assigning new workers to enterprises to recommending job applicants. However, due to lack of experience in the labour market, many SOEs still depend on labour bureaux for hiring new employees, making only limited attempts to recruit workers through market channels. Many large, long-established SOEs have their own affiliated vocational schools to provide technical training for their workers. These schools also enrolled a large number of children of employees and offered them jobs after they graduated as part of their employees' welfare programme.

In spite of significant disparities in recruitment channels, JVs and SOEs shared some similarities in selection criteria. All firms in the sample considered previous work experience and personal ability the most important criteria in selecting new recruits. Job interviews, and oral and written tests were used by joint ventures and SOEs alike as the primary method for choosing qualified employees.

Reward systems

Before the economic reforms, China adopted a centrally administered reward system, characterized by a flat structure which reflected an egalitarian mentality (Warner 1996). Wages were not closely linked to individual or corporate performance. The reform of the reward system was first attempted in the late 1970s and early 1980s by incorporating flexible, performance-based elements into the wage system. In addition to the basic wage, a variety of incentives were introduced, such as the functional wage (based on status or seniority), and the floating wage (based on performance). Piece-rates and daily-rates were restored, especially in labour-intensive industries. Decentralization in the state sector gave the SOEs greater authority in designing their wage and bonus schemes. The 1994 Labour Law further legitimized the rights of the employer in determining the form and level of reward according to the characteristics of business operations and profitability. The law tries to enforce minimum wage requirements across the country to guarantee the basic needs of employees.

Our survey examined the reward systems in the 62 sampled firms. Table 13.2 shows that employees, in general, were paid more in joint ventures than in SOEs. For example, in 1996, workers in JVs, on average, earned RMB1004 yuan per month, compared with RMB755 yuan per month earned by workers in SOEs. The exchange rate was just over 8 yuan to the US dollar at the time. Interviews in the surveyed firms revealed that senior managers in many JVs earned nearly three times as much as their counterparts in SOEs. It was also found that the wage structure in JVs was much steeper than in SOEs, as the wage differentials between a production worker and a senior manager in a JV could be as high as RMB5000, while in SOEs it was (nominally at least) no more than RMB600. The relatively flat wage structure in the SOEs clearly reflected a persistent egalitarian mentality.

Forms of reward were found to be similar in both JVs and SOEs, with both using basic salary plus bonus, and an array of allowances, although we found that the details varied. In most cases, the differentials in income were determined not by basic salary but by the performance-based bonuses, and allowances based on position, seniority and skills. Joint ventures for the most part designed their own wage systems and defined the scales of bonus and other rewards (though see Goodall and Warner 1997) for an example of an American JV with multiple Chinese partners which simply took on the SOE reward system). Although some SOEs asserted that they were still using the traditional eight-grade system, they had nonetheless introduced performance-related bonuses. Performance, corporate profit, ability and position were the most important elements used by the majority of sampled firms, both JV and SOEs, as criteria for determining rewards.

Social insurance system

Prior to the economic reforms, the fully company-funded 'iron rice bowl' comprehensive welfare benefits, covering illness, injury, pregnancy, death, or retirement, were an increasingly heavy financial burden for SOEs in the Chinese economy. The overall costs of welfare and labour insurance, as a percentage of the total wage bill, rose steadily, from 14 per cent in 1978 to 33 per cent in 1996, generating a mounting pressure for reform. The overall objective of reform was to establish a nationwide social insurance system, the costs of which would be shared by three parties: the state, the enterprise and the individual employee. The new labour law thus requires both employers and employees to make contributions to five separate funds: pension, accident and injury, maternity, unemployment and medical funds. Managed by local government agencies, the new social insurance system provides a safety net for employees in both JVs and SOEs in the event of their employers going bankrupt.

Our investigation found that both SOEs and JVs are conforming to the current legal requirements of the new social insurance system. Certain SOEs, however, have been unable or unwilling to fully modify their welfare arrangements, continue to take the lion's share of the responsibility, with employees making only nominal contributions. On the contrary, most JVs demand and achieve increased employees' contributions for their own welfare and benefits. One Shanghai-based JV, however, was paying employee contributions to social security funds as an explicit part of their recruitment and retention strategy (see Goodall and Warner 1997). Naughton (1997) similarly suggests that certain Chinese enterprises in the 'high-tech' sector, which have a requirement to recruit and retain highly qualified employees, continue to offer traditional work-unit benefits in order to support this need.

Labour turnover

With the demise of 'iron rice bowl' employment practices and the development of a nascent labour market, labour mobility (facilitated by reforms in the urban registration [*hukou*] system) has become much greater. Our study found that both SOEs and JVs reported substantially increased labour mobility. Interviews with SOE personnel directors revealed that in the course of large-scale downsizing, some workers had voluntarily resigned and opened their own businesses (*cai hai*), or moved to foreign-invested sectors. A higher turnover rate for workers was observed in SOEs than in JVs for this reason.

Role of personnel directors

Our study found a limited degree of change in the roles of personnel directors in SOEs, who were much less market oriented than those in joint ventures (see Table 13.2). Before the economic reforms, their role was limited to job assignment, record-keeping, and provision of welfare benefits (Child 1994). The framework of personnel management in Chinese enterprises has been changing since the economic reforms were set in place. Personnel directors in SOEs were increasingly involved in making decisions related to recruitment and selection, dismissal, promotion, reward and punishment, and in both JVs and SOEs, personnel managers were extensively involved in arranging vocational training programmes. However, our interviews showed that personnel management in JVs had more elements of human resource management (HRM) than in the SOEs. Moreover, personnel directors in JVs had greater autonomy with regard to their input to recruitment, promotion and the determining of reward and punishment systems.

Trade union and Workers' Congress

The two challenges facing trade unions in the years of economic reform are to promote economic development, and at same time help maintain social stability (Ng and Warner 1998; White 1996). The 1994 Labour Law further empowered the trade union in an enterprise to sign collective employment contracts with the employer on behalf of the employees. In cases of inappropriate termination of labour contracts and labour disputes, the trade union has the right to intervene to protect the interests of employees. The trade union is the executive agency of the Workers' Congress, which is, in theory, empowered to supervise the management of the enterprise and represent the voices of the workforce.

Our survey data (see Table 13.2) showed that trade union participation was less extensive in JVs than in SOEs. Although trade unions in both forms of organization were involved in housing allocation, organizing leisure activities, providing assistance in labour disputes and in individual and family problems, trade unions in SOEs participated to a larger extent in the business decision-making process than in JVs. The presence of the Workers' Congress was, overall, substantially less significant in JVs (Goodall and Warner 1997).

Further analysis

The data collected in the survey were further analysed to explore the extent to which type of ownership, size of the firm, and location have impacts on HRM practices. We hypothesized that:

1 Foreign direct investment will have a positive impact on HRM practices in Chinese enterprises.
2 The size of the firm will have a bearing on organizational inertia influencing the speed and extent of change.
3 The location of the firm, reflecting the openness of the business environment, will affect the general pattern of HRM prevailing in firms in that region.

In the course of our preliminary statistical analysis, a two-tail correlation test was conducted. Our main concern at this stage, given the limitations of space, is the direction of the correlations only; a further, more extended publication will discuss the detail of the relationships. A number of interesting significant correlations (significant at <.05 or above) were revealed. These included:

1 *Sales turnover* was positively related to employee size (.68).
2 *Employee size* was negatively related to year of establishment (.47), ownership type (.67), social insurance (.37), and the role of personnel directors (.48).
3 *Year of establishment* was positively related to ownership type (.67), social insurance (.33), role of personnel directors (.66).
4 *Ownership type* was positively related to social insurance (.33), role of personnel directors (.66) and labour turnover (.28).
5 *Location of the firm* was positively related to social insurance (.37).
6 *Labour turnover* was, as seen above, positively related to ownership type (.28).

Test of hypotheses

The results showed that *ownership type* was significantly and positively correlated with the following variables:

- the role of personnel directors (significant at <.001)
- social insurance (significant at <.01)
- labour turnover rate (significant at <.05)

at the levels noted above.

This confirms our hypothesis regarding the positive impact of foreign direct investment on HRM practices. JVs in general adopted more market-oriented approaches in managing human resources and in designing social insurance schemes. The employees in JV tended to have a higher labour turnover rate than in SOEs.

It is also noted that *ownership type* is significantly but negatively correlated with the following variables:

- participation in the trade union (−.25) (significant at <.05)
- the presence of workers' congresses (−.54) (significant at <.001)

This is consistent with our observation that JVs were less supportive of trade union activities than SOEs, and that trade unions and workers' congresses there played a less active role in enterprise management.

The *number of employees* was used as a proxy for the *size of the firm*. Nearly three-quarters of SOEs in the sample were large-sized enterprises with over 1500 employees. Our results showed that the number of employees was negatively related to the following variables:

- social insurance (.47) (significant at <.001 level)
- role of personnel directors (.28) (significant at <.05 respectively)

Large SOEs tended to retain old-style social insurance schemes, in which the company absorbed the bulk of the cost of welfare, with negligible contributions from employees. Changes in the role of personnel managers tended to be limited in these enterprises, due to the difficulty in implementing a new HRM system due to, among other considerations, organizational inertia.

The variable '*location*' was used to code cities on a north/south axis. Our results showed that the *location of the firm* was positively associated with the following variables:

- social insurance reforms (.37) but negatively related to
- trade union participation (−.38) (both significant at <.01)

The further south you go, therefore, the less trade unions count. This finding reflects the greater openness of cities in coastal and southern regions. The finding here might also mirror the greater number of joint ventures, which were more heavily concentrated in the southern region, where trade unions play a relatively less important role. Trade unions are generally not welcomed by Hong Kong and Macao investors, and most foreign-invested firms there have neither unions nor workers' congresses (Ng and Warner 1998).

Discussion

The results of this study provide evidence that HRM practices have undergone fundamental changes in Chinese enterprises in the last two decades of economic reforms, but this was most evidently the case in the foreign-funded sector. The old 'iron rice bowl' employment system is now being phased out as China steadily moves toward a market-oriented economy, and foreign direct investment has brought into China both the 'hardware' – the production facilities – and the 'software' – including HRM practices and systems. Yet it is clear that even in the case of JVs, the grafting of new managerial and organizational forms onto older SOE structures has hindered the advent of human resource practices. The degree of organizational inertia has, as our earlier research has suggested, been noteworthy.

Equity joint ventures have been the channel most preferred by the Chinese government for absorbing foreign technology (Tsang 1994). Our data revealed the positive impact of ownership type on HRM practices. This is due to the efforts made by the foreign partners in JVs to transfer Western HRM techniques and systems into joint ventures. Although problems and impediments have been reported (Fan 1998; Verburg 1996; Von Glinow and Teagarden 1988) JVs have frequently played a leading role in diffusing changes in HRM practices into Chinese enterprises, although in varying degrees, as we have seen.

With regard to location, our study found a significant correlation between location and the pattern of HRM practices. This is due to the differences in the level of economic development and degree of openness to foreign direct investment between the inland regions and the 'gold coast' provinces such as Guangdong, Fujian and Zhejiang. Child (1994: 149) similarly offers some evidence that in the southern province of Guangdong managers spent less time than their counterparts in Beijing or Shanghai on political, administrative or personnel issues and more time focused on business issues. The effect of location on human resource practices was also evidenced by Ding and Warner (1999).

Broadly, in the present sample, we can conclude the following:-

- the more northerly the location and the more distant from the coast, the greater the organizational inertia, and
- the more likely it is, therefore, that traditional attitudes and practices will still be in place in SOEs.
- The greater pace of economic reform in the south appears to be reflected in differences in SOE human resource practices, notably with regard to social insurance commitments, weaker trade union participation and higher staff turnover rates.

China's emphasis on revitalizing SOEs in recent years has also provided a momentum for HRM reforms in the state sector, but it is not necessarily referred to as such; the term 'personnel management' (*renshi guanli*) is still widely used. SOEs are under pressure to compete profitably with foreign-invested firms, and the downsizing of their workforces is a prerequisite for an improvement in their competitiveness. The reduction in the size of the workforce has been even more widely encouraged in the last few years as the government has tried to reduce the burden of loss-making SOEs.

Concluding remarks

If 1999 was the fiftieth year of the PRC for the Chinese to celebrate, the year 2000 was as important as it was the designated target date for achieving key goals, such as the elimination of poverty, illiteracy and so on. Premier Zhu Rongji had also set the date for the turn-round of the failing SOE industrial dinosaurs. Progress here has been painfully slow but discernable. This amelioration always depends on the growth of the economy, as China needs to grow at well above 8, even 9, per cent per annum to generate enough jobs for those seeking work. What has been dubbed 'Keynesianism with Chinese characteristics' may not prove to be enough, however. Deflation remains a formidable obstacle to reviving economic fortunes. Expert opinion predicts both costs and benefits from entry into the World Trade Organization (WTO), which is imminent.

More market-oriented management practices are no doubt expected to become more common in Chinese enterprises as the Open Door is opened even further but this will take time. Human resources development, for example, will unquestionably increase over the coming years (see Zhu 1999) but may be more narrowly defined than in Western or Japanese models. However, the concern for social stability (one reason for the growing political opposition to policies of pushing forward the reforms and moving into globally freer trade), as well as the persistence of organizational inertia in SOEs, has served as a brake on rapid change. In this regard, we would predict growing attempts at managerial innovation as China deepens its reform of the SOEs; however, regional and sectoral differences in levels of development are likely to remain as constraints for some years to come.

References

Child, J. (1994) *Management in China During the Age of Reform*, Cambridge: Cambridge University Press.

Ding, D. and Warner, M. (1999), ' 'Re-inventing China's' industrial relations at enterprise level: an empirical field-study in four major cities', *Industrial Relations Journal* 30: 243–60.

Fan, Y. (1998) 'The transfer of Western management to China', *Management Learning* 29(2): 201–21.

Goodall, K.W. and Warner, M. (1997) 'Human resources in Sino–foreign joint ventures: selected case studies in Shanghai compared with Beijing', *International Journal of Human Resource Management* 8(5): 569–94.

Goodall, K.W. and Warner, M. (1998) 'HRM dilemmas in China: the case of foreign-invested enterprises in Shanghai', *Asia Pacific Business Review* 4(4): 1–21.

Korzec, M. (1992) *Labour and the Failure of Reform in China*, London: Macmillan; New York: St. Martin's Press.

Lardy, N. (1998) *China's Unfinished Revolution*, Washington, DC: Brookings.

Lu, X. and Perry, E. (eds) (1997) *Danwei: The Changing Chinese Workplace in Historical and Comparative Perspective*, New York: Sharpe.

Naughton, B. (1996) *Growing out of the Plan*, Cambridge: Cambridge University Press.

Naughton, B. (1997) 'Danwei: the economic foundations of a Unique Institution', in X. Lu and E. Perry (eds) *Danwei: The Changing Chinese Workplace in Historical and Comparative Perspective*, New York: Sharpe.

Ng, S.H. and Warner, M. (1998) *China's Trade Unions and Management*, London: Macmillan; New York: St. Martin's Press.

Tsang, E.K.W. (1994) 'Human resource management problems in Sino–foreign joint ventures', *International Journal of Manpower* 9(10): 4–21.

Tsang, E.K.W (1998) 'Foreign direct investment in China: a consideration of some strategic options', *Journal of General Management* 24(1), Autumn: 15–35.

Vanhonacker, W. (1997) 'Entering China: an unconventional approach', *Harvard Business Review,* March–April: 130–40.

Verburg, R. (1996) 'Developing HRM in foreign–Chinese joint ventures', *European Management Journal* 14(5): 518–26.

Von Glinow, M.A. and Teagarden, M.B. (1988) 'The transfer of human resource management technology in Sino–US cooperative ventures: problems and solutions', *Human Resource Management* 27(2): 201–29.

Warner, M. (1996) 'Economic reforms, industrial relations and human resources in the People's Republic of China: an overview', *Industrial Relations Journal* 27(3): 195–210.

White, G. (1996) 'Chinese trade unions in the transition from socialism: towards corporatism or civil society?', *British Journal of Industrial Relations* 34: 433–57.

Yip, G.K.B. (1996) 'Labour management in domestic and foreign investment enterprises', in J. Smith and M. McFadden (eds) *Employment in China*, Hong Kong: THC Press.

Zhu, C.J. (1999) 'Major emerging issues in human resource management', in L. Kelley and Y. Luo (eds) *China 2000: Emerging Business Issues*, Thousand Oaks, CA, and London: Sage.

Zhuang, Q.D. (1994) 'Employment, wage distribution and social insurance', in G.M. Luo (ed.) *Ten Research Projects: Speeding up Reforms and Promoting Socialist Economic Construction in China (Shige Zhuanti Diaocha Yanjiu)*, Dalian: Press of Northeast University of Finance and Economics.

Chapter 14

South Korean management in transition

Chris Rowley

Introduction

An exploration and detailing of key aspects of management, its changes and transition in South Korea[1] is important and interesting for several reasons. First, Korea is often taken as an exemplar and possible role model of an economy that developed very rapidly from a predominantly agricultural society to an industrialized one, going on to become a world leader in several important sectors, including both the more 'traditional' (steel-making, shipbuilding) to 'newer' (electrical and electronics) ones. For example, Korea's Pohang Iron and Steel is the world's largest steel producer, with an output of 26.8 million tonnes in 2000 (by contrast, the Anglo-Dutch company Corus produced 18.4 million), Samsung was an important semiconductor and silicon chip producer. Second, this emergence and spectacular growth of a so-called Asian 'tiger' economy was due to several factors, including the influence of high doses of state intervention, direction and control. Furthermore, the interaction with Korea's large conglomerates, or *chaebol,* was also critical. These powerful corporations went on to become very well known around the world, producing familiar and popular consumer products. They also became overseas investors and set up operations in both developing (e.g. China) and more developed (e.g. the USA and the UK) economies and bought-up indigenous companies. Third, part of Korea's success is also seen as underpinned by its management, and especially its human resource management (HRM). Finally, all these aspects are now under stress and strain and are shifting, although there are some cultural and institutional constraints to rapid and deep change and transition. These areas form the framework and sections for the rest of this chapter.

The limits to this chapter will be briefly noted. It is not totally representative of all Korean management, neither by organizational size, sectors, nor functions. It does not include great detail on management in small firms, the service sector or public sector (see Kim and Rowley 2001; Kwun and Cho 2001). Likewise, the area of management in joint ventures or overseas corporations in Korea are also not detailed. The main focus beyond Korean management in general is the management of human resources (HRs).

Background and context

Korea's religious and philosophical beliefs include Confucianism, Buddhism and Christianity with Taoist traditions of holism with South East Asian neighbours

(Morden and Bowles 1998). Korea is almost 100,000 square kilometres in size, with a population which has rapidly grown and urbanized. Of its 20.2 million people in 1966, some 3.8 million lived in the capital, Seoul, with the Seoul Region accounting for 6.9 million (23.7 per cent of the population). By 1995 there has been a more than doubling of the population of Korea to 45.1 million and Seoul to 10.2 million, and the Seoul Region almost tripled to 20.1 million (44.7 per cent of the population) (Song 1997). Korea has a homogeneous workforce, with very few 'foreign' workers and its unemployment rate was just 2.6 per cent (1997) and the average nominal wage increase rates for all industries was 7 per cent, and real wage increase was 2.4 per cent (1997) (Kim, Bae and Lee 2000), with a move from labour surplus to short-age, especially of production workers and in small firms.

The development of the Korean model of industrialization and economic growth, internationalization, organizational capabilities and management has been detailed elsewhere (see Rowley and Bae 1998a; 1998b; 1998c; Rowley, Sohn and Bae 2001). The route was a developmental, state-sponsored, export-oriented and labour-intensive model of industrialization. In short, from the 1960s the Korean economy achieved remarkable growth and development. It rapidly moved on from being a rural backwater with limited natural resources, relatively small domestic market and a legacy of colonial rule and war with heavy dependence on US aid. With impressive growth rates in output, productivity and income, Korea was forged into a world-renowned industrial powerhouse and overseas investor and manufacturer, eventually becoming the world's eleventh largest economy and joining the Organization for Economic Co-operation and Development (OECD). Much of this development had been underpinned by exhortations and motivations such as national goals, includ-ing the need to escape the vicious circle of poverty, achieve economic superiority over North Korea, compete with the Japanese, repay debts and elevate Korea's image and honour.

Indicative of Korea's development are the following. Korea achieved gross domes-tic product (GDP) real annual growth rates of 9 per cent from the early 1950s to late 1990s, taking its $1.4 billion (1953) GDP to $437.4 billion (1994). In the three years of 1986–8 Korea achieved 11.6 per cent, 11.5 per cent and 11.3 per cent GDP growth respectively (Kim, Bae and Lee 2000) and annual rates of 7.5 per cent between 1990 and 1997. Korea's per capita GDP grew from $87 (1962) to $10,543 (1996), and gross national product (GNP) exploded from $3 billion (1965) to $376.9 billion (1994). From the mid-1960s to the late 1990s Korea achieved an annual manufacturing out-put growth rate of nearly 20 per cent and export growth of over 25 per cent, rising from $320 million (1967) to $136 billion (1997) (Kim and Rowley, 2001). The desti-nation of its foreign direct investment of $5,049 million (1996) was dominated by the USA and China (Chung, Lee and Jung 1997). There were also takeovers of Western companies, such as the US's Zenith (television equipment manufacturer) by LG and AST Research (manufacturer of personal computers) and Germany's Rollei (camera company) by Samsung, and a variety of former East German companies (Morden and Bowles 1998).

Within this picture of overall growth are variegated developments and shifts as Korea moved to a less agricultural and more industrial economy and society (from Song 1997). Between 1960 and 1995, as a percentage of GDP, agriculture's share declined from 39.9 per cent to 6.6 per cent and services grew slightly from 41.5 per cent to almost half, 49.9 per cent, while industry boomed, more than doubling its share, from 18.6 per cent to 43.5 per cent. Sectoral employment patterns also shifted. Between 1965 and 1995 agriculture's share of employment collapsed, from well over half, some 58.7 per cent, to just one-eighth, 12.5 per cent, while services' share almost doubled from 28.1 per cent to 54.6 per cent and industry's share more than doubled, from 13.3 per cent to 32.9 per cent. Again, within this there were differ-ences as the structure of manufacturing itself shifted. For instance, between 1960 and

1993, the share of employment declined in both food and beverages, which fell by almost two-thirds, from 36.5 per cent to 12.3 per cent, and also textiles and leather, by over two-thirds, from 25.2 per cent to 7.6 per cent. In contrast, metal products and machinery almost quadrupled their share, rising from 10.3 per cent to 39.6 per cent of manufacturing employment.

It seemed the sun would never set on this success story. Yet, it did coming to an abrupt halt and then reversal as the Korean economy was hit by the 1997 Asian financial crisis. For example, in 1998 Korea's GDP fell by 5.8 per cent (Plender 2000), GNP collapsed by two-thirds and the currency fell by 54 per cent against the US dollar. The number of establishments declined by 14 per cent (68,014) and 1 million jobs were quickly lost (Korea National Statistics Office 1999). The stock market plunged by 65 per cent between June 1997 and June 1998, while the widespread problems and bankruptcy of some well-known *chaebol* hit the press (*Economist* 1999). Smaller banks, such as Daedong, Dongnam, Donghwa, Kyungki, Chungchong, were closed. The low unemployment rate, which had been below 3 per cent during the 1980s, almost tripled to 8.6 per cent (2 million) by February 1999. Nominal wage increase rates declined to −2.5 per cent in 1998, while real wage rates decreased to −9.3 per cent. Partly in response, strikes increased by 65 per cent, from 78 (44,000 workers) to 129 (146,000 workers) between 1997 and 1998. This economic collapse led to much anxiety and incomprehension among politicians, policy-makers, management, workers and the general population, and produced much commentary as to how quickly and totally things had gone wrong. Even worse, for many ordinary Koreans it was a national humiliation and huge loss of face.

The Korean economy did strongly recover from 1999. For instance, GDP grew by 10.7 per cent in 1999 (Plender 2000). Many of the famous *chaebol* seemingly weathered the crisis and survived. Some companies made record profits, although unemployment remained above, and the wages of most workers below, pre-crisis levels, and income gaps widened. Also, this recovery may be a chimera and seems fragile. Korea remains plagued by poor, rather than glowing, behaviour, reports and publicity. Examples include problems at Hyundai, the bankruptcy of the construction company, Korea Industrial Development, which also hit sectoral share prices, bailouts by the state-run Korean Development Bank and strikes, such as those at Kookmin and Housing and Commercial banks, the National Health Insurance Company and the famous Lotte Store in Seoul and the Seoul Subway System in 1999. A major, high profile example concerns Daewoo's huge debt level and its owner's problems and £23 billion accounting fraud of its executives. Furthermore, Ford's abandonment of its interest in Daewoo Motor in September 2000 sent shock waves through Korea and its stock market.

The *chaebol*

While the *chaebol* were formerly frequently seen as the powerhouse of the economy, they are now often portrayed as part of the problem for the Korean economy and management. Most of the Korean large business sector is part of one or other of the *chaebol* networks. These large business groupings and conglomerates are broad in the scope of their interests and dominate the economy and some localities, even leading to company towns, such as Woosan (Hyundai) and Pohang (POSCO), housing and servicing large numbers of employees. There were more than 60 *chaebol*, although the top few dominate; in the 1990s the top five contributed 60 per cent of GDP.

Some of the *chaebol* became major international companies in the world economy and famous names. For example, LG Group, whose LG Electronics had sales of $9.3 billion and 22,800 staff in early 2000, is a global manufacturer of a range of electrical and electronic products. It had 59 branches, 18 sales subsidiaries and 31 manufacturing subsidiaries spanning 171 countries, with 26 R & D facilities in Korea (Kim

Table 14.1: **Example of *chaebol* diversification: Samsung**

Period	Interests
1930s	Fruit and sundry goods exporter
1950s	Sugar refiner, textile manufacturer
1960s	Paper, electronics, fertilizer, retailing, life insurance
1970s	Hotels, construction, electronics components, heavy industry, synthetic textitles, petrochemicals, shipbuilding
1980s	Aerospace, bio-engineering, semiconductors

From Chen 2000; Pucik and Lim 2001

2000). Samsung is the oldest, and leader in their development with aggressive diversification in manufacturing and services (see Table 14.1). Founded in the 1930s, it flourished in the 1950s and continued to expand. Its sales of $3 billion and staff of 45,000 (1980) grew to $96 billion and 267,000 employees (1998) (Pucik and Lim 2001). Within this, Samsung Electronics in 1998 had 21 worldwide production bases, 53 sales operations in 46 countries and sales of $16.6 billion, and was one of the world's largest producers of dynamic random access memory semiconductors.

The *chaebol* are characterized by a high degree of diversification, often unrelated, a broad scope and many subsidiaries run by 'a mixture of military commands combined with patriotic appeals' (Kang and Wilkinson 2000: 127). Koreans call them an 'octopus with many tentacles'. The chairman and the chairman's office are critical in the organization of the *chaebol,* augmenting the concentration of ownership and control structure (Oh 1999). They are usually family owned or controlled and kinship based, recruiting from certain clans or regions, while member firms own each other's shares and collaborate. Thus, ownership and management are not separated, clan members dominate positions of power, with kinship-based relationships with owners (*hyul-yun*), held together by an autocratic leader, with often competitive (and clan-based) tension and distrust between *chaebol* (Morden and Bowles 1998).

The growth of the *chaebol* was based on a variety of elements and circumstances (Rowley and Bae 1998c). Their success has been explained by some as due to organizational efficiency and by a range of theories, from neo-classical economics, Marxist perspectives, culture, network analysis, transaction cost economics to resource dependence and power theory (detailed by Oh 1999). In contrast, some argue it is the flux and flow of the state–military interactions with the *chaebol* that is the most important external factor, a politico-economic organization that substitutes for trust and efficiency and the market (ibid.). The links between the military, government and top executives has been damned as nepotism and 'crony capitalism'.

Thus, one key aspect for the *chaebol* and Korean management is the state. For instance, the Korean state became more integrated and strengthened, owning banks, and the *chaebol* were reliant on government for capital. State policy deliberately promoted *chaebol* as a development strategy in the 1960s and 1970s and directly intervened to maintain a quiescent workforce. The state's more recent democratic flavour was preceded by several military governments. These all impacted on Korean management.

Management

Korean management has been influenced by a range of factors, from cultural to institutional. The Korean management system has been influenced by three major factors: Japan, America and Confucianism (Chen 2000). These include both Japanese and American management approaches and systems. This is due to a colonial past and occupation when Koreans were restricted to lower positions in organizations and excluded from managerial roles. Other Japanese influences included infrastructural developments during the colonial period, Korean emigres, industrial policy imitation, and application of technology and techniques of operations management (Morden and Bowles 1998). Many Koreans subsequently studied the American management system, especially as most overseas students went to the USA. We must not forget the military's influence either. Korean ex-military personnel applied their US military and business management system experience to Korean enterprises. Key aspects of Korean management systems are noted in Table 14.2.

Some of the characteristics of Korean management are worthy of further detail. Important underpinnings to Korean management come from the cultural milieu. For Hofstede (1991) Korea was characterized by large power distance and authoritarianism, collectivism and communitarianism (associated with family and clan membership), and strong uncertainty avoidance. One important aspect is familial influence. Confucianism was the state religion for over 500 years, from the foundation of the Yi Dynasty (1392) to Japan's annex (1910). The influence of Confucianism on the values, attitudes and norms of Koreans 'spilled over to the fundamental underpinnings of the Korean management system and human relationships within Korean companies' (Song 1997: 192). With Confucianism, the values, ways of thinking and modes of conduct still centre on family life, which significantly impacts on Korean management as the role of the extended 'clan' (*chiban*) influences the organization and management of enterprises. For instance, founders often recruit, organize and manage on the basis of principles governing family life.

Another important underpinning of Korean management is the emphasis on hierarchical ranks. Korea is a highly homogeneous society built on vertical organizational principles. The influence of hierarchical traditional family systems makes Korean companies strongly hierarchical. The military influence is again important – many executives are ex-officers, while many employees were in the military and have regular military training, and companies even maintained reserve army training units (ibid.).

Thus, several cultural concepts (which can be compared and contrasted to Japanese ones) underpin Korean management (Song 1997). These include a sense of indebtedness (*un*) to organizations and fellow members, loyalty (*chung*) from subordinate to superior, integrity (*uiri*) to others in everyday life, and the process of informal consensus formation (*sajeonhyupui*) prior to making final decisions (ibid.). Personal qualities of respect, tolerance and patience are adhered to in business and there is the concept of resentment or frustration felt over unjust or inequitable treatment (*han*) (Morden and Bowles 1998), while personal entertainment and giving of gifts play important roles in building successful relationships (ibid.). The impact of such cultural aspects can be seen in the post-1997 crisis bailout by the International

Table 14.2: **Key characteristics of management in Korea**

Confucian influences
Company as family-type community
Sharp distinctions between owners, managers and workers
Emphasis on general hierarchical ranks
Loyalty and co-operation (to individuals)
Some lifetime emplyment
Seniority: age and service length
Military influences
Extensive training
Management recruitment from common ties: clan, geographical, school/university

Adapted and amended from Song 1997: 190

Monetary Fund (IMF) which was popularly perceived as a national humiliation and loss of face, and there were reports of people taking their gold and jewellery to contribute to national funds.

While these cultural-type aspects to Korean management retain some of their salience, cutting against them are some other trends. We may well expect some transition in this more traditional Korean management style. This could stem from the tension with professional managers, in particular those with experience of education or work in the USA and the West, increased by the influence of the globalization of Korean companies and takeovers, and the influx of foreign capital on management. For example, there may be developments with increased expectations, such as for transparency and openness in corporate affairs and decisions, improved information flows, and more 'professional' recruitment and selection.

These cultural underpinnings, and challenges and changes to them, have implications for the practice of Korean management. This is particularly so for the Korean system of HRM.

Human resource management

An important element of Korean management concerns its HRM policies and practices. In the *chaebol* there are links between the HR department and the powerful chairman's office, which makes many important HR decisions, 'Thus the HR function is closely tied to the highest level of the *chaebol*' (Kim and Briscoe 1997: 299). We will detail key aspects of HRM: employee relations, resourcing, development, labour markets and remuneration.

There was a dark side to the Korean economic miracle with physical brutality, fear and personal humiliation of workers. The pressure and exploitative nature of the labour process was indicated by the huge volume of industrial accidents, some 4,570 compared to smaller numbers in larger workforces (although with sectoral impacts, of course), such as 513 in the USA and 658 in the UK in 1987 (Kang and Wilkinson 2000). Before the 1980s state control of industrial relations was close with repressive labour policies (as part of its model of development). In terms of organization, the government decided that this should be industry based and it officially recognized the Federation of Korean Trade Unions. Post-1987 the institutions, framework and policies all shifted under pressures from political liberalization and civilian governments, joining the International Labour Organizations (ILO) (1991) and OECD (1996) and trade unions. From the 1980s unionization spread with more militant unions at the enterprise level, finally leading to the emergence of a second national federation, the Korean Confederation of Trade Unions (*minjunochong*).

Trade unionization was 12.6 per cent in 1970, peaking at 18.6 per cent in 1989 before falling back to 11.2 per cent by 1997. The number of labour disputes has varied, i.e. just four in 1970, 322 in 1990 (although with peaks of 3,749 in 1987 and 1,873 in 1988) and 78 in 1997 (ibid.). Obviously, this union density figure should not be taken as the only indicator of labour strength and influence as this also depends on environment and context, such as sector, legal constraints and opportunities it operates within and the nature and character of the disputes themselves. Korean industrial conflicts can be high profile, large scale and confrontational. For example, in 1992 the week long occupation of Hyundai Motor ended when 15,000 riot police stormed the factory, while strikes at LG Electronics in 1987 lasted ten days and stopped all work and in 1989 lasted 39 days, with another 23 strikes in LG companies (Kim 2000). Also, labour has played a large role in the democratization of the country.

The *chaebol* themselves are seen as prestige employers, traditionally recruiting graduates twice a year with preference for management trainees from prestigious universities (Kim and Briscoe 1997). Much of Korea's economic growth has been attributed to its highly skilled and well-educated workforce with heavy investment in the development of its HR. Many espoused the Confucian emphasis on education, with very strong commitment to it and traditional respect and esteem attached to educational attainment. This is indicated by high levels of literacy, the high proportion of scientists and engineers per capita, and that 70 per cent of the workforce graduated from high school (Morden and Bowles 1998). Many *chaebol* put strong emphasis on training and have their own well-resourced and supported training centres. There is often four weeks in-house induction training with new employees staying at training centres where they are inculcated in company history, vision and its songs (Kim and Briscoe 1997). These centres also provide ongoing training and a variety of programmes. In 1995 Samsung spent $260 million on training, Hyundai $195 million, Daewoo and LG $130 million each (Chung, Lee and Jung 1997). It was argued that the success of Pohang Iron and Steel Company was due in part to its employee development and regular training (Morden and Bowles 1998).

It seems that ideas of increased employee involvement, participation and partnership have blossomed. This is at both macro (neo-corporatism) and micro levels. Examples at the macro level include the Presidential Commission on Industrial Relations Reform (1996) and the tripartite Labour–Management–Government Committees (*nosajung owiwonhoe*) on Industrial Relations of January and June 1998 (for details see Yang and Lim 2000). At the micro level is the example of LG Electronics which looked at practices in plants in the US (Saturn, Motorola) and Japan.

Some aspects of traditional Korean HRM indicate Japanese influences, including lifetime employment and seniority pay, although with some differences. For instance, employee loyalty was 'chiefly to an individual, be it the owner or chief executive' (Song 1997: 194), with little to organizations as such, producing a 'quasi-long-term employment ideal' (in contrast to Japanese organizational commitment). While limited to regular, particular male employees in large companies, normative practice extended to smaller firms (Kim and Briscoe 1997). Traditionally, the system and practice of performance appraisal was not important as it did not affect promotion or pay.

There have been some attempts to alter HRM practices and reform labour laws, now with the added twist of change driven by post-1997 IMF bailout conditions. These are compared and contrasted in Table 14.3.

Key aspects of these changing characteristics in HRM revolve around shifts from seniority and regulation towards more flexibility in labour markets (with easier job shedding) and remuneration (with greater focus on performance elements). One way to try to deliver these changes is via the performance appraisal system. Given the importance of these aspects, they will be detailed further.

Employment adjustment

Korea's flexibility was classified as 'low' numerically and 'moderately high' functionally (Bae *et al.* 1997). However, since then flexibilities have seemingly swiftly and extensively increased and spread, as indicated in Table 14.4. Numerical flexibility increased and it is argued that in 1999 the number of temporary, contract and part-time workers were more than 50 per cent of the workforce (Demaret 2001; Kang and Wilkinson 2000). Also, functional type flexibility spread via redeployment, especially to other departments.

The extent of transition is also indicated by another survey of 300 firms in January–November 1997 and December 1997–March 1998 (Choi and Lee 1998). During the first period, virtually one-third (32.3 per cent, some 97 firms), adjusted employment. By the second period this coverage almost doubled to 60.3 per cent (181 firms). For the first period, specific types of employment adjustment (firms made multiple responses) were: worker numbers (19.7 per cent, some 59 firms), working hours (20 per cent, 60 firms) and functional flexibility (12.7 per cent, 38 firms). In the second period, numbers experiencing employment adjustment massively increased in all these types; worker numbers more than doubled (43.7 per cent,

Table 14.3: **Key characteristics of traditional and new HRM in Korea**

HRM areas	Traditional characteristics	New characteristics
Core ideology	• Organizational first • Collective equality • Community oriented	• Individual respected • Individual equity • Market principle adopted
HR flow	• Mass recruitment of new graduates • Job security (lifetime job) • Generalist oriented	• Recruitment on demand • Job mobility (lifetime career) • Development of professional
Work systems	• Tall structure • Line and staff; function based • Position-based	• Flat structure • Team systems • Qualification-based
Evaluation and reward systems	• Seniority (age and tenure) • Pay equality • Evaluation for advancement in job grade and job • No appraisal feedback • Single-rater appraisal	• Ability, perfomance (annual systems) • Merit pay • Evaluation for pay increases • Appraisal feedback • 360° appraisal
Employee influence	• Less involvement • Less information sharing	• Involvement of knowledge workers • Information sharing

From Bae and Rowley 2000

Table 14.4: **Changes in Korean employment adjustment practices***

Flexibility	Practices	1996	1998	Difference
Numerical internal	Working hours reduction	5	61	56
	Restriction of overtime	11	104	93
	Temporary leave of absence, unpaid	5	24	19
	Temporary leave of absence, paid	2	26	24
Numerical external	Postponement of recruitment	6	29	23
	Reduction of recruitment	33	148	115
	Dismissal	2	53	51
	Voluntary retirement	22	72	50
	Outsourcing	19	45	26
Financial	Base pay reduction	0	41	41
	Freezing of wages	1	78	77
	Bonus reduction	0	116	116
	Fringe benefits reduction	4	141	137
Functional	Dispatch to affiliated company	11	21	10
	Redeployment after training	5	19	14
	Redeployment as salesperson	12	53	41
	Redeployment to departments of shortage	19	95	76

Note: * N=286, multiple responses from firms, conducted November 1998 across various industries.
Various tables from Park and Ahn 1999

some 131 firms), while working hours (36.7 per cent, 110 firms), and functional flex-ibility (24.3 per cent, 73 firms), almost doubled. There was a more than doubling in both 'freezing or reducing recruitment', from 15 per cent (some 45 firms) to 38.7 per cent (116 firms), and 'dismissal' from 7 per cent (21 firms) to 17.3 per cent (52 firms), with rises in 'early retirement' from 5.7 per cent (17 firms) to 8 per cent (24 firms).

Some company cases also highlight changes. Samsung Electronics is an important example as it has been something of a trendsetter in HRM for Korean firms. Its 60,000 employees (1997) were massively reduced by about one-third to 40,000. LG Group in 1998 dismissed 14,000 (11.6 per cent of its total) employees (Kim 2000). Daewoo Motor shed 3,500 jobs despite violent protests and strikes by unions (Burt 2001). Some 30,000 at public companies like Korea Telecom, Korea Electric Power Company and Korea National Tourist Organization were to be dismissed, while another 30, 000 (10 per cent) of local public servants were dismissed by the end of 1998 (Park and Park 2000). Korea Telecom made some movements towards increased adjustment via changes in job categories, transfers and promotions (Kwun and Cho 2001).

However, there were limits to these developments. Even though the economic and legal contexts had changed, neither the government nor the conglomerates seemed overly keen to put the new legislation to use (*Economist* 1999: 7). This inertia can be seen in the following cases where adjustment has been constrained. Rather than dis-missal, a Samsung subsidiary asked for both men and women to take unpaid 'pater-nity leave', while Kia remained 'proud' of its 'no-lay-offs' agreement and Seoul District Court protected jobs by refusing to close Jinro (ibid.). One high-profile exam-ple concerns Hyundai Motor, whose initial plan to dismiss 4,830 of its 45,000 work-ers was diluted to 2,678 and then 1,538. The union went on strike in 1998, followed by six illegal strikes and about 50 instances of physical conflict with management until a negotiated compromise was reached. The final agreement provided for just 277 dismissals (with 167 of these from the canteen), along with lump-sum severance pay.[2] As a result, while Hyundai's workforce fell to 35,000, this was mainly due to 7,226 voluntary retirements plus about 2,000 who will return after 18 months' unpaid leave (ibid.). Indeed, some collective dismissals, such as the 1,500 figure at Hyundai Motor, were regarded as 'illegal' and 'unreasonable' (Lee 2000).

Remuneration adjustment

There have been changes in remuneration systems in Korea, with a de-emphasizing of seniority and an increasing importance attached to 'performance' in its calcula-tion. Some of the reasons for this were: pay system rigidity making labour almost a quasi-fixed cost; weak individual-level motivational effects; and changing environ-mental factors (Kim and Park 1997). Data in Table 14.4 indicates some financial changes. Data from the earlier survey (Choi and Lee 1998) indicated remuneration flexibility almost quadrupled from 10.7 per cent (some 32 firms) in 1997 to 38.7 per cent (116 firms) by 1998. Table 14.5 shows that about one-third (33 per cent) of firms now had performance-based – (3) or (4) – systems. There seem to be common trends across sectors, although with some greater change in use of (4) in non-manufactur-ing vis-à-vis manufacturing. Slightly more variation by size of organization would be somewhat expected given size is a powerful variable across many HRM areas. Some-what counter-intuitively, (1) was used by slightly more 'smaller' (although defined at a relatively high employment level here) firms, while more than twice the percent-age (although still a small total percentage) compared to 'larger' ones, used (4).

The example of annual pay in Korea (salary based on individual ability or per-formance) presents a striking contrast to traditional remuneration systems. A survey of 4,303 business units (with over 100 employees) in January 1999 found 15.1 per cent (some 649) had already adopted annual pay, 11.2 per cent (481) were preparing for it and 25 per cent (1,077) were planning to adopt it (Korea Ministry of Labor 1999). Hence, just over one -quarter (26.3 per cent) of firms had either made, or were

Table 14.5: **Variations in Korean pay systems by size and sector (percentage)**

System options	Sector Manufacturing (N = 210)	Non-manufacturing (N = 68)	Size (employees) Less than 300 (N = 144)	More than 300 (N = 134)	All firms
(1)Traditional seniorityism	42.4	42.6	43.8	41.3	42.4
(2) Seniority-based with performance factor*	25.2	22.1	22.8	26.0	24.5
(3) Performance-based with seniority factor	29.0	29.4	27.8	30.5	29.1
(4) Ability/performance-based	3.4	5.9	5.6	2.2	4.0

*Note: *Original labelled this 'Ability-based system, but seniority-based operation'.
From Park and Ahn 1999*

preparing to make, changes. Indeed, just over half (51.3 per cent) of firms were in some stage of changing pay systems. Again, there seem to be common trends across organizational size.

The operation of annual pay systems can also be seen in specific cases. Instances among the *chaebol* are shown in Table 14.6. All used forms of annual pay systems. Samsung and Hyosung adopted a 'zero-sum' method, reducing salary for poorer performers while increasing pay by the same amount of reduced salary for better performers. Doosan, Daeang and SK used a 'plus-sum' method, increasing salaries of good performers without reducing those of poor performers. Finally, some firms accumulated performance evaluation results.

The example of Samsung is important given its size, high profile and influence. It has made shifts in its remuneration (as well as hiring, selection and promotion) systems. Samsung introduced its 'New HR Policy' in 1995 with its greater emphasis on performance. Pertinent points in this are compared and contrasted in Table 14.7. Remuneration in its former system was composed of base pay (based on seniority), plus extra benefits (long service, etc.). By way of contrast, in the new system remuneration was composed of base pay (common pay, cost of living), plus merit pay (competence and performance based) (Kim and Briscoe 1997; Pucik and Lim 2001).

Other cases of remuneration adjustment can be noted. LG Group in 1998 introduced new practices to determine pay based on ability and performance (Kim 2000). LG Chemical introduced a system of performance-related pay at its Yochon plant (*Economist* 1999). Hyundai Electronics in December 1999 introduced share options, with some 13 per cent (6 per cent in 1998) of companies listed on the Korean Stock Exchange giving employees share options, while Samsung Electronics introduced profit sharing, with some 18 per cent (4 per cent in 1998) of 5,116 large companies sharing profits in January 2000, while another 23 per cent planned to do so by year end (Labor Ministry survey reported in *The Economist* [*Economist* 2000]). Korea Telecom made some movement from seniority towards more performance and flexibility in remuneration (Kwun and Cho 2001).

The key lever in operationalizing this movement towards increasing performance elements is the system and process of performance appraisal, as promotion and remuneration were now heavily dependent on it. Given this, Samsung's appraisal system was revamped and made more sophisticated in the search for greater objectivity and reliability. It was now composed of several elements: supervisors' diary; 360-degree (supervisors, subordinates, customers, suppliers) appraisal; forced

Table 14.6: **Comparison of annual pay systems among Korean *chaebols***

	Doosan	Daesang	Hyosung	SK	Samsung
Adopted	1994	1995	1997	1998	1998
Target group	Section chief and above	College graduates and above	College graduates and above	Deputy general managers and above	Section chief and above
Composition of annual pay	–Basic annual –Performance	–Basic –Ability –Performance	–Seniority –Job-based –Ability –Performance	–Individual annual –Incentives	–Basic annual –Performance (individual and group)
Base-up	No	Yes	Yes	No	Yes
Plus-sum	Yes	Yes	No	Yes	No
Cumulative	Yes	Yes	No	Yes	No

Adapted from Yang 1999: 232

Table 14.7: **Traditional and new HRM in Samsung**

Area	Traditional HRM	New HRM
Promotion	Seniority: Minimum tenure then promotion	Performance: 'Qualification' based on capability + performance points in appraisal Increased job hierarchy (8 to 11) = more steps for promotion
Remuneration	Position and seniority: – basic (50%) – allowance (10%) – bonus (40%) several months basic 4–6/year; more if better than average year	Individual incentives: – basic (position + seniority) – varied % of performance pay (individual performance ratings) – varied special bonus to top 2%

distribution; and two interviews (with the supervisor and 'Day of Subordinate Development'). The 'Evaluation of Capability Form' used was composed of interesting items, such as 'Human Virtues', e.g. 'morality': willingness to sacrifice (sic) themselves to help colleagues (Kim and Briscoe 1997).

Again, the extent of these remuneration adjustments need to be considered. Some of these changes are relatively limited in coverage and spread. For instance, data in Table 14.5 indicates that traditional seniority remained in large numbers of firms (nearly 43 per cent), with little variation in usage by size or sector. Indeed, some form of seniority – (1) or (2) – accounted for the pay systems of over two-thirds (67 per cent) of firms, again with little size or sector variation in usage. Likewise, data in Table 14.6 indicates most firms applied practices only to certain groups, such as managers or the higher educated. Some firms, such as Samsung, Daesang and Hyosung, used 'base-up' methods, a uniform increase of basic pay regardless of performance or ability levels. Similarly, Hyundai's vaunted stock option policy covered just 7 per cent of the workforce, while Samsung's profit sharing was limited to 'researchers' (*Economist* 2000). At LG, although employee evaluation systems are in place, in most instances compensation 'does not reflect evaluation results as it is largely determined by seniority' (Kim 2000: 178).

Thus, as well as the exact coverage, we can also question the depth and acceptance of any transformation and HRM changes. The rhetoric may well be different from the reality of positions. More recent qualitative data[3] can be used to support these sorts of developments, counter-trends and ambivalence. In late 2000 a variety of types of executives, managers and HR practitioners in several large *chaebol* and other businesses on the whole mostly professed the need to change key aspects of the traditional system of HRM. They argued frequently for the requirement to replace it with moves towards greater flexibility and performance in labour markets and remuneration. These managers seemed well aware of the problems of the Korean model (and the Japanese variant), such as the perceived inflexibility and unfairness in employment and remuneration. For instance, there were concerns that junior, younger workers were paid lower, and older workers higher, than their respective contributions. These problems were seen to stifle recognition and reward of differential performance. These manages also had a view on the 'benefits' of the US model of flexible labour markets, such as employment generation and more closely rewarding performance.

Yet, these very same managers were equally unaware of the potential disadvantages and costs of other models, for instance, in terms of social costs, and the potential collapse in morale, loyalty and training with increased labour mobility, disposability and 'poaching'. Neither were they aware of any possible alternatives, such as a European (social market) model and its possible benefits. This may partly be due to the dominance of the USA in Korea in its business and educational spheres (and the unquestioning views of some management). For instance, perceived 'inflexibilities', such as seniority and long-term employment, can generate loyalty and commitment to company success and also flexibilities such as willingness to change and stimulate innovation and long-term development. In contrast, some 'flexibilities', as when workers face easier dismissal, can produce problems and inflexibilties, such as when companies look to solve problems in a short-term fashion by cutting labour and training at the cost of long-term and dynamic growth and morale. If this latter route is more constrained with obstacles, then organizations and management would be forced to look at and consider other alternatives (Rowley 1997a; 1997b). Another area of ambivalence is that, critically, many of these firms continued to maintain workforces and expend large amounts on broad and deep training.

There are also many, seemingly ignored or at least underplayed, problems with trying to link HR performance via appraisals. These concern performance appraisals in general, when linked to rewards, and in Asian contexts. For instance, there are well-known tendencies in human nature that lead towards subjective aspects in appraisals. Furthermore, it is very common in the prescriptive and practitioner type literature to strongly recommend that performance appraisals should not be linked with remuneration. Finally, there are cultural biases to be aware of (see review in Taylor 1998; also Farh, Dobins and Cheng 1991). For example, it has been noted that Korean managers are often unwilling to give too negative an evaluation as *inhwa* emphasizes the importance of harmony among individuals who are not equal in prestige, rank and power, while supervisors are required to care for the well-being of their subordinates and negative evaluations may undermine harmonious relations (Chen 2000). Another Korean value, *koenchanaye* ('that's good enough'), also hampers performance appraisals as it encourages tolerance and appreciation of people's efforts, and not being excessively harsh in assessing sincere efforts (ibid.). These all impact on the use of performance appraisals and should warn against any naïve acceptance of their usefulness.

These cases and issues highlight several points concerning Korean management. They contain conflicting messages on adjustment. That actual dismissals and pay changes were attempted and practised could give strong signals that others might follow this route. However, Hyundai was an example that unions could alter some redundancies. The demonstrations, May Day 2000 rallies and general strike threats by unions were generated partly by fear of job loss and reflected the severe dislocation that Korean employees face. Layoffs also tore apart many families and workers, and managers took their lives. For example, an average of 25 people a day committed suicide in the first quarter of 1998, a 36 per cent increase from the previous year (Business Week 1998). There is only a limited 'safety net' with many denied social protection or benefits, and the unemployment budget has been reduced by 50 per cent (Demaret 2001).

Thus, the spread, and certainly level of acceptance and usefulness, of these HRM changes and practices can be questioned. The limits to such 'New HRM' in Korea stem from both culture and institutions (Bae and Rowley 2000; Rowley and Benson 2000c).

Conclusion

This chapter has outlined some of the key underpinnings, elements, transitions and challenges in the area of Korean management, especially its HRM. There remain some key difficulties for Korean management. First, there is the problem of demographics – there is an ageing workforce (as in many economies). For example, in 1990 the economically active population aged 15–19 was 639,000, by 1995 it was 441,000, while over the same period the numbers for those aged 40–54 increased by 8 per cent (Lee 2000). Second, there remains the need for greater debate and understanding of the possible applicability of Western concepts of HRM, such as performance-related remuneration and performance appraisals. This links to the wider picture of possible convergence of HRM and its remaining divergence of practices (see Rowley 1997a; 1997b; Rowley and Benson 2000a; 2000b). Third, there is the problem of trying to maintain employee commitment, loyalty and teamwork, and their attendant benefits, in an era of easier dismissal and greater focus on individual, sometimes short-term, performance.

The Korean economy has emerged from the ruins of the financial crisis of the late twentieth century. However, in the early part of the new millenium it is still difficult to predict how well or robustly the economy has recovered or the role of Korea management in it. Nevertheless, what we can see is that the view of Korean management has radically changed, from the often posited role of 'saviour' during the long boom of the post-1960s, to be replaced by the now common label of 'sinner' from the late 1990s. Both these may be naïve. What may have usefully emerged from all of this is a greater balance as to management's role in the success of economies, which ultimately rest on an amalgam of other foundations. Also, there may be less hagiography of management and pointless search for the elixir of some magic 'one best way' to manage, which, as we should not forget, remains complex and specific.

Endnotes

1 Korea is used for shorthand from now on.
2 Severance pay was equivalent to 7 months' gross salary for those who had worked for less than 5 years, 8 months' for 5–10 years, and 9 months' for over 10 years.
3 Based on meetings, interviews and fieldwork in Korea during September 2000.

References

Bae, J. and Rowley, C. (2000) 'Globalisation and transformation in HRM: the Korean case', Working Paper.
Bae, J., Rowley, C., Kim, D.H. and Lawler, J. (1997) 'Korean industrial relations at the crossroads: the recent labour troubles', *Asia Pacific Business Review* 3(3): 148–60.

Business Week (1998) report *Business Week* 17 August: 20.

Chen, M. (2000) 'Management in South Korea', in M. Warner (ed.) *Management in Asia Pacific*, London: Thomson.

Choi, R. and Lee, K. (1998) *Employment Adjustment in Korean Firms, Survey of 1998*, Seoul: Korea Labor Institute

Chung, K.H., Lee, H.C. and Jung, K.H. (1997) *Korean Management: Global Strategy and Cultural Transformation*, Berlin: De Gruyter.

Demaret, L. (2001) 'Korea: two speed recovery', *Trade Union World* (12-1), December–January: 21–2.

Economist (1999) 'A survey of the Koreas', *The Economist* 10 June: 1–16.

Economist (2000) 'Business in South Korea', *The Economist* 1 April: 67–70.

Farh, J., Dobins, G.H. and Cheng, B.S. (1991) 'Cultural relativity in action: a comparison of self-ratings made by Chinese and US workers', *Personnel Psychology* 44: 129–47.

Hofstede, G. (1991) *Cultures and Organisations*, London: McGraw-Hill.

Kang, Y. and Wilkinson, R. (2000) 'Workplace industrial relations in Korea for the 21st century', in R. Wilkinson, J. Maltby and J. Lee (eds) *Responding to Change: Some Key Lessons for the Future of Korea*. Sheffield: University of Sheffield Management School.

Kim, D. and Park, S. (1997) 'Changing patterns of pay systems in Japan and Korea: from seniority to performance', *International Journal of Employment Studies* 5(2): 117–34.

Kim, D.O., Bae, J. and Lee, C. (2000) 'Globalization and labour rights: the case of Korea', in C. Rowley and J. Benson (eds) *Globalization and Labour in the Asia Pacific Region*, London: Cass.

Kim, J. and Rowley, C. (2001) 'Managerial problems in Korea: evidence from the nationalized industries', *International Journal of Public Sector Management,* 14(2): 129–48.

Kim, S. and Briscoe, D. (1997) 'Globalization and a new human resource policy in Korea: transformation to a performance-based HRM', *Employee Relations* 19(4): 298–308.

Kim, Y. (2000) 'Employment relations at a large South Korean firm: the LG Group', in G. Bamber, F. Park, C. Lee, P. Ross and K. Broadbent (eds) *Employment Relations in the Asia-Pacific*, London: Thomson.

Korea Ministry of Labor (1999) Korea national statistics, Seoul, Government publications.

Korea National Statistics Office (1999) *Korea National Statistics*. Seoul, Government publications.

Kwun S.C. and Cho, N. (2001) 'Organisational Change and Inertia: Korea Telecom', in C. Rowley, T.W., Sohn and J. Bae, (eds) *Managing Korean Businesses: Organization, Culture, Human Resources and Change*, London: Cass.

Lee, C. (2000) 'Challenges facing unions in South Korea', in G. Bamber, F. Park, C. Lee, P. Ross and K. Broadbent (eds) *Employment Relations in the Asia-Pacific*, London: Thomson.

Morden, T. and Bowles, D. (1998) 'Management in South Korea: a review', *Management Decision* 36(5): 316–30.

Oh, I. (1999) *Mafioso, Big Business and the Financial Crisis: The State-Business Relations in South Korea and Japan*, Aldershot: Ashgate.

Park, J. and Ahn, H. (1999) *The Changes and Future Direction of Korean Employment Practices*, Seoul: The Koran Employers' Federation (in Korean).

Park, F. and Park, Y. (2000) 'Changing approaches to employment relations in South Korea', in G. Bamber, F. Park, C. Lee, P. Ross and K. Broadbent (eds) *Employment Relations in the Asia-Pacific*, London: Thomson.

Plender, J. (2000) 'Emerging from the gloom', *Financial Times*, 11 April: 22.

Pucik, V. and Lim, J.C. (2001) 'Transforming HRM in a Korean Chaebol: a case study of Samsung', in C. Rowley, T.W. Sohn and J. Bae, (eds) *Managing Korean Businesses: Organization, Culture, Human Resources and Change*, London: Cass.

Rowley, C. (1997a) 'Comparisons & perspectives on HRM in the Asia Pacific', *Asia Pacific Business Review* 3(4): 1–18.

Rowley, C. (1997b) 'Reassessing HRM's Convergence', *Asia Pacific Business Review* 3(4): 198–211.

Rowley, C. and Bae, J. (1998a) 'The Icarus Paradox in Korean business & management', *Asia Pacific Business Review* 4(2): 1–17.

Rowley, C. and Bae, J. (1998b) 'Korean business & management: the end of the model', *Asia Pacific Business Review* 4(2): 130–9.

Rowley, C. and Bae, J. (1998c) *Korean Businesses: Internal and External Industrialization*, London: Cass.

Rowley, C. and Benson, J. (2000a) 'Global labour: issues & themes', *Asia Pacific Business Review* 6(3/4): 1–14.

Rowley, C. and Benson, J. (2000b) 'Globalization, labour & prospects', *Asia Pacific Business Review* 6(3/4): 300–8.

Rowley, C. and Benson, J. (2000c) (eds) *Globalization and Labour in the Asia Pacific Region*, London: Cass.

Rowley, C., Sohn, T.W. and Bae, J. (2001) *Managing Korean Businesses: Organization, Culture, Human Resources and Change*, London: Cass.

Song, B.-N. (1997) *The Rise of the Korea Economy*, Oxford: Oxford University Press.

Taylor, S. (1998) *Employee Resourcing*, London: IPD.

Yang, B. (1999) 'The annual pay systems in Korean firms', *Proceedings of the International Conference of Korean Association of Personnel Administration on the Change of HRM Paradigm and Annual Pay*, Seoul.

Yang, S. and Lim, S. (2000) 'The role of government in industrial relations in South Korea: the case of the Tripartite (Labour–Management–Government) Committee', in R. Wilkinson, J. Maltby and J. Lee (eds) *Responding to Change: Some Key Lessons for the Future of Korea*, Sheffield: University of Sheffield Management School.

Chapter 15

The Japanese employment model revisited

Philippe Debroux

Introduction

Large Japanese firms' employment and human resource management practices were devised during a period of sustainable high growth and constant expansion of the firms' activities. Now, Japanese economy and society have reached a stage of maturity. Long-term economic growth rate will probably be in the range of 2–2.5 per cent, about the same as the main European economies. Indeed, large Japanese firms were successful in developing and maintaining stable employment practices during the post Second World War period. The structural moderate growth expected in the future, coupled with the opening of the Japanese economy to the world, requires a change of logic. The priority given to permanent employment and long-term job guarantee is not attuned to the new economic reality and does not reflect either the diversification or the needs and expectations of the employees. It is unsustainable and bound to drag down further the firms' profitability if it is not reconsidered. The constraints put on the development of atypical types of employment were probably justified in the past in order to protect workers against possible abuse from the employers. However, they impede now the creation of new job opportunities. Devised to protect the workers, they maintain paradoxically the discrimination between the minority holders of permanent jobs and the majority of the others, those who because of their age, gender or lifestyle would prefer more flexible types of employment.

Under pressure from the market and the society transformation, a new regulatory environment is slowly replacing the older one. The gradual transformation reflects the pragmatism of Japanese authorities, management and trade unions. Nikkeiren, the Japan Federation of Employers' Associations and Rengo (1999), the biggest Union Confederation, are showing a lot of realism in their proposals to transform the Japanese human resource management system (Nikkeiren 1995). Japanese government has identified the problems facing Japanese firms in dealing with rigid employment practices. It is also well aware of the necessity to find a solution to the long-term expected labour shortage due to the drastic ageing of the population and the low fertility rate. Female and elder workers' contributions will be crucial in that respect. New opportunities have to be offered to make them stay on in the labour market. All the measures have to be devised and implemented with respect to the balance between work and family (Araki 1998). It also means that a number of non-permanent types of occupations, for instance, temporary or part-time work, must be recognized as legitimate activities responding to the needs of certain segments of the working population. They should not be considered a priori as second-class jobs as it was until recently (Yashiro 1998). Therefore, upgrading the ability and skill level of a large part of the population is of utmost importance. Reform of the education system is gaining pace and the great success of training programmes organized for the working population shows that Japanese people are aware of the importance of the issue (Debroux 2000). The protracted and, so far, often inconclusive debate concerning recent regulatory changes of the Labour Standards Law and the Part-Time Labour Law has shown that it is difficult to satisfy the parties on all points. The grey zone of uncertainty is still very large. Nevertheless, in regulating properly the new labour market and finding the right balance between liberalization and protection, Japan can avoid a collapse of its system, a sudden surge of the unemployment rate and large regional imbalances such as those that have plagued Western Europe during the last 20 years. The system can certainly not survive in its previous form but it can still be restructured in a manner and at a pace acceptable to the main stakeholders.

Contradictions of the human resource management system during a low-growth period

In a low economic growth period, it is necessary to adopt flexible employment practices to maintain stable employment and stabilize the system in the long term. Current practices allowed Japan to keep a lower unemployment rate than the other developed countries during the last 50 years. Long-term job guarantee was linked to a training policy, considered as an investment by both management and employees in large companies (see chapter 13). Training was mainly an internal matter. It was organized on the job sites, reinforced constantly by a comprehensive skill-grading system and job rotations inside the whole company. Firms were not likely to accept readily losing the fruit of their training investment because of the mobility of their workforce. They always did their best to keep the cost of the redundant workers as low as possible through an optimization of the results during the high-growth periods and collaboration with related companies. At the same time, they devised reward policies aimed to limit the potential mobility of their core employees. Job security and the wage system based on lifetime needs were not merely the result of yearly trade unions–management negotiations. It was a give and take process with a long-term rationale for both employees and employers. The costs of job change increased a lot because of the complementarity between two kinds of factors. The first is related to the firm itself such as retirement pay, mandatory retirement, welfare policy and the almost exclusive recruitment of young graduates. In the first part of his or her career, the employee accepted a salary lower than his or her productivity. It was offset by the expectation of a higher salary during the second part of his or her career. Promotion was slow but guaranteed to some extent. Large firms always managed to keep the system competitive in organizing systematically the competition among employees of the same cohort (Aoki 1994). Any departure from such career pattern was financially penalized (Hanada and Hirano 2000). The lump sum was not portable and could only be received in full by remaining in the same company during the whole career. The second is related to external factors such as the interfirm hierarchy, the mediocre public welfare services until recently, and the very high cost of education and housing. The differed salary made the employees key stakeholders in their company without becoming shareholders. Such a forced savings system helped companies to support their investments when high economic growth was sustainable (Tsuru 1993). For the employees, it was considered a better investment than individual savings in a bank offering very low interest rate. Common investments by stakeholders, employees and management, provided a strong incentive. Profits coming from the high commitment and high skill level of the employees were redistributed via the company-based union. Cross-shareholdings among industrial groups' firms developed a committed and patient capital, and the subsequent absence of takeovers provided for the financial stability.

However, the system required a pyramidal structure of companies and workers to operate smoothly. The '*shukko*' system, allowing the temporary dispatching of redundant workers in related companies, could only work with a large young workers' basis at the bottom of the pyramid and with continuous high economic growth. Women had to accept to play for ever a subordinate role on the labour market. Workers in small and medium-sized enterprises (SMEs), representing the large majority of the labour population, had to work under inferior conditions in terms of compensation and fringe benefits, and endured a much more unstable labour market. Under such conditions, Japanese-style human resource management had a strong rationale. The implicit mutual long-term contract between employees and the firms could bring growth and prosperity. Wage and fringe benefits differentials between the prestigious large companies and SMEs could be legitimized by the meritocratic education system. Products of the élite schools naturally entered large firms to get the best jobs. The distinctness of male and female roles in the marriage relationship, and in society at large, determined the acceptability of a large difference between the terms and conditions under which young unmarried and older married women were recruited and compensated (Dore 2000). On the whole, it was just the result of social norms accepted by both men and women at that time (Hunter 1993). Thanks to a spill-over effect and a tight labour market, the prosperity of large firms did trickle down to SMEs. In the 1960s and 1970s, nominal wages increased almost at the same rate in all sizes of firms. Workers in SMEs got better working conditions and a number of them adopted a human resource management system operating under the same basic principles as the large firms. Meanwhile, housewives could have a more comfortable life in better housing with a number of appliances making their house chores less absorbing. Starting from a miserable economic condition after the war, many Japanese people were indeed entitled to believe that they belonged to a large middle class, able to buy cars and houses and to provide the best education for their children. In that sense, the Japanese welfare corporatism and the 'capitalism without capitalists' developed in large firms was indeed a major success (Dore 1987).

Optimal employment and human resource management practices cannot perpetuate with a disregard for economic changes just because they are based on a mutual agreement between employees and management and the tacit understanding of the other main stakeholders. If basic conditions change fundamentally, it is necessary to pass to another logic. The psychological contract and employees' loyalty are important for the company but if growth slows down and business cycles shorten and become erratic, long-term job guarantee and seniority-based wages become a heavy burden for any company. In the same way, the optimal level of mutual investment in training, as well as the capital investment, depend on the profit expectations. If long-term growth declines, the optimal level of training lowers also. In the logic of the firm, it is necessary to reduce the relative weight of the permanent employees and use a more atypical labour force of part-timers, temporary and dispatched workers. Since the 1970s, Japanese firms had adopted a 'low-growth management'. Competition had become extremely fierce among subcontractors of the same rank. It helped large companies to implement a restructuring and reorganization of their production process, to reduce their costs and cope with the difficult economic circumstances. It had already appeared that it was much easier for a large company to co-ordinate employment and wages with subcontractors utilizing effectively non-regular workers (Isogai, Uemura and Ebizuka 2000). As a matter of fact, the number of female non-regular employees had already started to increase in the beginning of the 1980s, with the introduction of information technology. After the subsequent burst of high growth culminating with the bubble economy of the second part of the

1980s, the 'low-growth' management way of thinking came back to the fore on a much larger scale in the 1990s adjustments.

In the current low-growth period, both employees and management can take advantage of the changes in the mutual investment logic. The demise of a number of large firms during the second half of the 1990s has made employees aware of the risks of relying too much on firm-specific skills. The risks are bound to further increase in the future, creating strong incentives for a firm to develop more widely marketable capabilities on its own, even at private expense if necessary. The changes in the system started by companies such as Matsushita Electric, Komatsu and Fujitsu provide good examples. In giving employees the opportunity to cash in pensions from the beginning of their careers by incorporating the retirement lump sum into salary, they give more flexibility to management. But, in facilitating a move to another firm it also reflects the willingness of the employees not to make so easily long-term binding mutual investments. The intensification of international competition and the widening range of values to which workers subscribe also contribute to the demand for change. A growing heterogeneity of the employees' needs and expectations is observed. It reflects the growing weight of service industries and of white-collar jobs, and the diversification of female employment. Then contradictions appear between different needs and expectations. A number of employees may still give priority to job guarantee and salary reflecting the household's lifetime needs with the counterpart of long working hours, job rotations, transfers within Japan and abroad. Indeed, in most large companies the permanent male employees continue to be the core of the labour–management compromise (Benson and Debroux 1998). Others may accept a flat career without large salary rise, but select their working place and refuse overtime work. A growing segment of female employees wants to be given the opportunity to make a career on an equal footing with the male employees, but many of them may prefer to stay on the labour market as part-timers or dispatched workers. However, even in those latter cases, not all of them are ready to accept as usual purely routine jobs. Without aiming to achieve managerial positions, growing numbers of women give more importance to their vocational ability and skills. They expect to be rewarded for their ability and productivity by getting promotion and higher compensation (Ministry of Labour 1999). More elder workers may be willing to work after retiring because of the necessity to retain an income before receiving the retirement allowance, but with a flexible schedule and a workplace close to their home as their most important conditions.

A transitional stage of departure from the traditional employees' model of employment

To establish stable employment practices on the new labour market it is necessary to conciliate those contradictory requests. The recent labour law reforms and those of the retirement system requested by both management and the employees are departing somewhat from the principles that developed during the high-growth period (Yashiro 1998). Until recently, all the types of jobs that did not assure employment stability in a given company were frowned upon. They were considered 'bad' jobs and constraints were imposed on their development to avoid any abuse from the employers. In a structural low-growth period, such a way of thinking is impeding the creation of new jobs opportunities. To maintain the advantages of the minority of permanent employees in large companies, the system prevents those willing to work under more flexible conditions from finding the kind of job they want. It means that it is time to rethink a pattern of labour relations that have been almost exclusively centred on trade unions–management deals involving permanent male employees (Yashiro 1998). It is true that the Japanese labour market was always sufficiently flexible to cope with the vagaries of the business cycles. But it was essentially because of its segmentation. Working conditions in SMEs are harsh and most often based on strict monitoring in a Taylorist-type of production process. The same can be said about the non-permanent workers in large firms. Compared with the highly institutionalized wage setting for male employees in large firms, the wage determination in SMEs was always strongly influenced by conditions in the spot labour market. Different wage determination mechanisms have always coexisted for female workers in large companies. The growing recourse to the courts by female employees shows that it is now considered by many of them as a breach of the principle of equality (Debroux 2000). So, many workers would like to be given opportunities to get away with the dichotomy between first-class permanent status and second class non-permanent status. A crucial point when considering part-time workers and non-permanent employees is to respect their vocational abilities. They are eager to improve their vocational abilities in order to achieve a professional life independent of their employers. Female workers in particular are anxious to have a wage system that focuses on the content of the task (Ministry of Labour 1999). Despite some attempts to organize independently from the traditional unions, for the time being, with so many uncertainties in the regulatory environment and lingering conservative attitude concerning the role of women in society, recognized expertise is about the only solution to avoid being discriminated against.

The trade unions recognize fully the necessity of an adaptation of the system. Rengo is making a proposal in that regard. It calls for the introduction of Japanese-style work-sharing by reducing the amount of overtime, and for the implementation of Rengo-version job placement service. It is even ready to start its own training programmes (Rengo website 2000). Finally, Rengo did not oppose the end to the revision of the fixed-term contract law (see details later) but pushed for the enactment of a comprehensive employment contract law that would provide strict guidelines for the dismissal of employees. Such a conciliatory attitude surely reflects Rengo's current weakness. The voice of the workers has been weakened during this long crisis. Unions have been unable to defend efficiently the workers' jobs at a time of drastic restructuring. Therefore, they suffer from a lack of credibility even among their members (Tsuru 1995). Nevertheless, it shows also a flexibility of mind on their part. The debate is now open inside the unions to foresee change before it happens and to act before the government and employers, even if it means giving up some of their vested interests. Labour unions recognize they have been too slow in organizing non-regular employees. In 1996, Rengo established guidelines for organizing such workers, and founded 'regional unions' to which individual part-time workers in a region could affiliate. Rengo plans to put more effort into these units in order to better organize non-regular employees (Ohki 1998).

Part-timers and temporary workers were always hired on an ad hoc basis and their salary considered in the same way as the purchase of raw material or components. It explains the large gap between employees benefiting from seniority-based wages, receiving a yearly bonus and fringe benefits, and those whose wages just reflected the market conditions and who served as a cushion to smooth the impact of the business cycles' downturns. From the point of view of wages and employment the contractual differences have become institutionalized status differences. Indirectly, because of the concentration of female employment in SMEs, the companies using the most part-time and temporary workers, it has created the largest gap in terms of wages and working conditions between men and women in the developed world (ILO 2000).

The Maruko Alarms case in 1996 was probably a turning point as regards the issue of the unequal treatment of part-time workers because they are non-permanent employees. The court decision concerned the alleged gender discrimination against 28 married women who had worked for the company during periods of from 6 to 27 years under continuously renewed two-month contracts and were engaged in the same duties for the same working hours and days as permanent employees. The court considered that it was unfair for part-time workers doing relatively simple tasks under working conditions similar to those of permanent employees for a long period of time to receive 20 per cent less than regular employees (Kezuka 2000). The judgement brought to light the important problem of the part-time workers' working conditions and called for regulatory action. A 'Study Group Concerning Employment Management of Part-Time Workers' was formed and it released a report in April 2000. The key feature of the report is the elaboration of a 'balanced' approach to equal treatment in cases where part-time workers are performing identical tasks to those of permanent workers and, specifically, the stipulation of identical methods to determine treatment and standards for labour conditions. The idea of 'balance' seem to assume implicitly equal treatment in the sense that wages should be equal if the tasks are the same. However, it does not reject the idea of reasonable compensation differences between the two kinds of employees performing the same tasks because of different obligations concerning overtime, holidays and transfers to other workplaces. In the case of difference in the tasks performed by the part-time workers from those performed by permanent employees, the report recommends that wages, bonus and retirement allowances be considered in relation to the duties and levels of the workers in question. In cases where part-time workers' ability improves with time the improvement should be reflected in their treatment. Moreover, opportunities should be provided for education and training. On the whole, difficulties remain because the report does not present any clear criteria for assessing the equal treatment of part-time workers, especially those engaged in different activities from permanent employees. Nevertheless, it is significant because it asks labour and management to explain any difference in treatment of the different types of employees, and it attempts to make the differences quantitatively specific (Kezuka 2000). The situation is thus getting better but the task is not over. The legal norm aspect of the Part-Time Work Law needs to be reinforced with a provision prohibiting management from treating part-time workers differently from permanent workers without clear and verifiable reasons. The Labour Standards Law (LSL) has been comprehensively revised for the first time in 50 years. The revised Part-time Work Law, which came into effect at the same time (April 1999) requires companies to provide a hiring notification when employing a part-time worker. One recommendation of the Study Group was related to the fact that most part-timers work under fixed-term contracts. The termination of employment means that firms do not extend a contract after the expiration of a fixed-term of employment, such as three or six months. If a company stops renewing a contract with a part-time worker who had had his or her contract renewed several times previously and where the contract could be expected to be renewed again, there are now grounds for the case to be considered as a dismissal under case law (Ministry of Labour 2000).

Nevertheless, laws cannot by themselves be expected to correct the unequal treatment of part-time workers. Eventually, the external aspect is the most important element. It is the responsibility of public authorities to foster the development of an external labour market in which a fair wage mechanism is based on the professional ability of workers. It is not the case for the time being because of the low level of specialization of the workers and the blurred lines between tasks that exist in most firms. Moreover, any comprehensive solution will require also a reform of the tax and social assurance systems that affect the way part-timers, especially women, work (Ministry of Labour 2000).

The Equal Employment Opportunity Law of 1986 was also revised in 1999. The new version has stronger 'claws' than the older one that just requested companies to 'endeavour efforts' not to discriminate against female labour. Although widely criticized because of the weakness of its enforcement power and its ambiguity (Hanami 2000), the new law calls nevertheless for a stricter control in the case of gender discrimination related to recruitment, training, promotion and compensation. The Japanese tradition of conciliation and persuasion has probably made the law less compelling than it would have been in a Western context. But it fundamentally brings into question the traditional system of gender role differentiation on the labour market. Among other measures, the revision removed most of the regulations devised with the objective of protecting supposedly weak female workers. They were often conducive to indirect discrimination practices. Many companies used the constraints imposed on female labour as a pretext not to hire them or offer them equal career opportunities. So, in this sense it was a step in the direction of gender-neutral rules promoted by the International Labour Organization (ILO). For instance, the revised law allows women to work at night between 10p.m. and 5a.m. the following morning, a practice which had been prohibited in the past. They can also perform as many overtime hours as the male workers. Rengo recognized fully the need for such liberalization as it was supported by the majority of women. However, the Union Confederation added that liberalization should be part of a policy limiting working hours for both male and female workers. Freeing women from a number of regulatory constraints cannot be considered as real social progress if it means that they have to work very long hours with very little holidays like the current male permanent employees (Rengo website 1999). De facto, only a very narrow segment of the female population would be able to benefit from it and the majority of the others may well see a degradation of their working conditions because of the liberalization. Public authorities are trying to respond to those demands. The Ministry of Labour instituted a system of certification and awards for 'family-friendly' firms which help their employees to manage both work and childcare or other nursing responsibilities at home. The measures enabling their employees to have flexible working conditions were timed to coincide with the full enforcement of the Child Care and Family Leave System in the existing Child Care Leave System in April 1999. The awards were founded to make the aims and contents of the new law better known and to promote the adoption of work practices which allow employees to achieve a better balance between work and the family (Sato 2000). However, for the time being, the large majority of SMEs employing female workers cannot afford to comply with the law requirements, for financial reasons and because of a shortage of qualified personnel. Therefore, changes are expected to be gradual.

The amendments to the Labour Standards Law show also a willingness to accommodate individual needs in labour contracts. Until now, there was almost nothing between part-time jobs and full-time permanent employment. The LSL was amended in response to the call for deregulation of working hours. It also allowed labour to be hired on fixed-term contracts for up to three years. Although fixed-term employment contracts are linked to job insecurity, they also offer new jobs opportunities. It should be true of the new three-year contractual agreement, although it will be limited to jobs that require sophisticated and professional knowledge. Nikkeiren had called for an extension of work-related contracts to five years. Perhaps reflecting a concern that such provisions may be abused by employers, the legislator has settled for a three-year period as a compromise.

The amendments to the LSL will allow discretionary work schemes to be applied across a broader range of occupations, such as R & D, planning and analysis of information management systems, gathering information and editing in the mass media, and designing. In the case of such white-collar work, there is no proportional relation between the number of hours worked and the output. The increase in the discretionary work schemes weakens the relations between working hours and wages. It may be a good method to shift from wages based on the number of working hours to a performance-based system. It also gives the opportunity to white-collar workers to develop their capabilities and acquire new skills on their own, in order to be clearly appraised on an individual basis. In the end, it may lead to a decrease in working hours and a rise in productivity per hour. The expansion of provisions allowing for more discretionary work was strongly supported by management. Rengo was not opposed to the system as it has recognized that the revision of the LSL can be a significant step toward establishing fair labour–management relations suitable for a changed labour market. In the end a compromise was found. Rengo concentrated its efforts on obtaining a ministerial ordinance that would allow labour unions to be involved in the implementation of new arrangements for working hours. Nikkeiren accepted the scheme although it declared that the meticulously detailed provisions for the scheme will mean that the productivity benefits are less likely to be achieved. The scheme for planning and for project-type work obliges firms to obtain the unanimous agreement of their worker–management committee and to pay due attention to the health of the employees. Despite the strict regulations, it seems to be popular among a growing number of firms. Most of the time the schemes are applied in conjunction with the introduction of new wages systems such as annualization (Japan Labour Bulletin 2000).

Ageing of the population means that in Japanese society most 65-year-old people will be assumed to be still at work in the future. The minimum pensionable age is gradually increasing to 65, whereas the current system of re-employment is at 60 after mandatory retirement. It is necessary to take into account the differences in professional capability and other factors such as health. Therefore, a new wage system entirely disconnected from the current employment would not respect the diversity of individual situations (Yashiro 1998). In line with this issue, the Ministry of Labour released the results of the fiscal 2000 year *Survey on Employment Management*, focusing on retirement management. As for employment extension and re-employment schemes, many companies want to apply a wage system different from that for younger employees. Apart from that, the most often mentioned challenges are the reappraisal of duties and the work environment, preventing a decline in work efficiency, pay arrangements and the shortage of posts, the need to reappraise working hours and working patterns (Ministry of Labour 2000). All those problems are very difficult to handle. Many companies recognize that they will need elder workers in the years to come. However, they also intend to be very selective in their choice of the workers who could be reinstated. Companies whose unions belong to the Japanese Electrical, Electronic and Information Unions affiliated to Rengo (Rengo Electric) are those that have adopted the most comprehensively employment extension schemes (Rengo website 2000). Thus, some active steps are being taken, although most practical measures are still debated in most firms at this stage.

Increasing private presence in the human resource management business

The law revision easing restrictions on private job placement companies is an important element in the reform. Until recently, this was a public monopoly with private services playing only a marginal role. Now, the labour market is dominated by white- collar types of work, with varied skill requirements. So, the mismatch between job offers and job applicants in the labour market has become more pronounced in terms of age and job type due to such changes in the industrial structure and the attitude of job applicants towards work. Job placement services were strongly geared to non-qualified or semi-qualified blue-collar workers, introduced for free in an undifferentiated manner to employers. The system was an outdated remnant of a period during which there was perhaps some reason to fear abuse by employers and non-respect of working conditions, but it was completely out of tune with the new labour market needs. From now on, private job placement companies will be involved in almost all areas. It will not be of help only to unemployed people, but may greatly help the personnel department in many companies who find it difficult to dispatch redundant personnel to related companies. SMEs are also in trouble. They may need workers but often not middle-aged generalist managers. Moreover, many of them want to relinquish dependence on a large firm (Debroux 2000). Therefore, large companies need to find new outlets for their underemployed workforce. Proof of the change in the environment can be seen in the behaviour of Rengo. After a constant opposition during the debates concerning the relaxation of the restrictions in the mid-1900s, the Union Confederation has decided to offer job placement services to union and non-union members. It shows a departure from a protracted opposition to the system towards a more pragmatic approach responding to the dire needs for finding jobs for the growing number of unemployed people.

Dispatched work was always considered inherently 'bad' and had to be strictly controlled. However, on a Japanese labour market still very regulated despite the gradual liberalization, it offers the rare opportunity to select one's own work and place of work. The revision of the Worker Dispatching Law abolished general restrictions on types of work which dispatched employees could undertake with the adoption of a negative list system by which only listed activities were prohibited. However, once again, a compromise had to be found between the management position and that of the trade unions. The dispatched employee is to be allowed to stay in the same company for no more than one year lest it might put into jeopardy permanent employment. The Law has also strengthened workers' protection. The dispatching agency must inform the client company whether the dispatched worker is enrolled in social and labour insurance. Dispute resolution procedures are improved. A dispatched worker can report to the Ministry of Labour the fact that a dispatching agency or the client company has violated provisions of the Law. Retaliatory treatment against the reporting worker is prohibited. Employment Security offices are to counsel a dispatched worker and provide necessary advice and other assistance (Ministry of Labour 2000).

Conclusion

With the rise of the number of non-permanent part-time workers, older workers and married women on the labour market, the diversification of needs increases. The demand for long-term job guarantees and wage rises goes along with specific demands related to workplaces, working hours and other varied conditions. The wage schemes that linked age, tenure and head of household position are replaced by a system where individual merit is more explicitly recognized. Non-permanent types of work acquire a new legitimacy and a regulatory framework is put into place in order to maintain fairness and avoid labour conflict. For a long time, although over regulated in many respects, the Japanese human resource management system worked by keeping unclear many points related to employment conditions. Therefore, in view of the numerous 'loose ends' built into the system, it is not surprising that many problems come to the fore in a period of liberalization. The new Worker Dispatching Law is causing a number of social troubles. The number of complaints is running high and recourse to the courts has increased (Nikkei Weekly 1999). A fair treatment of the part-time workers will still require a lot of regulatory and non-regulatory changes (Japan Labour Bulletin, November 2000). It concerns workers with such different status that it makes it difficult to establish general rules. For the same reason, there are a number of inconsistencies in the legislation concerning female workers. A consensus on the understanding and interpretation of the concepts of protection and equality has not yet been reached. Such confusion is mainly due to the remaining attitudinal problems related to the position and role of women in Japanese society. It would take time to solve them whatever the regulatory environment. The new Equal Employment Opportunity Law (EEOL) is certainly a step in the right direction but it should not be the last.

Japanese public authorities, management and labour representatives do not intend to rock the boat. They intend to change the system and makes it more dynamic and attuned to the economic and social evolution, while keeping intact the Japanese stable social fabric. Indeed, despite ten years of very low growth, Japanese society remains stable. Income redistribution is increasingly skewed and the income gap is growing but the Japanese Gini coefficient seems to remain at an acceptable level in a country very sensitive to social inequality (Economic Planning Agency 1999). Little by little employment practices are departing from the traditional model privileging long-term job guarantee. Under the revised LSL, the Ministry of Labour is urging employers and workers to consult each other as frequently as possible. The Japanese system is at the preliminary stage of adjustment. The situation is fluid and it may still take a long time and many new incremental changes to find the right balance. However, assessment of the progress so far, the quality of the debate on the key issues and the initiatives taken by both employers and unions justify a reasonable optimism. This seems to indicate that in the end it can be expected that both Japanese firms and employees will find their marks and create a new system responding to their respective needs and interest.

References

Aoki, M. (1994) 'The Japanese firm as a system of attributes', in M. Aoki and R. Dore (eds) *The Japanese Firm: The Sources of Competitive Strength*, New York: Oxford University Press.

Araki, T. (1998) 'Recent legislative developments in equal employment and harmonization of work and family life in Japan', *Japan Labour Bulletin*, 37(4): 5–10.

Benson, J. and Debroux, P. (1998) 'HRM in Japanese enterprises: trends and challenges', in C. Rowley (ed.) *Human Resource Management in the Asia Pacific Region*, London: Cass.

Debroux P. (2000) 'The role of the venture business culture in the renewal of Japanese industry', *International Business Review*, 9: 657–68.

Dore, R. (1987) *Taking Japan Seriously*, Stanford, CA: Stanford University Press.

Dore, R. (2000) *Stock Market Capitalism: Welfare Capitalism*, Oxford: Oxford University Press.

Economic Planning Agency (1999) *White Book on Japanese Life-style*, Tokyo: EPA.

Hanada, M. and Hirano, Y. (2000) 'Industrial welfare and company-ist regulation', in R. Boyer and T. Yamada (eds) *Japanese Capitalism in Crisis,* London: Routledge.

Hanami, T. (2000) 'Equal employment revisited', *Japan Labour Bulletin*, January: 5–10.

Hunter, J. (1993) *Japanese Women Working*, London and Geneva: Routledge.

International Labour Organization (ILO) (2000) *Yearly Work Statistics*, ILO.

Isogai, A., Uemura, H. and Ebizuka, H. (2000) 'The hierarchical market–firm nexus as the Japanese mode of regulation', in R. Boyer and T. Yamada (eds) *Japanese Capitalism in Crisis*, London: Routledge.

Kezuka, K. (2000) 'Legal problems concerning part-time work in Japan', *Japan Labour Bulletin*, 1 September: 6–12.

Japan Labour Bulletin (2000) 'Update on the Discretionay Work Scheme', *Japan Labour Bulletin*, 1 August: 2–3.

Ministry of Labour (1999) *Survey on Women Workers' Employment Management*, Tokyo: MoL.

Ministry of Labour (2000) *Survey on Employment Management*, Tokyo: MoL.

Nikkeiren, (1995) *Shin Jidai no Nihonteki Keiei (A New Era for Japanese-Style Management)*, Tokyo: Nikkeiren.

Nikkei Weekly (1999) 'A fair treatment for dispatched workers?' *Nikkei Weekly*, 6 November: 7.

Ohki, K. (1998) 'New trends in enterprise unions and the labour movement', in H. Hasegawa and G. Hook (eds) *Japanese Business Management: Restructuring for Low Growth and Globalization*, London: Routledge.

Rengo website (1999) and (2000) http://www.jtuc-rengo.org.jp.

Sato, H. (2000) 'The current situation of "family-friendly" policies in Japan', *Japan Labour Bulletin*, 1 February: 5–10.

Tsuru, S. (1993) *Japan's Capitalism*, New York: Cambridge University Press.

Tsuru S. (1995) 'The determinant of union decline in Japan', *Labour Issues Quarterly*, (26), Winter: 14–16.

Yashiro N. (1998) *Koyo Kaikaku no Jidai (Time for Employment Reform)*, Tokyo: Chuo Shinsho.

Chapter 16

Business and management in Australia

Russell Lansbury

Overview

Australia is a highly urbanized, advanced industrial society with a population of 19 million. During the past 30 years, major changes in the composition of the Australian workforce have occurred with cyclical fluctuations of the overall economy. Between 1965 and 1999, the proportion of the Australian workforce employed in agriculture declined from almost 10 per cent to less than 5 per cent while those in industry declined from 40 per cent to 20 per cent. Conversely, the service sector grew susbstantially from employing 50 per cent to 75 per cent in 1999. Unemployment rose to around 11 per cent in 1993 but had declined to 7 per cent by 1999.

The Australian management environment has been significantly affected in the past few decades by the injection of overseas investment. Some industries are almost entirely foreign controlled: 90 per cent of vehicle building, 75 per cent of pharmaceuticals and aluminium. Apart from the large-scale, predominantly foreign owned corporations, Australia also possesses a large number of small Australian owned enterprises. The typical firm in Australia is family owned or owner managed and employs fewer than 100 people. Only 600 enterprises employ more than 1000 people. Yet half the value added by the manufacturing industry is contributed by the largest 200 firms, half of which are at least one-quarter foreign controlled. The decisions of these top 200 corporations greatly affect Australian industry because they employ about half of the total workforce engaged in manufacturing and account for 60 per cent of the fixed capital expenditure. These firms also exercise considerable influence on the national economy through their pricing and investments as well as their general competitive capacity; in industrial relations matters, large firms set the pattern for smaller ones.

Although located in one of the fastest-growing economic regions of the world, in recent years the Australian economy has not fared as well as some of its trading partners. According to the Institute of Management Development (IMD)–World Economic Forum's 1999 *World Competitiveness Report*, Australia was ranked twelfth out of 23 Organization for Economic Co-operation and Development (OECD) countries, compared with tenth place in 1989. While Australia scored well for business efficiency, with comparatively good levels of productivity, its managers were regarded as deficient in long-term orientation, strategic skills and international experience. A 1995 report (Karpin Committee 1995) commissioned by the Australian government, and known as the Industry Task Force on Leadership and Management

Skills (the Karpin Report), argued that a lack of depth within the ranks of Australian management had contributed to poor economic performance. Furthermore, Australia's history of protectionism and prevailing educational culture have resulted in limited attention being paid to the personal and integrative skills of managers. Accordingly, the Karpin Report called for a programme of management reform that would lead to employment growth and improved living standards. Key proposals in the Karpin Report included upgrading management education at all levels, workplace reform and developing a positive enterprise culture through education and training.

The Business Council of Australia (BCA) issued a report, *Managerial Leadership in the Workplace*, in 2000 in which they expressed concern about the capacity of Australian enterprises to grasp and create new opportunities emerging from globalization, technological change and the knowledge economy (BCA 2000). A survey of chief executive officers (CEOs) by the BCA revealed that they estimated that 55 per cent of potential improvement in their business was achievable through better managerial leadership, while 26 per cent of potential improvement in business was available from improved capability, performance and alignment of employees. Although the industrial relations system was seen as an impediment to workplace reform, only 19 per cent of potential business performance improvement was regarded as flowing from a better industrial relations system. In other words, the view of Australia's senior CEOs was that better managerial leadership was the key to improving national economic performance.

Managers' characteristics and employment

Managers comprise approximately 7 per cent of the total workforce, while professional employees account for around 18 per cent. There is an overlap between these categories as some professional employees, such as engineers and accountants, occupy managerial positions but are classified as professional in workforce statistics. Nevertheless, while there was a steady increase in the number of managers recorded by the census and workforce survey from the end of the Second World War until the early 1980s, the recent past has witnessed a decline in numbers. This has been largely due to the economic recession of the 1980s and 1990s when most large corporations (in both the private and public sectors) undertook programmes of restructuring, downsizing (reducing the number of employees) and outsourcing (contracting to external providers work previously conducted internally). After each recession, many companies continued to operate with fewer managers, and those who remained assumed greater workloads.

The distribution of managers throughout Australian industry is uneven. The wholesale and retail sector has the highest percentage of managers, while agriculture has the lowest. The financial sector, which is one of the newest and more dynamic industries, has the second highest percentage of managers. In making these interindustry comparisons, it should be noted that the census of occupational categories is frequently applied in a rather broad way to different industries. In some sectors, such as retailing, the term manager is used to describe a wide range of functions, from someone in charge of a small section in a store to the person responsible for the whole store itself. Similarly, it appears that in the rapidly expanding and relatively new field of finance, the term 'manager' is applied to technical specialists who are not necessarily in charge of other staff.

The public sector, which employs approximately one-quarter of the total workforce, has a large proportion of Australian managers. Since the Second World War, with the rapid expansion of Commonwealth powers, a vast new managerial élite within the public service was created and given the security of tenure and considerable powers. However, the position of managers in the public sector has become much less secure in the past decade or so as many large government business organizations have been corporatized or privatized. Furthermore, many government departments and statutory authorities now appoint many middle to senior managers on fixed contracts.

Management in Australia has not acquired the prestige or status accorded to executives and business people in many other advanced industrial societies. Byrt and Masters (1978; 29) lament that: 'In Australia, the achievement of success through business does not appear to be a feat worthy of admiration'. Generally, managers are not held in high esteem by the Australian public. A national survey of occupational status and prestige by Congalton (1969), for example, revealed that the manager of a large industrial enterprise was ranked only twelfth. Yet chief executives and senior government officials command not only some of the highest salaries but exert considerable power within Australian society. For the most part, however, they maintain a low profile and avoid public attention.

Women and management

The Karpin Report (Karpin Committee 1995) noted that Australia had one of the lowest figures in the industrialized world for women in management. In 1999, less than 4 per cent of women were employed as managers compared with approximately 12 per cent of men. The four industries in which more than 15 per cent of managers are women are either of the nurturing kind, such as health and community services, or are relatively new industries such as finance. The need for specialized staff in these latter industries has grown so rapidly that new opportunities for women have been created. Little progress has been made by women into the managerial and professional ranks of traditionally male-dominated industries such as manufacturing, mining or construction.

Many of the women who have moved into managerial or professional positions are in the human resources or personnel area, and women constitute almost one-third of all personnel specialists in Australia. The personnel function includes many 'caring' tasks and is therefore consistent with the traditional female stereotype. In addition, women are typically found in lower-level occupations, especially those involving part-time or casual work with little or no career prospects. Although some women do reach more senior positions, it is only in relatively small numbers and usually in newer areas that are less subject to traditional male dominance.

Even though women have made some inroads into human resources and some other specialist areas, their numbers are still relatively small. The growing demand for highly trained specialists, especially in the finance industry, has undoubtedly widened opportunities for women. In the words of one senior bank executive:

> Among our 3,400 managers there would probably be only about 30 women, but we would have another 150 who are not classified as managers but are being paid managerial salaries for market-related reasons. In other words, they have been hired for special skills in a particular area and we are paying them equivalent to our lower levels of management.

> (*Lansbury and Quince 1989: 102*)

Women have advanced more strongly in the management ranks of the public service sector than in the private sector. In the senior executive service of the Australian public service, women held 16 per cent of positions by the mid-1990s, compared with only 4 per cent in 1984. In 1993, 26 per cent of promotions into this level went to women. Furthermore, both the state and Commonwealth governments are under pressure from a variety of women's groups and have created a number of specialized departments for women's needs. These departments have given female public servants the opportunity to progress into managerial positions at a much faster rate than if they had moved up through the normal career channels. The problem these women now face is whether their experience and seniority will be recognized if they move into other areas of public or private sectors.

A study of the perceptions of women managers by Still and Jones (1984) found a number of stereotypical attitudes towards women in managerial positions. Typical views expressed included: women are too emotional and therefore react badly under stress; women are not career oriented; women tend to become pregnant; they lack initiative and motivation; they tend to be away from work all the time because of family problems; and women have an alternative role as wives and mothers. They conclude: 'The Australian community still has a long way to go before women will be generally accepted in positions of power and influence' (Still and Jones 1984: 294).

While many Australian organizations have formal policies that encourage women to move into managerial positions, the statistical evidence suggests that very little is done to achieve this. It would appear that the programmes sponsored by the Australian government and the threat of US-style affirmative action legislation have made some impact on both private and government organizations, at least in terms of their 'formal policies', but progress remains very slow vis-a-vis corporate cultures.

Women face many hidden barriers to remaining in the workforce and moving into managerial and professional areas in the absence of childcare services. Unless such services are made more readily available, career opportunities now opening up to women may be out of the reach of many who would like careers in management.

A more recent study by Still (1993) indicates that progress by women within management ranks may have slowed if not reversed in recent years. Support for these findings comes from a 1993 survey of Australia's leading 100 accounting firms (Still 1993: 35). Although women comprised 17 per cent of management staff in the top 20 firms, the number of women in senior management in the 100 firms had declined from 2.4 per cent to 1.9 per cent since the mid-1980s.

The Karpin Report claimed that the 'glass ceiling' for women in management seemed thicker in Australia than other industrialized countries. It argued that Australian industry needed to do more in order to capitalize on the talents of women and recommended that the 'peak' bodies in the private sector set 'broad and achievable targets' for the number of women to achieve senior managerial positions by the year 2000. Evidence from the International Labour Organization (Still 1993: 26) shows that Australia has the lowest percentage of female managers in the industrialized world and recorded one of the slowest percentage increases in the previous decade.

Management recruitment and mobility

The methods used by organizations to recruit managerial staff depend on whether they are recruiting people for senior or junior positions. At the junior level, organizations typically recruit directly from within their own ranks. One method of recruitment for senior management positions, which has expanded since the mid-1980s in the private and public sectors, is executive search or headhunting. The growth and acceptance of executive search agencies have undoubtedly been related to the increasing need for organizations to recruit senior managerial and professional staff externally. A decade ago, executive search was seen as something of an undercover method in Australia, whereas today it is accepted as a legitimate method of recruitment. However, it is difficult, if not impossible, to ascertain the proportion of senior positions filled by executive search methods.

Traditionally, interfirm mobility has been limited as managers followed a career path within one organization. However, the past five to ten years have seen the emergence of managers who do not view their careers in terms of organization only. This development is related to the needs of Australian organizations in response to the rapidly changing economic environment that has included oil crises, recessions and the internationalization of Australian business.

A study by Lansbury and Quince (1989) showed a tendency by companies to reposition people either during training or while they are still at a junior management level. Once people reach the more senior levels, organizations tend to be reluctant to move them across functions. This reflects, in part, a lack of sophistication among most Australian employers in regard to career planning and development. However, overseas experience within a firm appears to be increasingly important, and is undoubtedly related to the internationalization of Australian business. It was felt that Australian managers and professionals would have to be given greater international training and experience as their organizations moved into world markets and international organization moved into Australia. Banks in particular have become convinced that their managers need foreign experience.

Remuneration

One of the most important changes in the past decade has been the development of uniform salary schemes, that is, a system where all salary levels for managerial staff are arrive at by predetermined criteria rather than on an ad hoc basis in response to market forces or personal whim of senior managers. The criteria commonly used to determine salary levels are job sizing and market comparisons. Organizations are placing greater emphasis on establishing and maintaining salary levels that are comparable with market rates. This process has been assisted and stimulated by the growth in job evaluation, as it enables more meaningful comparisons to be made between organizations.

Market comparisons are conducted mainly by using independent salary surveys or information from events such as the Canberra Salary Conference, a privately sponsored conference of private and public sector organizations conducted each year to ascertain market rates for managerial salaries. In the Noble Lowndes–Committee for Economic Development (CED) (1989) survey, 53 per cent of companies said that independent salary surveys were the key factors in establishing salary levels, and another 34 per cent said they were the secondary factor.

Recent years have also witnessed the growing use of fringe benefits, greater emphasis on market orientation and emergence of the concept of pay for performance. The extent to which these changes have penetrated different industries has varied, but no industry has entirely escaped their effects. However, in expanding industries, such as finance, banking and retailing, the effects of these changes are most pronounced. The reasons underlying these changes include increasing incidence of corporate mergers, taxation, the growing emphasis on diversification and the impact of international markets on Australia.

As the need for more sophisticated compensation systems has emerged, the number of remuneration consultants has expanded to meet the demand. Many of these consultants have encouraged organizations towards a more structured approach to remuneration, supply support services and market data for the new systems. Several major remuneration consultants, who came to Australia originally to service multinational enterprises, have made a considerable impact on Australian business.

While the proliferation of benefits has been closely related to the desire of employers to use tax-effective forms of remuneration, it has been a product of the recruitment policies of employers seeking to attract managers and professionals away from rival organizations. In the study by Lansbury and Quince (1989), it was apparent that firms open to external recruitment at senior levels were more likely to offer an extensive array of discretionary non-taxable benefits than those organizations not open to such recruitment. Organizations in competitive industries where external recruitment was the norm were forced into providing packages and benefits to attract and retain staff.

Career planning, appraisal, training and development

In order to control and utilize their management and professional staff more effectively, Australian organizations have adopted the practices of succession planning, career planning, performance appraisal and managerial traineeships. There are two advantages to the development of such systematic human resources policies and practices. On the one hand, they allow companies to organize their managerial staff in a more efficient and effective manner. On the other hand, senior management gains greater control over its employees and their future careers within the organization. Many managers become locked into the company system, which then determines where and how their career should progress.

The value of employees as a strategic resource has come into sharp focus during the past ten years. Once managers are perceived as a strategic resource it becomes obvious that they must be trained, nurtured and motivated to achieve their full potential. The roles and functions of human resource managers and management consultants have expanded to fill this need.

Additionally, human resource managers in most large organizations are becoming highly qualified and often act as internal consultants to senior management, but this has been a slow and uneven process. Their sphere of influence is beginning to encompass a wider array of issues and policies, including: strategic planning, policy information, training and development, career path and success planning, and performance appraisal. However, these aspects are still underdeveloped in many Australian organizations.

The economic recession of the 1990s caused organizations to focus more directly on maximizing the efficiency of their staff. Most large organizations have reduced their number of managers during the past five years. The result is that the remaining staff are expected to work harder and perform more effectively. As a direct consequence of this quest for efficiency, there has been a growing emphasis on the need for performance appraisal. However, while an increasing number of companies indicate that they are introducing formal systems of performance appraisal, there is evidence of a high attrition rate among appraisal plans owing to problems of design and implementation (Lansbury 1980; 1995).

On-the-job experience remains the main route to a management position, although increasing importance is being given to management training both within and outside organizations. Internal courses tend to involve job-related skills while external courses provide broader, general management skills. The typical Australian manager spends about six days per year on formal education and training. A survey of Australian managers commissioned by the Karpin Task Force (Karpin Committee 1995) revealed that they believed their Australian colleagues had a poor commitment to learning, and lacked vision, strategic direction and teamwork abilities. Their counterparts in Asia saw Australian managers failing in overall management skills and educational attainment.

The Karpin Report (Karpin Committee 1995) noted that the formal qualifications of Australian managers lagged significantly behind those of managers in the world's major trading nations. Less than 30 per cent of Australian managers held a degree (or its equivalent) compared with more than 60 per cent of German and French managers and more than 80 per cent of Japanese and US managers. Included among the recommendations of the Karpin Report were the design of funding arrangements for postgraduate management education to encourage greater responsiveness by management schools to consumer and industry demand; greater focus by management schools on small business; improved articulation between various educational institutions which provide management courses; and an open learning network for the delivery of management education to small and medium-sized enterprises and professional firms.

Factors influencing managerial success

In an Australian study of 420 chief executives within both private and public organizations, Mukhi (1982) developed a profile of the personal characteristics his respondents perceived as required for the achievement of managerial success. The four characteristics ranked as most important by both private and public sector executives were: having a need to achieve results; the ability to work with a wide variety of people; being able to influence people; and negotiating skills. Public and private sector executives, however, differed in terms of how they ranked other characteristics. Executives in the private sector, for example, rated as very important the desire to seek new opportunities, leadership experience at an early stage in their career and strong family support, while public sector executives gave higher ratings to having more ideas than other colleagues, possessing sound technical training and having a manager as a model early in one's career.

Mukhi concluded that 'private sector managers reach top positions through achieving results via their own initiative, whereas public sector managers reach high positions not basically through results (although this does not mean to say that achieving results is not important) but through generating ideas' (Mukhi 1982: 26). The profile of the successful private sector manager that emerges from Mukhi's study is of one 'who has been thrown in the deep end to gain leadership experience' early in his or her career, has worked long hours, has attended an élite school, taken a university degree (preferably in finance or accountancy), worked for more than three organizations and held more than eight jobs. Having done all this, the individual should have reached a senior management position by the age of 33 and be in the top job by age 40.

The study by Lansbury and Quince (1989) found that younger senior managers typically had a wider range of experience. Approximately half the respondents indicated that their organizations had turned away from the idea of the specialist manager and were encouraging a more generalist approach. This reflects the changing nature of Australian organizations, the move towards decentralized organizational structures and also increasing diversification. Several respondents spoke of the need for managers to be able to understand a range of different functions and to have had experience in both line and staff areas. Based on responses from organizations in the study, intra-firm mobility, especially early in one's career, appears to be important for managerial success. It is becoming increasingly apparent that people who remain too long in a highly specialized area will find it difficult to transfer into managerial ranks later in their career.

Successful managers need knowledge and experience in a wide variety of functional areas and industries. Those who possess these characteristics can command very high salaries. Such individuals used to be highly mobile and are found in expanding industries such as finance and banking. This trend towards a high degree of mobility among managers is likely to continue as more organizations open up their senior positions to external recruitment.

Unionization of managers

A number of unions, especially those covering white-collar and professional workers, include managers among their numbers. However, with some minor exceptions, few unions cover managers. Many existing unions are interested in extending their coverage of managerial employees and strongly challenge the formation of new managerial unions. An example is provided by a small Institute of Middle Management that formed in 1983 with the aim of recruiting private sector managers. So far, however, it has failed to obtain registration under the Australian Industrial Relations Act owing to opposition from other unions and hence has been unsuccessful in attracting many members.

The most significant feature of managerial and professional unionization in Australia is that it is strongest in the government sector. A survey by the Australian Bureau of Statistics (1993) found that 22.5 per cent of managerial employees in Australia belong to a union. However, 66.4 per cent of government sector managers are unionized, compared with only 12.5 per cent of private sector managerial employees. A similar pattern emerges with professionals where 37.9 per cent are union members. However, only 8.6 per cent of professionals are unionized in the private sector, compared with 55.4 per cent of government-employed professionals.

It is difficult to predict future trends in unionization among managers. There is often hesitation on the part of managers about joining a union that includes other levels of employees. This may be due not only to a fear of losing status by becoming a union member, but also because of concern about a conflict of interest between representing the employer and having an allegiance to a union. Yet managers are increasingly aware that without the collective strength offered by a union they have little bargaining power with their employers. During periods of recession, it also becomes apparent that managers, like shop-floor employees, are likely to suffer a reduction in their conditions of employment as well as the loss of their jobs.

Issues of managerial pay and working conditions are now much more openly discussed than in the past and many managers increasingly express their dissatisfaction with their situation, especially at lower levels in the hierarchy. Hence, at the most basic level, managers are beginning to look for ways in which they might defend or enhance their position through collective action. The increasing size of organizations is another factor that has influenced managers to consider unionization. In a large bureaucratic structure, many managers, especially at the lower and middle levels, feel remote from the source of decision-making.

A union may be seen as a forum in which managers' interests can be discussed and provide a channel for communication to higher-level management. A union may also act as a pressure group to gain concessions for managers, especially when unions representing other groups of employees are seen to exercise considerable influence. The fact that managers have become more unionized in the public sector may be the result of experiencing a greater feeling of powerlessness in large government bureaucracies.

In the private sector, a closer sense of identity may still exist between managers and their companies but may also be more difficult to sustain as organizations become increasingly large and diffuse. Security of tenure for private sector managers is rapidly disappearing and the level of performance required of senior executives has increased. Thus, private sector managers may yet follow the example of their public sector colleagues and become highly unionized.

Management and employment relations

During the decade from the late 1980s to the late 1990s, the Australian economy was opened up to greater global competition. This was achieved by deregulating banks and other financial institutions, reducing tariff protection for manufacturing industry and decentralizing the industrial relations system. The process was begun by the Labour government but continued with greater momentum by the Conservative Coalition government from the mid-1990s. An important area of reform, which impacted on Australian management, was industrial relations. Until the late 1980s, the system remained rather centralized with the Australian Industrial Relations

Commission (AIRC) playing a key role in regulating the labour market. Under pressure from the BCA and other employer bodies, and with the co-operation of the trade unions, the Labour government spearheaded the introduction of enterprise bargaining. This was designed to encourage employers and unions to negotiate agreements at the enterprise level rather than relying on the centralized system of arbitration to determine wages and conditions (see Davis and Lansbury 1998).

After the change of government in 1996, the process of enterprise bargaining was accelerated and the role of the AIRC further diminished. The union movement became increasingly concerned at rising unemployment, the decline in union membership and the government's policy of encouraging non-union agreements as well as individual contracts. The government argued that the reforms would ensure that managers and employers would take more direct responsibility for employment relations at the enterprise level and result in greater productivity. The evidence suggested, however, that enterprise bargaining (among other things) had led to declining real wages, increased wage differentials and longer working hours, often as unpaid overtime.

The changing role of management in employment relations is reflected in the results of two major Australian Workplace Industrial Relations Surveys (AWIRS) conducted in 1990 and 1995 (see Callus *et al.* 1991 and Morehead *et al.* 1997). Among the most significant changes which the surveys revealed between 1990 and 1995 were the increase in formalized management practices, the decline in union influence at the workplace level and a growth in the diversity of pay systems. In terms of management practices, the most significant changes included the use of disciplinary procedures, training for supervisors on employee relations and the use of consultative committees. However, while there appeared to be an increase in the formal avenues open to employees to communicate with management, the majority of employees reported that they were not consulted about changes which affected them and had only limited opportunities to directly influence decisions. While an increasing number of organizations utilized employment relations managers or specialists (46 per cent in 1995 compared with 34 per cent in 1990), there was little change in the influence of the employee relations function within organization.

Hence, it would appear that while managers are being required to take a more active role in employment relations issues, as the industrial relations system becomes more decentralized, changes have focused mainly on introducing more structured and formalized systems rather than involving or 'empowering' employees at the workplace level (see also Davis and Lansbury 1996).

Conclusion

Having traced the growth and development of managerial employees in Australia we can conclude that not only is the old-style manager being replaced by the younger, more highly educated professional, but the nature of the managerial function is also changing. A diverse array of specialists now share many of the technical aspects of what was formerly the managers' exclusive role. The fragmentation of managerial activity has also affected first-line and middle-level managers. Industrial relations and human resources specialists, for example, have taken over many of the responsibilities for recruitment, training and even termination of staff that previously were the prerogatives of line management. The power of unions, not only at the shop-floor level but also within the ranks of clerical and administrative employees, has also restricted the freedom of managers to organize and distribute work at their own discretion. Pressures for greater employee involvement in decision-making have caused many managers to reassess their role in the enterprise and to consider becoming unionized as a defensive measure.

One of the most significant areas of change has been in the labour market processes involving managerial employees. As a result of extensive changes in the Australian economic environment in recent years, including the internationalization of business and stronger competition in the marketplace, there has been much greater mobility among managers between organizations. This has eroded traditional single-organizational careers, whereby most senior management positions were filled by internal recruitment.

Two distinct managerial and professional groups are emerging in Australia: those who have been promoted from lower levels within one organization and who tend to be older and have less formal qualifications, and those recruited into middle or senior positions externally who tend to be younger with wider experience and greater formal qualifications. Often the managers who have been recruited externally enjoy a higher level of remuneration and perquisites than their internal counterparts since they are recruited on the basis of a special package of salary and conditions. This development has been assisted by the growth of executive search consultants and headhunters who specialize in procuring the services of senior managers from other organizations.

In the area of remuneration, a great deal of attention has been paid to devising tax-effective packages that will attract and retain managers whose skills are in high demand. Such systems are now facing changes in tax laws that are designed to minimize the opportunities for tax avoidance. This is likely to remain a dynamic area of change in the future.

It is possible that Australia will follow the trend established in other advanced industrial societies towards greater differentiation within management between a small but powerful group at the top and a middle- to lower-level group that feels powerless and demoralized. There is evidence of this trend, especially with the emergence of a cadre recruited externally and given special nurturing and developmental opportunities. This division is likely to deepen in the public sector where organizations are often larger and more bureaucratic and the distance between the top decision-makers and middle managers often appears to be greater. However, private sector managers are also increasingly vulnerable to retrenchment and dismissal as the result of the increasing number of takeovers and mergers. The concept of lifetime employment, particularly for managers, is no longer as tenable in either the public or private sectors. Managers in Australia therefore face a dynamic but uncertain future.

References

Australian Bureau of Statistics (1993) *Annual Review of Trade Union Membership*, Canberra: Australian Government Publishing Service.

Business Council of Australia (BCA) (2000) *Managerial Leadership in the Workplace*, Melbourne: Business Council of Australia.

Byrt, W.J. and Masters, P.R. (1978) *The Australian Manager*, Ringwood: Penguin.

Callus, R., Morehead, A., Cully, M. and Buchanan, J. (1991) *Industrial Relations at Work: The Australian Workplace Industrial Relations Survey*, Canberra: Australian Government Publishing Service.

Congalton, A.A. (1969) *Status and Prestige in Australia*, Melbourne: Longman Cheshire.

Davis, E.M. and Lansbury, R.D. (eds) (1996) *Managing Together: Consultation and Participation in the Workplace*, Melbourne: Addison Wesley Longman.

Davis, E.M. and Lansbury, R.D. (1998) 'Employment relations in Australia', in G.J. Bamber and R.D. Lansbury (eds) *International and Comparative Employment Relations: A Study of Industrialised Market Economies*, Sydney: Allen & Unwin; London: Sage.

IMD–World Economic Forum (1999) *World Competitiveness Report*, Lausanne: IMD.

Karpin Committee (1995) *Enterprise Nation: Report of Industry Task Force on Leadership and Management Skills* (Karpin Report), Canberra: Australian Government Publishing Service.

Lansbury, R.D. (ed.) (1980) *Performance Appraisal: Managing Human Resources*, Melbourne: Macmillan.

Lansbury, R.D. (1995) 'Performance appraisal: the elusive quest?', in G. O'Neill and R. Kramar (eds) *Australian Human Resource Management*, Melbourne: Longman.

Lansbury, R.D. and Quince, A. (1989) 'Australia', in M. Roomkin (ed.) *Managers as Employees: An International Comparison of the Changing Character of Managerial Employment*, New York: Oxford University Press.

Morehead, A., Steele, M., Alexander, M., Stephen, K. and Duffin, L. (1997) *Changes at Work: The 1995 Australian Workplace Industrial Relations Survey*, Melbourne: Addison Wesley Longman.

Mukhi, S.K. (1982) 'Leadership paths and profiles', *Human Resource Management Australia* 20(3): 20–6.

Noble Lowndes–CED (1989) *Annual Review of Executive Salaries in Australia*, Sydney: Noble Lowndes–CED.

Still, L.V. (1993) *Where To From Here? The Managerial Woman in Transition*, Sydney: Business and Professional Publishing.

Still, L.V. and Jones, J.M. (1984) 'Perceptions of the Australian woman manager', *Search* 15(9–0): 278–84.

Further reading

Australian Bureau of Statistics (1998) *Labour Statistics*, Canberra: Australian Government Publishing Service.

Australian Bureau of Statistics (1993) *Annual Review of Trade Union Membership*, Canberra: Australian Government Publishing Service.

Australian Department of Employment and Industrial Relations (1983–94) *Labour Statistics*, Canberra: Australian Government Publishing Service.

Blandy, R. (1982) 'The senior executive', in R. Blandy and S. Richardson (eds), *How Labour Markets Work*, Melbourne: Longman Cheshire.

Business Council of Australia (2000) *Managerial Leadership in the Workplace*, Melbourne: Business Council of Australia.

Byrt, W.J. and Masters, P.R. (1978) *The Australian Manager*, Ringwood: Penguin.

Callus, R., Morehead, A., Cully, M. and Buchanan, J. (1991) *Industrial Relations at Work: The Australian Workplace Industrial Relations Survey*, Canberra: Australian Government Publishing Service.

Congalton, A.A. (1969) *Status and Prestige in Australia*, Melbourne: Longman Cheshire.

Davis, E.M. and Lansbury, R.D. (eds) (1996) *Managing Together: Consultation and Participation in the Workplace*, Melbourne: Addison Wesley Longman.

Davis, E.M. and Lansbury, R.D. (1998) 'Employment relations in Australia', in G.J. Bamber and R.D. Lansbury (eds) *International and Comparative Employment Relations: A Study of Industrialised Market Economies*, Sydney: Allen & Unwin; London: Sage.

IMD–World Economic Forum (1999) *World Competitiveness Report*, Lausanne: IMD.

Karpin Committee (1995) *Enterprise Nation: Report of Industry Task Force on Leadership and Management Skills* (Karpin Report), Canberra: Australian Government Publishing Service.

Lansbury, R.D. (1978) *Professionals and Management*, St Lucia: University of Queensland Press.

Lansbury, R.D. (ed.) (1980) *Performance Appraisal: Managing Human Resources*, Melbourne: Macmillan.

Lansbury, R.D. (1995) 'Performance appraisal: the elusive quest?', in G. O'Neill and R. Kramar (eds) *Australian Human Resource Management*, Melbourne: Longman.

Lansbury, R.D. and Quince, A. (1989) 'Australia', in M. Roomkin (ed.), *Managers as Employees: An International Comparison of the Changing Character of Managerial Employment*, New York: Oxford University Press.

Morehead, A., Steele, M., Alexander, M., Stephen, K. and Duffin, L. (1997) *Changes at Work: The 1995 Australian Workplace Industrial Relations Survey*, Melbourne: Addison Wesley Longman.

Mukhi, S.K. (1982) 'Leadership paths and profiles', *Human Resource Management Australia* 20(3): 20–6.

Noble Lowndes–CED (1989) *Annual Review of Executive Salaries in Australia*, Sydney: Noble Lowndes–CED.

Still, L.V. (1993) *Where To From Here? The Managerial Woman in Transition*, Sydney: Business and Professional Publishing.

Still, L.V. and Jones, J.M. (1984) 'Perceptions of the Australian woman manager', *Search* 15(9–0): 278–84.

Chapter 17

Whither South African management?

Frank M. Horwitz

Overview

South Africa's re-entry into competitive global markets in the 1990s created new managerial challenges. The legacy of apartheid is systematically being eroded, with some 30 per cent of South African managers being black. Employment discrimination is being replaced by policies and practices aimed at recruiting and developing black managers. Management development, changes in corporate culture and black advancement have become more prominent. Legislation such as the Employment Equity Act (1998) and Promotion of Equality Bill (1999) require employers of more than 50 people to develop an employment equity plan with specific measures to remove discriminatory employment practices.

Following Western approaches to management there is an emphasis on general management at middle to senior levels. These skills are acquired through career path planning experiences such as job rotation, project assignments and cross-functional appointments. General management education programmes such as an MBA or a shorter executive development programme, either at one or more of South Africa's seven business schools, or through international business schools which have recently entered the management education market, are popular. Management consulting firms also play an important role.

Decades of economic isolation created tough but inward-looking managers in South Africa who were hands-on and results oriented. Managers tended to be individualistic and directive in their styles, with a masculine orientation. Other than in the retail sector, fewer than 20 per cent of managerial jobs are held by women. Managers are appointed to such positions following five to ten years' work experience in a functional discipline or occupation such as engineering. With affirmative action and the impact of external factors, such as globalization, new technology and intense competition, this internal focus has begun to make way for greater internationalization, an export orientation and an opening of business practices to international best practice

Introduction

Management work in South Africa has, since the 1990s, been influenced by a fluid and sometimes uncertain political climate. Complexity and change have become standard features of the decision-making process now that simple 'right or wrong' responses of the past no longer work. Since the latter 1990s, however, greater stability prevailed and democracy has also been accompanied by higher economic growth, predicted to be around 3 per cent per annum in the early part of the twenty-first century.

There are certain watershed events which have shaped management practices in South Africa since 1970. These include the 1973 Natal strikes for improved working conditions and trade union recognition, the Soweto riots of 1976, the legalization of industrial relations rights and the impact of sanctions and disinvestment in the 1980s. The state of emergency introduced in 1986 created a siege economic strategy with inward-looking managerial practices, and further isolated South African business from international competition and new technology. This mindset made re-entry into world markets in the post-apartheid era more difficult, especially for the manufacturing and service sectors. However, since the first democratic election in 1994 several South African firms such as the Old Mutual insurance company, South African Breweries, Investee, Didata and SAPPI (paper and timber) have adapted quickly to global challenges and compete successfully in international markets.

Context

Labour and political rights

Several factors are important in the evolution of management in South Africa. Rapid growth of the trade union movement since 1980, from less than 10 per cent to over 30 per cent and around 3 272 999 members, has changed the nature of managerial work. The changes have consisted primarily of increasing support for human resource management, fair employment practices and equitable treatment. Authoritarian managerial styles and unilateral decisions have been eroded as expectations increased as apartheid structures were gradually eaten away. Managers have faced demands in which the separability of political and workplace issues is unclear. As a result they have experienced a steep learning curve, being forced into acquiring negotiating skills and getting used to dealing with complex issues.

Socio-economic factors

While a positive increase in economic growth has occurred since 1993, in the decade up to 1993 economic growth averaged at 1 per cent; this compared with a population growth rate of 2.5 per cent and unemployment of over 5.5 million, estimated at nearly 30 per cent of the economically active population. Whereas retrenchment in the 1980s focused primarily on blue collar employees, the 1990s and early 2000s saw job cuts at managerial and professional levels following organizational restructuring, delayering, downsizing and outsourcing. Rising costs, poor labour and capital productivity and intense competition as South Africa re-enters global markets, coupled with poorer economies of scale and higher wage costs than the Pacific Rim economics, have led to job losses at all levels. Meanwhile, the hoped-for high level of foreign investment necessary for employment creation, has not been attained. Managerial work in South Africa is therefore influenced by a mix of socio-political and labour market factors and the prevailing organizational culture.

The labour market

A structural inequality in the skill profile exists: a shortage of occupationally and managerially skilled workers is contrasted with an excess of unskilled labour. Meanwhile fairly low economic growth and a lack of managerial skills have led to a comparatively low level of spending on training and development. The *World Competitiveness Report* (1999) has indicated, however, that organizational investment in training and development is a decisive competitive factor. In comparison to developed market economies, South Africa's per capita output is one-sixth of Switzerland's, one-fifth of that of the USA and one-quarter of Japan's. Ultimately, labour and capital productivity is a managerial function.

While more than 35 per cent of managers have tertiary educational qualifications, nearly 60 per cent of formal sector employees working for them do not have a high school education. South African companies under apartheid did not invest sufficiently in human capital. This neglect has hampered successful large-scale re-entry into global markets. Though improving, South Africa is still rated lowly by the *World Competitiveness Report* among emerging industrial countries in terms of human resource priorities. Socio-economic and labour market issues remain pressing managerial challenges in the transition to a post-apartheid South Africa. The government has relaxed legislative provision on basic conditions of employment to allow greater flexibility for small firms, and is encouraging better education and training through the Skills Development and Employment Equity Acts (1998).

Structural factors
Apartheid created a distorted labour market with economic power concentrated in a few white hands. Economic power was, until recent moves to disaggregate or unbundle large corporations such as Gencor and Barlow Rand, concentrated in eight conglomerates which controlled over 70 per cent of the share capital on the Johannesburg Stock Exchange. There is also a concentration of managerial control through a system interlocking directorates where the same person(s) serve on the boards of several corporations. This social closure has limited the upward mobility of black managers and women. However, South Africa's re-entry into the international business community has forced an awareness about its relative competitiveness in the manufacturing and services sectors. Recently, the impetus has also been towards employment equity and diversity at all levels. There have been several black directors appointed to boards of directors. Although less than 20 per cent of South Africa's company directors are black or women, this is likely to change significantly by the year 2005.

Specific features
Management styles
Managerial styles reflect both Western values based on individualism and meritocracy and the authoritarian legacy of apartheid. Indigenous models of leadership have slowly begun to emerge. The concept of *ubuntu* (humaneness) underlines traditional group decision-making. Transformational leadership styles are exceptional, for example Albert Koopman, former Chief Executive of Cashbuild, a building supply company, and Leon Cohen, former Chief Executive of PG Bison Ltd and Dr Mamphela Ramphele, former Vice Chancellor of the University of Cape Town. Managerialism – a focus on administrative systems and risk aversion – has been reinforced by an inward-looking economy. Nonetheless, increasing globalization of markets coupled with rising costs and low productivity has resulted in reassessment of organizational strategies, restructuring and downsizing, and an experimentation with Japanese work methods such as self-directed work teams and employee empowerment through task-level participation and multiskilling. South African management now emphasizes co-operative teamwork and communal decision-making, where the core is the group and not the individual. Companies such as Pick 'n Pay in retailing and SA Breweries, where significant black advancement has occurred, are examples of this new approach. Organizational culture in South Africa thus reflects the coexistence of both Western and African leadership styles. A synergy of these ostensibly different leadership approaches is part of organizational development in the post-apartheid era. This is evident in black-owned insurance companies such as African Life and Metropolitan Life and in New Africa Investments Ltd (NAIL).

Unfair labour practice jurisprudence has also eroded unilateralism and ensured more participative managerial styles. While managers retain traditional rights to hire and dismiss, how they may do so has changed. Procedural and substantive fairness are a cornerstone of managerial labour relations practice reinforced by the Labour Relations Act (1995), which defines managers as 'employees' and thus entitled to fair treatment such as a proper disciplinary hearing. Traditional managerial styles are increasingly questioned by employees. However, although behavioural change has occurred in this regard, a shift in mindset is important for developing suitable styles for managing diversity.

Managerial culture

Management styles reflect organizational and national cultural patterns. In South Africa, while achievement is valued, group and organizational conformity is also important. Although little research has occurred on managerial culture in South Africa, a masculine dominance across ethnic groups, is evident, underlined by individualist values and a societal culture with a relatively large power distance between groups. This is based on historical racial disparities. However, an emergent black middle class has begun to occupy decision-making positions in business and government sectors, and this class mobility is likely to have an impact on managerial culture and inform a debate about desirable values, rituals and organizational practices. Managerial ideologies also reflect unitarist ideas – the organization as a 'happy family' or team with organizational loyalty, and conflict avoidance – which are similar to the Japanese notion of industrial familism. Organizational realities in South Africa reflect diversity and pluralism and the procedural regulation of inherent conflicts. The late 1990s however saw a significant move to unbundle or disaggrate large corporations to focus on their core business.

Management development

Management development programmes are run internally in larger organizations. The Skills Development Act (1998) levies firms 1–1.5 per cent of their payroll cost to encourage investment in human resource development through sectoral education and training authorities (SETAS). Many organizations send managers to MBA programmes and executive development at one or more of South Africa's business schools, international business schools in South Africa, or abroad. Average expenditure on training and development is around 2 per cent of salary budgets, with a small number of companies spending around 6 per cent. Of this expenditure, 21 per cent goes on management training. Black management development has been neglected historically, but employment equity policies and programmes have now been introduced in more than 35 per cent of medium and large organizations. These policies seek to remove discriminatory policies and practices and to actively recruit and develop black managers. In terms of the Labour Relations Act (1995) discriminatory employment practices constitute an unfair labour practice.

Creating employment equity in organizations dominated by white males is an important aspect of employment equity. Black empowerment includes both advancement into positions of executive authority and the provision of equity and profit-sharing. Most management development programmes set numerical goals based on workforce requirements and labour market supply of relevant occupations. Employers reject quotas in favour of a goals and timetable approach. An important lobby group, the Black Management Forum (BMF), formulated a blueprint of management development, which stresses the process, and importance, of increasing the supply of suitable managers with requisite skills. This blueprint advocated that by the year 2000, 40 per cent of middle management positions must be held by black people, 30 per cent of senior management posts and 20 per cent of executive directors. This goal was not achieved by 2000, but progress is being made. The Employment Equity Act requires employers of more than 50 people to submit employment equity plans with targets, timetables and measures to redress past discrimination.

Subtle discrimination still acts as a barrier to occupational mobility. This is mitigated by pressure to build non-racial organizational structures emanating from trade unions, lobby groups, foreign multinational companies and legislation. However, perceptions of black inferiority have developed a white managerial mindset, which often doubts the ability of black people to perform managerial work. Although higher economic growth coupled with a new political order may stimulate management development efforts, until significant numbers of black people have the decision-making authority to affect organizational outcomes, the corporate culture of South African organizations will change gradually. Nonetheless, a restructuring of the workforce at all levels to reflect a visible non-racial diversity is occurring, for example in parastatal organizations such as Transnet.

The historically small black managerial class is a function of a defunct political dispensation. The presence of black majority government means more emphasis is being placed on the upward mobility of black managerial staff. The questions of employment equity and black advancement are more complex in South Africa than in post-colonial African countries. The upper echelons of state bureaucracy were dominated by an Afrikaner cultural ethos: the civil service élite was predominantly male, but a rapidly increasing proportion are now held by black managers. There is concern among skilled and experienced civil servants that patronage appointments will occur. This has in fact been the case, in reverse, historically.

Conclusion

Participative practices are an example of a collective orientation towards motivation and work design. This is more a feature of European and Japanese organizations than the individualism of North American managerial culture. An important question is the extent to which teams with multicultural and interfunctional diversity can be fostered in South African organizations. A shift from a traditional to a flexible organization requires a move away from a command and control style towards co-operation and motivation. Managers will have to learn new principles and practices if South African organizations are to compete effectively. This is also essential because employee expectations and attitudes to work are changing; socio-political change and a workforce which is becoming more educated mean higher levels of expectations for personal growth, fair treatment and better income.

Participative practices are more successful where management has restructured to create a delayered organization in which authority and responsibility are delegated to lower levels and where employees are empowered through information sharing, knowledge and skills, recognition and rewards, and the opportunity to influence decisions. In South Africa such approaches are increasing and include a range of organizations such as Anglogold, Cape Cabinets, Escom, SA Nylon Spinners, Pick 'n Pay retailers and the Delta Motor Corporation. Although not extensive, flexible work practices, multiskilling and performance-based pay have become issues in the field of human resource management.

There is a need to reduce racial polarization, erode a tradition of adversarialism and nurture a sense of common purpose. The latter requires the visible advancement and economic empowerment of black people in order to create employment equity and the stability necessary for economic growth. The diversity of South African organizations creates an insistent need to find common goals, shared values and foster reconciliation after the divisiveness of apartheid. Raising managerial competence in strategic management, resource utilization, negotiation and operations is vital for organizational effectiveness. Performance improvement, greater accountability and active measures to address racial and gender mixes in the occupation structure are necessary. While management development emphasizes planned interventions, informal experiences often provide meaningful learning.

There is no uniform approach to management development. Differing cultural contexts imply that for management initiative to have a lasting effect, integration with corporate objectives, organizational structure and job design, reward systems and corporate culture is necessary.

Further reading

Adam, H. and Moodley, E. (1993) *The Negotiated Revolution: Society and Politics in a Post-Apartheid South Africa*, Los Angeles, CA: University of California Press.

Barker, F. (1999) *The South African Labour Market*, Pretoria: Van Schaik.

Blunt, P. and Jones, M. (1993) *Managing Organisations in Africa*, Berlin: De Gruyter.

Bowmaker-Falconer, A., Hortwitz, F.M. and Searll, P. (1994) 'Affirmative action and equal opportunity', *Breakwater Monitor Update* 1: 5–10.

Bowmaker-Falconer, A., Horwitz, F., Jain, H. and Tagger, S. (1998) 'Employment equity programmes', *Industrial Relations Journal* 29(3): 1–12.

Horwitz, F.M. (1993) 'Elements in participation, teamwork and flexibility in South Africa', *International Journal of Human Resources Management* 4(4): 917–31.

Horwitz, F.M. (1998) 'The Employment Equality Bill', *South African Labour Bulletin* 22(3): 80–2.

Horwitz, F. and Smith, D. (1998) 'Flexible work practices and human resource management: a comparison of South African and foreign owned companies', *International Journal of Human Resource Management* 9(4): 590–607.

Horwitz, F.M., Bowmaker-Falconer, A. and Searll, P. (1995) 'Employment equity, human resource development and institution building in South Africa', *International Journal of Human Resource Management* 6(3): 671–85.

Human, P. and Horwitz, F.M. (1992) *On the Edge: How South African Companies Cope with Change*, Kenwyn: Juta.

Visser, J. (1994) 'Why South Africa is not a winning nation', *Human Resource Management* 9(10): 26–8.

World Competitiveness Report (1999) University of Lausanne: World Economic Forum and the Institute for Management Development.

Part III

Cross-cultural issues

Chapter 18

The role of social science in the study of economic and cultural transformation

Frank Heller

Introduction

Recent research shows that economic and cultural transformation, particularly in Central and Eastern Europe, does not conform with popular and journalistic generalizations (Pearce and Frese 2000). What kind of information could be helpful for countries undergoing transformation? Are cultural-historical differences between countries a hindrance to the transfer of ideas or practices or are they successful recipes capable of being adapted in certain circumstances? If adaptation is possible, what are the conditions that facilitate or obstruct the process of transition or change in organizations?

Practice has leapt ahead of theory and evidence, so after 1945 Western Europe was impressed by the obviously successful American organizational practices and set about learning from their experience. Thirty years later, Japan was the model that led America and Western Europe to copy some of their practices – not always successfully. Later, South Korea, Taiwan and Singapore have been studied by organizational analysts to discover what other countries can learn from the Asian tiger economies. Then in the 1990s the tigers lost their teeth; their economies were in various stages of collapse and the United States returned to its former position as a role model. How did these cycles affect countries in Central and Eastern Europe? Poland, the Czech Republic, Hungary and Russia had particularly acute problems in adjusting their over-centralized economic structures and organizational practices to the prevailing market-oriented Western models. Which examples and experiences are relevant for them (Koopman and Heller 1999)?

Several social science disciplines, economics, sociology, psychology and anthropology, have carried out extensive studies on transformation practices and some of their findings are beginning to provide useful guidelines to policy makers. In this paper I will confine myself to discussing five topics related to transformation on which reasonably reliable evidence is available. The topics are: the importance of understanding equilibrium needs when planning for change; the necessity of developing institutional structures before the introduction of market mechanisms; the advantages for motivation and efficiency of some measure of influence-sharing within hierarchical organizations; the relevance of the work ethic; and the need to use a longitudinal analysis in which provision is made for different conditions to apply to different phases of the transformation process.

It is not claimed that these five topics are more important than any others, or that they will satisfactorily answer the questions I have asked, but I believe that organizations subjected to economic and cultural transformation will find that useful guidelines for change can be derived from the social science evidence presented on the five topics.

Equilibrium needs

A much neglected but almost universal factor in the life of organizations is the need for continuity and equilibrium equivalent to the biological need for homeostasis. (Schön 1971). This is the basis of resistance to change which students of organization observe everywhere. It operates at the level of individuals as well as organizations and has been neglected because in the second half of the twentieth century the opposite trend, namely turbulence, unpredictability and the need to adjust to competition and new technology, has been much in evidence.

The synchronic need for equilibrium and the diachronic need for change can and do coexist in an uneasy and potentially conflictual relationship which has to be understood and managed. However, a considerable volume of recent literature has supported the desirability for rapid change and pretended that it can be achieved easily and with low cost (Dawson 1994; McCalman and Paton 1992). At the organizational level a front runner was re-engineering, advocated by Hammer and Champy (1994) and in economics a strong supporter was Harvard's Jeffrey Sachs, one of the early consultants to President Yeltsin's advisers in Russia. These approaches have run into many difficulties.

The case for rapid and painless change is often based on the writings of consultants who take a broad universalistic, rather than a contingency, approach to change. A contingency approach would carefully distinguish between situations where incremental or rapid change is more appropriate and successful. Two very experienced organizational analysts have come to the conclusion that claims of having achieved lasting and successful reforms are greatly exaggerated (Brunsson and Olson 1993).

In the last four decades China has gone through several very radical political upheavals but at the level of organization, in spite of extensive management development plans and new legislation, progress has been very slow (Child 1994; Warner 1995a; Whitley 1992) but has nevertheless achieved a very high rate of growth (see chapter 13).

Compared with China, Japan had until the 1990s (Economist 2001) an uneventful, relatively tranquil four decades and with one or two exceptions, organizational life had retained its basic characteristics, most of which have deep historic roots. One exception is in its treatment of quality, which was notoriously poor in the 1950s but within a decade and a half had established an enviable reputation for reliability which western countries are even now trying to emulate. This remarkable turn around was achieved through a combination of adopting an American statistical quality control programme (Deming 1982), building quality into its traditional group collaboration culture and adapting the ideas derived from British and Norwegian research on semi-autonomous work groups plus the rapid establishment of a government quality control agency. In this remarkable transformation, the important culturally sanctioned role of the government agency is sometimes underestimated.

Institutional infrastructure

The strong corporatist influence exerted directly and indirectly by the Japanese government on industry is often cited as one of the reasons for the remarkable Japanese economic success in the 1980s. In 1960, the International Labour Office sent a French expert to Japan and a British expert to Argentina to help with their respective economic development. Both countries were then classified as under-developed. The two ILO experts contributed to one of the first cross-national comparative studies on managerial attitudes and values (Haire, Ghiselli and Porter 1966). The results of this study show that Japan occupied an attitudinal value position significantly different from Europe, Argentina and Chile. By the 1970s, Argentina and Chile were still classified as underdeveloped, while Japan was beginning to attract the attention of American business school academics who wanted to discover the secret of their rapid progress (see chapter 15).

The different rates of economic development would be explained by the new school of institutional economics in terms of what North (1990) calls the 'rules of the game'; that is to say, the institutional constraints or facilitators that provide a structure to everyday life and, in particular, to economic activity. North makes the important point that neo-classical economics cannot explain why poor or underdeveloped countries should not easily catch up simply by emulating the economic policies of the more successful economies. To explain why this catching up does not occur and why the differences are frequently perpetuated over long periods, one has to look at the institutional infrastructures, one of which is the educational system. Furthermore, one of the missing links in traditional economic theory is 'an understanding of the nature of human co-ordination and co-operation' (ibid.: 11) and he mentions uniformities that are transmitted from one generation to the next and can be called 'culture' (ibid.: 36–7). He gives examples of informal conventions in modern society that solve co-ordination problems. An example is the punctuality habit, which is more highly developed in economically successful than unsuccessful societies. Economists see the outcome of informal conventions and habits, for instance the acceptance of 'my word is my bond' in terms of low transaction costs. Conventions acquire a moral force that has economic benefits.

If one looks at the different values between Argentina and Chile on the one hand and Japan on the other, as shown in the Haire, Ghiselli and Porter study (1966) and adds the institutional conditions listed by North, the differential rate of economic development of these two parts of the world is unsurprising.

Then there are formal institutional arrangements, like rules of contract, patent law, and clearly formulated property laws, monopoly rules, stock exchange regulation and surveillance and so on. These rules have to be accepted and enforced. At this point it is worth remembering that North is not only an economist but a recent Nobel laureate who goes on to disagree with most of his neo-classical colleagues by supporting a clear and important role for the state and an acceptance that voluntarism does not often work, so that formal social rules have to be coercively enforced (North 1990: 58). He keeps his analysis largely in terms of transaction costs, saying that the successful enforcement of a purely voluntary system is prohibitively costly. He gives the example of countries that spend large amounts of scarce financial resources on higher education when investment in elementary education has a much higher social rate of return in Third World countries. In such cases, he argues, governments should have stepped in when the market did not allocate resources appropriately (ibid.: 80).

The same theoretical approach would also explain the coexistence of rapid privatization and ferocious criminal activity in the former Soviet Union, where no attempt was made to impose the kind of legal-structural control mechanisms which are taken for granted in countries practising a competitive market economy. North is not afraid to make simple, almost banal points, like drawing attention to the cost of useless inspection or multiple form-filling which one finds very much in evidence in China and South America. Central and East European countries often use bureaucratic procedures to create employment as well as to control dishonesty; they were more successful in the former than in the latter intention. These procedures continue when they have outlived their original function. For instance in 1994, trying to buy a ticket for an international train at Budapest's main station was an obstacle course. However, it was quite easy to pay on the train, where the conductor would pretend that he had temporarily run out of tickets so that he could keep the cash.

Japan, on the other hand, had used bureaucratic procedures intelligently and was prepared to incur transaction costs for elaborate inspection procedures, form-filling and delaying tactics to slow down or restrict the importation of foreign products. However, since the 1990s it has become apparent that Japan had failed to apply control and inspection procedures to their banking system; this had disastrous consequences.

Two other points from Douglass North's institutional economics are important for understanding issues of transformation. One is his emphasis on skills and competence to produce *adaptive efficiency* which is concerned with developing the rules and structures that support a growing economy through time and are quite different from the traditional emphasis on *allocative efficiency*. Adaptive efficiency emphasizes the acquisition of knowledge and supports risk and innovation leading to the second point, which shows that societal and economic changes are marginal adjustments in an incremental process based on routines, customs, traditions and conventions supported by formal rules and informal conventions. Adaptation and change are slow processes.

Most of the new angles in North's economics, in particular his stress on the role of formal and informal institutions, have extensive antecedents in other social science disciplines since the writings of Herbert Spencer (*First Principles*, 1862). However, this analysis has now become more important by being linked with transaction costs and economics, which is a discipline that has easy access to policy-makers. Policy-makers in transforming economics have been heavily preoccupied by the important role of the market as the centrepiece of a system which, according to Hayek (1945), will fairly automatically regulate prices and other factors to return to equilibrium. However, institutional economics pays much more attention to actors inside organizations, their motivation and effectiveness (Williamson 1985). Another important theoretical approach which substantially reduces the role of the market is put forward by Herbert Simon (1991) who bases his arguments on empirical socio-psychologically oriented research. He strongly supports the need for transforming economies to pay attention to intra-organizational mechanisms like co-ordination, incentives, power, authority, quality and employee satisfaction. Simon concludes that the economies of modern industrialized society can more appropriately be called organizational economies than market economies (Simon 1991: 42).

Distribution of organizational power

The industrial organizational models we admire change over time. In the nineteenth century the preferred role models came from Britain; in the early part of the twentieth century, under the influence of Frederick Winslow Taylor, they came from the USA. After the Second World War, there were three models in rapid succession: first, the USA, sheltered from the immediate ravages of the war, then Scandinavia, and third, Japan from about 1975. Then, as already mentioned, Japan's influence as a role model declined precipitously in the 1990s and North America emerged as the exemplar. Who next?

In the 1960s a number of influential publications explored the reason why American business earned a higher return on invested capital than European business (Caves, and associates 1968; Diebolt 1968; OECD 1968). Was the efficiency gap due to technology, inventiveness, capital investment, or the quality of management? A considerable body of informed opinion came to the conclusion that the gap was managerial (Granick 1962; Haenni 1969; PEP 1965; Smith 1968). Servan-Schreiber, in his influential *The American Challenge* (1967) looked at the various alternative explanations and came to the conclusion that American organizations were more democratically run than European organizations. To check this view, an eight-country cross-national research project was designed to explore the possibility that American business executives shared influence more extensively than their European counterparts (Heller and Wilpert 1981). While very significant country differences were found, the USA–Europe gap in democratic decision making was only partly confirmed. Swedish top and second level managers practised more participation than USA managers, but top level American managers behaved more democratically than their counterparts in the Netherlands, Germany, the UK, and Spain. More important than participation differences among countries was the finding that democratic decision making practices, wherever they occur, liberate competence.

Since then, this topic (under a variety of names) has become an important focus of analysis in comparative studies of managerial efficiency between countries. The terms used include: leadership styles, participation, involvement, semi-autonomous groups, team working, empowerment, co-operation, consensus management, and organizational democracy (Heller *et al.* 1998)

The extraordinarily rapid and successful economic growth of Japan in the period up to 1990 has led to attempts all over the world to copy quality circles and other participative practices. At least one well-known American consultant and academic went on record with the view that if American industry wants to compete in the world, it has to adopt Japanese-style democratic decision making practices (Lawler 1986). Presumably such a recommendation would apply to any country or organization eager to compete in the world.

However, the transfer of allegedly successful practices from one country to another has not always been easy, smooth or effective. There are several reasons: one is the ubiquitous resistance to change analysed earlier, another is a misunderstanding of the essential ingredients of the practice or the attempt to cut corners and, of course, there is always the possibility that certain practices have, as Douglass North has argued, long incrementally developed gestation periods which cannot be instantly adopted in a different socio-economic setting. The failure of quality circles in other countries has been well documented. (Drago 1988; Lawler, Ledford and Mohrman 1992).

Doubts have been raised about the uniqueness of the Japanese system or understanding it correctly in the popular literature (Abegglen 1958; Dale 1986; Ouchi 1981). Some comparative studies have found surprisingly little difference between the Japanese leadership style and that used in other countries (Misumi 1984). Xu (1989), for instance, compared large samples of Chinese managers with Misumi's findings on Japanese managers and found almost no difference.[1] A replication study in China of managerial decision styles in Britain also found only small differences (Ma and Heller 1991).[2] The stereotyped view that all important decisions in Japanese companies are taken by the bottom up *ringi seido* method is a gross oversimplification (Heller and Misumi 1987). It has even been alleged that a substantial element in the Japanese organizational culture can be traced back to the fairly pervasive impact of Taylorism on Japanese companies, starting with the introduction of motion studies into Nippon Electric in 1908 and the translation of Taylor's *Scientific Management* into Japanese in 1912 (Warner 1994).

Similarly, it is not possible to analyze the Chinese management system today without an understanding of the heavy and perseverating influence of the 'legacy of High Stalinism' which became deeply entrenched in all large-scale Chinese enterprises during the 1950s (Kaple 1994). Even so, a knowledge of historic-cultural differences does not substantially help policy-makers who want to speed up the process of transformation. For instance, there is little doubt that the distribution of power in organizations plays an important part in understanding the process of economic development looked at in a historic perspective. Given our present knowledge about the positive effect influence-sharing practices have on liberating hidden resources of skill and innovation and how much they contribute to flexible group-determined work practices, it is tempting to advise countries in transition from statism to a market system to adopt such practices, often abbreviated into the acronym HRM (Human Resource Management). Such advice could be counter-productive.

In the case of China, two experienced analysts (Child 1994; Warner 1995a, 1999) agree 'that HRM is too culturally infused with Western values to be as yet on the Chinese menu' (Warner 1995b). We must also remember that several of the East Asian 'Little Dragon' countries have used very controversial autocratic hierarchical structures with no power distribution and such autocracy is often credited with being functional in early stages of development (McRae 1994).

In the case of some Central and East European countries one could expect that their historic cultural alignment with Western Europe would soon lead enterprises to use HRM practices, but this is not yet in evidence (Koopman and Heller 1999). In this connection the role of joint ventures may be very important in Central and Eastern European countries as they have been in China. For instance, a joint Hungarian-British food processing company has developed a high profile in HRM practices, almost certainly influenced by the fact that the British partner in the joint venture has for many years had an excellent reputation for participative, joint consultative management (Markóczy 1993). For an American example, see Balaton (1994).

Work-related values

The relation of work values to economic development has become an important issue since the well-known work of Max Weber (1930) and Richard Tawney (1926). Both, in different ways, came to the conclusion that the rise and growth of capitalism in Western Europe was significantly influenced by Protestantism; hence the term 'the Protestant Work Ethic'. While this historic relationship was well documented, its post-modern validity was worth examining.[3] A multinational team from Germany, Belgium, Israel, the United States, Japan, the Netherlands, Yugoslavia and Britain conducted extensive research and came to the somewhat unexpected conclusion that the work ethic was alive and well in Japan, Israel and Yugoslavia – countries in which Protestantism was conspicuously absent. At the same time, the Work Ethic, or more precisely the values which gave centrality to working in people's lives compared with other activities, came low in Britain, Germany and the Netherlands (MOW 1987).

One interpretation of this finding is to associate high work centrality scores with people who were ambitious to achieve high real standards of life[4] and who lived in countries that had become industrialized later than the countries that scored low on work centrality (Heller 1987). In this interpretation, one would expect the Little Dragon as well as Central and Eastern European countries to have high work centrality, but one would also expect work centrality to diminish as the real standard of life increases and offers people a choice of other activities. In this interpretation there need be no connection between the work ethic and productivity.

A closer look at the work ethic statistics produces a useful policy-oriented finding that brings us back to the discussion on the distribution of organizational power (Heller and Ruiz 1998). If we take the total seven-country sample of over 14 000 individuals and divide them by the nature of their work, we find that irrespective of country, work centrality is consistently higher in jobs that enjoy a measure of autonomy and self-direction (MOW 1987: 261–3).[5] In policy terms this means that if countries in transition from centralized to decentralized economies want to benefit from a population that identifies with a high work centrality, then it would be worth persuading companies to redesign as many jobs as possible to give them a higher degree of influence or even to legislate for a measure of organizational democracy, as Germany did after the Second World War (IDE 1981b). In other words, decentralizing a command economy at the macro level or organizational ownership could be paralleled by a decentralization of the intra-organizational command structure.

History, longitude and phases

In a way, everything I have said so far shows that the analysis of transition issues requires a historic-longitudinal design or interpretation. I want to underscore this now with a few examples from each of the sections covered so far.

I have started by showing that equilibrium rather than change is the natural and preferred condition for individuals as well as society. This does not preclude development and adjustment in conformity with changing circumstances. It does call into question the functionality of a deliberate imposition of rapid alien conditions.

Institutional economics, looking at the historic development and evolution of organizational life comes to similar conclusions by showing that the growth of formal and informal rules of the game is an incremental process, although there is no reason why this should take as long as it does in many of the underdeveloped countries.

Institutional theories have looked at the transformation processes in Eastern Europe and have concluded that 'the reforms have been based on the unrealistic assumption that the spontaneous market mechanism does exist' whereas they would argue that

> markets cannot be established overnight and, moreover, they require conscious and deliberate action by the state; consequently, the argument goes, it was a mistake to attempt to stabilize the post-socialist economies with purely market-oriented macro economic measures which may be effective only under properly functioning market mechanisms, implying rational behaviour at the micro level.
>
> (*Rosati 1994: 429*)

These arguments are not against the use of markets but in support of a carefully phased and planned introduction.

Most of the arguments and nearly all the research on the distribution of organizational power neglect the developmental aspect and I have given a number of examples. In addition, it can be shown that differences in influence distribution occur at different phases of the decision process and can be justified functionally. The first systematic cross-national investigation of power in the longitudinal decision process was reported by Heller *et al.* (1988). It took place in the Netherlands, Yugoslavia and Britain. Some years later this research design was replicated on a sample of Chinese and British companies (Ma and Heller 1991). The decision process was divided into four phases: start up, development, finalization and implementation. In strategic decision, the cycle could take over a year. The amount of influence (participation) exercised by employees differed significantly over the four phases. Lower-level employees had almost no influence in the first three phases, but were able to participate to some extent in the implementation phase. Foremen had some influence in the start up phase and more in implementation. At these two levels the Chinese results were very similar to Britain's. At the Representative Body level there were important differences. In the Chinese companies, the Representative Body had much less influence in all phases, but least in the final phase. British Representative Bodies exercised on average more influence than workers and foremen and were particularly influential during the implementation of the decision. The policy implication of this finding is that democratization is not an all or nothing process; by having influence distributed by phases, it is possible to take account of skill differences in the process of transformation and, nevertheless, to achieve some of the beneficial motivating and competence utilization outcomes which modern research has demonstrated (for an overview see Heller 2000).

Summary and concluding remarks

Comparative studies of the process of transforming economies from one system to another are sometimes geared towards issues that have little policy relevance. In this chapter we have dealt with five topics derived from social science research that have potentially practical implications for organizational policy makers.

We started by asking a few questions. Given that we recognize important historic, legal, structural and socio-cultural differences between countries, what scope is there for learning from each other? Are the differences so profound that each country has to find its own unique transformation path? Alternatively, is the economic success of one politico-economic system so overwhelmingly obvious that the best option for developing or transforming countries is to adopt all the main characteristics of the successful model?

These questions and possible alternatives between positions will be debated for a long time and require a very extensive review of evidence and choices between different theories. There is a tendency for these debates to be strictly discipline-oriented so that theories derive, *inter alia*, from economics, or from sociology or social psychology, but I believe that ultimately, solutions require a problem-oriented systems perspective in which disciplinary knowledge will be used sparingly (Bertalanffy 1993).

In the meantime, the present chapter tries to make a limited contribution to the problems faced by economies in transformation by analysing a number of policy-relevant topics which straddle the major disciplines.

In the first place, I argue that change, particularly radical change, is not a natural process for either individuals or organizations. While change is with us all the time and has become more ubiquitous and fast moving in recent decades, it is usually resisted and often sabotaged. Successful reform or transformation has to be carefully planned for timing, phasing, appropriate speed, and socio-cultural considerations.

Second, a relatively new school of economics which would support the psycho-social evidence on the problematics associated with rapid change, also stresses the need for a careful build up of formal and informal structures to facilitate the transformation process. While structural economics accepts the market as a mechanism, it gives more important emphasis to an analysis of processes and transactions between and within organizations and their costs. The transactions are facilitated or obstructed by structures and control mechanisms, many of which are most appropriately carried out or monitored by the state. Attempts to move quickly from a centralized to a market system without the necessary structural, social, legal and political institutions firmly in place, is likely to be disastrous.

Then there is the question of the distribution of power from the state to organizations, between organizations (monopoly or competition) and within organizations (organizational democracy). The location of power at these levels varies extensively between highly and less highly developed economies. Economic success seems to be positive with different models of power concentration (Far East versus Western economies) but it seems that in a longitudinal analysis, power concentration is more usual in early phases of development, while decentralization occurs in later phases.

The longitudinal-phase approach in relation to the problems of transition and power needs to be developed much further and should be conceptualized in a system perspective from macro, via meso, to micro levels of change. The important role of the work ethic in stimulating economic development for instance can, it seems, be traced back to the difference between centralized (hierarchical) versus decentralized (semi-autonomous) job design, irrespective of country. This means that under the hierarchical Tayloristic organizational designs practised in the countries under Russian influence, the work ethic would be low. As these countries try to adjust to a more decentralized market-oriented behaviour, they could also attempt to design work to give individuals and groups more influence over their work cycle. The research findings suggest that democratizing organizational decision making could significantly increase the work ethic, thus facilitating economic transformation (Heller and Ruiz 1998). This could explain why Japan, Israel and Yugoslavia scored high on the work ethic. Many years later, when economies are highly developed and produce a satisfactory standard of life, other life interests will take precedence and the work ethic can then afford to take up a lower priority. This could explain the relatively low work centrality scores of Germany, Netherlands and the UK (MOW 1986: 88).[6] This example further supports the need for treating economic and cultural transformation within a longitudinal phase model so as to obtain more accurate policy-relevant guidelines.

Endnotes

1 The comparison was based on an extensively validated scale called PM developed by Misumi and derived from the well-known Ohio Leadership study distinction between concern for people compared with concern for productivity.
2 The scale used in this research was based on the Influence-Power-Continuum (IPC) extensively used in previous research, for instance Heller 1971; IDE 1981a.
3 Following Toynbee, I use the term 'post-modern' to describe the period between the two world wars and beyond (Docherty 1993: 2).
4 I endorse Erikson's (1993) assessment that 'by the 1950s, it had already become clear that, in spite of its widespread use, per capita GNP is an insufficient measure of the well-being of citizens. A real standard of life includes living space, opportunities to travel and choose to practice a variety of sports and leisure activities.'
5 This comes out particularly clearly in a subsample of 6000 who were chosen to represent certain 'target groups', some of which were skilled and others not.
6 In this schema, a low work ethic score can characterize countries or organizations at an early as well as a late stage of economic development. It applies to an early stage if work structures are hierarchical and non-participatory but also to a late stage when standards of living have risen to a point where people choose to reduce the centrality of work in order to give more time and weight to leisure, family, or social pursuits.

References

Abegglen, J.C. (1958) *The Japanese Factory: Aspects of its Social Organisation*, Glencoe, IL: Free Press.
Balaton, K. (1994) 'Implementing corporate management system abroad: General Motors in Hungary', in C. Makó and P. Novoszáth (eds) *Convergence versus Divergence: The Case of the Corporate Culture* Institute for Social Conflict Research, Hungarian Academy of Sciences.
Bertalanffy, L. von (1993) *General System Theory: Foundation, Development, Applications*, revised edition, New York: Braziller.
Brunsson, N. and Olsen, J. (1993) *The Reforming Organization*, New York and London: Routledge.
Caves, R.E. and associates (1968) *Britain's Economic Prospects*, London: Allen & Unwin.
Child, J. (1994) *Management in China During the Age of Reforms*, Cambridge: Cambridge University Press.
Dale, P. (1986) *The Myth of Japanese Uniqueness*, London: Croom Helm.
Dawson, P. (1994) *Organizational Change: A Processual Approach*, London: Paul Chapman Publishing.
Deming, W.E. (1982) *Quality, Productivity and Competitive Position*, Boston, MA: MIT Centre for Advanced Engineers Studies.
Diebolt, J. (1968) 'Is the gap technological?' *Foreign Affairs* 46: 276–91.
Docherty, T. (ed.) (1993) *Postmodernism: A Reader*, London: Harvester Wheatsheaf.
Drago, R. (1988) 'Quality circle survival: an exploratory analysis', *Industrial Relations* 27: 336–51.
Economist (2001) 'China's confident bow', *The Economist*, 10 March: 79.

Erikson, R. (1993) 'Descriptions of inequality: the Swedish approach to welfare research', in M. Nussbaum and A. Sen (eds) *The Quality of Life* Oxford: Clarendon Press.

Granick, D. (1962) *The European Executive*, London: Weidenfeld and Nicolson.

Haenni, P. (1969) 'Management gap in a world context: a spectral analysis'. *Progress, Unilever Quarterly*, 2: 106–14.

Haire, M., Ghiselli, E.E. and Porter, L.W. (1966) *Managerial Thinking: An International Study*, New York: Wiley.

Hammer, M. and Champy, J. (1994) *Reengineering the Corporation: A Manifesto for Business Revolution*, London: Brealey.

Hayek, F. (1945) 'The use of knowledge in society', *American Economic Review*, 35: 519–30.

Heller, F.A. (1971) *Managerial Decision-Making: A Study of Leadership and Power Sharing among Senior Managers*, London: Tavistock.

Heller, F.A. (1987) 'The disappearing work ethic', *Business and Economics Review*, 3, Cardiff Business School, UWIST.

Heller, F. (2000) *Managing Democratic Organizations Vol 1 and 2 Classic Studies in Management*, Dartmouth: Ashgate.

Heller, F.A. and Misumi, J. (1987) 'Decision making', in *Organizational Psychology: An International Review* in B. Bass, P. Drenth and P. Weissenberg (eds), Beverly Hills, CA: Sage.

Heller, F. and Ruiz, A.Q. (1998), 'Work ethic' in M. Poole and M. Warner (eds) *The IEBM Handbook of Human Resources Management*, London: International Thomson Press.

Heller, F.A. and Wilpert, B. (1981) *Competence and power in Managerial Decision Making: A Study of Senior Levels of Organization in Eight Countries*, Chichester: Wiley.

Heller, F.A., Drenth, P., Koopman, P. and Rus, V. (1988) *Decisions in Organizations: A Longitudinal Study of Routine, Tactical and Strategic Decisions*, London and Beverly Hills, CA: Sage.

Heller, F.A., Pusic, E., Strauss, G. and Wilpert, B. (1998) *Organizational Participation: Myth and Reality*, Oxford: Oxford University Press.

Industrial Democracy in Europe Research Group (IDE) (1981a) *European Industrial Relations*, Oxford: Oxford University Press.

Industrial Democracy in Europe Research Group (IDE) (1981b) *Industrial Democracy in Europe*, Oxford: Oxford University Press.

Kaple, D. (1994) *Dream of a Red Factory: The Legacy of High Stalinism in China*, Oxford: Oxford University Press.

Koopman, P. and Heller, F. (1999) 'Privatization and transformation: lessons from six cases in Hungary' in L.A. ten Horn, B. Sverko and I.L. Zinovieva (eds) *Organizational Psychology and Transition Processes in Central Eastern Europe* Proceedings of a conference held in Dubrovnic, 30 September–3 October, Zagreb Work and Organizational Psychology Unit, University of Zagreb, Croatia.

Lawler, E. (1986) *High Involvement Management: Participative Strategies for Improving Organizational Performance*, San Francisco: Jossey-Bass.

Lawler, E., Ledford, G. and Mohrman, S. (1992) *Employee Involvement and Total Quality*, San Francisco: Jossey-Bass.

Ma, J.H. and Heller, F.A. (1991) 'A phase-related analysis of influence distribution within organizations: A China-Britain comparison'. *Tavistock Institute paper*.

Markóczy, L. (1993) 'Managerial and organizational learning in Hungarian-Western mixed management organizations'. *International Journal of Human Resources Management*, 4: 273–304.

McCalman, J. and Paton, R. (1992) *Change Management: A Guide to Effective Implementation*, London: Paul Chapman Publishing.

McRae, H. (1994) *The World in 2020*, London: Harper Collins.

Meaning of Working (MOW) (1987) *The Meaning of Working*, London: Academic Press.

Misumi, J. (1984) 'Decision making in Japanese groups and organizations', in B. Wilpert and A. Sorge (eds) *International Yearbook Of Organizational Democracy*, volume 2, Chichester. Wiley.

North, D.C. (1990) *Institutions, Institutional Change and Economic Performance*, Cambridge: Cambridge University Press.

Organization for Economic Co-operation and Development (OECD) (1968) *The Technological Gap: General Report*, Paris: OECD.

Ouchi, W.G. (1981) *Theory Z – How American Business Can Meet the Japanese Challenge*, Reading, MA: Addison-Wesley.

Pearce, J.L. and Frese, M. (2000) 'Introduction to the special issue on applied psychology from transitional economies in Eastern Europe' *Applied Psychology: An International Review* 49(4): 613–18.

PEP Report (1965) *Thrusters and Sleepers*, London: Allen & Unwin.

Rosati, D.K. (1994) 'Output decline during transition from plan to market: a reconsideration'. *Economics of Transition*, 2: 419–41.

Schön, D.A. (1971) *Beyond the Stable State*. The 1970 Reith Lectures, London: Temple-Smith.

Servan Schreiber, J. (1967) *The American Challenge*, London: Hamilton.

Simon, H.A. (1991) 'Organizations and markets' *Journal of Economic Perspectives 1991*, 5: 25–44.

Smith, D. (1968) 'The "gap" that is a chasm', *International Management*, May.

Spencer, H. (1862) *First Principles*, London: Williams and Moorgate.

Tawney, R.H. (1926) *Religion and the Rise of Capitalism: A historical study*. Holland Memorial Lectures 1922, London: Murray.

Warner, M. (1994) 'Japanese culture, Western management: Taylorism and human resources in Japan'. *Organization Studies*, 15: 509–33.

Warner, M. (1995a) *The Management of Human Resources in China*, Basingstoke: Macmillan.

Warner, M. (1995b) 'Managing human resources in East Asia'. *The International Journal of Human Resource Management*, 6: 177–80.

Warner, M. (ed.) (1999) *China's Management Revolution*, London: Frank Cass.

Weber, M. (1930) *The Protestant Ethic and the Spirit of Capitalism*, London: Allen & Unwin.

Whitley, R.D. (1992) *Business Systems in East Asia: Firms, Markets and Societies*, London: Sage.

Williamson, O.E. (1985) *The Economic Institutions of Capitalism*, New York: Free Press.

Xu, Lian-cang (1989) 'Comparative study of leadership between Chinese and Japanese Managers based upon PM theory' in B.J. Fallon, H.P. Pfister and J. Brebner (eds). *Advances in Industrial Organizational Psychology* North Holland: Elsevier Science.

Chapter 19

Global leadership: women leaders

Nancy J. Adler

> Women will change the nature of power;
> power will not change the nature of women.
>
> *(Bella Abzug, State of the World Forum 1996)*

Global leadership and the twenty-first century

In his speech accepting the Philadelphia Liberty Medal, Vaclav Havel (1994: A27), President of the Czech Republic, eloquently explained that:

> There are good reasons for suggesting that the modern age has ended. Many things indicate that we are going through a transitional period, when it seems that something is on the way out and something else is painfully being born. It is as if something were crumbling, decaying and exhausting itself, while something else, still indistinct, were arising from the rubble.

Havel's appreciation of the transition that the world is now experiencing is certainly important to each of us as human beings. None of us can claim that the twentieth century exited on an impressive note, on a note imbued with wisdom. As we ask ourselves which of the twentieth century's legacies we wish to pass on to the children of the twenty-first century, we are humbled into shameful silence. Yes we have advanced science and technology, but at the price of a world torn asunder by a polluted environment, by cities infested with social chaos and physical decay, by an increasingly skewed income distribution that condemns large proportions of the population to poverty (including people living in the world's most affluent societies) and by rampant physical violence continuing to kill people in titulary limited wars and seemingly random acts of violence. No, we did not exit the twentieth century with pride. Unless we can learn to treat each other and our planet in a more civilized way, is it not blasphemy to continue to consider ourselves a civilization (Rechtschaffen 1996)?[1]

The dynamics of the twenty-first century will not look like those of the twentieth century; to survive as a civilization, twenty-first century society must not look like the twentieth century. For a positive transition to take place, the world needs a new type of leadership. Where will society find wise leaders to guide it toward a civilization that differs so markedly from that of the twentieth century? While many people continue to review men's historic patterns of success in search of models for twenty-first century global leadership, few have even begun to appreciate the equivalent patterns of historic and potential contributions of women leaders (Adler 1996). My personal search for leaders who are outside traditional twentieth-century paradigms has led me to review the voice that the world's women leaders are bringing to society. This chapter looks at the nature of global leadership and the role that women will play at the most senior levels of world leadership.

Leadership: a long history

To lead comes from the latin verb *agere* meaning to set into motion (Jennings 1960). The Anglo-Saxon origins of the words *to lead* come from *laedere*, meaning people on a journey (Bolman and Deal 1991). Today's meaning of the word 'leader' therefore has the sense of someone who sets ideas, people, organizations and societies in motion; someone who takes the worlds of ideas, people, organizations and societies on a journey. To lead such a journey requires vision, courage and influence.

According to US Senator Barbara Mikulski, leadership involves 'creating a state of mind in others' (Cantor and Bernay 1992: 59). Leaders, therefore, are 'individuals who significantly influence the thoughts, behaviors, and/or feelings of others' (Gardner 1995: 6). Beyond strictly focusing on the role of the leader, leadership should also be thought of as interactive, as 'an influence relationship among leaders and followers who intend real changes . . . [reflecting] their mutual purposes' (Rost 1991: 102). In addition, according to Bolman and Deal (1995: 5), true leadership also includes a spiritual dimension:

> [T]wo images dominate in concepts of leadership: one of the heroic champion with extraordinary stature and vision, the other of the policy wonk, the skilled analyst who solves pressing problems with information, programs, and policies. Both images miss the essence of leadership. Both emphasize the hands and heads of leaders, neglecting deeper and more enduring elements of courage, spirit and hope.

Thus leadership must be viewed as something more than role and process – something more than the extent to which a particular leader has been influential. To fully appreciate leadership, we must also ask the ends to which a leader's behaviour is directed. From this process and outcome perspective, leaders can be viewed as people whose vision, courage, and influence set ideas, people, organizations, and societies in motion toward the betterment of their organization, their community, and the world.

While comprehensive, this definition of leadership cannot be considered historically agreed upon; indeed, no such agreed upon definition exists. After reviewing more than 5000 published works on leadership, neither Stogdill (1974) in the 1970s nor Bass (1991) in the 1990s succeeded in identifying a commonly agreed upon definition of leadership. As Bennis and Nanus (1985: 4) concluded:

> Decades of academic analysis have given us more than 350 definitions of leadership. Literally thousands of empirical investigations of leaders have been conducted in the last 75 years alone, but no clear and unequivocal understanding exists as to what distinguishes leaders from non-leaders and, perhaps more important, what distinguishes effective leaders from ineffective leaders . . .

Rather than adding once again to the already over-abundant supply of leadership definitions, this chapter simply adds two dimensions to the historical definitions of leadership: the first is a global perspective and the second is the inclusion of women leaders and their experience in a field that has heretofore focused almost exclusively on men.[2]

Global leaders: global leadership

Global leadership involves the ability to inspire and influence the thinking, attitudes, and behaviour of people from around the world. Thus from a process and an outcome perspective, global leadership can be described as 'a process by which members of . . . [the world community] are empowered to work together synergistically toward a common vision and common goals . . . [resulting in an] improv[ment in] the quality of life' on and for the planet (based on Astin and Leland 1991: 8; Hollander 1985). Global leaders are those people who most strongly influence the process of global leadership.

Whereas there are hundreds of definitions of leadership, there are no global leadership theories. Most leadership theories, although failing to state so explicitly, are domestic theories masquerading as universal theories (Boyacigiller and Adler 1991; 1996). Most commonly, they have described the behaviour of leaders in one particular country, the USA (and, as will be discussed later, of one particular gender, men). This is particularly unfortunate for understanding global leadership since 'Americans' extreme individualism combined with their highly participative managerial climate, may render U.S. management practices [including leadership] unique; that is, differentiated from the approaches in most areas of the world' (Dorfman 1996: 292; see also Dorfman and Howell 1988; Hofstede 1991). Recent research on leadership supports this conclusion in finding that the USA is unique in several respects among all of the Eastern and Western cultures that have been studied (Howell *et al.* 1994). For example, based on 221 definitions of leadership from the twentieth century, Rost (1991) concluded that leadership has most frequently been seen as rational, management-oriented, male, technocratic, quantitative, cost-driven, hierarchical, short term, pragmatic and materialistic. Not surprisingly, many of these listed descriptors reflect some of the core values of American culture. For example, relative to people from most other cultures, Americans tend to have a more short-term orientation (e.g. they emphasize this quarter's results and daily reported share prices), a more materialistic orientation (e.g. 40 per cent of American managers still think that 'the bottom line' is the criterion for corporate health, whereas no other nation can find even 30 per cent of its managers who take this view; see Hampden-Turner 1993), and a more quantitative orientation (e.g emphasizing measurable contributions and results rather than relying on less easily quantified qualities such as success in relationship-building).[3]

Of those leadership studies and theories that are not US based, most still tend to be domestic, with the only difference from the American theories being that their cultural focus reflects the values and context of a country other than the USA; such as descriptions of Israeli leaders in Israel (e.g. Vardi, Shrom and Jacobson 1980) or Indian leaders in India (e.g. Kakar 1971). The fundamental global leadership question is not 'do American leadership theories apply abroad?' (Hofstede 1980b), nor is it the comparative question of attempting to determine the extent to which behaviours of leaders in one culture replicate those of leaders in other cultures. Both questions frame leadership within a domestic context; the only distinction being that the former focuses on a single country (descriptive domestic theories) whereas the later focuses on multiple countries (comparative multidomestic theories) (see Boyacigiller and Adler 1991; 1996).

Global leaders, unlike domestic leaders, address people worldwide. Global leadership theory, unlike its domestic counterpart, is concerned with the interaction of people and ideas among cultures, rather than with either the efficacy of particular leadership styles within the leader's home country or with the comparison of leadership approaches among leaders from various countries – each of whose domain is limited to issues and people within their own cultural environment. A fundamental distinction is that global leadership is neither domestic nor multidomestic; it focuses on cross-cultural interaction rather than on either single-culture description or multi-country comparison. The Secretary General of the United Nations (UN) cannot change his message for each of the UN's more than 100 member states. Similarly the chief executive officer (CEO) of a global company cannot change her message for each of the countries and cultures in which her company operates. As we move toward the twenty-first century, the domain of influence of leadership is shifting from circumscribed geographies to globally encompassing geographies; from part of the world – e.g. a nation or domestic economy – to the whole world. Historically, such transnational leadership '. . . that goes beyond the nation-state and seeks to address all human beings' has been 'the most important, but rarest and most elusive, variety of leadership' (Gardner 1995: 20). However, the essence of such transnational leadership was captured already centuries ago by Diogenes in his assertion to his fellow Athenians, 'I am not an Athenian or a Greek but a citizen of the world' (cited in Gardner 1995: 51), and again much more recently by Virginia Woolf (1938), one of the twentieth century's thought leaders:

As a woman, I have no country.
As a woman, I want no country.
As a woman, the whole world is my country.

Within this emerging cross-culturally interactive context, global leaders must articulate a vision which, in and of itself, is global; that is, global leaders articulate the meaning within which others from around the world work and live. According to Britain's Anita Roddick (1991: 226), founder and CEO of the highly successful global firm, The Body Shop:

Leaders in the business world should aspire to be true planetary citizens. They have global responsibilities since their decisions affect not just the world of business, but world problems of poverty, national security and the environment. Many, sad to say, [have] duck[ed] these responsibilities, because their vision is material rather than moral.

Roddick's view of global leaders as 'true planetary citizens' echoes Bolman and Deal's (1995: 5) observation that strictly emphasizing the hands and the head of leaders misses the essence of leadership by neglecting the deeper and more enduring elements of courage, spirit and hope. The vision of a global leader, by definition, must be broader than the particular organization or country that he or she leads.

Beyond having a worthy vision, global leaders must be able to communicate their vision in a compelling manner to people from around the world. According to leadership expert Howard Gardner (1995: 8–9), 'Leaders achieve their effectiveness chiefly through the stories they relate', both by communicating the stories and by embodying them. 'Nearly all leaders are eloquent in voice', with many being 'eloquent in writing as well' (Gardner 1995: 34). As leaders, 'they do not merely have a promising story; they can [also] tell it persuasively' (Gardner 1995: 34).

Gardner (1995: 11) goes on to distinguish between leaders of a domain and leaders of a society. Leaders of a domain address an audience which 'is already sophisticated in the stories, the images, and the other embodiments of that domain. To put it simply, one is communicating with experts' – such as when a medical doctor addresses other physicians. Leaders of a society 'must be able to address a public in terms of the commonsense and commonplace notions that an ordinary inhabitant absorbs simply by virtue of living for some years within a society' (Gardner 1995: 12). According to Ireland's President, Mary Robinson (1996, cited in Pond, 1996: 59):

a woman leader often has a distinctive approach as the country's chief 'storyteller, [personifying] a sense of nationhood and [telling] a story that also [helps] shape people's sense of their own identity.' This is leadership by 'influencing [and] inspiring' rather than by commanding.

As society goes global, the audience of a leader also goes global. What members of a global audience have in common is only that which is most fundamentally human to each individual. Global leaders, to a much greater extent than their domestic counterparts, must be able to communicate in terms of what is common sense and commonplace for people worldwide; they must therefore communicate in the most fundamental terms of humanity. Global leaders do not enjoy the simplified reality that their domestic predecessors enjoyed of speaking primarily to people from one culture, one country, one organization, or one discipline.

Global leaders: women leaders

The feminization of leaders and of leadership is a significant development in our understanding and in the governance of global political, economic and societal structures.[4] As we approached the end of the twentieth century, the number of women in the most senior global leadership positions was increasing and, at the same time, the style of global leadership was increasingly incorporating approaches most frequently labelled as feminine. It appears that 'the economic exigenc[ies] of global competition . . . [are making] feminine characteristics admirable in both men and women' (Calas and Smircich 1993: 71–81).

This chapter focuses on women with positional power, women in the most senior leadership roles in major global companies and nations. The focus goes beyond the assumption that scholarship on women leaders must limit itself to women's historically more traditional mode of influence – that of influencing, primarily from behind the scenes, the men who hold society's most élite positions of power while the women themselves hold no positional power. See, for example, contemporary discussions of the influence on their respective presidential husbands of American first ladies, including the more than 50 books published on Hillary Rodham Clinton and the extensive literature on Eleanor Roosevelt (Goodwin 1995). While the feminist literature has tended to champion the non-hierarchical notion of broadly dispersed leadership – that is, the empowerment of many leaders within society (see Astin and Leland, 1991, among many others) – in contrast to traditional, role-based, hierarchical, and more exclusive notions of leadership, this chapter attempts to bring the two notions back together. It asks what the nature of élite role leadership, as exhibited by women, will be in the organizationally flattened world of the twenty-first century.

Women leaders: numbers increasing

The 'feminization of an occupation or a job refers to women's disproportionate entry into a customarily male occupation' (Fondas 1997: 258, based on Cohn 1985 and Reskin and Roos 1990). Thus the feminization of global leadership would be the disproportionate entry of women into the most senior political and business leadership roles in the world. Is there reason to believe that we will see the feminization of global leadership in the twenty-first century? Yes. While rarely recognized or reported in the media, one inescapable trend is that the number of the most senior global women political leaders – presidents and prime ministers of countries – is rapidly increasing, albeit from a negligible starting point. As shown in Figure 19.1, no women presidents or prime ministers came to office in the 1950s, three came to office in the 1960s, five in the 1970s, eight in the 1980s, and 29 in the 1990s. More than half of all women who have ever served as political leaders – 29 of 46 – have come into office since 1990. More than twice as many women became president or prime minister in the 1990s as ever served before. As shown in Table 19.1, countries as dissimilar as Sri Lanka, Ireland and Rwanda have had women lead them.[5]

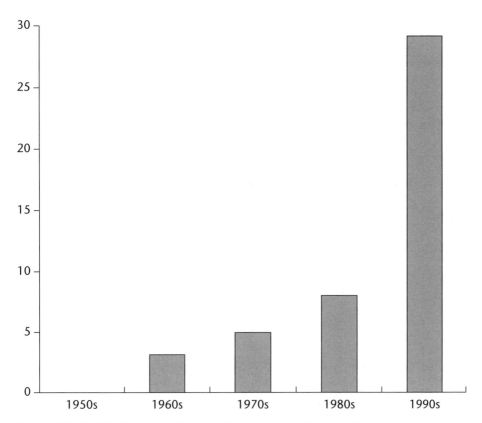

Figure 19.1 **Political Leaders: the number of women is increasing**

Do we see similar increases in the number of women leading major world businesses as we see among women presidents and prime ministers? Whereas the pattern among global business leaders is not yet clear, initial surveys suggest that there are very few women CEOs.[6] According to the United Nations' 1995 report, *The World's Women*, there are no women running the world's largest corporations (as reported in Kelly 1996: 21). Catalyst reports that only 2.4 per cent of the chairmen and CEOs of *Fortune* 500 firms are women (Wellington 1996). Moreover, only in 1997 did Britain gain its first woman chief executive of a *Financial Times* (FT-SE) 100 firm, Marjorie Scardino at Pearson Plc (Pogrebin 1996).

Contrary to popular belief, however, women's scarcity in leading major corporations does not mean that they are absent as leaders of global companies. Unlike their male counterparts, most women chief executives have either created their own businesses or assumed the leadership of a family business. A disproportionate number of women have founded and are now leading entrepreneurial enterprises. According to the Small Business Administration, for example, women currently own one-third of all American businesses. These women-owned businesses in the USA employ more people than the entire *Fortune* 500 list of America's largest companies combined (Aburdene and Naisbitt 1992). As the list of women business leaders in Table 19.2 attests, the reality is that women from around the world are leading major companies. Moreover, contrary to what many people believe, these global women business leaders neither come strictly from the West nor predominantly from the West (see Adler 1997a).

There is, of course, a fallacy in assuming that because global women leaders are still so few in number they are not important (Bunch 1991: xi–xii). In fact, as

Table 19.1: Global women leaders: a chronology

Country	Name	Office	Date
Sri Lanka	Sirimavo Bandaranaike	Prime Minister	1960–1965; 1970–1977, 1994–2000
India	(Indira Gandhi)	Prime Minister	1966–1977, 1980–1984
Israel	(Golda Meir)	Prime Minister	1969–1975
Argentina	(Maria Estela [Isabel] Martínez de Perón)	President	1974–1976
Central African Rep.	Elizabeth Domitien	Prime Minister	1975–1976
Portugal	Maria de Lourdes Pintasilgo	Prime Minister	1979
Bolivia	Lidia Gveiler Tejada	Interim President	1979–1980
Great Britain	Margaret Thatcher	Prime Minister	1979–1990
Dominica	Mary Eugenia Charles	Prime Minister	1980–1995
Iceland	Vigdís Finnbógadottir	President	1980–1996
Norway	Gro Harlem Brundtland	Prime Minister	1981; 1986–1989; 1990–1996
Yugoslavia	Milka Planinc	Prime Minister	1982–1986
Malta	Agatha Barbara	President	1982–1987
Netherland–Antilles	Maria Liberia-Peters	Prime Minister	1984; 1989–1994
The Philippines	Corazon Aquino	President	1986–1992
Pakistan	Benazir Bhutto	Prime Minister	1988–1990; 1993–1996
Lithuania	Kazimiera-Danute Prunskiene	Prime Minister	1990–1991
Haiti	Ertha Pascal-Trouillot	President	1990–1991
Myanmar (Burma)	Aung San Suu Kyi	Opposition Leader**	1990–**
East Germany	Sabine Bergmann-Pohl	President of the Parliament	1990
Ireland	Mary Robinson	President	1990–1997
Nicaragua	Violeta Barrios de Chamorro	President	1990–1996
Bangladesh	Khaleda Zia	Prime Minister	1991–1996
France	Edith Cresson	Prime Minister	1991–1992
Poland	Hanna Suchocka	Prime Minister	1992–1993
Canada	Kim Campbell	Prime Minister	1993

Country	Name	Title	Dates
Burundi	Sylvia Kinigi	Prime Minister	1993–1994
Rwanda	(Agatha Uwilingiyimana)	Prime Minister	1993–1994
Turkey	Tansu Çiller	Prime Minister	1993–1996
Bulgaria	Reneta Indzhova	Interim Prime Minister	1994–1995
Sri Lanka	*Chandrika Bandaranaike Kumaratunga	Executive President & Former Prime Minister	1994–*
Haiti	Claudette Werleigh	Prime Minister	1995–1996
Bangladesh	*Hasina Wajed	Prime Minister	1996–*
Liberia	*Ruth Perry	Chair, Ruling Council	1996–*
Ecuador	Rosalia Artega	President	1997
Bermuda	Pamela Gordon	Premiere	1997–1998
Ireland	*Mary McAleese	President	1997–*
New Zealand	Jenny Shipley	Prime Minister	1997–1999
Guyana	Janet Jagan	Prime Minister	1997–1999
Bermuda	*Jennifer Smith	Premier	1998–*
Lithuania	Irene Degutienė	Acting prime minister	4–18 May 1999
Mongolia	Nyam-Osorily Tuyaa	Acting prime minister	22–30- July 1999
Switzerland	Ruth Dreifuss	President	1999
Latvia	*Vaira Vike-Freiberga	President	1999–*
Panama	*Mireya Moscoso	President	1999–*
New Zealand	*Helen Clark	Prime Minister	1999–*

Notes: () = No longer living
      * = Currently in office;
      ** = Party won 1990 election but prevented by military from taking office; Nobel Prize laureate.

Source: Adapted and updated from Adler, Nancy J. (1996) "Global Women Political Leaders, An Invisible History, An Increasingly Important Future," *Leadership Quarterly*, 7 (1):136.

© Nancy J. Adler, 1997

Table 19.2: **Women leading global companies**

Selected women who lead major global companies in countries around the world. Table states annual revenues, or, in the case of banks, assets in US$.

Argentina

Amalia Lacroze de Fortabat, $700 million, President, Grupo Fortabat. Richest woman in Argentina, with nine cement companies, a rail cargo line, eighteen ranches, a news paper, four radio stations, part-ownership in a satellite-communications company.

Ernestina Herrera de Noble, $1.2 billion, President and editorial director, Grupo Clarin. The largest-circulation Spanish newspaper in the world.

Australia

Imelda Roche, $237 million, President, Nutri-Metics International Holdings Pty. Ltd. Skin cream and beauty products sold by 250 000 sales people in 20 countries.

Brazil

Beatriz Larragoiti, $2.9 billion, Vice President and Owner, Sul America S.A. Insurance company with 20% of the Brazilian market.

Canada

Maureen Kempston Darkes, $18.3 billion, President and General Manager of General Motors of Canada.

Costa Rica

Donatella Zigone Dini, $300 million, Chairman, Zeta Group. Fifth largest business in Central America, conglomerate.

Egypt

Nawal Abdel Moneim El Tatawy, $357 million, Chairman, Arab Investment Bank.

France

Colette Lewiner, $800 million, Chairman and CEO, SGN-Eurisys Group. World's largest nuclear fuels reprocessing company with contracts in Japan, Jordan, Pakistan, Indonesia, and the USA.

Annette Roux, $139 million & $31.9 million, CEO of Beneteau and of Roux S.A. Beneteau is one of world's most respected yacht builders with employees in 28 countries and exports accounting for 60% of sales. Roux is one of France's largest hardware companies.

Anne-Claire Taittinger-Bonnemaison, $100 million & $230 million, CEO, Baccarat and Vice President, ELM Leblanc. Company represents 40% of France's handmade crystal production; 70% of sales are exports.

Germany

Ellen R. Schneider-Lenné, $458 billion. Member of the board of managing directors, Deutsch Bank AG. Responsible for operations in the UK.

Hong Kong

Joyce Ma, $112 million, CEO, Joyce Boutique Holdings, Ltd. Designer clothes boutiques throughout Asia in China, Hong Kong, Malaysia, the Philippines, Taiwan, and Thailand, and The Joyce art gallery in Paris.

Sally Aw Sian, $237 million, Chairman, Sing Tao Holdings Limited. Publishes one of Hong Kong's largest Chinese-language daily newspapers, *Sing Tao Daily*; also publishes overseas from Sydney to San Francisco.

Nina Wang, $1 to $2 billion in assets, Chairlady, Chinachem. Property development, primarily in Hong Kong and China.

India

Tarjani Vakil, $1.1 billion in assets. Chairperson and managing director, Export-Import Bank of India. Highest ranking female banking official in Asia; bank promotes Indian exports and helps Indian companies set up businesses abroad.

Israel

Galia Maor, $35.6 billion, CEO of Bank Leumi le-Israel.

Jamaica

Gloria Delores Knight, $1.86 billion, President and managing director, The Jamaica Mutual Life Assurance Society. Largest financial conglomerate in English-speaking Caribbean.

Japan

Mieko Morishita, $85 million, President, Morishita Jintan Co., Ltd. Leading manufacturer of breath fresheners in Japan, with soft capsule technique in demand both in Japan and abroad.

Sawako Norma, $2 billion, President of Kodansha Ltd. Largest publishing house in Japan. One of the company's international divisions publishes general trade books, including English translations of classic Japanese novels.

Harumi Sakamoto, $13 billion, Senior managing director, The Seitu Ltd. A supermarket and shopping centre operator expanding throughout Asia; Sakamoto opened stores in Hong Kong, Indonesia, Japan, and Singapore, and plans to expand to China and Vietnam.

Yoshiko Shinohara, $330 million, President of Tempstaff Co. Ltd. Second largest personnel agency in Japan; benefiting from demand boom for temporary services, including translation.

Malaysia

Khatijah Ahmad, $5 billion, Chairman and Managing Director of KAF Group of Companies. Financial services group.

The Netherlands

Sylvia Tóth, $166 million, CEO of Content Beheer. One of the Netherland's top temporary-placement agencies; also conducts training.

The Philippines

Elena Lim, $114 million, President of Solid Corporation. Diversified company makes Sony- and Aiwa-brand electronic products exported to Japan, Europe, and the Middle East; is the Philippines' largest exporter of prawns, and produces Kia Pride subcompact cars for the domestic market.

Singapore

Jannie Tay, $289 million, Managing Director of The Hour Glass Limited. High-end retail watches, with boutiques throughout South Asia region from Thailand to Australia.

South Africa

Aïda Geffen, $355 million, Chairman and managing director, Aïda Holdings Limited. Residential commercial real estate firm.

Spain

Mercè Sala i Schnorkowski, $1.1 billion, CEO, Renfe. Spain's national railway system, currently helping to privatize Columbian and Bolivian rail and selling trains to Germany.

Sweden

Antonia Axson Johnson, $4.7 billion, Chairman, The Axel Johnson Group and of Axel Johnson AB. Retailing and distribution, more than 200 companies.

Switzerland

Elisabeth Salina Amorini, $2.28 billion, Chairman of the board, managing director, and chairman of the group executive board, Société Générale de Surveillance Holding S.A. The world's largest inspection and quality control organization, testing imports and exports in more than 140 countries.

Taiwan

Emilia Roxas, $5 billion, CEO Asiaworld Internationale Group. Multi-national conglomerate.

Thailand

Khunying Niramol Suriyasat, $200 million, Chairperson, Toshiba Thailand Co. High technology. Started first company in 1963; established new companies in 1964, 1969, 1973, and 1976; in 1989 became director of real estate company in joint venture with Mitsui Corporation.

UK

Ann Gloag, $520 million, Executive director, Stagecoach Holdings PLC. Europe's largest bus company, with 7400 additional buses running in Malawi, Hong Kong, Kenya, and New Zealand.

Anita Roddick, $338 million, Founder and chief executive, The Body Shop International Plc. Body creams and lotions, with more than 1300 stores in 45 countries.

Marjorie Scardino, $3.6 billion, Chief executive, Pearson. A publishing and entertainment comglomerate, including the *Financial Times* and *The Economist*.

USA

Sally Frame Kasaks, $658 million, CEO of Ann Taylor Inc. Women's clothing retailer.

Loida Nicolas Lewis, $1.8 billion, Chairman and CEO, TLC Beatrice International Holdings. Food conglomerate with operations outside of the USA.

Linda Joy Wachner, $266 million, Chairman, The Warnaco Group, Inc. and of Authentic Fitness Corporation. Owner of both Warnaco, a lingerie maker, and Authentic Fitness Corp.

Zimbabwe

Liz Chitiga, $400 million, General manager and CEO, Minerals Marketing Corporation of Zimbabwe. In foreign-currency terms, the biggest business in Zimbabwe; administers Zimbabwe's sales and exports of minerals.

(Based on Kelly 1996: 20–31)

Charlotte Bunch (1991: xii), Director of the Center for Global Issues and Women's Leadership suggests, perhaps the most important question to ask is 'why so little attention has been paid to the women who have become [global] leaders and why the styles of leading more often exhibited by women are particularly useful at this critical moment in history.'

The feminization of global leadership

In addition to increasing numbers, feminization also refers to 'the spread of traits or qualities that are traditionally associated with [women] ... to ... people [and processes] not usually described that way' (Fondas 1997: 258 based on Douglas 1997 and Ferguson 1984). Hence, the feminization of global leadership – beyond strictly referring to the increasing numbers of women who are global leaders – refers to the spread of traits and qualities generally associated with women to the process of leading organizations with worldwide influence. Whereas this certainly has not been true of traditional twentieth-century leadership models which have primarily reflected American men and their norms, it appears that twenty-first century global leadership is increasingly being described in terms that neither reflect the masculine ideal nor the American ethos.

What is a feminine style of leadership? 'Feminine is a word that refers to the characteristics of females' (Fondas 1997: 260). Many authors argue that 'there are character traits, interaction styles, and patterns of reasoning, speaking, and communicating that are culturally ascribed as feminine attributes' (Fondas 1997: 260). Although theorists debate whether these traits are biologically given or socially constructed, most researchers credit women

> with some or all of the following qualities: empathy, helpfulness, caring, and nurturance; interpersonal sensitivity, attentiveness to and acceptance of others, responsiveness to their needs and motivations; an orientation toward the collective interest and toward integrative goals such as group cohesiveness and stability; a preference for open, egalitarian, and cooperative relationships, rather than hierarchical ones; and an interest in actualizing values and relationships of great importance to community (Belenky, Clinchy, Goldberger, & Tarule, 1986; Chodorow, 1978; Dinnerstein, 1976; Eisler, 1987; Ferguson, 1984; Gilligan, 1982; Glennon, 1979; Grace, 1995; Hartsock, 1983; Iannello, 1992; Klein, 1972; McMillan, 1982; Miller, 1976; Scott, 1992; Spender, 1984; Tannen, 1990, 1994).
>
> *(Fondas 1997: 260)*

By contrast, as Fondas (1997: 260) summarizes,

> traits culturally ascribed to men include an ability to be impersonal, self-interested, efficient, hierarchical, tough minded, and assertive; an interest in taking charge, control, and domination; a capacity to ignore personal, emotional considerations in order to succeed; a proclivity to rely on standardized or 'objective' codes for judgment and evaluation of others; and a heroic orientation toward task accomplishment and a continual effort to act on the world and become something new (cf. Brod & Kaufman, 1994; Gilligan, 1982; Glennon, 1979; Grace, 1995; Kanter, 1977; Seidler, 1994).

Studies focusing specifically on women managers – as opposed to women in general or senior-level women leaders (on whom there is as yet no body of literature) – document their 'orientation toward more participative, interactional, and relational styles of leading' (Fondas 1997: 259 based on Helgesen 1990; Lipman-Blumen 1983, Marshall 1984; and Rosener 1990). Frequently labelled as the feminine advantage (e.g. Chodorow 1978; Helgesen 1990; Rosener 1990), some authors have suggested that all managers today need to incorporate a more feminine leadership style (Fondas 1997: 259). As Fondas (1997: 259) observes, these findings,

> when juxtaposed against calls for companies to improve their competitiveness by transforming themselves into learning, self-managing, empowering, and continuously improving organizations – transformations that rely upon more interactional, relational, and participative management styles – [lead] . . . some writers to conclude that . . . [women] are well-suited for managerial roles in contemporary organizations and that male [managers] need to cultivate feminine leadership traits (Aburdene & Naisbitt, 1992; Godfrey, 1996; Grant, 1988; Peters, 1989).

The current implication is that both female and male leaders also need to cultivate such feminine characteristics in their styles of leadership.

However, leadership approaches that frequently have been labelled as feminine in the North American management literature – including more co-operative, participative, interactional and relational styles – appear to reflect male/female patterns specific to the American culture, rather than broader, universally valid patterns. Relative to American men, male managers in many other parts of the world, including in the fastest growing economies of Asia, exhibit a more supposedly feminine style than do American men. As Cambridge management scholar Charles Hampden-Turner (1993: 1) notes:

> America's ultra-masculine corporate value system has been losing touch progressively with the wider world. It needs a change of values, desperately, or it will continue to under-perform, continue to lose touch with the value systems of foreigners, which ironically are much closer to the values in which American women are raised . . . .
>
> American women, who are socialized to display values antithetical yet complementary to American men, have within their culture vitally important cures for American economic decline.

It appears that some of the male/female cultural distinctions documented in the USA among domestic American women and men have been overgeneralized.

For example, as the economy shifts from the twentieth century's emphasis on mass production capitalism to the twenty-first century's emphasis on mass customization – that is, from the twentieth century's machine-age emphasis on huge production runs of essentially undifferentiated products to the emerging era of products and services made in short runs and in great variety – the importance of interactional and relational styles increases. Why? Because 'the future for developed economies lies in products [and services] uniquely fashioned for special persons' (Hampden-Turner 1993: 6). Whereas the more typically male (from a North American perspective) universalistic approach of treating everyone the same according to codified rules worked well for mass-producing products such as jeans, colas, and hamburgers sold to a mass domestic market, a more typically feminine (from a North American perspective) particularist approach works best for developing products and services – such as software – which must be tailored to the individual client and his or her particular needs. To understand particular markets and particular clients well enough to fashion suitable products and services to their needs, one must develop deep relationships. Not surprisingly, relational skills (labelled by the anthropologists as particularism and by North Americans as typically feminine) outperform the seemingly more objective approach of following the same rules with everyone (labelled as universalism by the anthropologists and as typically male by North Americans). The distinction does not appear to be strictly male/female, but rather a difference between the approach of most American male managers and that of most other managers around the world. Results of research by Trompenaars (1993) and Hampden-Turner (1993) show that American male managers strongly prefer universalism (the less relational style), whereas executives from many very strong economies, such as Hong Kong, Japan and South Korea, emphasize more relational values which are opposite to those of their American male colleagues (Hampden-Turner 1993). As Hampden-Turner (1993: 6) summarized, at the close of the twentieth century: 'Most American male executives suddenly find themselves ill-suited to the wider world, trying to codify the uncodifiable, flanked by a huge surplus of lawyers using cumbersome rules where other nations enter trusting relationships with subtle communications'.

According to the research, American women display a relational style of communicating that is closer to the style of most non-American managers around the world than to that of most American male managers. Given American women managers' concurrence with the relational styles of their non-American colleagues, it is not surprising that, on average, American women expatriate managers outperform their American male counterparts (Adler 1994). It is not that the distinction between women and men identified in the American managerial literature is either incorrect or inconsequential, but only that it is incomplete. Without appreciating American male managers as outliers, it is impossible to begin to appreciate what men's and women's approaches can bring to global leadership in the twenty-first century.

Global women leaders: an emerging portrait

Beyond knowing that their numbers are increasing and that their approaches to leadership appear to differ from those of men, what do we know about the women who are global leaders that might help us to better plan for the twenty-first century?[7]

Diversity defines pattern

The dominant pattern in the women leaders' backgrounds as well as in the countries and companies that select them to lead is diversity. As highlighted in Tables 19.1 and 19.2, the 46 women political leaders and their business counterparts span the globe. They come from both the world's largest and smallest countries, the richest and poorest countries, the most socially and economically advantaged and disadvantaged countries and from every geographical region. Countries led by women represent six of the major world religions, with four women prime ministers having led predominantly Muslim countries (see Adler 1996; 1997a).

Many people believe that female-friendly countries and companies select more women leaders. They do not. Seemingly female friendly countries (for example, those that give equal rights to women) do not elect a disproportionate number of women presidents and prime ministers. Similarly, companies that select women for their most senior leadership positions are not those that implement the most female-friendly policies, such as day-care centres and flexitime (Wellington 1996, as reported in Dobrzynski 1996). For example, among the 61 *Fortune* 500 companies employing women as chairmen, CEOs, board members or one of the top five earners, only three are the same companies that *Working Woman* identified as the most favourable for women employees (Dobrzynski 1996).

The fact that the countries that elect women presidents and prime ministers or have women serving as CEOs of major companies are so diverse suggests that the overall pattern is toward selecting more women as senior leaders, rather than toward a particular group of supposedly female-friendly countries and companies (such as the Scandinavian countries, companies such as Avon Products or organizations such as Britain's National Health Service) valuing women per se. The dominant pattern is that women are increasingly being selected to serve in senior leadership positions, not that a few countries, companies or organizations with particularly feminine cultures are choosing to select women to lead them.

People's aspirations: hope, change and unity

Why would countries and companies, for the first time in modern history, increasingly choose to select women for senior leadership positions? It appears that people worldwide increasingly want something that women exhibit (e.g. feminine values and behaviour) and/or something that they symbolize.

Women leaders' most powerful and most attractive symbolism appears to be change. Women's assumption of the highest levels of leadership brings with it the symbolic possibility of fundamental societal and organizational change. The combination of women being outsiders at senior leadership levels previously completely controlled by men and of beating the odds to become the first woman to lead her country or company produces powerful public imagery about the possibility of broad-based societal and organizational change.

As 'firsts', women assuming senior leadership positions literally bring change. When a woman is visibly chosen to become president, prime minister or CEO when no other woman has ever held such an office and when few people thought that she would be selected, other major organizational and societal changes become believably possible. Mary Robinson's presidential acceptance speech captures the coupling of the unique event of a woman being elected Ireland's first non-male president with the possibility of national change:

> I was elected by men and women of all parties and none, by many with great moral courage who stepped out from the faded flags of Civil War and voted for a new Ireland. And above all by the women of Ireland . . . who instead of rocking the cradle rocked the system, and who came out massively to make their mark on the ballot paper, and on a new Ireland.
> *(RDS, Dublin, 9 November 1990, as reported in Finlay 1990: 1)*

In addition to symbolizing change, women leaders appear to symbolize unity. For example, both Nicaragua's Chamorro and the Philippines' Aquino became symbols of national unity following their husband's murders. Chamorro even claimed 'to have no ideology beyond national "reconciliation"' (Benn 1995). Of Chamorro's four adult children, two are prominent Sandinistas while the other two equally prominently oppose the Sandinistas, not an unusual split in war-torn Nicaragua (Saint-Germain 1993: 80). Chamorro's ability to bring all the members of her family together for Sunday dinner each week achieved near legendary status in Nicaragua (Saint-Germain 1993: 80). As 'the grieving matriarch who can still hold the family together' (Saint-Germain 1993: 80), Chamorro gives symbolic hope to the nation that it too can find peace based on a unity that brings together all Nicaraguans. That a national symbol for a woman leader is family unity is neither surprising nor coincidental.

Based on similar dynamics in the Philippines, former president Corazon Aquino, as widow of the slain opposition leader, was seen as the only person who could credibly unify the people of the Philippines following Benigno Aquino's death. Although Aquino was widely condemned in the press for *naïveté* when she invited members of both her own and the opposition party into her cabinet, her choice was a conscious decision to attempt to reunify the deeply divided country.

Given that women leaders symbolize unity, it is perhaps not surprising that a woman business leader, Rebecca Mark, chief executive of Enron Development Corporation, and not a male executive, was the first person to successfully negotiate a major commercial transaction following the Middle East peace accords. Mark brought the Israelis and Jordanians together to build a natural gas power generation station.

When, as Vaclav Havel (1994: A27) says, the world is 'going through a transitional period, when something is on the way out and something else is painfully being born', it is not surprising that people worldwide are attracted to women leaders' symbolic message of bringing change, hope and the possibility for unity.

Driven by vision, not by hierarchical status

What brings the women themselves into the most senior levels of leadership? Most women leaders are driven by a vision, mission or cause. They are motivated by a compelling agenda that they want to achieve, not primarily by either a desire for the hierarchical status of being president, prime minister or CEO, or a desire for power per se. Power and the presidency are means for achieving their mission, not the mission itself.

As children, none of the women leaders dreamed about becoming her country's leader, as have so many male politicians, including America's Bill Clinton and Bob Dole, and Britain's Michael Heseltine. For example, Golda Meir's mission was to create the state of Israel and to ensure its survival as a Jewish state. Not only did she not dream of becoming prime minister, she rejected the position when it was initially offered to her. Similarly, Anita Roddick (1991: 126), CEO of The Body Shop, describes her contemporary vision as 'corporate idealism'. Her vision transcends traditional, narrowly defined economic goals; she is neither motivated to be a traditional CEO nor to focus singularly on maximizing either profits or shareholder wealth.

That women have not imagined, let alone dreamed about, leading a country or a major company is not surprising. For all of the women political leaders – except Sri Lanka's current executive president, Chandrika Kumaratunga, who followed her prime minister mother Sirimavo Bandaranaike into office, and Bangladesh's Hasina Wajid – and most of the women corporate leaders, there have been no women predecessors and therefore no women role models. What is important for twenty-first century leadership is that society, if it is to survive as a civilization, can no longer tolerate nor support the leadership of self-aggrandizement at the expense of the greater, now highly interrelated whole, at the expense of the world's entire population and its physical, spiritual and natural environment.

Source of power: broadly-based

Who supports women in becoming senior leaders? Women leaders tend to develop and to use broadly based popular support, rather than relying primarily on traditional, hierarchical party or structural support. This is particularly apparent among the women who become political leaders who often are not seriously considered as potential candidates by their country's main political parties. They are consequently forced to gain support directly from the people, and thus foreshadow the dynamics of leadership in an organizationally flattened world.

Mary Robinson, for example, campaigned in more small communities in Ireland than any previous presidential candidate before either her party or the opposition would take her seriously. The opposition now admits that they did not seriously consider Robinson's candidacy until it was too late to stop her (Finlay 1990). Similarly, Corazon Aquino, whose campaign and victory was labelled the People's Revolution, held more than 1000 rallies during her campaign, while incumbent Ferdinand Marcos held only 34 (Col 1993: 25). Likewise, Benazir Bhutto, who succeeded in becoming Pakistan's first woman and youngest-ever prime minister, campaigned in more communities than any politician before her. Her own party only took her seriously when more people showed up upon her return to Pakistan from exile than either they, the opposition or the international press had ever expected (Anderson 1993; Weisman 1986).

In business, the disproportionate number of women who choose to become leaders of entrepreneurial businesses, rather than attempting to climb the corporate ladder and break through the glass ceiling to senior leadership positions in established corporations, echoes the same pattern of broadly based popular support – as opposed to traditional hierarchical support – that women political leaders enjoy. The only difference being that the entrepreneurs' support comes from the marketplace rather than from the electorate. In both cases, the base of support is outside of the traditional power structure and therefore more representative of new and more diverse opinions and ideas. The source of support, and therefore of power, more closely reflects the flattened network of emerging twenty-first century organizations and society than it does the more centralized and limited power structure of most twentieth-century organizations.

Path to power: lateral transfer

How do the women leaders gain power? Rather than following the traditional path up through the hierarchy of the organization, profession or political party, most women leaders laterally transfer into high office. For example, Gro Harlem Brundtland was a medical doctor; six years later she became Norway's first woman prime minister. Similarly, Charlotte Beers became both Ogilvy & Mather Worldwide's first woman chief executive as well as their first CEO brought in from outside the firm (Sackley and Ibarra 1995). Marjorie Scardino, Pearson's first woman chief executive, is a double outsider. As the first American CEO brought in to lead this traditional British firm, she is a cultural outsider. In addition, because *The Economist*, where Scardino previously served as managing director, is only 50 per cent owned by Pearson, she is an organizational outsider. The general public was so surprised by Pearson's selection of Scardino that Pearson's stock dropped initially on the announcement of her appointment (Pogrebin 1996).

Today's global organizations and society can only benefit from the dynamics of lateral transfers. The twenty-first century needs integration across geographies, sectors of society and professions. It can no longer tolerate leaders with 'chimney stack' careers that, in the past, have resulted in deep expertise in one area, organization, or country without any understanding of the context within which their particular organization or country operates. Transferring across organizations, sectors of society and areas of the world allows leaders to develop alternative perspectives and an understanding of context that is almost impossible to acquire within a single setting. Due to the historic pattern of promoting men and failing to promote women to the most senior leadership positions from within organizations – most often referred to as the 'glass ceiling' – women appear to have inadvertently become the prototypes of a career pattern that is needed more broadly among all twenty-first century leaders.

Global leadership: global visibility

What difference does it make that a global leader is a woman? For the women who become global leaders, it is always salient that they are women. For example, the single most frequently asked question of former British prime minister Margaret Thatcher (1995) was 'What is it like being a woman prime minister?' (to which Thatcher generally responded that she could not answer because she had not tried the alternative).

Women are new to the most senior levels of leadership. As mentioned previously, of the 37 women presidents and prime ministers, only two – in Bangladesh and Sri Lanka – followed another woman into office. All the rest of the women leaders are 'firsts'. Because women leaders are new, they have the advantage of global visibility. Their unique status as their countries' first woman president or prime minister attracts worldwide media attention, thereby leveraging historically domestic leadership positions into ones with global visibility and the concomitant potential for worldwide influence. For example, following the election of Mary Robinson as Ireland's first woman president:

> Newspapers and magazines in virtually every country in the world carried the story
> ... [T]he rest of the world understood Ireland to have made a huge leap forward
> ... Mary Robinson had joined a very small number of women ... who had been
> elected to their country's highest office. It was, quite properly, seen as historic.
>
> (*Finlay 1990: 149–50*)

Similarly, President François Mitterand purposely created a worldwide media event by appointing Edith Cresson as France's first woman prime minister. Likewise, in contrast to Benazir Bhutto's male predecessor who not only complained about receiving insufficient worldwide press coverage while abroad but also fired the Pakistani embassy's public relations officer when too few journalists showed up to cover his arrival in London, Pakistan's former Prime Minister Benazir Bhutto always received extensive media coverage no matter where in the world she travelled.

Because of the worldwide media attention given to women leaders, women today are becoming global, rather than domestic, leaders as they assume roles that were primarily domestic when previously held by men. Whether by intention or consequence, the senior women leaders are at the forefront of learning how to move beyond a domestic focus to communicate on the world stage to a global audience.

Whereas many of the dynamics affecting senior women leaders are quite different from those that affect women managers (see Adler 1997a), it should be noted that international businesswomen also receive more visibility than their male colleagues. Women expatriate managers as well as women on international business trips, for example, report being remembered more easily than their male counterparts (Adler 1994). Compared with business men, global business women gain access more easily to new clients, suppliers and government officials; receive more time when meeting with international contacts; and are more frequently remembered (Adler 1994).

The future: global leaders, women leaders

The confluence of twenty-first century business, political, and societal dynamics gives leaders a chance to create the type of world that they, and we, would like to live in. It demands, as Vaclav Havel (1994: A27) reflected, that leaders find 'the key to insure the survival of . . . [our] civilization[,] . . . a civilization that is global and multicultural'. The increasing number of women political and business leaders brings with it a set of experiences and perspectives that differ from those of the twentieth century's primarily male leaders. The interplay of women's and men's styles of leadership will define the contours and potential success of twenty-first century society. The risk is in encapsulating leaders, both women and men, in approaches that worked well in the twentieth century but foretell disaster for the twenty-first century. As Dr Frene Ginwala, Speaker of the South African National Assembly stated, 'the institutions that discriminate are man-shaped and must be made people-shaped. Only then will women be able to function as equals within those institutions'. Ginwala's fundamental belief is that 'women's struggle is not a struggle to transform the position of women in society but a struggle to transform society itself' (Iqtidar and Webster 1996: 10). Recognizing the growing number of women leaders is the first step in creating and understanding the type of global leadership that will lead to success in the twenty-first century.

Acknowledgement

The author would like to thank Soraya Hassanali and Kirsten Martin for their research support and insight on this chapter.

Endnotes

1 The opening section of this article is based on Adler's 'Societal leadership: the wisdom of peace' (1997b).
2 For contemporary discussions of some of the widely read leadership theories and approaches, see Bennis 1989; Bennis and Nanus 1985; Conger 1989; Conger and Kanungo 1988; Gardner 1995; Kotter 1988; and Rosen 1996, among many others.

3 For descriptions of American societal and managerial culture contrasted with those of many other countries, see, among others, Hofstede 1980a; Kluckhohn and Strodbeck 1961; Laurent 1983; Trompenaars 1993.
4 Based on Fondas' (1997: 257) observation 'that the feminization of managers and managerial work is a significant development in management thinking'.
5 The Republic of San Marino, a city state with a population of less than 25 000 people has been led since 1243 by a consul, the Co-Captain Regent, who acts as both head of government and head of state, and is elected for a period of six months. In modern history, four women have held the position of Co-Captain Regent, Maria Lea Pedini-Angelini (1981), Glorianna Ranocchini (1984, 1989–90), Edda Ceccoli (1991–2), and Patricia Busignani (1993). Due to the small size of the country and the frequency of changing leaders, San Marino has not been included in the statistics on global women leaders.
6 Although the results are not yet available, the author is currently involved in a major worldwide survey to identify women who head global businesses with annual revenues in excess of $250 million.
7 For a more indepth discussion of the issues raised in this section, see Adler (1997a).

References

Aburdene, P. and Naisbitt, J. (1992) *Megatrends for Women*, New York: Villard Books.
Adler, N.J. (1994) 'Competitive frontiers: women managing across borders', in N.J. Adler and D.N. Izraeli (eds) *Competitive Frontiers: Women Managers in a Global Economy*, Cambridge, MA: Blackwell.
Adler, N.J. (1996) 'Global women political leaders: an invisible history, an increasingly important future', *Leadership Quarterly* 7(1): 133–61.
Adler, N.J. (1997a) 'Global leaders: a dialogue with future history', *International Management* 1(2): 21–33.
Adler, N.J. (1997b) 'Societal leadership: the wisdom of peace', in S. Srivastva (ed.) *Executive Wisdom and Organizational Change*, San Francisco: Jossey-Bass.
Anderson, N.F. (1993) 'Benazir Bhutto and dynastic politics: her father's daughter, her people's sister', in M.A. Genovese (ed.) *Women as National Leaders*, Newbury Park, CA: Sage.
Astin, H.S. and Leland, C. (1991) *Women of Influence, Women of Vision*, San Francisco: Jossey-Bass.
Bass, B. (1991) *Bass & Stogdill's Handbook of Leadership*, 3rd edition, New York: Free Press.
Belenky, M.F., Clinchy, B.M., Goldberger, N.R. and Tarule, J.M. (1986) *Women's Ways of Knowing: The Development of Self, Voice, and Mind*, New York: Basic Books.
Benn, M. (1995) 'Women who rule the world', *Cosmopolitan* February.
Bennis, W. (1989) *Why Leaders Can't Lead: The Unconscious Conspiracy Continues*, San Francisco: Jossey-Bass.
Bennis, W. and Nanus, B. (1985) *Leaders: Strategies of Taking Charge*, New York: Harper & Row.
Bolman, L. and Deal, T. (1991) *Reframing Organizations: Artistry, Choice and Leadership*, San Francisco: Jossey-Bass.
Bolman, L. and Deal, T. (1995) *Leading with Soul*, San Francisco: Jossey-Bass.
Boyacigiller, N. and Adler, N.J. (1991) 'The parochial dinosaur: the organizational sciences in a global context', *Academy of Management Review* 16(2): 262–90.
Boyacigiller, N. and Adler, N.J. (1996) 'Insiders and outsiders: bridging the worlds of organizational behavior and international management', in B. Toyne and D. Nigh (eds) *International Business Inquiry: An Emerging Vision*, Columbia, SC: University of South Carolina Press.
Brod, H. and Kaufman, M. (eds) (1994) *Theorizing Masculinities*, Thousand Oaks, CA: Sage.
Bunch, C. (1991) 'Foreword' to H.S. Astin and C. Leland, (1991) *Women of Influence, Women of Vision*, San Francisco: Jossey-Bass.
Calas, M.B. and Smircich, L (1993) 'Dangerous liaisons: the "feminine-in-management" meets "globalization"', *Business Horizons* 36(2): 71–81.
Cantor, D. and Bernay, T. (1992) *Women in Power*, New York: Houghton Mifflin.
Chodorow, N. (1978) *The Reproduction of Mothering*, Berkeley, CA: University of California Press.
Cohn, S. (1985) *The Process of Occupational Sex-Typing: The Feminization of Clerical Labor in Great Britain*, Philadelphia, PA: Temple University Press.
Col, J.-M. (1993) 'Managing softly in turbulent times: Corazon C. Aquino, president of the Philippines', in M.A. Genovese (ed.) *Women as National Leaders*, Newbury Park, CA: Sage.

Conger, J.A. (1989) *The Charismatic Leader: Behind the Mystique of Exceptional Leadership*, San Francisco: Jossey-Bass.

Conger, J. A. and Kanungo, R. (1988) *Charismatic Leadership*, San Francisco: Jossey-Bass.

Dinnerstein, D. (1976) *The Mermaid and the Minotaur*, New York: Harper & Row.

Dobrzynski, J.H. (1996) 'Somber news for women on corporate ladder', *New York Times*, 6 November: D1.

Dorfman, P.W. (1996) 'International and cross-cultural leadership', in B.J. Punnett and O. Shenkar (eds) *Handbook for International Management Research*, Cambridge, MA: Blackwell.

Dorfman, P.W. and Howell, J.P. (1988) 'Dimensions of national culture and effective leadership patterns: Hofstede Revisited', *Advances in International Comparative Management*, volume 3, Greenwich, CT: JAI Press.

Dorfman, P.W. and Ronen, S. (1991) 'The universality of leadership theories: challenges and paradoxes', paper presented at the National Academy of Management annual meeting, Miami, Florida.

Douglas, A. (1977) *The Feminization of American Culture*, New York: Avon Books.

Eisler, R. (1987) *The Chalice and the Blade*, San Francisco: HarperSanFrancisco.

Ferguson, K.E. (1984) *The Feminist Case against Bureaucracy*, Philadelphia, PA: Temple University Press.

Finlay, F. (1990) *Mary Robinson: A President with a Purpose*, Dublin: O'Brien Press.

Fondas, N. (1997) 'The origins of feminization', *Academy of Management Review* 22(1): 257–82.

Gardner, H. (1995) *Leading Minds: An Anatomy of Leadership*, New York: Basic Books.

Gilligan, C. (1982) *In a Different Voice: Psychological Theory and Women's Development*, Cambridge, MA: Harvard University Press.

Glennon, L.M. (1979) *Women and Dualism*, New York: Longman.

Godfrey, J. (1996) 'Mind of the manager', *Inc.* 18(3): 21.

Goodwin, D.K. (1995) *No Ordinary Time: Franklin & Eleanor Roosevelt: The Home Front in World War II*, New York: Simon & Schuster.

Grace, N.M. (1995) *The Feminized Male Character in Twentieth-Century Literature*, Lewiston, NY: Mellen Press.

Grant, J. (1988) 'Women as managers: what can they offer organizations?', *Organizational Dynamics* 16(1): 56–63.

Hampden-Turner, C. (1993) 'The structure of entrapment: dilemmas standing in the way of women managers and strategies to resolve these', New York City, Global Business Network meeting, 9–10 December.

Hartsock, N.C. (1983) *Money, Sex, and Power: Toward a Feminist Historical Materialism*, New York: Longman.

Havel, V. (1994) 'The new measure of man', *New York Times*, 8 July: A27.

Helgesen. S (1990) *The Female Advantage: Women's Ways of Leadership*, New York: Doubleday.

Hofstede, G. (1980a) *Culture's Consequences: International Differences in Work-Related Values*, Beverley Hills, CA: Sage.

Hofstede, G. (1980b) 'Motivation, leadership, and organization: do American theories apply abroad?', *Organizational Dynamics* 9(1): 4–21.

Hofstede, G. (1991) *Cultures and Organizations: Software of the Mind*, London: McGraw-Hill.

Hollander, E.P. (1985) 'Leadership and power', in G. Lindzey and E. Aronson (eds) *Handbook of Social Psychology*, New York: Random House.

Howell, J.P., Dorfman, P.W., Hibino, S., Lee, J.K. and Tate, U. (1994) *Leadership in Western and Asian Countries: Commonalities and Differences in Effective Leadership Processes and Substitutes across Cultures'*, Center for Business Research, New Mexico State University.

Iannello, K.P. (1992) *Decisions without Hierarchy: Feminist Interventions in Organization Theory and Practice*, New York: Routledge.

Iqtidar, H. and Webster, L.J. (1996) 'Frene Ginwala: speaker of the South African National Assembly', McGill University, Faculty of Management (unpublished).

Jennings, E. (1960) *The Anatomy of Leadership*, New York: Harper & Row.

Kakar, S. (1971) 'Authority patterns and subordinate behavior in Indian organizations', *Administrative Science Quarterly* 16(3): 298–308.

Kanter, R.M. (1977) *Men and Women of the Corporation*, New York: Basic Books.

Kelly, C. (1996) '50 world-class executives', *Worldbusiness* 2(2), March–April: 20–31.

Klein, V. (1972) *The Feminine Character: History of an Ideology*, Urbana, IL: University of Illinois Press.

Kluckhohn, F.R. and Strodtbeck, F.L. (1961) *Variations in Value Orientations*, Evanston, IL: Row, Peterson.

Kotter, J. (1988) *The Leadership Factor*, New York: Free Press.

Laurent, A. (1983) 'The cultural diversity of Western conceptions of management', *International Studies of Management and Organization* 13(1–2): 75–96.

Lipman-Blumen, J. (1983) 'Emerging patterns of female leadership in formal organizations', in M. Horner, C.C. Nadelson and M.T. Notman (eds) *The Challenge of Change*, New York: Plenum Press.

Marshall, J. (1984) *Women Managers: Travellers in a Male World*, New York: Wiley.

McMillan, C. (1982) *Reason, Women and Nature: Some Philosophical Problems with Nature*, Princeton, NJ: Princeton University Press.

Miller, J.B. (1976) *Toward a New Psychology of Women*, Boston, MA: Beacon Press.

Peters, T. (1989) 'Listen up, guys: women fit profile of execs of future', *Seattle Post-Intelligencer*, 11 April: B6.

Pogrebin, R. (1996) 'Pearson picks an American as executive', *New York Times*, 18 October: D7.

Pond, E. (1996) 'Women in leadership: a letter from Stockholm', *Washington Quarterly* 19(4): 59.

Rechtschaffen, S. (1996) *Timeshifting*, New York: Bantam. Audio version, Doubleday Dell Audio Publishing.

Reskin, B.F. and Roos, P.A. (1990) *Job Queues, Gender Queues: Explaining Women's Inroads into Male Occupations*, Philadelphia, PA: Temple University Press.

Robinson, M. (1996) Speech to International Women's Leadership Forum, Stockholm, May.

Roddick, A. (1991) *Body and Soul*, New York: Crown.

Rosen, R.H. (1996) *Leading People*, New York: Viking.

Rosener, J. (1990) 'Ways women lead', *Harvard Business Review* 68(6): 119–25.

Rost, J. (1991) *Leadership for the 21st Century*, New York: Praeger.

Sackley, N. and Ibarra, H. (1995) 'Charlotte Beers at Ogilvy & Mather Worldwide', Harvard Business School, Case 9-495-031.

Saint-Germain, M.A. (1993) 'Women in power in Nicaragua: myth and reality', in M.A. Genovese (ed.) *Women as National Leaders*, Newbury Park, CA: Sage.

Scott, A.F. (1992) *Natural Allies: Women's Associations in American History*, Urbana, IL: University of Illinois Press.

Seidler, V.J. (1994) *Unreasonable Men: Masculinity and Social Theory*, London: Routledge.

Spender, D. (1984) *Women of Ideas and What Men Have Done to Them from Aphra Behn to Adrienne Rich*, Boston, MA: Routledge & Kegan Paul.

Stogdill, R. (1974) *Handbook of Leadership*, New York: Free Press.

Tannen, D. (1990) *You Just Don't Understand: Women and Men in Conversation*, New York: Ballantine Books.

Tannen, D. (1994) *Talking from 9 to 5: How Women's and Men's Conversational Styles Affect Who Gets Heard, Who Gets Credit, and What Gets Done at Work*, New York: Morrow.

Thatcher, M. (1995) *Path to Power*, New York: HarperCollins.

Trompenaars, F. (1993) *Riding the Waves of Culture: Understanding Cultural Diversity in Business*, London: Economist Books.

Vardi, Y., Shrom, A. and Jacobson, D. (1980) 'A study of leadership beliefs of Israeli managers', *Academy of Management Journal* 23(2): 367–74.

Weisman, S.R. (1986) 'A daughter returns to Pakistan to cry for victory', *New York Times*, 11 April: 12.

Wellington, S.W. (1996) *Women in Corporate Leadership: Progress and Prospects*, New York: Catalyst.

Woolf, V. (1938) *Three Guineas*, London: Harcourt Brace.

Chapter 20

Managing to learn: from cross-cultural theory to management education practice

Keith Goodall

The anthropologist, Clifford Geertz, reflecting on 40 years of cultural studies, had this to say about the experience,

> Questions rained down, and continue to rain down, on the very idea of a cultural scheme ... Questions about continuity and change, objectivity and proof, determinism and relativism, uniqueness and generalization, description and explanation ... Anthropology, or anyway the sort that studies cultures, proceeds amid charges of irrelevance, bias, illusion, and impracticability.

> *(Geertz 1995: 42–3)*

The rain of questions falling on the heads of scholars and practitioners in the field of cross-cultural management and organization is no less intense – though reactions to this particular downpour encompass apparent indifference, as well as more or less skilful avoidance. What is faced here are critical colleagues from other 'harder' disciplines (and the effects of what Redding 1994 calls 'physics-envy'), demands for 'rigour' from within the discipline (see, for example, Bartholomew and Adler 1996: 25–7) and pressure from managers for pragmatic, digestible 'solutions'. In the face of such pressures, the attraction of treatments of cross-cultural interaction which are ever more reassuringly solid, 'objective' and amenable to 'technique' is then fairly clear.

The broad object of this chapter is, however, to challenge such responses, and to offer a critique of what, I will argue, are interrelated tendencies in the cross-cultural management literature to reify cultural difference, to assume a rational-technical view of management and organization and, in educational terms, to therefore risk treating managers as passive, neutral absorbers of instrumental knowledge. By way of conclusion, I will attempt to ground this critique in recent experiences of three intercultural management programmes run by the Cambridge Programme for Industry at Cambridge University.[1]

Despite claims that global management styles will eventually converge (Kerr, Dunlop and Myers 1960; Kidger 1991), arguments for the importance, in a globalizing economy, of managerial cross-cultural competence have been well rehearsed (Adler 1983; 1997; Gomez-Mejia and Palich 1997; Hofstede 1980; Laurent 1983; Schneider and Barsoux 1997). Accepting the need for managers to operate effectively across cultures, what exactly is it that they should learn, and how should they learn it? In order to address these questions it is useful to clarify assumptions about the nature of culture, management and management education – clarifications that are seldom offered in the cross-cultural management literature.

The chapter is therefore organized in four sections: the first deals with 'traditional' assumptions about the nature of management and, in particular, what Roberts (1996) has called 'the limits of technical rationality'. The second section then looks at what has been characterised as the 'orthodox' view of management education, and its connection to technicist views of management. The third section considers the ways in which 'culture' has been presented in various texts, and the extent to which these presentations are congruent with what have been called 'orthodox' views of management and management education (Grey, Knights and Willmott 1996). The final section offers alternative perspectives on management, management education and culture, before drawing on examples from recent programmes in intercultural management in order to support claims for a pedagogy informed by interpretivist views of both management and culture.

Traditional management

Tsoukas (1994) likens what he calls the 'traditional view' of management to being 'in a control room checking certain variables on a panel of instruments and pressing buttons or pulling levers in order to bring any deviating variables within their normal range of operation' (1994: 3). This is, he suggests, a view of management as 'social engineering' which 'equates management with control' (see also Alvesson and Willmott 1992, and Morgan 1997: 11–31, for a treatment of the machine metaphor of organization). Underlying the 'social engineering' view of management are, according to Tsoukas, several important assumptions: that organizations consist of sets of stable regularities, expressable as propositional (if/then) statements, which can be influenced at will; that the relationship between manager and organization is external (like that between an individual and an inanimate object), so that he or she can accurately map the outside world 'in a way that is not affected by his or her relationship with it' (Tsoukas 1994: 5); that, because organizations are orderly, explanatory and predictive knowledge about them can be collected and used to steer towards desirable objectives; and, finally, that reliable knowledge about organizations should be produced by the scientific method:

> Thus, organizational behaviour, broadly understood as the discipline of the social sciences concerned with the human side of organization and management, is supposed to search for the regularities exhibited by social systems, establish their validity and codify them in the form of rules (that is 'if/then' statements) which managers would then be able to put into practice with confidence . . .
>
> *(ibid.: 5; see also Grey, Knights and Willmott 1996).*

In a similar vein, Roberts (1996) follows MacIntyre (1981) in suggesting that the orthodox view of the manager is as a 'morally neutral technician' (Roberts 1996: 55). Roberts goes on to outline a notion of management dominated by 'technical rationality' to the extent that management practice 'comes to be equated with the application of technique' (ibid.: 57). That such views of management and organization have been seized upon by managers is hardly surprising: what is apparently offered is a tool-kit which will deliver rational, predictable control. Arguably, managers have been aided and abetted in the pursuit of this dream by management educators. The next section briefly explores this claim.

'Traditional' management education

Traditional management education has been characterized as inviting

> students and practitioners to acquire knowledge of relevant facts and techniques that, in principle, are of universal relevance. The world is assumed to have the status of an exterior independent object which can be known about. By acquiring a body of knowledge, the student or practitioner becomes an expert who can better use, manipulate and control human and material resources.
>
> (*Willmott 1997: 169*)

Self-development is, in this context, 'unimportant' (ibid.). In the context of such a view of education, it is then necessary, in the classroom presentation of 'best practice', that 'conflicts, debates, tensions, and uncertainties' are concealed (Roberts 1996: 55). From this perspective, what participants on management training courses and MBA programmes expect, and what educators must deliver, is clarity, certainty and instrumental rationality. The knowledge that is transmitted thus remains 'unproblematized', and 'staff development' in universities, for example, focuses on efficient and effective means of delivery of management knowledge (Grey, Knights and Willmott 1996).

Looked at more broadly, it would appear that management education in both the UK and the USA is firmly weighted in favour of the technical and the functional (Fox 1997; Grey and Mitev 1995). Much management education, certainly in America and Great Britain, treats management as a context-free activity – there are things to learn, and ways of learning them which have a universal validity (Cunningham and Dawes 1997). The similarities between even this brief account of traditional management education and both Tsoukas's and Roberts' characterization of the dominant values of orthodox management are striking. Both are inextricably entwined in positivist assumptions about the relationship between the knower and the known, and both emphasize the primacy of technique as applied to unproblematical fact.

The temptation, then, is to run courses in intercultural management as if cultural difference simply presented a technical problem, amenable to managerial technique. The next section looks at representations of 'culture' in the literature in order to see to what extent these images might be aligned with the traditional views of management and management education outlined above.

Culture

Having briefly traced the conceptually intertwined values of 'orthodox' management and 'traditional' management education, where might 'culture' fit? The academic literature suggests that culture is important in business. In a review of over 28 000 articles in 73 academic and professional journals published between October 1985 and September 1990 (Bartholomew and Adler 1996), just over 70 per cent of international organizational behaviour and human resource management articles were found to include the concept of culture, whether as 'mind-state', 'social enactment' or an 'ecological variable' (though, interestingly, neither these specific terms, nor 'culture' in general are defined by the authors). Of the 28 000 articles, 541 concluded that culture 'makes a difference', while 28 found it makes no difference. The difference that it makes is, of course, often destructive (Shenkar and Zeira 1990; Parkhe 1995). Yet there are also suggestions in the literature that synergies are to be found in intercultural relations which can result in, for example, greater innovation or responsiveness (Adler 1997; Brannen and Salk 2000; Heenan and Perlmutter 1979; Schein 1986).

It would appear, however, that, like St Augustine pondering the notion of time, we know what culture is until we try to define it (see chapter 8). A consistent criticism in the academic literature is that we do not have a widely accepted definition of 'culture' (Child 1981; Redding 1994; Triandis 1992). Usunier (1998: 15) notes, for example, that culture can be defined in 'various ways': as collective mental pro-grammes (Hofstede 1991); a shared system of representations and meanings (Geertz 1983; Goodenough 1971), or as basic assumptions or value orientations (Kluckhohn and Strodtbeck 1961). He goes on to suggest that culture can be understood as 'learned and forgotten norms and behavioural patterns' (Usinier 1998: 16), before finally giving in and acknowledging that culture is 'somewhat all-encompassing' (ibid). Similarly Kluckhohn, in 27 pages of intellectual gymnastics, produces 11 different definitions of culture and concludes with three largely incompatible simi-les: of culture as map, sieve and matrix (*Mirror for Man*, noted in Geertz 1995: 4–5). More recently, Adler (1997: 14–15), in a potentially useful text aimed at managers, offers five separate glosses on culture in a single page. Alternative techniques for deal-ing with the conceptualization of culture are to offer a single definition with no com-ment, or no definition at all, assuming culture to be a taken-for-granted concept.

Our uncertainty about what culture might be is rather under-reported in the man-agerial literature, and the study of culture which is most frequently clung to for reas-surance and certainty is that of Hofstede (1984). Hofstede's work is both valuable, and, I will argue, dangerously seductive. He famously describes similarities and dif-ferences in values between national groups along four dimensions: masculini–femininity; uncertainty avoidance; individualism–collectivism; and power distance. A fifth, 'Confucian' dimension of long-term versus short-term orientation was later added (Hofstede and Bond 1988). These dimensions of difference are correlated with national differences in organizational and managerial preferences, and the problems likely to arise when two given cultures meet are then predicted. Hofstede's original study, drawing on over 116 000 IBM questionnaires from 72 national subsidiaries, was welcomed as providing the rigorous research design, systematic data collection and theory development that were seen by some as missing from the field (Sondergaard 1994). On publication, however, reviewers pointed to possible prob-lems: that the dimensions developed were artefacts of the period of analysis; that the research population was uniquely from one company, IBM, and therefore of ques-tionable generalizability; that values had been inferred from an attitudes-only survey; that culture is equated by Hofstede with national boundaries (ibid.).

Although there is a clear temptation to do so, Hofstede himself offers a clear admo-nition that samples of culture should not be confused with samples of individuals, 'We do not compare individuals, but we compare . . . central tendencies in the answers from each country' (Hofstede 1991: 253). He goes on to caution against using the country scores in his study for the purpose of stereotyping individuals, and emphasizes the impact of gender, social class, occupation and education, among oth-ers, on questionnaire responses. Further, Hofstede notes that the absolute value of the scores in the survey has no meaning: 'The national culture scores . . . only describe differences between countries' (ibid.: 255). Elsewhere, he points out that his dimensions of difference are not real, but are simply theoretical constructs which may help us think about culture. Hofstede suggests that his scores are, however, use-ful for understanding the dominant values of a country, and their impact on social systems such as organizations. In preparing to do business with the Suzuki Corpora-tion, for example, 'we had better assume their organization to be built on collectivist values' (ibid.: 254). These clarifications and cautions are helpful, yet in managerial texts Hofstede's dimensions of difference tend to be presented without any such caveats. And so the appearance of solid, objective knowledge is constructed, and we are still left with the problem of how to move from this national level of analysis to its implications for contextualized social interaction.

Hofstede also offers a widely quoted definition of culture – a definition that clearly illustrates the dangerously seductive appeal of his work, at least to those of a deterministic bent. For Hofstede, culture is 'The collective programming of the mind which distinguishes the members of one human group from another' (Hofstede 1991: 5). 'Programming' here suggests, by analogy with computing, a set of predictable responses. The danger of this definition (and precisely the reason for its popularity, perhaps) is that what apparently remains is for managers and educators to simply set out 'the programmes' (similarly, see Hall's 1959 'social glue'). The manager is then able, presumably, to study how 'the French', for example, are culturally 'programmed'. He or she can then apply suitable techniques in managing them. Cross-cultural difference is thus reified, and becomes an object amenable to managerial technique – technique that can now be conventionally taught.

Hampden-Turner and Trompenaars (2000) similarly offer a list of dimensions along which national cultures differ (universalism–particularism; individualism–communitarianism; specificity–diffusion; achieved status–ascribed status; inner direction–outer direction; sequential time–synchronous time). Like Hofstede, these authors work from a large database (in their case some 46 000 managers responding to a 'dilemmas' questionnaire). The cross-cultural data upon which Hampden-Turner and Trompenaars draw is derived from a forced choice methodology. Respondents are presented with a series of dilemmas and forced to choose between two responses. What is measured, as the authors now acknowledge, is 'not just the responses of managers, but the "conditions of siege" that they themselves have created' (Hampden-Turner and Trompenaars 2000: 353). The findings are again at a considerable distance from whatever might be the 'realities' of located intercultural encounters. This criticism remains true no matter how many dilemma options are offered in the new questionnaire. A great virtue of Hampden-Turner's theorizing of cultural dimensions is that he insists that values of individualism and communitarianism, for example, are both important in any society. Americans may, stereotypically, prefer to begin with and emphasize individualist values, but must, nonetheless, also deal with how to be part of a community. This way of presenting values mitigates a tendency to polarize them and allocate, say, individualism to America and communitarianism to Japan.

Both Hofstede, and Hampden-Turner and Trompenaars are, however, open to the same criticism: they begin with a priori definitions of relevant groups and units of analysis, and treat culture as a reified construct (Brannen and Salk 2000). Generalized cultural traits, such as those generated by Hofstede, have been used in the cross-cultural management literature to produce what has been called a 'two-billiard ball' view of cultural interaction (Wolf 1982, cited in Brannen and Salk 2000: 454): national cultures collide with each other, leading to failed ventures, or miss one another, remaining untouched. There are other long-standing criticisms of the treatment of culture that have been made in the academic literature. Child (1981), for example, identifies five problems: culture is not clearly defined; cultural boundaries which do not overlap with national boundaries are normally taken to do so; cultural factors are used as explanatory variables without any explanation of their functioning or of their origins in the history of the society; not enough has been done to specify which components of which cultures are relevant to organizations, nor to specify which aspects of organizational behaviour are influenced; the measurement of culture continues to be hindered by conceptual and operational problems. Triandis (1992) is similarly critical. Yet many of these criticisms themselves tend to be rooted in quasi-positivist assumptions about the role of social science. Nonetheless, even these caveats, hesitancies and reservations tend to get stripped out when culture is re-presented for a managerial audience.

I have so far argued that what may be called traditional views of management, management education and culture form an 'unholy trinity', sharing a common tendency to reify social processes and relationships, and to therefore see in them nothing more than stability and predictability. Clearly, reified notions of culture sit comfortably both with managers seeking to apply technique in the context of controllable interactions, and with educators looking for objective truths to deliver. In the next section I want to return to management, management education and culture in order to examine an alternative, interdependent view of all three.

Alternatives

In a review of the state of comparative management theory, which includes, of course, intercultural studies, Redding notes that one of the greatest challenges is 'the bankruptcy of empirical positivism – which has sent the subject round in circles for thirty years' and 'the weakness of the deterministic mechanical causal model, and the false assumptions on which it is based' (Redding 1994: 345). The main opposition to this empiricism comes, as Redding notes, from interpretive approaches. As an example of the latter, he cites Geertz (1973), with whose rain of questions we began the chapter,

> The concept of culture I espouse – is essentially a semiotic one. Believing, with Max Weber, that man is an animal suspended in webs of significance that he himself has spun, I take culture to be those webs, and the analysis of it to be therefore not an experimental science in search of laws, but an interpretive one in search of meaning.
>
> *(Geertz 1973: 5, cited in Redding 1994: 345)*

From this perspective, culture theory, as Redding goes on to suggest, stays close to what it describes; is not predictive; does not 'accumulate upon itself, except that an accretion of conceptual tools allows for deeper and more incisive probes into the same things' (Redding 1994: 346). It does not pretend, in other words, to be a natural science whose findings facilitate the control and manipulation of its object of investigation. In the interpretive tradition what we become interested in is the examination in detail of the actions and perceptions of human actors, and the context within which those actions and perceptions happen (Klein and Myers 1999). From this perspective the human actor and the world are inextricably linked through the actor's lived experience, and our understanding of 'reality' is then produced through social constructions made in situated contexts (Berger and Luckman 1966; Giddens 1995; Schutz 1967). Our interest must necessarily be in the perceptions and actions of the managers we teach, as well as of those they plan to interact with, since the two are interdependent. The relationship between teacher and taught, their actions and perceptions must also be liable to examination. Grey, Knights and Willmott (1996) describe, for example, an approach to management education based on critical theory, in which a wide range of assumptions, including those concerning pedagogical methods are subject to scrutiny as part of the programme.

Giddens (1995) offers a view of social relations which has important consequences for any understanding of culture. He insists, first, on seeing the human actor as a 'knowledgeable agent', arguing that much social theory has treated him or her as considerably less knowledgeable than they really are (a view that would be equally true of the assumptions underlying many treatments of culture). Giddens explicitly distinguishes human knowledgeability from 'the sort of "knowledgeability" displayed in nature, in the form of coded programmes' (ibid.: 2), reinforcing the sense that Hofstede's 'programming' definition is less than helpful in aligning conceptions of culture with knowledgeable human behaviour. One of the consequences of our knowledgeability, and of our ability to reflexively monitor and respond to the ongoing flow of social life is, according to Giddens, that with regard to social norms 'a variety of manipulative attitudes are possible' (ibid.: 4). This suggests, of course, that a wide range of responses to an awareness of cultural norms is possible: yet none of the treatments of culture so far discussed takes seriously the idea that knowledgeable agents in specific contexts can and will make their own particular sense of cultural 'norms'. Giddens goes on to say that much of the 'mutual knowledge' available to actors in their encounters is not directly accessible to their consciousness Hofstede recently modified his definition in a way that brings it closer to the path Giddens is taking here, though still retaining the analogy with programming, 'Maybe "pre-programming" is an even better term, because the programming is only partial: it is up to the individual what he or she does with it' (Hofstede 1996: 151). Though again, the modification is seldom quoted in the literature, nor does Hofstede pursue the implications of his redefinition for the way we research and present intercultural encounters.

Our knowledgeability as agents, Giddens suggests, 'is largely carried in practical consciousness' which consists of 'all the things which actors know tacitly about how to "go on" in the contexts of social life without being able to give them direct discursive expression' (Giddens 1995: xxiii). Giddens usefully distinguishes here between unconscious motivations and cognition; practical consciousness; and discursive consciousness. Between discursive consciousness and practical conscious-ness 'there are only the differences between what can be said and what is character-istically simply done' (ibid.: 7). While there is a bar between discursive consciousness and the unconscious, centred mainly on repression, the division between discursive and practical consciousness 'can be altered by many aspects of the agent's socializa-tion and learning experiences' (ibid.: 7). So while the bulk of the knowledge about how to behave day-to-day is in practical consciousness, much of it can be accessed, through learning experiences, in discursive consciousness. The aim then of intercultural training must be to learn about our own unarticulated behaviours in a way that makes them available to discursive consciousness, since it is only then that the possible impact of our tacit behaviour across cultures can begin to be talked about, and possibly modified.

Giddens also helps to articulate broader limits to the control exercised by the man-ager, by locating human activity in the context of both unacknowledged conditions of action and unintended consequences of action. We can neither know completely the context of our actions, nor can we control the results of what we do. Similarly, MacIntyre (1981: 101) points to the fact that our social order is not under anyone's control, not least because of, as Roberts (1996) glosses it, the unpredictability 'created by individual's attempts to escape the predicative behaviour of others' (ibid.: 58). The consequence of this state of affairs, Roberts suggests, is that 'the most important product of a management education should be an insistence that the student recog-nizes that he or she is not in control and instead begin to develop the habits of mind and action consistent with the reality of organizational interdependencies' (ibid.).

Looking again at culture in the context of Giddens's analysis of human behaviour, what is striking about many definitions (see Brown 1995 for a list of 15 definitions of organizational culture) is precisely that for the most part they simply emphasize some kind of stability, patterning, shared-ness or perpetuation. They share a deter-ministic quality, as if human actors were, in Garfinkel's terms, 'judgemental dopes'. While this quality of culture is clearly important, it is, if we accept Giddens' treat-ment of the knowledgeable agent, not sufficient. These definitions fit very well, of course, with the views of traditional organization, management and education outlined at the start of this chapter. Interestingly, it is the earliest definition of organizational culture offered by Brown – that by Jaques (1977) – that is distinctive in two important ways,

> The culture of the factory is its customary and traditional way of thinking and of doing things, which is shared to a greater or lesser degree by all its members, and which new members must learn, and at least partially accept, in order to be accepted into service in the firm. Culture in this sense covers a wide range of

behaviour: the methods of production; job skills and technical knowledge; attitudes towards discipline and punishment . . . the objectives of the concern; its way of doing business; the methods of payment . . . and the less conscious conventions and taboos.

(Jaques 1977: 251)

There are three things to note about this definition which are relevant to the discussion so far of national cultures. First, it is only in this definition that there is a degree of hesitancy over how completely a culture might be shared and accepted. Second, Jaques also insists on the relevance of organizational practices in determining a culture. Third, he recognizes 'less conscious' elements in a culture. Culture here then is contested (or at least is differentially accepted), is partly the product of attitudes and beliefs which are unconscious (and therefore not amenable to rational management 'technique' either in its production or reinforcement) and is partly the product of specific, situated organizational practices. These are three conditions of the production of culture, which, I want argue, are insufficiently acknowledged in discussions of culture noted so far.

Goffman (1974: 14) makes an important observation about culture which is in line with the views of both Giddens and Jaques: 'Culture concerns systems of meaning, ideas and patterns of thought. It represents more a model for the behaviour of members of a given group than a model of their behaviour' (quoted in Van Maanen and Laurent 1992: 276). The observation is important because it restores the notion of agency (Giddens 1995) to human behaviour with regard to culture. Such an understanding of culture takes us away from Hofstede's deterministic analogy with 'programmed' behaviour: an image which is dangerous because it offers false hope that behaviour can be predictably understood and therefore managed. However, Goffman seems to suggest that there is one culture at work here. Yet we may belong to several different cultures – corporate, ethnic, national, social or sporting, for example. My behaviour will then partly depend on which culture I see as 'operational', which one helps me 'to decide what is, what can be, how one feels about it, what to do, and how to go about doing it' (Goodenough 1971, cited in Usunier 1998: 17).

So what is the relevance of these insights to the ways in which culture might be written and taught? Having refused the assumptions of what has been labelled as traditional management and management education, what might be the relevance of aggregate models of culture, such as Hofstede's? Recent cross-cultural research seems to offer hope of embracing an interpretive perspective of human being and doing, while not abandoning work such as this altogether. Brannen and Salk (2000), for example, offer valuable insights into the realities of intercultural management. The idea of a 'negotiated culture' is central to their analysis, which focuses on the product of cultural negotiations and interactions between, in this case, German and Japanese partners in the 'contested terrain' of a joint venture. They begin with an interest in the dynamic, situated aspects of intercultural encounters, and a view of culture as 'a set of symbols, meanings and practices that are created and reproduced through the interactions of group members . . . historically situated and emergent, shifting and incomplete meanings and practices generated in webs of agency and power' (ibid.: 454). This is a formulation of culture which, although the authors do not make this explicit, sits well with Giddens' treatment of the embodied, knowledgeable agent. The authors provide rich, contextualized descriptions of these negotiations, pointing out that aggregate models of cultural difference (such as that produced by Hofstede) are of use only in as much as they serve as latent conceptual anchors – an observation that reproduces Goffman's insight that culture should be seen as a model for, rather than a model of, behaviour. These aggregate attributes are, according to Brannen and Salk (2000: 483), 'important, but are not effective determinants of organizational culture formation in complex cultural systems'.

Further, they conclude that national cultural traits are unreliable predictors of the issues and differences that might emerge in mixed culture organizations. The authors rather describe a range of personal fit with national cultures of origin in a range from 'marginal' to 'hyper-normal' – the latter embodying national cultural attributes to a very strong degree. They further note that individuals might have different cultural stances depending on the cultural attribute in question, for example, one might be hyper-normal with regard to the importance of lifetime employment but marginal-normal with regard to loose boundaries between business and personal life.

Determinants of the course of the cultural negotiations that they describe are taken by Brannen and Salk to include the history of the joint venture, the relative power and influence of both individuals and cultural groups, the complexity of the issues being faced and prior knowledge of the other's culture. This again responds, as the authors acknowledge, to Child's insistence that culture be seen as part of a wider political and socio-technical context for action (see chapters 4 and 5).

Brannen and Salk, writing within what I take to be an interpretivist paradigm, provide rich descriptions of situated interaction, and of the perceptions of the knowledgeable agents in that situation. They do not attempt prediction, and their theorizing stays close to what they describe. In so doing they are able to place aggregate models such as Hofstede's in a useful perspective for managers. Their research is a model, I would argue, of what an interpretivist view of culture might produce, and sits well with a view of the manager as knowledgeable agent. In the next section, drawing on recent work on intercultural programmes in Cambridge, I briefly describe the implications of this viewpoint for management education

Alternative management education

One commentator suggests that in signing up for British management education, managers can leave their 'guts at the door' and just bring in their brains (Mant 1983: 150). On this reading management education has a literally disembodied quality. An alternative view is to see management as a form of embodied practice which requires mutual recognition of our interdependence (Roberts 1984). Rather than being taught simply how to manage others, then, programmes must incorporate an understanding of how managers manage themselves both in one-to-one relationships and in groups. Roberts goes on to describe participants on an MBA programme working in unstructured groups to confront '[T]he habitual nature of practice, the tacit nature of most knowledge, the reality of individual differences of perceptions, the uncertainty, difficulty and causal circularity of reciprocal dependence (Roberts 1996: 70).

I want now to indicate some of the thinking behind the first module on the Diploma in Intercultural Management run by the Cambridge Programme for Industry in association with the Cambridge-based cross-cultural consultancy, TCO. The course is taught by myself and two of the TCO consultants, and this in itself has produced what we hope is a fruitful tension between the managerialist urge to deal in facts and practicality, and the academic preference for ideas and experimentation.

Although this is a programme focused on intercultural management skills we do not begin with culture, nor do we continue with it as an exclusive topic. As Redding (1994: 350) suggests, we attempt to '[a]void seeing culture a single cause of anything and get accustomed to claiming its position as a necessary, but not sufficient determinant of social outcomes'. To begin with culture as an object of 'expert' study and technique would perhaps allow participants to fall too easily into the traditional views of both management and management education described above. The worst place to start thinking about culture, then, is with culture. Instead we begin with trying to establish how, in Geertz's terms, we spin the webs in which we are suspended. The object of the first morning's work is to destabilize any sense that there might be 'objective facts' about the world that do not depend on our interpretation. Facing a group of managers who have signed up to become more expert in intercultural management, we begin with the Latin tag 'Homo semper tyro est' – people are always beginners – and spend the rest of the morning exploring why this might be the case. Since the arguments here might be either too easily rejected (or too easily accepted without real understanding) a lot of this early work is experiential. We take it that these experiences offer the best hope of moving participants (and ourselves) from practical to discursive consciousness. To a large extent these exercises therefore produce the content of the early stages of the course. Using, for example, pictures that appear 'real' but are in part the projective product of our perceptions, and an exercise in which the meaning of an apparently simple text evaporates in a cloud of multiple interpretations, we attempt to illustrate Heidegger's (1977) observation that perception is always guided by conception, and that representation is 'projective'. The world, he tells us, is enacted and organized by assumptions that help us select what to pay attention to. We then use a 'Prisoner's Dilemma' exercise to explore the notion, whose importance is repeatedly stressed by Roberts, of interdependence, and the illusion (commonly held, it appears) that we can unilaterally act on others as if somehow standing outside the system. What is problematized in these exercises and experiences is the possibility of ever becoming a detached expert on human relationships and 'reality'.

What then remains on the course is to explore the consequences of our perpetual beginner status for interpersonal relationships of any sort. The problems of intercultural relationships cannot, we suggest, be seen in isolation from an awareness of what it is to be an embodied human actor dealing with other knowledgeable agents. The purpose of the course is established, we hope, as less about knowing – the accumulation of intercultural facts and techniques – and more about embodied understanding. The course begins, then, not with 'culture' as an exterior independent object, but rather with notions of self-awareness, self-development and interpretation.

The next step, in the afternoon of day 1, is to try to diminish the importance of culture in the analysis of organizational problems. Because the course is ostensibly about culture, there is a natural tendency to see cultural factors as having almost magical explanatory power. Following a brief presentation of Chinese cultural values, partly using Hofstede's dimensions of power distance and individualism–collectivism, and of the Chinese *danwei* system, a video of a Chinese locomotive factory is shown. There is then a discussion of the video which has, as its main purpose, to show how much of the behaviour we have seen is explicable in terms of political and organizational constraints (Child 1981; Goodall and Warner 1997). A case study (Goodall 2001) dealing with a change process in a Chinese joint venture is subsequently set as an assignment, and so far the tendency has still been to try to explain behaviour in the case in terms simply of national cultural stereotypes, largely ignoring the industrial context.

The aim, then, of the first stage of the programme is to avoid culture as far as possible, and when we meet it, to try to put it, as Redding (1994) advised, in some kind of perspective as one among many possible explanatory variables. By the third module this message appears to have registered with the majority of participants. We are willing to be hesitant about knowing exactly what 'culture' might be in precise definitional terms, we emphasize participant's individual distance from their national stereotype wherever possible, look for organizational and political explanations of behaviour wherever possible, and repeatedly return in exercises and management games to the problems presented by our own assumptions about the world. The aim is to avoid seeing problems 'out there'which are amenable to simple technique. The response to these elements of the opening module appears to have ranged so far from guarded interest to bemused uncertainty by way of blank incomprehension. By module 2, when we test understanding of and revisit some of these ideas, there is much more willingness to engage with them. We have not yet lost anybody.

Concluding remarks

My aim, in exploring alternative conceptions of management to those characterized above as 'traditional', has not been to deny the importance of technique in management, but rather to suggest that our treatment of cross-cultural issues should be held in a productive tension with, rather than be subsumed, by this dominant view. Managers are necessarily engaged in instrumental activities which bring about changes in nature, and produce goods and services (Alvesson and Wilmott 1992: 18). What is objected to in the traditional view is that other important elements of management are ignored. In the 'social engineering perspective', for example, what is underestimated, according to Tsoukas, is the significance in management of 'interpretation, narrative understanding, enacting organization and recognizing patterns' (Tsoukas 1994: 8). Managers traditionally have aquired legitimacy for their exercise of power in large part through technical expertise, supported by the 'objective' facts that the application of technique generates. The resulting 'dominance of instrumental reason' can be seen to feed and foster what Habermas calls a 'technocratic consciousness' in which the relationship to the body, self and others comes to be seen exclusively in instrumental terms' (Roberts 1996: 141) and aims at some kind of behavioural control. An alternative to the traditional view, I have suggested, is to see management as a form of embodied practice which requires mutual recognition of our interdependence, and acknowledges that managers are, and must work with, knowledgeable agents whose ability to see 'reality' is, to say the least, severely constrained.

Managers who wish to learn to manage interculturally must, I have argued, first manage to learn. Learning, however, given the skilful collusion of the managers themselves, and writers and educators, may often be an early casualty of management education. I began with Geertz' 'rain' of questions – 'Questions about continuity and change, objectivity and proof, determinism and relativism, uniqueness and generalization, description and explanation' – and in conclusion will briefly return to them. Taking each of his couplets in turn: I have tried to suggest that there is a danger in overemphasizing continuity in culture, and failing, therefore to take note of its contested, fragile nature; that the search for objectivity and proof leads us towards quantitative methods and a 'scientific' stance from which to view management and organization, yet, as Brannen and Salk, Giddens and Roberts have powerfully argued, quantitative methods alone are inadequate; that deterministic views of culture ('He is Chinese and therefore will . . . ') provide a dangerously seductive fit with 'traditional' views of organization, management and management education, but yet fail to capture the complexity of human interaction; that a balance is needed between generalization and uniqueness, and that this balance is currently too generously tipped in favour of generalization, and 'billiard-ball' models of culture; similarly, we are short of both rich descriptions of cross-cultural interaction, and theoretical explanations of the same. Geertz goes on, 'Anthropology, or anyway the sort that studies cultures, proceeds amid charges of irrelevance, bias, illusion, and impracticability'. Studies of cross-cultural management can fairly, I think, be charged with a degree of irrelevance and impracticability, to the degree that we continue to rely on large sample questionnaires using a priori categories, and fail to engage with the nature of negotiated culture as one element of organizing understood in its social and political context. Interpretivist studies, such as that of Brannen and Salk, however, offer a potentially useful way forward.

Endnote

1   The Diploma in Intercultural Management, offered as an external programme for managers, is validated by Cambridge University, and administered by the university's Programme for Industry. The framework for the course was established, with input from university staff, by Nigel Ewington, of the cross-cultural consultancy, TCO. The programme consists of three residential modules of two days each, with assignments and readings set between each module, and a concluding research project. The first open course was run in 1998, followed by an in-company version for the Italian energy company ENI in Rome and Cambridge. The third open course is nearing completion at the time of writing. More information about this course at Cambridge University can be obtained by email (info@cpi.cam.ac.uk) or on the CPI website (www.cpi.cam.ac.uk).

References

Adler, N. (1983) 'Cross-cultural management research: the ostrich and the trend', *Academy of Management Review* 8(3): 226–32.

Adler, N. (1997) *International Dimensions of Organizational Behavior*, 3rd edition, Cincinnati, OH, South Western College.

Alvesson, M. and Willmott, H. (eds) (1992) *Critical Management Studies*, London: Sage.

Bartholomew, S. and Adler, N. (1996) Building networks and crossing borders', in P. Joynt and M. Warner (eds) *Managing Across Cultures: Issues and Perspectives*, London: International Thomson Business Press.

Berger, P. and Luckman, T. (1966) *The Social Construction of Reality*, New York: Anchor Books.

Brannen, M. and Salk, J. (2000) 'Partnering across borders. Negotiating organizational culture in a German–Japanese joint venture', *Human Relations* 53(4): 451–87.

Brown, A. (1995) *Organisational Culture*, London: Pitman.

Child, J. (1981) 'Culture, contingency and capitalism in the cross-national study of organizations', in L.L. Cummings, and B.M. Staw (eds) *Research in Organizational Behavior*, volume 3, Greenwich, CT: JAI Press.

Cunningham, I. and Dawes, G. (1997) 'Problematic premises, presumptions, presuppositions and practices in management education and training', in J. Burgoyne and M. Reynolds (eds) *Management Learning: Integrating Perspectives in Theory and Practice*, London: Sage.

Fox, S. (1997) 'From management education and development to the study of management learning', in J. Burgoyne and M. Reynolds (eds) *Management Learning: Integrating Perspectives in Theory and Practice*, London: Sage.

Geertz, C. (1973) *The Interpretation of Cultures*, New York: Basic Books.

Geertz, C. (1983) *Local Knowledge*, New York: Basic Books.

Geertz, C. (1995) *After the Fact – Two Countries, Four Decades, One Anthropologist*, Cambridge, MA: Harvard University Press.

Giddens, A. (1995) *The Constitution of Society*, Cambridge: Polity.

Goffman, E. (1974) *Relations in Public*, New York: Harper & Row.

Gomez-Mejia, L.R. and Palich, L.E. (1997) 'Cultural diversity and the performance of multinational firms', *Journal of International Business Studies* 28(2): 309–35.

Goodall, K.W. (2001) 'Lafarge in China', unpublished case study produced for the China Europe International Business School, Shanghai, China.

Goodall, K.W. and Warner, M. (1997) 'Human resources in Sino–foreign joint ventures: selected case-studies in Shanghai compared with Beijing', *International Journal of Human Resource Management* 8(5): 569–94.

Goodenough, W.H. (1971) *Culture, Language and Society*, Reading, MA: Addison-Wesley.

Grey, C. and Mitev, N. (1995) 'Management education: a polemic', *Management Learning* 26: 73–90.

Grey, C., Knights, D. and Willmott, H. (1996) 'Is a critical pedagogy of management possible?', in R. French and C. Grey (eds) *Rethinking Management Education*, London: Sage.

Hall, E. (1959) *The Silent Language*, New York: Doubleday.

Hampden-Turner, C. and Trompenaars, F. (2000) *Building Cross-Cultural Competence: How to Create Wealth from Competing Values*, London: Wiley.

Heenan, D.A. and Perlmutter, H. (1979) *Multinational Organization Development*, Reading, MA: Addison-Wesley.

Heidegger, M. (1977) *The Question Concerning Technology and Other Essays*, New York: Harper & Row.

Hofstede, G. (1980) *Culture's Consequences*, London: Sage.

Hofstede, G. (1984) *Culture's Consequences: International Differences in Work-Related Values*, Beverley Hills, CA: Sage.

Hofstede, G. (1991) *Culture and Organisations: Software of the Mind, Intercultural Cooperation and its Importance for Survival*, London: McGraw-Hill.

Hofstede, G. (1996). 'Images of Europe: past, present, and future', in P. Joynt and M. Warner (eds) *Managing Across Cultures, Issues and Perspectives*, London: International Thomson Business Press.

Hofstede, G. and Bond, M.H. (1988) 'The Confucius connection: from cultural roots to economic growth', *Organizational Dynamics* 16(4): 4–21.

Jacques, E. (1977) *A General Theory of Bureaucracy*, London: Heinemann.

Kerr, C., Dunlop, J.T. and Myers, C.A. (1960) *Industrialism and Industrial Man*, Cambridge, MA: Harvard University Press.

Kidger, P.J. (1991) 'The emergence of international human resource management', *International Journal of Human Resource Management* 2(2): 149–63.

Klein, H.K. and Myers, M.D. (1999) 'A set of principles for conducting and evaluating interpretive field studies in information systems, *MIS Quarterly* 23(1): 67–93.

Kluckhohn, F. and Strodtbeck, F.L. (1961) *Variations in Value Orientations*, Westport, CT: Greenwood Press.

Laurent, A. (1983) 'The cultural diversity of Western conceptions of management', *International Studies of Management and Organization* 13(1/2): 97–118.

MacIntyre, A. (1981) *After Virtue*, London: Duckworth.

Mant, A. (1983) *Leaders We Deserve*, Oxford: Blackwell.

Morgan, G. (1997) *Images of Organization*, London: Sage.

Parkhe, A. (1995) 'Joint venture research: accessing the past, present and future', in B.J. Punnett and O. Shenkar (eds) *Handbook of International Management Research*, Cambridge: Blackwell.

Redding, G. (1994) 'Comparative management theory: jungle, zoo, or fossil bed?', *Organization Studies* 15(3): 323–59.

Roberts, J. (1984) 'The moral character of management practice', *Journal of Management Studies* 21(3): 287–302.

Roberts, J. (1996) 'Management education and the limits of technical rationality: the conditions and consequences of management practice', in R. French and C. Grey (eds) *Rethinking Management Education*, London: Sage.

Schein, E. (1986) 'International human resource management: new directions, perpetual issues, and missing themes', *Human Resource Management* 25(1): 169–76.

Schneider, S.C. and Barsoux, J.-L. (1997) *Managing Across Cultures*, London: Prentice Hall.

Schutz, A. (1967) *The Phenomenology of the Social World*, trans. G. Walsh and F.N.W. Lehnert, Urbana, IL: University of Illinois Press.

Shenkar, O. and Zeira, Y. (1990) 'Role conflict and role ambiguity of chief executive officers in international joint ventures', *Journal of International Business Studies* 23: 5–75.

Sondergaard, M. (1994) 'Hofstede's consequences: a study of reviews, citations, and replications', *Organization Studies* 15(3): 447–56.

Triandis, H.C. (1992) 'Cross-cultural industrial and organizational psychology', in M.D. Dunnette (ed.) *Handbook of Industrial and Organizational Psychology*, volume 4, Palo Alto, CA: Consulting Psychologists Press.

Tsoukas, H. (1994) 'Introduction: from social engineering to reflective action in organizational behaviour', in H. Tsoukas (ed.) *New Thinking in Organizational Behaviour*, Oxford: Butterworth-Heinemann.

Usunier, J.-C. (1998) *International and Cross-Cultural Management Research*, London: Sage.

Van Maanen, J. and Laurent, A. (1992) 'The flow of culture: some notes on globalization and the multinational corporation', in S. Ghoshal and E. Westney (eds) *Organization Theory and the Multinational Corporation*, New York: St Martin's Press.

Willmott, H. (1997) 'Critical management learning', in J. Burgoyne and M. Reynolds (eds) *Management Learning: Integrating Perspectives in Theory and Practice*, London: Sage.

Wolf, E. (1982) *Europe and the People without History*, Berkeley, CA: University of California Press.

Chapter 21

Globalization and management: the role of the transnational capitalist class

Leslie Sklair

Introduction

It is widely acknowledged that globalization, however defined, has penetrated, albeit to varying depths, into all major facets of social, economic, political and cultural life (see, for example, Lechner and Boli 2000). Management is no exception and, indeed, it is not difficult to argue that managing across borders has become one of the most powerful globalizing practices (see Parker 1998). The purpose of this chapter, however, is to focus on the agents of these practices rather than the practices themselves.

It is important at the outset to distinguish between three distinct but often confused conceptions of globalization. The first is the *international* or *state-centrist* conception of globalization where internationalization and globalization are used interchangeably. This usage signals the fact that the basic units of analysis are still nation states and the pre-existing, even if changing, system of nation states. This is the position of most of those who are in globalization denial, for example those who continue to believe that 'national systems of management' can adequately cope with the demands of a rapidly globalizing world economy. The second is the *transnational* conception of globalization, where the basic units of analysis are transnational practices, forces and institutions. In this conception, states (or, more accurately, state agents and agencies) are just one among several factors to be taken into account and, in some theories of globalization, no longer the most important. The third is the *globalist* conception of globalization, in which the state is actually said to be in the process of disappearing.[1] It is obviously important that all those who write about globalization are clear about the sense in which they use the term, but not all are, with resultant confusions. In order to make my own position clear, I should note that I use the terms 'transnational' and 'globalizing' interchangeably, in order to signal that the state – or rather, some state actors and agencies – do have a part to play in the globalization process, however diminished relative to their previous roles. This highlights the distinction between 'globalizing' and 'globalist' approaches.

The concept of globalization propounded here rejects both state-centrism and globalism (the end of the state). The transnational conception of globalization postulates the existence of a global system. Its basic units of analysis are transnational practices (TNP), practices that cross state boundaries but do not originate with state agencies or actors. Analytically, TNPs operate in three spheres: the economic, the political and the cultural-ideological. The whole is the global system. While the global system is not synonymous with global capitalism, what the theory sets out to demonstrate is that the dominant forces of global capitalism are the dominant forces in the contemporary global system. The building blocks of the theory are the transnational corporation, the characteristic institutional form of economic transnational practices, the transnational capitalist class in the political sphere and in the culture-ideology sphere, the culture-ideology of consumerism (see Sklair 1995).

The transnational capitalist class (TCC)

The transnational capitalist class can be analytically divided into four main fractions.

- owners and controllers of TNCs and their local affiliates
- globalizing bureaucrats and politicians
- globalizing professionals
- consumerist elites (merchants and media)[2]

The exact disposition of these four fractions and the people and institutions from which they derive their power in the system can differ over time and place. To study globalization and the state, for example, it makes most sense to couple globalizing bureaucrats and politicians, while for other issues other alliances may be more appropriate. It is also important to note, of course, that the TCC and each of its fractions are not always entirely united on every issue. Nevertheless, together, leading personnel in these groups constitute a TCC. The TCC is opposed not only by anti-capitalists who reject capitalism as a way of life and/or an economic system, but also by capitalists who reject globalization. Some localized, domestically oriented businesses can stand out against global corporations and prosper, but most cannot and perish. Influential business strategists and management theorists commonly argue that to survive, local business must globalize (Kanter 1996). Similarly, though most national and local politicians claim to represent the interests of the constituents on whose votes they depend, those who entirely reject globalization and espouse extreme nationalist ideologies are comparatively rare, despite the recent rash of civil wars in economically marginal parts of the world. And while there are anti-consumerist elements in most societies, there are few cases of a serious anti-consumerist party winning political power anywhere in the world.

The TCC is transnational (or globalizing) in the following respects:

1 The economic interests of its members are increasingly globally linked rather than exclusively local and national in origin. As rentiers, their property and shares are becoming more globalized through the unprecedented mobility of capital that new technologies and new global political economy have created.[3] As executives, their corporations are globalizing in terms of four criteria: foreign investment, world best practice and benchmarking, corporate citizenship and global vision. The analysis of how the TCC has constructed a discourse of globalization and how this is translated into globalizing practices of management below will focus on these criteria. The intellectual (or, perhaps more accurately, ideological) products of the TCC serve the interests of globalizing rather than localizing capital, expressed in free market neo-liberalism and the culture-ideology of consumerism. This follows directly from the shareholder-driven growth imperative that lies behind the globalization of the world economy and the increasing difficulty of enhancing shareholder value in purely domestic firms. While for many practical purposes the world is still organized in terms of discrete national economies, the TCC increasingly conceptualizes its interests in terms of markets, which may or may not coincide with a specific nation state, and the global market, which clearly does not.

2 The TCC seeks to exert economic control in the workplace, political control in domestic, international and global politics, and culture-ideology control in every-day life through specific forms of global competitive and consumerist rhetoric and practice. The focus of workplace control is the threat that jobs will be lost and, in the extreme, the economy will collapse unless workers are prepared to work longer and for less in order to meet foreign competition. A term first introduced around 1900 to describe how the capitalist class controls labour – the race to the bottom – has been rehabilitated by radical critics to characterize the effects of economic globalization.[4] This is reflected in local electoral politics in most countries, where the major parties have few substantial strategic (even if many tactical) differences, and in the sphere of culture-ideology, where consumerism is rarely challenged within 'realistic' politics. As we shall see below, this process is reinforced through the discourse of national and international competitiveness.

3 Members of the TCC have outward-oriented global rather than inward-oriented local perspectives on most economic, political and culture-ideology issues. The growing TNC and international institutional emphasis on free trade and the shift from import substitution to export promotion strategies in most developing countries since the 1980s have been driven by members of the TCC working through government agencies, political parties, élite opinion organizations, and the media. Some credit for this apparent transformation in the way in which big business works around the world is attached to the tremendous growth in business education with a global focus, notably international, and increasingly global MBAs, in recent decades all over the world.

4 Members of the TCC tend to share similar lifestyles, particularly patterns of higher education, and consumption of luxury goods and services. Integral to this process are exclusive clubs and restaurants, ultra-expensive resorts in all continents, private as opposed to mass forms of travel and entertainment and, ominously, increasing residential segregation of the very rich secured in gated communities by armed guards and electronic surveillance, from Los Angeles to Moscow, from Mexico City to Beijing, from Istanbul to Mumbai.

5 Finally, members of the TCC seek to project images of themselves as citizens of the world as well as of their places and/or countries of birth. Leading exemplars of this phenomenon include Jacques Maisonrouge, born in France, who became in the 1960s the chief executive of IBM World Trade; Percy Barnevik, born in Sweden, who created the infrastructure and electronics conglomerate Asea Brown Boveri, often portrayed as spending most of his life in his corporate jet; Helmut Maucher, born in Germany, former Chief Executive Officer (CEO) of Nestlé's far-flung global empire; David Rockefeller, born in the USA, said to have been one of the most powerful men in the USA; the legendary Akio Morita, born in Japan, the founder of Sony and widely credited with having introduced global vision into Japan; and Rupert Murdoch, born in Australia, who took US nationality to pursue his global media interests.

The discourse of capitalist globalization: competitiveness

One need not indulge in the fantasy of conspiracy theory to understand why politi-cians and professionals have been so engrossed with contentious ideas of the national interest and national competitiveness. Krugman's (1996) devastating critique, 'Competitiveness: a dangerous obsession' explains the latter (though not necessarily the former) with admirable clarity. The argument, briefly, is that only cor-porations and similar institutions can compete with one another and that the idea that nations can compete with one another is a 'dangerous obsession' that interferes with the economic efficiency of business. While Krugman's neo-liberal assumptions about the impossibility of industrial strategies can be challenged, the logic of his case on the incoherence of the idea of national competitiveness appears more convincing. This is central to the way in which politicians, bureaucrats and professionals in the service of the transnational capitalist class relate to the state.

A good illustration of these processes at work is provided by the political trajectories of five individuals who fit well into my category of globalizing politicians and professionals, what Jorge Dominguez (1997) terms 'technopols'. These five technopols are F.H. Cardoso, president of Brazil, A. Foxley in Chile, D. Cavallo in Argentina (relative successes), P. Aspe in Mexico and Evelyn Matthei in Chile. They all take seriously ideas that are cosmopolitan and meet normal international professional standards, and they succeed by selling sound economic policy in their own countries. Technopols are technocrats with added characteristics: they are political leaders, they go beyond narrow specialisms, and they are active in the politics of remaking damaged social and political systems. Democratic technopols choose freer markets (this can be translated as 'support of globalizing business') over state intervention because it is what their professional training has taught them to do. Technopol support for free markets also makes them more liable to favour democracy but this is the democracy of pluralist polyarchy and not any wider conception of representative democracy. In a statement redolent with meaning for those who would dare to oppose global capitalism, Dominguez (1997: 3) argues: 'only democratic political systems embody the compromises and commitments that may freely bind government and opposition to the same framework of a market economy'.

The careers of these five notables illustrate how technopols in Latin America and, I would argue, globalizing politicians and professionals all around the world, are made in five settings: élite schools, religious and secular faiths, policy-oriented teams, the world stage and specific national contexts. The Latin American five all studied either directly in the USA or were inspired by those who had (notably in the economics and political science departments at Chicago, the Massachusetts Institute of Technology (MIT) and Harvard). They made their moves when statist democrats (Alfonsin in Argentina, Sarney in Brazil, Allende in Chile, for example) failed, and when economic crisis facilitated acceptance of some version of the neo-liberal consensus. Technopols, thus, incorporate two transnational pools of ideas – one favouring free markets, the other democracy. It is also important to note that technopols are not extreme neo-liberals out to kill off the state, but politicians and professionals who want to recraft the state from 'fat to fit', to encourage growth with a measure of equity. Above all, technopols understand that corporations and those who own and control them expect policy continuity to safeguard their investments. This means technopols need to develop a political, professional and, increasingly, a globalizing agenda to establish a cosmopolitan vision to lock in their countries to free markets, international trade agreements and globalization. In addition, they have to create political openings to bring all important social groups on side for 'national development in a competitive international marketplace'.

The significance of these examples, and they could be reinforced by many others from all over the world (see Sklair 2001), is that they undermine the popular misconception that globalization is a Western imperialist plot. While there is no doubt that the global economy is still largely dominated by corporations domiciled in Western countries, globalization has transformed the meaning of this fact. Crude dependency ideas of American corporations exploiting Latin America as instruments of the US state or British corporations exploiting Africa as instruments of the British state have given way to more nuanced theories of globalizing alliance capitalism and global shift to accommodate new technologies of production, financing and marketing (see Dicken 1998; Dunning 1998) (see chapter 6).

Major corporations indulge these views for obvious reasons. Many major corporations interpret globalization in terms of being global locally. Corporations cope with the responsibilities of being local citizens globally by mobilizing national competitiveness on behalf of their mythical national interest in whatever part of the world the corporation happens to be doing business. Those fractions of the TCC whose role it is to support the owners and controllers of TNCs (notably globalizing bureaucrats, politicians and professionals) work hard to ensure that all businesses, particularly the 'foreign' corporations who have traditionally felt themselves discriminated against (sometimes true, often not), receive at least equal treatment and, where possible, privileges. These privileges, in the form of development grants, fiscal holidays, training subsidies and other 'sweeteners', are routinely justified by the argument that attracting foreign investment will enhance the national interest. This can happen directly, with the addition of world-class manufacturing facilities, and/or indirectly, with the introduction of new ideas, methods, and incentives for local supplier industries. The ability of corporations seeking such investment opportunities to show that they are world class and thus could enhance the industrial environment they seek to enter, is a political requirement for these privileges. Without this promise of increases in national prosperity, a corollary of global competitiveness, subsidies for 'foreign firms' would be much more difficult to sell to local populations who might see better uses for their taxes.

The insertion of the nation state into the global capitalist system is facilitated by the TCC through the discourse of national competitiveness. The TCC achieves this through facilitating alliances of globalizing politicians, globalizing professionals and the corporate sector. Globalizing politicians create the political conditions for diverting state support of various types (financial, fiscal, resources, infrastructure, ideological) towards the major corporations operating within state borders under the slogan of 'national competitiveness'. Such support represents direct and indirect subsidies to the TCC and, in the context of foreign direct investment, often involves state regulation in the interests of the major corporations. Politicians deliver these aids to industry and commerce through their campaigning and votes in support ofcapital-enhancing labour, trade and investment legislation. Parliamentary democracies based on geographical constituencies encourage this, resulting in 'pork-barrel politics' in the USA and its equivalents elsewhere. Globalizing politicians, therefore, need global benchmarks in a generic sense to demonstrate that they are internationally competitive. Their 'national' corporations and, by extension, their 'nation', has to seek out world best practice in all aspects of business. Global capitalism succeeds by turning most spheres of social life into businesses, by making social institutions – such as schools, universities, prisons, hospitals, welfare systems – more businesslike. Various forms of benchmarking are used in most large institutions to measure performance against actual competitors or an ultimate target, zero defects, for example. The term 'world best practice' (WBP) is widely used as a convenient label for all measures of performance, achieved through various systems of benchmarking.

While globalizing politicians are responsible for creating the conditions under which world best practice becomes the norm for evaluating the effectiveness of any social institution, they rarely become involved in its techniques. This is the responsibility of the globalizing professionals. The role of globalizing professionals is both technical and ideological. Their technical role is to create and operate benchmarking systems of various types; their ideological role is to sell these systems as the best way to measure competitiveness at all levels and, by implication, to sell competitiveness as the key to business (and national) success. It is, paradoxically, the way that national economic competitiveness has been raised to the pinnacle of public life that explains the empirical link between world best practice, benchmarking and globalization.

World best practice is bound to be a globalizing practice in the global capitalist system. It is quite conceivable that benchmarking could be restricted to small, localized communities of actors and institutions interested solely in providing a local service in terms of agreed criteria of efficiency. Examples of this can be found in the tourist industry, where several small competing firms offer almost identical services to unique, local attractions. They may systematically compare what they offer and upgrade (or possibly downgrade) their services to match the practices of more successful competitors. In a global economy, however, there are relentless pressures on small local businesses to become more global, either through predatory growth or, more typically, by allying themselves with major globalizing corporations. Therefore, to become world class it is not necessary to be big but it is necessary to compare yourself with what the big players in your business sector do, and to do better what you always do (see, notably, Kanter 1996). Benchmarking is the measure through which all social institutions, including the state, can discover whether they are world class.

Benchmarking is normally defined as a system of continuous improvements derived from systematic comparisons with world best practice. The idea of continuous improvement was introduced by the New York University professor and soon-to-be management guru William Edwards Deming shortly after the end of the Second World War. This became the driving force behind the total quality management (TQM) movement which has had profound though uneven effects on big business all over the world. However, Japanese corporations working with state agencies first adopted these ideas, seeing in them the best way to rebuild their war-shattered economy. The Deming Prize for the best quality circles was established in Japan in 1951. These quality circles became a central mechanism for the spread and development of the new quality movement. By the 1990s their numbers exceeded 100 000 with about 10 million members throughout Japan. Total quality management, world best practice and benchmarking were given added impetus by the increase in global competition as protectionist walls have been breached all over the world and as rapidly growing new companies, particularly in the high-tech sector, have threatened the market dominance of their older and, perhaps, less innovative rivals.

The Malcolm Baldrige National Quality Award was established in the USA in 1987, then the European Quality Award was introduced in 1991, followed by a veritable flood of quality initiatives covering almost all sectors of industry all over the world. These gave public recognition throughout business and beyond to the TQM movement that had swept through boardrooms, office complexes and shop floors whenever an enterprise was faced with competition, particularly from 'foreign' companies, from the mid-1980s. An important aspect of these awards and quality standards and the movements they were part of was the centrality of the role of leadership, particularly the leadership of the most senior executives, in the quest for continuous improvement. Not since the robber barons in the nineteenth century had the leaders of big business been in the limelight to such an extent. And what the leaders of the major corporations were saying, almost unanimously, was that business success lay in putting the customer first and that customer satisfaction depended on quality.

World best practice and benchmarking are logical strategies for globalizing corporations because when competition can, in principle, come from anywhere in the world, it is necessary for companies who wish to hold on to their market share, let alone increase it, to measure their performances against the very best in the world. 'The very best', of course, is a highly contentious idea. It can mean 'best returns on capital invested' or 'best stockmarket price increase' or 'best environmental performance' or 'best employer' or any number of other things. An additional and crucial factor is that most major corporations are in industries in which most of their products are quite similar to (sometimes virtually identical with) those of their competitors. Thus, it is vital to ensure that any competitive advantage that a product has, however small, is matched by competitive advantages in bringing it to market. That is why world best practice, benchmarking and related performance-enhancing measures are so important. The TQM movement ensured that all aspects of company performance, from manufacturing widgets to answering telephones, from delivering and servicing the product to monitoring energy use in factories and offices, were liable to be benchmarked. The numerous criteria included for both the Deming Prize in Japan and the Baldrige National Quality Award in the USA were significant motivators in operationalizing the idea of total quality for customer-driven business. Many major corporations had their own versions of these quality packages.[5]

The pioneers in global benchmarking were technology-intensive companies whose very survival depended on continuous innovation, like Motorola and Xerox. Also influential in the theory and practice of benchmarking were global management consultants, notably Andersen Consulting and McKinsey. There are literally hundreds of different quality measures, some firm specific, others product or industry specific, some specifically aspiring to zero defects. Some cover environmental standards, others citizenship standards. Some are regional in scope (the USA, UK, European Union and Japan, for example, all have various types of quality standards) and some are virtually global (for example, the International Standards Organization [ISO] series).

The links between state agencies and corporations in the creation of benchmarking and best practice systems can be briefly illustrated with the cases of Australia, Brazil and the USA. In Australia and Brazil, the globalizing fractions of the state and business were united in their belief that the protectionism of the past could no longer be maintained if they were to enter the global economy. The two governments embarked on two different paths to implement world best practice but with the same end in view, to make their companies internationally competitive. In Australia, best practice was seen largely as a problem of changing labour practices, and a Best Practice Demonstration Program was introduced in 1991 by the Department of Industrial Relations, working with the Australian Manufacturing Council. The rationale for the Program was clearly stated in the pamphlet 'What is best practice?' issued in 1994: 'As the Australian economy becomes increasingly integrated into the global market, Australian enterprises must become internationally competitive to succeed'. DuPont, ICI and BHP in Australia are cited as enthusiastic supporters of the Program. The official magazine of the Best Practice Program was entitled *Benchmark* and its pages in the 1990s exemplified the alliance between globalizing politicians, bureaucrats, professionals, big and small business, all striving for the quality improvements that would enhance national competitiveness.

In Brazil, the government agency responsible for quality standards was the National Institute for Standardization, Metrology and Industrial Quality (Inmetro). The President of Inmetro declared to an international meeting in Holland in 1998 that:

> The efforts made by Brazilian firms to improve the quality of their goods is linked to the beginning of competition in Brazil's economy. Up to 1990, when the economy was closed to imports, our companies did not bother about quality. After the opening of the economy in 1992, the need grew to show international standards of quality'.

> *('Brazilian companies invest in quality', advertisement in the Financial Times, 26 August 1998)*

Inmetro worked closely with the Brazilian Program for Quality and Productivity and the Brazilian Foreign Trade Association, for enhanced quality in Brazil was necessary not only to compete against imports but, more importantly, to increase the potential for companies in Brazil to export.

In the USA, while quality standards and benchmarking have come largely from private industry initiatives, the Baldrige National Quality Award, perhaps the most prestigious mark of quality in the USA, was established in 1987 as a joint venture between government and industry. Although modelled on the Japanese Deming Prize, the Baldrige process is transparent and provides an audit framework which companies could use for self-assessment. Cole has gone so far as to predict the death of the quality movement as quality improvement becomes part of normal management activity (Cole 1999).

This is not the case outside the USA and a few major economies. While over 70 countries were reported as having agencies for accreditation and inspection of technical standards laboratories in the 1990's, it is commonly accepted that standards vary from place to place. An International Accreditation Forum (IAF) was established precisely to ensure comparability of standards and by 1998 had 18 member countries, with more applications, including Inmetro, in the pipeline. Accreditation by IAF meant recognition for technical standards in the US, Canadian, Chinese, Japanese and European Union markets, and a reasonable guarantee that the WTO technical rules were less likely to be used to block imports, often seen as a form of disguised protectionism. What the three cases of Australia, Brazil and the USA suggest is that globalizing state agents and professionals have joined forces with corporations to promote best practice in the service of national competitiveness. In this way the globalizing capitalist class uses the discourse of national and international competitiveness to impose more intensive discipline on the workforce and in some cases to impose unnecessarily high standards that drive smaller competitors out of the market. In addition, the imposition of world best practice and benchmarking beyond the narrow confines of manufacturing industries is another important step in the commodification of everything that is closely connected with the culture-ideology of consumerism.

The corporate capture of sustainable development

Similar processes can be observed in the management of environmental problems. For decades, theorists of a singular ecological crisis have argued over the future prospects for life on the planet with those who conceive of the issue in terms of multiple, but manageable environmental problems. Major corporations always tried to keep these ideas apart but disasters like the *Torrey Canyon* (1967) and Santa Barbara (1969) oil spills, toxic contamination that provoked hundreds of anti-pollution suits in Japan in the 1970s, Bhopal in 1984 and *Exxon Valdez* in 1989, exacerbated the problems. The argument climaxed in the late 1980s and early 1990s under the pressures of globalization just as the discourse of sustainable development was emerging as the common language for those who were thinking about almost any environmental issue (Sklair 2001: ch. 7).

We can trace the first indication that some members of the corporate élite were beginning to take the ecological crisis seriously to the publication of *The Limits to Growth*, sponsored by the Club of Rome.[6] This gave a modicum of business respectability to the profoundly anti-capitalist thesis that growth had limits but, in general, those who spoke for global capitalism were able to shrug off the deeper lessons of the 'limits to growth' school as alarmist and naïve. However, the problem would not go away and the more forward-thinking members of the global business community knew that they were going to have to deal with it, eventually. By the late 1980s it became clear that the rhetoric of sustainable development provided a convenient solution and it was eagerly taken up by globalizing corporations as they tried to manage what many were calling an ecological crisis.

The corporate response in the USA and Europe to a spate of environmental catastrophes, notably Bhopal, evolved gradually throughout the 1980s. The chemical industry was clearly under pressure to be seen to be taking decisive action. An initiative of the Chemical Manufacturers Association (CMA) in 1988 in the USA resulted in the Responsible Care Program. This was adopted by more than 170 members of the CMA, including Union Carbide, and announced to the investing public and concerned citizens in full-page advertisements in the *New York Times* and the *Wall Street Journal* on 11 April 1990. The British Chemical Industries Association had adopted its Responsible Care Programme in 1989.

Not only industry but international organizations of various types took it upon themselves to 'do something' about the environment. The European Community introduced a Community-wide environmental auditing scheme in 1993. The World Bank had been discussing the environmental aspects of lending since the 1970s, with controversial results. Similarly, the Environmental Committee of the Organization for Economic Co-operation and Development (OECD) has been discussing the issue since the early 1980s. Why has it proved so difficult to enact effective legislation to protect the environment? One factor was clearly the phenomenon of poacher-turned-gamekeeper in the leadership of some bodies charged with environmental protection. It is clear from the evidence of the 1980s that even anti-regulatory right-wing governments like those of Reagan and Thatcher, could no longer entirely ignore environmental violations. For example, while the Reagan administration was 'pulling the teeth' of the Environmental Protection Agency, at the same time it permitted the establishment of a powerful Environmental Crimes Unit in the Department of Justice.

The major corporations were not, of course, standing idly by while the struggle over the environment was accelerating. Globally, big business response was orchestrated by the International Chamber of Commerce (ICC), which had been promoting an environmental agenda since the first United Nations (UN) environment conference in Stockholm in 1972. The ICC had members in more than 100 countries, though it was most active in Europe. It founded its own Commission on Environment in the 1970s, and its first World Conference of Environmental Management in 1984 attracted 500 leaders of industry, government and environmental groups from 72 countries. The ICC was chosen to give the official business community input to the Bergen Ministerial Conference that led to the report of the UN World Commission on Environment and Development where the concept of sustainable development was firmly established. In the frank words of an ICC analyst of this process: 'the Brundtland Report called on the cooperation of industry . . . the business community is willing to play a leading role, and to take charge' (Willums 1990: 3). And take charge of sustainable development it did.

An immediate consequence of the work of ICC was the Global Environmental Management Initiative (GEMI) of 1990 formed to implement the Business Charter for Sustainable Development. Nineteen leading US transnational corporations announced their support for GEMI, including Union Carbide, desperate to rebuild its reputation after Bhopal. GEMI soon took on an institutional form in Washington, DC. The organization that eventually resulted from these efforts, the World Business Council for Sustainable Development (WBCSD), was probably the most influential of the many green business networks that were established in the 1990s. For all their differences – local, national or global, general or industry specific, well or less well resourced – they all had one thing in common, their emphasis on self-assessment and voluntary codes where possible, but a decisive input into regulation where necessary. In this respect, the globalizing neo-liberal revolution associated with the Thatcher-Reagan attempt to mould state legislation to promote rather than to restrict the corporate interest, or 'free enterprise' as it was ideologically constructed, was very successful.

The roots of the distinctive global capitalist theory of sustainable development can be traced to the discussions around the Brundtland Report, *Our Common Future*, presented to the General Assembly of the United Nations in 1987. The uneasy compromise between conceptualizing the problem as a set of environmental challenges and as a much more serious singular – indeed, planetary life-threatening – ecological crisis suited big business very well. An insight into corporate thinking on the issue was given by Stephan Schmidheiny, a Swiss billionaire who was to play a crucial role for big business at the Rio Earth Summit in 1992. In a series of high-profile articles, public pronouncements and consultations, Schmidheiny (1993) argued that environmental protection had been a defensive, negative, anti-progress concept, but environmentalists and industrialists were beginning see each other's points of view and to compromise. Thus, the idea of 'sustainable growth' had replaced the idea of 'conservation' and industry could get on with its job. Limits to growth were not, as originally thought, limits on supplies but rather limits on the disposal of resources used and transformed in the productive process. Accepting that industry has to operate within existing frameworks it can, nevertheless, act to use these frameworks for its own advantage by taking the offensive and shaping ecological legislation.

Thus, the negative environmentalism that had forced industries to respond to specific challenges on pollution and toxic hazards gave way to more general conceptions of 'sustainable growth' and 'sustainable development', entirely compatible concepts in the corporate analysis. Corporate environmentalism, therefore, both as a social movement and as a discourse, coexisted easily with this moderate conception of sustainability. From this powerful conceptual base big business successfully recruited much of the global environmental movement in the 1990s to the cause of sustainable global consumerist capitalism. This achievement is an object lesson in how dominant classes incorporate potential enemies into what Gramsci called new historical blocs.

Historical blocs are fluid amalgamations of forces that coagulate into social movements to deal with specific historical conjunctures, reflecting concrete problems that have to be confronted by different social groups. In the struggle for hegemony, historical blocs form and dissolve and reform. Big business mobilized a sustainable development historical bloc against what it saw as a threatening counter-culture organized around the powerful idea of the singular ecological crisis, the deep green or ecological movement.

The sustainable development historical bloc began in earnest in the period leading up to the Earth Summit in Rio in 1992. The close relationship between Maurice Strong, the virtual CEO of the Earth Summit, and Stephan Schmidheiny is a matter of public record. The environmental arm of the ICC, the Business Council for Sustainable Development, represented big business in Rio and was successful in keeping any potential criticism of the TNCs off the official agenda (Panjabi 1997). There was, as a consequence, formidable corporate input into the formation of the UN Commission on Sustainable Development (CSD), the major institutional result of the United Nations Conference on Environment and Development (UNCED). The CSD has become a major transnational environmental organization in its own right. It evolved into a Division for Sustainable Development at the UN, and its major task was to monitor how member governments tested, developed and used over 100 indicators of sustainable development. The extent to which it redirects attention away from the singular ecological crisis that threatens the very existence of global capitalism onto the multiple environmental challenges that corporations can cope with and global capitalism can live with, will be a critical test for the success of the sustainable development historical bloc. The signs are not promising for deep ecologists. The basis on which the CSD approached its task of measuring consumption and production was as follows:

> Sustainable consumption and production are essentially two sides of the same coin. Sustainable consumption addresses the demand side, examining how the

goods and services required to meet peoples' needs and improve the quality of life, can be delivered in a way that reduces the burden on the Earth's carrying capacity. The emphasis of sustainable production is on the supply side, focussing on improving environmental performance in key economic sectors such as agriculture, energy, industry, tourism and transport.

(United Nations 1998: n.p.)

From the ecological point of view this approach is based on a series of fallacies. The first is the anthropocentric approach itself, where sustainability for people and societies takes precedence over sustainability for the planet. The second fallacy is the idea that 'sustainable consumption' and 'sustainable production' are essentially two sides of the same coin, For ecologists, the real issue is not 'sustaining' production and consumption, but reducing them absolutely. In addition, ecologists argue that it is fallacious to assume that 'meeting needs', 'improving quality of life' and 'improving environmental performance' are parts of the solution to the ecological crisis. They are not. They are parts of the problem, particularly in terms of distinguishing real from artificial needs and establishing universal norms for an ecologically sound quality of life. It need hardly be said that those who hold these views – radical ecologists – are a small minority, even in the environmental movement,[7] but the capture of the discourse of sustainable development from the environmental movement by the TCC has made it even more difficult to mount a radical critique of capitalist consumerism than would otherwise have been the case.

The combination of the discourse of sustainable development with that of national and international competitiveness provides powerful weapons for the TCC. Globalization is not a 'Western' but a globalizing capitalist ideology, whose discourse and practices are necessary to negate the growing class polarization and ecological crises characteristic of this latest stage in the long history of capitalism.

Conclusion

The combination of the discourse of sustainable development with that of national and international competitiveness provides a powerful weapon for the TCC and its effort to manage the global system. Global system theory, as outlined in this chapter, argues that capitalism is organized politically on a global scale through the TCC. Each of the four fractions of the TCC tends to be represented, to a greater or lesser extent, in movements and campaigns on behalf of the interests of the global capitalist system. Local, national, international, and global trade and industry associations are mainly composed of TNC executives and their affiliates all over the world. Chambers of commerce and business, educational, and philanthropic organizations are also prime sites for the study of how TNC executives and their local affiliates work in the community on behalf of the capitalist global project. The political activities of what are wryly called civil servants in some societies provide ample evidence of the role of globalizing state bureaucrats in pro-capitalist movements all around the world, including many states officially hostile to global capitalism in previous decades. Not all managers, like not all bureaucrats in all government departments and agencies, are entirely and wholeheartedly in favour of the global capitalist project – far from it.

Global system theory sets out to explain the transition from a capitalism that is circumscribed by national interests to one in which globalizing bureaucrats, politicians and professionals in local and national governments increasingly begin to see their interests best served by a more open adherence to the practices of global capitalism and in more open alliance with the TNCs and their globalizing management practices. Substantial lobbying efforts by globalizing bureaucrats, politicians and professionals on behalf of corporate interests in the General Agreement on Tariffs and Trade (GATT), World Trade Organization (WTO), Codex Alimentarius and countless other international bodies are particularly important markers of this transition. The point of all this activity is to defuse and marginalize the growing crises of class polarization and ecology that capitalist globalization appears to be making worse rather than resolving. It is not certain that managers at all levels in the transnational capitalist class will have either the capacity or the will to carry out these tasks under the existing system.

Endnotes

1 Few writers take this extreme position, and of these Kenichi Ohmae (1995) has been the most influential. If Ohmae did not exist then anti-globalization theorists would have had to invent him!
2 See Sklair (2001), from which some material is borrowed and adapted for this chapter.
3 Despite the arguments that national governments still exert regulatory powers over capital flows and that most financial corporations are still focused mainly on their home economies, it is nevertheless true to say that there has been a globalization of capital in recent decades. Certainly, in my own interviews with executives in *Fortune* Global 500 financial corporations (banks of various types and insurance companies) the constant theme was 'we have to globalize because our clients are going global' (Sklair 2001: ch. 3).
4 The race to the bottom can be connected with the class polarization crisis of global capitalism, that is the simultaneous enrichment of some rapidly increasing minorities and impoverishment of other rapidly increasing and more numerous minorities all over the world.
5 For an analysis of these, including Six Sigma, see Sklair (2001: ch. 5).
6 Meadows *et al.* (1972). A second edition published in 1992 received relatively little attention.
7 I would not wish to appear entirely negative about the Division on Sustainable Development. The 'Success Stories' distributed from 1997 onwards are quite inspiring.

References

Cole, R. (1999) *Managing Quality Fads: How American Business Learned to Play the Quality Game*, New York: Oxford University Press.

Department of Industrial Relations (1991) 'What is best practice', pamphlet issued by the DoIR and the Australian Manufacturing Council, Canberra.

Dicken, P. (1998) *Global Shift: Transforming the World Economy*, 3rd edition, London: Paul Chapman publishing.

Dominguez, J. (ed.) (1997) *Technopols: Freeing Politics and Markets in Latin America in the 1990s*, University Park: University of Pennsylvania Press.

Dunning, J.H. (1998) *Alliance Capitalism and Global Business*, London and New York, Routledge.

Kanter, R.M. (1996) *World Class: Thriving Locally in the Global Economy*, New York: Simon & Schuster.

Krugman, P. (1996) *Pop Internationalism*, Boston, MA: MIT Press.

Lechner, F. and Boli, J. (eds) (2000) *The Globalization Reader*, Oxford: Blackwell.

Meadows, D.C., Meadows, D.L., Randers, J. and Behrens W.W., III, (1972) *The Limits to Growth*, New York: New American Library.

Ohmae, K. (1995) *The End of The Nation State*, New York: Free Press.

Panjabi, R. (1997) *The Earth Summit at Rio: Politics, Economics and the Environment*, Boston, MA: Northeastern University Press.

Parker, B. (1998) *Globalization and Business Practice: Managing across Boundaries*, London: Sage.

Schmidheiny, S. (1993) *Changing Course: A Global Business Perspective on Development and the Environment*, Cambridge, MA: MIT Press.

Sklair, L. (1995) *Sociology of the Global System*, 2nd edition, Baltimore, MD: Johns Hopkins University Press.

Sklair, L. (2001) *The Transnational Capitalist Class*, Oxford: Blackwell.

United Nations (1998) 'Workshop on indicators for changing consumption and production patterns', pamphlet issued by the Division for Sustainable Development, New York: 2–3 March.

Willums, J.O. (1990) *The Greening of Enterprise: Business Leaders Speak Out*, Bergen: International Chamber of Commerce.

Index